IRISH ROMANTICISM

What does 'Irish romanticism' mean and when did Ireland become romantic? How does Irish romanticism differ from the literary culture of late eighteenth- and nineteenth-century Britain, and what qualities do they share? Claire Connolly proposes an understanding of romanticism as a temporally and aesthetically distinct period in Irish culture, during which literature flourished in new forms and styles, evidenced in the lives and writings of such authors as Thomas Dermody, Mary Tighe, Maria Edgeworth, Lady Morgan, Thomas Moore, Charles Robert Maturin, John Banim, Gerald Griffin, William Carleton and James Clarence Mangan. Their books were written, sold, circulated and read in Ireland, Britain and America and as such were caught up in the shifting dramas of a changing print culture, itself shaped by asymmetries of language, power and population. Connolly meets that culture on its own terms and charts its history.

CLAIRE CONNOLLY FLSW MRIA IntFRSE is Professor of Modern English at University College Cork. She is the author of the award-winning *A Cultural History of the Irish Novel, 1790–1829*, as well as many essays and articles on eighteenth- and nineteenth-century Irish culture.

IRISH ROMANTICISM

A Literary History

CLAIRE CONNOLLY
University College Cork

Shaftesbury Road, Cambridge CB2 8EA, United Kingdom

One Liberty Plaza, 20th Floor, New York, NY 10006, USA

477 Williamstown Road, Port Melbourne, VIC 3207, Australia

314–321, 3rd Floor, Plot 3, Splendor Forum, Jasola District Centre, New Delhi – 110025, India

103 Penang Road, #05–06/07, Visioncrest Commercial, Singapore 238467

Cambridge University Press is part of Cambridge University Press & Assessment, a department of the University of Cambridge.

We share the University's mission to contribute to society through the pursuit of education, learning and research at the highest international levels of excellence.

www.cambridge.org
Information on this title: www.cambridge.org/9781107579538

DOI: 10.1017/9781316443392

© Claire Connolly 2026

This publication is in copyright. Subject to statutory exception and to the provisions of relevant collective licensing agreements, no reproduction of any part may take place without the written permission of Cambridge University Press & Assessment.

When citing this work, please include a reference to the DOI 10.1017/9781316443392

First published 2026

A catalogue record for this publication is available from the British Library

Library of Congress Cataloging-in-Publication Data
NAMES: Connolly, Claire author
TITLE: Irish romanticism : a literary history / Claire Connolly, University College Cork.
DESCRIPTION: Cambridge, United Kingdom ; New York, NY : Cambridge University Press, 2026. | Includes bibliographical references and index.
IDENTIFIERS: LCCN 2025025273 | ISBN 9781107131613 hardback | ISBN 9781316443592 ebook
SUBJECTS: LCSH: Romanticism – Ireland | English literature – Irish authors – History and criticism | LCGFT: Literary criticism
CLASSIFICATION: LCC PN751 .C65 2026 | DDC 809/.9145/09361–dc23/eng/20250709
LC record available at https://lccn.loc.gov/2025025273

ISBN 978-1-107-13161-3 Hardback
ISBN 978-1-107-57953-8 Paperback

Cambridge University Press & Assessment has no responsibility for the persistence or accuracy of URLs for external or third-party internet websites referred to in this publication and does not guarantee that any content on such websites is, or will remain, accurate or appropriate.

For EU product safety concerns, contact us at Calle de José Abascal, 56, 1°, 28003 Madrid, Spain, or email eugpsr@cambridge.org

Contents

List of Figures		*page* vi
Acknowledgements		vii
	Introduction: People, Places, Pasts	1
1	Bookish Histories, 1780–1815	26
2	Watery Prospects, 1815–1830	75
3	Darkening Skies, 1830–1850	116
	Afterword: Frieze Coats and the Fabric of Irish Romanticism	164
Notes		182
Select Bibliography		218
Index		236

Figures

1.1 Robert Rainey, diary giving accounts of political affairs in Dublin, business and social activities while working at Crampton Court and Dame Street. National Library of Ireland MSS 34.395/1. *page* 41

1.2 Charlotte Edgeworth, *John Langan with Little Harriet and Sophy*. Bodleian Libraries, University of Oxford. MS. Eng. misc. c. 903. 43

1.3 Mary Tighe, title page of *Mary, a Series of Reflections during Twenty Years*. 8.5 × 13.5 cm. *EC8 T4484 811m, Houghton Library, Harvard University. 67

3.1 Gabriel Beranger, *Timoleague Castle, Abbey and Town*, c. 1770–1799. Watercolour. 29.5 × 24 cm. RIA MS 3 C 30/68. By permission of the Royal Irish Academy © RIA. 157

A.1 George Petrie, *Hanging Washing in Lord Portlester's Chapel, Saint Audeon's, Dublin*, n.d. Graphite and wash on paper. 14.3 × 23.1 cm. NGI.6002. 165

A.2 Henry McManus, *Reading 'The Nation'*, 1850s. Oil on canvas. 30.5 × 35.5 cm. National Gallery of Ireland. NGI.1917. 166

A.3 A late sixteenth-century coat recovered from Killery Bog, County Sligo in 1824. © National Museum of Ireland. 169

A.4 Nathaniel Grogan, *The Country Schoolmaster*, n.d. Mezzotint and etching. 36.4 × 52.8 cm. The British Museum. 1977, U.1225. 170

Acknowledgements

Irish Romanticism: A Literary History describes a culture made of tough stuff. My sporadically fragile efforts in its writing would not have come to much without the robust good sense and companionship of those whose names are recorded here. Bethany Thomas commissioned *Irish Romanticism* for Cambridge University Press and, with support from George Paul Laver, provided excellent guidance. The people who read this book in outline, in part and in its emerging entirety – including Cambridge University Press's anonymous readers, Tina Morin, Breandán Mac Suibhne and Tríona Ní Shíocháin – gave vital support. James Chandler, Jane Moore and Porscha Fermanis read the whole thing and each one of them went above and beyond in their responses and encouragement. I feel lucky to count all three as friends. Thanks to Andy Bielenberg for answering my questions about economic history, to David Dickson for telling me about Robert Rainey and to Peadar Ó Muircheartaigh for advice on manuscript culture. For continued encouragement in the messy business of making books, I thank Patricia Coughlan, Margaret Kelleher and Moynagh Sullivan. And for highly practical and efficient support in the same business, warmest thanks to Brandon Yen. I hold the memory of the late Tom Dunne dear and hope to have done justice to the stylishness, verve and insight of his formative work on Irish romanticism.

For sustaining conversations and advice along the way, I thank: Ros Ballaster, Luisa Calè, Matt Campbell, Nicholas Canny, Linda Connolly, Mary Ann Constantine, Nick Daly, Greg Dart, David Duff, Ian Duncan, Liz Edwards, Penny Fielding, Nuala Finnegan, Roy Foster, Katie Garner, Peter Garside, Sonia Hofkosh, Bob Irvine, Nigel Leask, Joep Leerssen, Deirdre Lynch, Barry McCrea, Ailbhe McDaid, Tetsuko Nakamura, Finola O'Kane, Danielle O'Donovan, Clare O'Halloran, Anna Pilz, Stephanie Rains, Katharina Rennhak, Ann Rigney, Diego Saglia, James Louis Smith, Clair Wills and Yuri Yoshino.

I completed work on *Irish Romanticism* while Burns Fellow at Boston College and every page of the book bears the signature of the support afforded by the university and its stellar community of Irish studies scholars. Special thanks to Guy Beiner, Christian Dupont, Marjorie Howes, Joe Nugent, Vera Kreilkamp, Erin Scheopner, Jim Smith and Colleen Taylor. An earlier phase of research as Parnell Fellow in Irish Studies allowed for a vital period of reading and thinking among the fellowship of Magdalene College, University of Cambridge. Thanks especially to Eamon Duffy for that opportunity. Much of the research was conducted at the Bodleian Library, Oxford, Cambridge's University Library, the Houghton Library at Harvard, the National Library of Ireland, the library of Trinity College Dublin, the National Library of Scotland and the library of the Royal Irish Academy. At University College Cork, I am extremely grateful for the support of friends and colleagues, including Helena Buffery, Mary Costello, John Cryan, Conor Delaney, Aoife Dowling, Anne FitzGerald, John FitzGerald, Adam Hanna, Elaine Harrington, Lee Jenkins, Heather Laird, Máirín MacCarron, Órla Murphy, Georgina Nugent, Clíona Ó Gallchoir, Crónán Ó Doibhlin, Maureen O'Connor, Aisling O'Leary, James O'Sullivan and Jay Roszman. I know that they join me in remembering Eibhear Walshe and Chris Williams. For help in chasing down permissions, my thanks to Claudia Kinmoth, Avice-Claire McGovern, Leeanne Quinn and Aoife Ruane. I gratefully acknowledge the Research Support Fund of University College Cork's College of Arts, Celtic Studies and Social Sciences, along with the Publications Fund of the National University of Ireland.

For cousinly chats about everything apart from this book, thanks to Catherine Kirwan and Marcia Kirwan. The threads of family connection – especially my relationship with my late father Jim Connolly, my mother Ann Connolly, my late aunt Maura Cullinan and my siblings Ciara Connolly, Cliona Connolly and John Connolly – are the stuff of which not just a book but a world is made. At home, Paul O'Donovan pushed me to seek out new horizons while Olan O'Donovan kept my feet on the ground. Their cat, Hickey, was no help at all. The book is dedicated to Paul, who will have to forgive the typos that he will find.

Introduction
People, Places, Pasts

Between the mid-eighteenth century and the mid-nineteenth century, the population of Ireland soared – growing every decade from about 1750 until 1840 – only to fall back dramatically as a result of the Great Famine. Considering the scale and intensity of the changes experienced, the historian Niall Ó Ciosáin asserts that the hundred or so years from the middle of the eighteenth to the middle of the nineteenth century can be treated as 'a single, fairly coherent, unit', at least from the perspective of the majority of the rural population.[1] What happens if we treat those same years as a unit in literary history? Susan Wolfson and William Galperin already made a similar case for a British 'Romantic Century' when they proposed 1750–1850 as 'an intellectually and historically coherent century-long category'.[2] For Ireland, I argue in this book, a slightly briefer span of time, the years between about 1780 and 1850, can be understood as a meaningful period in the making of a romantic Ireland.

Nestled within that century lie folds and splits that lend a distinctive texture to Irish romantic culture. Not least of these is the relationship between the majority Catholic population and the mainly elite Protestant women writers who inaugurated an Irish romantic literature. That all began to change as middle-class Catholic writers, mostly men, came into voice from about 1800. Meanwhile, Irish romantic literature registers and responds to a palpable history of unjust colonial land settlements, revolution and war, a rural society in transition, famine and displacement. The encounter happens in the English language, on the flat plane of the printed page. A commitment to distinct cultural voices emerging from peripheral places gives force and energy to writers as varied as Maria Edgeworth, Sydney Owenson and Thomas Moore. Despite their many differences – one the offspring of a midlands landlord who made her name with prestigious publications in prose, the next a more or less self-made actor's daughter who worked as a governess even as she made her way into publishing and the last the son of a Dublin shopkeeper who worked tirelessly to achieve income and reputation – the three writers share a self-consciously historical imagination and helped to invent a distinctly Irish literature. Although Edgeworth's and Owenson's fictions and Moore's satires and melodies are partitioned in many histories, all share the same cultural ground prospected in this book.

Despite the familiarity of Edgeworth and Owenson on our pages or Moore on our ears, however, we remain literate outsiders to a culture that moved freely between oral, performed and print modes, forever on the other side of a barrier erected by colonialism, cultural privilege and recurrent catastrophes. Comprised of texts written in English by Irish writers whose class position ranges downward from elite to ordinary, Irish romantic literature partakes in particular ways of the problems outlined by Peter Burke in his classic study of popular culture. Imaging the latter as 'elusive quarry', Burke describes problems of access across time, language and class.[3] In Ireland, the experiences of death, emigration and language loss heralded by the Great Hunger eroded cultural links still further. The late eighteenth- and early nineteenth-century compositions discussed in this book were written in one world and increasingly came to be read or heard within another: we are the inheritors of this process.

But neither can it be right, as Vincent Morley has shown us, to consign 'the bulk of the Irish people to the role of non-speaking extras' in our history.[4] Using popular Irish-language poetry and songs as his source, Morley finds evidence of a collective sense of identity shared by the majority of the Irish people, resting on a belief in Ireland's status as an ancient kingdom loyal to the Stuarts and the Pope, eagerly awaiting the overthrow of the Williamite settlement. Such a worldview, Morley shows, was remarkably resilient and responsive, able to adapt to a variety of political events, including the American Revolution and the United Irish uprising, and later passing into Anglophone idioms of political democracy.[5]

Only traces of such popular understandings come into view in this book. Yet their marks are present and they helped to shape a modern Irish literature written in the English language that carried with it questions of history, language and identity, in their turn imprinted by issues of representation, population and demographic change. Beginning in the optimistic aftermath of the American Revolution with the performative politics of the Volunteers, the decades discussed witnessed innovations in literary genres, the flourishing of individual reputations and a brief literary renaissance. William Drennan's poem 'Glendalloch' imagines an Ireland 'stung' into activity by 'trans-atlantic glory' and the 'eloquence and virtue' of the Irish parliament.[6] The French Revolution severed older Irish ties, both commercial and religious, and prepared the grounds of modernity, while Ireland also felt the reverberations of the Haitian Revolution of 1791–1804. Toussaint Louverture lay dying in a French prison during Maria Edgeworth's visit to Paris in 1803, where she closely followed news of Napoleon's losses in Saint Domingue, discussed Britain's future in Bengal and heard tell of the Louisiana Purchase. In terms of empire more broadly, Ireland over these years transitioned from a 'colonial outpost for much of the eighteenth century to sub-imperial centre by the beginning of the nineteenth', a change that meant much tighter ties into imperial commerce.[7] But these same years tell also of disease, violence and the creeping horrors of hunger. Growing wealth for the middle and upper classes did little to counteract the effective pauperisation of most of the country as the sub-division of land proceeded apace, early efforts at industry failed, vagrancy increased and social dislocation ensued. Widening inequalities, disease, contagion, famine and recurrent agrarian violence were notable features of Irish life even as the state extended its reach during the period after the 1801 Act of Union.

Still, the case for linking the lives of Ireland's majority rural population with the emergence of Irish literature is not an easy one to make. Rather than any clear alignment between the lives of the people and the literature of Ireland, we encounter questions, demands, doubts and entreaties that take shape in particular ways from about the 1780s onwards. These of course are quintessentially literary modes, and to track them is to begin to map a relationship between vernacular culture, learned Irish-language texts, popular classicism and new developments in imaginative literature. That latter body of work, the realm of polite letters across Britain and Ireland, is now most readily identified with romanticism but contains within itself those other, older, forces.

Defining Irish Romanticism

The broad outlines of the usual story of the emergence of Irish literature from the middle of the eighteenth century are well known, and there have been important and ongoing efforts to frame and analyse the brilliant literary achievements of the Banims, William Carleton, Maria Edgeworth, Gerald Griffin, James Clarence Mangan, Charles Robert Maturin, Thomas Moore, Lady Morgan and Mary Tighe. But it remains a challenge to bring these authors into dialogue with one another and to understand them in the context of the culture at large, the result perhaps of a tendency to conceive of Irish romanticism as an inherently broken cultural moment, of interest because of the ways in which its own fragmented state enacts a kind of prototypical romantic predicament. As it is usually told, the story of Irish romanticism comes equipped with a high-flown rhetoric of loss and defeat: a culture 'on a collision course with Britishness and the ideology of empire'.[8] But while it is possible to make such a case based on a selective reading of key scenes and images from a range of writers, the wider context is too often ignored: Irish literature of the Romantic period still needs what Marilyn Butler described as a 'methodology which gives weight both to the collection of evidence and to analysis as opposed to synthesis' and that is just what is offered here.[9]

So, what does 'Irish romanticism' mean and when did Ireland become romantic? How does Irish romanticism differ from the literary culture of late eighteenth- and nineteenth-century Britain, and what qualities do they share? I propose an understanding of romanticism as a temporally and aesthetically distinct period in Irish culture, during which literature flourished in new forms and styles. Books by Irish authors were written, sold, circulated and read in Ireland, Britain and America and as such were caught up in the shifting dramas of a changing print culture. Not all of these writers knew each other personally, but they shared networks that crossed the Irish Sea: with the exception of Mangan, all published in Britain or lived or spent time there. At the same time, each of these writers is aware of their distance from the larger island, and in particular from London: at once centre of colonial power and capital of an expanding culture industry. Romanticism is perhaps the period when Irish literature most needs Britain in order to chart its history and create a cultural narrative. Where Victorian literature seems to belong to Britain and its expanding empire, and where modernism sees Irish writers make their own global moment, it is striking to reflect upon the extent to which romanticism is a quintessentially archipelagic cultural formation shaped by back-and-forth movement between the two islands and across the empire. British romanticism in turn is shaped at countless points by a relationship with Ireland, from the influence of Edgeworth on Scott or Bishop Percy on Wordsworth to the role of the Catholic question in the quarrel between the *Edinburgh* and the *Quarterly* reviews or the friendship of Moore and Byron.

In 1814, Jane Austen advised her niece Anna not to locate any part of the action of a novel in progress in Ireland: 'you had better not leave England', she wrote, 'Let the Portmans go to Ireland; but as you know nothing of the Manners there, you had better not go with them. You will be in danger of giving false representations. Stick to Bath & the Foresters. There you will be quite at home.'[10] Austen herself made only brief, allusive references to Ireland, but these also express a reluctance to engage with the place, as when in *Emma* 'the not going to Ireland' becomes the motive for one of the heroine's many misunderstandings about Jane Fairfax and her secret relationship with Frank Churchill. Mrs Bates quite trusts Jane's preference for 'her native air', though she has to correct her language from that of 'different kingdoms' to the more nuanced post-Union term, 'different countries'. As the Union hovers in the background of Austen's great paean to Englishness, Frank's clandestine gift of a piano accompanied by the sheet music for some *Irish Melodies* further seeks to secure Ireland within that framework, joining native airs to Irish ones. When Jane plays one song from this imagined collection – 'Robin Adair' – it is a popular English composition set to an old Irish air (also used by Thomas Moore and Gerald Griffin and mentioned in *The Wild Irish Girl*), 'Eileen Aroon'.[11] The exchange testifies not only to the pervasive place of the *Melodies* in wider cultural conversations but also to the ease by which they might be appropriated: in the late 1820s, Felicia Hemans, at once lamenting the loss of her mother and commencing work on her *Records of Woman*, wrote that she herself resembled 'an Irish melody', with its 'quick and wild transitions from sadness to gaiety'.[12]

Austen's best unionist efforts aside, Irish literature of the late eighteenth and early nineteenth centuries rings with accusations of 'false representations'. Much of the writing of the late eighteenth and early nineteenth centuries served as so many retorts to the linking of Ireland to barbarity and savagery, a common historic association still in need of address. Austen shows us she has this string to her bow too, when Emma makes a nasty joke about Jane's 'odd' and 'outrée' curled hair resembling 'an Irish fashion', as if recalling the wild Irish hairstyles and glibs outlawed in the sixteenth century.[13] Present since medieval times, such prejudices took on a distinctly colonial dimension in the sixteenth and seventeenth centuries in the work of writers including Sir John Davies, Edmund Spenser and Fynes Moryson. Attacking Moryson in particular, Sydney Owenson took aim at these early modern 'prejudiced and abject' commentators on Ireland, 'scribblers, who in the Elizabethan day, endeavoured to write themselves into the favour of the English government by calumniating the natural as well as the moral state of Ireland'.[14] She framed her own fiction in opposition to such assumptions and wrote, she says, her landmark novel *The Wild Irish Girl*, 'against a host of gigantic prejudices'.[15]

Following the success of *The Wild Irish Girl*, Owenson went on to write national tales set in Greece (*Woman: or, Ida of Athens*, 1809) and India (*The Missionary*, 1811), reminding us that Ireland requires analysis in a multiplicity of modes: variously, as comprised of specific places and internal frontiers; equivocally, as a bilingual culture where accents and voices compete and overlap; and imperially, via locations such as Greece, Peru and India. Irish romanticism not only emerges against a backdrop of political, religious, social and cultural conflict but also comes equipped with a strong sense of diverse communities, often made manifest in an awareness of layered and overlapping readerships.

In the Romantic period, the perennial question of knowing Ireland took on a new charge, informed by rebellion and union as well as increased travel between the two islands. The journeys avoided by Austen were undertaken by others, as acts of imagination as well as material movements. Speaking in the House of Lords in favour of the Catholic cause in 1812, Byron countered that objection 'that I never was in Ireland' with an assertion that 'it is as easy to know something of Ireland without having been there, as it appears with some to have been born, bred, and cherished there, and yet remain ignorant of its best interests'.[16] And in 1800, Thomas De Quincey accompanied his school friend Lord Sligo on a visit to Ireland, undertaking a thirty-hour journey to Dublin along the 'high road to the Head', as he described it in his *Confessions of an English Opium-Eater* (1821), and finding himself in Dublin even as the Act of Union passed into law.[17] That same summer of 1800 saw William Godwin in Ireland, spending time with the lawyer John Philpott Curran and the veteran politician Henry Grattan as well as meeting Margaret Mount Cashell and Joseph Cooper Walker. Writing home, Godwin made little of the challenges of the journey – the sea was but 'a river sixty miles broad' – though in the end his return was delayed by high winds.[18] Later, among the additions to the 1856 edition of *Confessions*, we find De Quincey's reckoning with the 'massy' infrastructure joining up the disparate parts of the United Kingdom, in which he imagines his own person, transported to London as part of a 'huge tonnage' that includes 'all that weight of love and hatred which Ireland had found herself able to muster through twenty-four hours in the great depôt of Dublin, by way of donation to England'.[19]

Austen, De Quincey and Byron all witnessed, participated in and resisted a broader reframing of British imperialism in the aftermath of the Peninsular and Napoleonic Wars. Tim Fulford and Peter Kitson have described the 1820s and 1830s as 'a watershed' in British colonialism, 'witnessing a move from a protectionist colonial system … to a free-trade empire with a political and moral agenda'.[20] Changes included rights for Catholics and dissenters, the abolition of slavery in the empire and parliamentary reform. Some Irish Catholics benefited from this 'historic settlement across nation and empire' as the bonds of union grew closer, and these imperial affiliations are also explored in the book.[21]

Romanticism by the Numbers

From the mid-eighteenth century to the end of the Great Famine, Ireland was 'an intensely bilingual and diglossic society'.[22] Over 40 per cent of the population still spoke Irish at the turn of the nineteenth century, while the absolute number of Irish speakers continued to increase until the 1840s, growing as the population did. Language change was 'a lengthy, largely silent and ad hoc process, its pace and impact varying greatly according to region, class and even individual experiences'.[23] Literacy was typically acquired via English, and the idea of 'literature', even when prefixed with the adjective 'Irish', was strongly associated with imaginative Anglophone writing. Across these decades, a 'vibrant culture of partial literacy' took on new meaning in the rapidly changing world of Anglophone print.[24]

To these asymmetries of language and power, we must add population size. The question of the popular exerts a special force in my argument, and I show across the book how significant the sheer size of the population is for an Irish literature in the making. Though contemporary historians largely contradict the notion that Ireland's impoverishment in the pre-Famine period was caused by overpopulation, it remains true that pressure on population is clearly linked to poor-quality housing, illiteracy and poverty.[25] Contemporaries, including Thomas Malthus, saw such factors in stark terms not least because of differences across the islands: by 1841, the island's population was three times that of Scotland and half that of England. The vast majority of those people, counted and charted across a series of state exercises that gathered momentum from the 1820s, were poor Catholics. A minority Presbyterian population also played a role, feared for their part in the great turnout of 1798 but later thought of as a bulwark against a Catholic threat. In the words of William Hamilton, the loyalist rector and scholar whose assassination is discussed in Chapter 2, Presbyterians might be 'ungracious and litigious' but nonetheless possessed a value inherent in their balancing power within the population: 'one must estimate their worth as a miner often does his ore, rather by its weight than its splendour'.[26]

Remarks on the numerousness of the Irish people are so common as to be virtually invisible, and yet acts of calculation exerted particular kinds of cultural pressure. Edmund Burke's criticism of the economists and calculators of France takes some of its force from the Irish context, while a classic statement of the chasm that divided the Anglo-Irish minority of 'thousands' from the millions that they governed is found in his 'Letter to Hercules Langrishe': 'Sure I am', Burke writes, 'that there have been thousands in Ireland, who have never conversed with a Roman catholick in their whole lives, unless they happened to talk to their gardener's workmen, or to ask their way, when they had lost it, in their sports; or, at best, who had known them only as footmen, or other domesticks, of the second and third order.' Such 'a state of things', writes Burke, results in 'alienation on the one side and pride and insolence on the other.'[27] Burke's description of an unknown and alienated Catholic majority and a proudly unknowing Anglo-Irish minority carries something of the energy and vitality of Irish romanticism itself: a drama of oppression and resistance rooted in the material facts of numbers. The liberal Protestant MP and writer William Parnell spelled the numbers out yet more clearly when he complained that 'a Protestant of seven hundred a year is more looked up to than a Catholic of seven thousand a year'.[28] In John Banim's novel *The Anglo-Irish of the Nineteenth Century* (1828), an anxious Anglo-Irish group replay fears of the combination of Catholics and Presbyterians in 1798, as they worry about 'the Popish Rockites' and predict that they will soon be joined by 'the discontented weavers'. The alliance is made inevitable by numbers and may well topple a system sustained only by history and faith: 'Providence – who, since the first planting of English interests in this miserable country, has wonderfully upheld those interests, against an immense numerical odds of the Papist people – may, indeed, be pleased to avert our danger.'[29] In such accounts, the presence of what Lady Morgan named 'seven millions of Irish Catholics' in pre-Famine Ireland is always felt.[30] Still, the story could be told differently. Many saw the Union as a correction to an imbalanced set of accounts, as suggested by Richard Musgrave: 'In a menacing tone, the papists have told us for some years "we are 3 to 1". With the Union, we may retort "we are 11 to 3".'[31]

When the census of 1821 was taken, the population of Ireland was measured at 7 million, compared to 8.6 million in England and 1.6 million in Scotland. Irish romanticism took shape in the context of a thickly populated country, subject to mass mortality and emigration. Famines and epidemics claimed thousands of lives, notably during the decade after 1815. The thirty years before 1845 were characterised by recurrent patterns of emigration; reaching new and unprecedented heights during and immediately after the Great Famine. Along with the findings of the new statistical science and the efforts of the political economists, the population of Ireland was often remarked upon in terms of wonder and awe: a miserably poor place and yet *'the most densely peopled country in the world'*, according an *Edinburgh Review* article published in 1825. In same article, Ireland is calculated to contain, 'on an average, 215 persons to each square mile!'[32] Reviewing Edward Newenham's study of Ireland's population for the *Edinburgh*, Malthus reported that the country might potentially come to 'contain *twenty millions*' in the course of the nineteenth century and remarked that such a people would have a 'physical force' that would demand political change.[33]

When Percy Bysshe Shelley confronts the asymmetries of population size and power in Britain in the immediate aftermath of the Peterloo Massacre in 1819, it was to call up an 'unvanquishable' popular force: 'YE ARE MANY – THEY ARE FEW'.[34] Already in 1812, Shelley had visited Ireland with his first wife, Harriet, motivated by the improbable plan of finding a publisher in post-Union Dublin for material including a book of poems, an Irish pamphlet and his *Declaration of Rights*. Paul O'Brien suspects that Shelley used John Stockdale as the printer, speculating that the newly arrived poet was not to know that the formerly radical publisher had already turned government informer.[35] In any case, Shelley's address to the Irish people stressed reform over revolution. 'Temperance, sobriety, charity, and independence will give you virtue', declared Shelley's pamphlet *Address to the Irish People* (1812), 'and reading, talking, thinking, and searching will give you wisdom; when you have those things you may defy the tyrant.'[36] As with Coleridge's praise for Irish 'strength and vivacity' in 1800,[37] Shelley's belief in Ireland as a place ripe for a non-violent revolution in 1812 meant thinking of a country as a moral laggard that might yet reform. His *Address* expresses a note of hesitant hope that mixes revolutionary language with a fine-grained gradualist theory of political change: 'May every sun that shines on your green island see the annihilation of an abuse, and the birth of an embryon of melioration!'[38] While Shelley's philosophy of non-violence did not make a notable impression on Irish romantic literature, his later criticisms of Lord Castlereagh resounded in song and story: lines from 'The Masque of Anarchy' are collected as part of the 'Stories, Songs and Ballads of '98' in the Irish Schools Collection, compiled in the 1930s.[39]

Rather than a Shelleyan cry for justice, what we find most commonly in Irish literature is a growing attention to numbers and their meanings, a process that tends towards realism as it follows the data, but does not forget its origins in injustice, war and revolution. There are however connections with Shelley's own *Philosophical View of Reform*, written after Peterloo but not published until the 1920s. Arguing against the idea that 'the evils of the poor arise from an excess of population', Shelley protests that Malthus wishes to take away even legitimate pleasures, having 'the hardened insolence to propose as a remedy that the poor should be compelled … to abstain from sexual intercourse'.[40] Just such a shocked, dramatic and vital understanding of population numbers, as they press on culture and shape a literary legacy, continues up to W. B. Yeats, a writer who measured and enumerated his own literary inheritance in relation to romanticism.[41] And within Irish romantic literature itself, the size of the Irish population was not an inert political problem but rather 'a force for cultural change', to borrow Breandán Mac Suibhne's terms.[42] John Gamble phrased the need to bring the full spectacle of the people into view via some dismissive remarks about 'topography, or the natural curiosities of the country': instead of describing views, his tour of Ireland's northern counties in 1812 focuses on 'human passions, human actions, and human beings'. Gamble puts his point bluntly as he delivers a slight to the famed spectacle of the Giant's Causeway: 'Men and women', he writes, 'are of more importance than pillars or columns'.[43]

James Orr's poetry addresses the ethical debate about people and place via a notably sceptical account of landscape writing in his 'A Fragment of an Epistle to Mr. W. H. D –', a poem addressed to the Presbyterian minister and former United Irishman, William H. Drummond. The poem, written in Ulster Scots vernacular and using the Standard Habbie stanza, imagines a natural world that eludes the poet's abilities and continually returns his vision to real scenes. A 'purplin' morn and pensive eve' call for the poet's pen, but acts of artistic representation are rebuffed by a sensuously rendered world: 'O Nature! cud I set your stage, / Wi' a' its scen'ry on my page!' – 'My cliff sud frown, my echo rave, / My shamrock smell, / My night appear as gran'ly grave / As night hersel'. Orr's sense of responsibility to atmosphere and environment might be understood in the context of the extractive economy of colonialism, as it moves from 'Hill, wood, an' grove' and 'rough cascades' to people and their lives:

> Or cud my manners-paintin' rhymes
> 'Haud up the mirror' to the times,
> I'd sing how *av'rice* gnaws folks wymes,
> How *folly* tipples,
> An' how *ambition* thins the climes
> That *love* re-peoples.

Focussing as it does on partial or fragmentary insights into 'the times', Orr's poem links an anti-Malthusian re-peopling of an impoverished landscape (a place to be populated by '*love*') with a quietly insistent literary force:

> I needna strive. My want and woe
> Unnerves the energies, you know;
> Yet Nature prompts my muse, tho' slow
>   An' faints her fires:
> The cuckoo sings obscurely low,
>   The lark aspires.
> Coy science spurn'd me frae her knee,
> An' fortune bad my shuttle flee;
> But, a' the while, smit strangely wi'
>   The love o' sang,
> I rudely rhyme the scenes I see,
>   Whare'er I gang.[44]

Orr's defence of his rude rhymes and Gamble's invocations of 'men and women' both assert the value of ordinary Irish voices. But these can be difficult to pin down, braided as they often are with forms of silence that include narrative pauses, lyrical hesitations and unfinished speculations. It may even be that the rhetoric of silence and reticence affords Irish romanticism at least part of its distinctive cultural shape: not only the silence of harps or bowers, but that of people and places. When the Donegal schoolmaster Hugh Dorian described the customs and ceremony surrounding the opening of letters from America, including the reading aloud by the local 'scholar', he notes that 'In every family letter there is always something which strangers have no right to know.'[45] The Cambridge academic John Lee noted not only secrecy of Irish but also their pertinacious efforts to extract information from travellers themselves. The question of secrecy moves into the mode of mystery in William Makepeace Thackeray's *Irish Sketchbook* (1842), where the fictional narrator arrives at 'a dilapidated hotel and posting-house' near Leighlinbridge in County Carlow and, finding himself surrounded by noisy children and preying beggars, asks 'How do all these people live?': 'One can't help wondering; – these multifarious vagabonds, without work or workhouse, or means of subsistence?' Citing the Poor Law report, Thackeray notes 'that there are twelve hundred thousand people in Ireland, a sixth of the population, who have no means of livelihood but charity, and whom the state, or individual members of it, must maintain.' Repeating his wonderment at how the state can 'support such an enormous burthen', Thackeray also tries to peer into everyday lives of the wandering poor: 'What a strange history it would be, could one but get it true, – that of the manner in which a score of these beggars have maintained themselves for a fortnight past!' Such questions generate some remarkable rhetoric, starting with Malthus' 'astonishment and curiosity' and continuing through Thackeray's pronouncement that 'It is awful to think that there are eight millions of stories to be told in this island'.[46] Keats' observation about a sick and elderly woman seen as he passed through Belfast, discussed in Chapter 2 – 'What a thing would be a history of her Life and sensations?' – adopts the same tone of dazed dismay.

Others tried to tell at least some of the stories. Sydney Owenson's *Patriotic Sketches* (1807) returns us to the silent suffering of a crowded West of Ireland place, as she vividly after the manner of Burke, evokes a scene of 'alienation', 'where prerogative rests on one side, and submission on the other'.[47] Owenson went to Connaught on the advice of Joseph Cooper Walker, who suggested the value of visiting a 'primitive' part of Ireland while 'Your name is … *up*', following the publication of *The Wild Irish Girl* (1806).[48] Her account of the densely populated landscape of Sligo around 1807 imagines a silent peasantry in aggregate, even as her own individualised, lyric response to poverty takes on a Yeatsian solemnity: 'I have seen the feet of the heavily-laden mother totter through winter snows beneath her tender burthen', she wrote, 'I have met them wandering over those heaths, which afforded no shelter to their aching brows, amidst the meridian ardours of a summer's day; … I have met them at the door of magisterial power, and seen them spurned from its threshold … I have seen them cheerfully received into the cabin of an equally humble, but more fortunate compatriot, where their wants were a recommendation to benevolence, and their number no check to its exertion.'[49]

If *Patriotic Sketches* tries on an anaphoric rhetoric in a lyric voice whose power is achieved in the name of the people, Owenson's novels from *The Wild Irish Girl* onwards occupy themselves with the deep past of that same population, their books, traditions, customs, clothing and plants. The narrative preoccupation with the material of Irish life belongs to a post-Enlightenment nationalising moment embodied in such forms as antiquarian histories, travels and collections of ballads and vernacular poetry. Also present at its birth of Irish romanticism is a vibrant popular classicism that played its part, vividly evoked by Owenson in the figure of the poor scholar, a restive type who captured the attention of William Carleton in the 1840s, Padraic Colum in the 1950s and Seamus Heaney and Brian Friel in the 1980s.

While there have been challenges to accounts of British romantic literature as moving away from classical and neoclassical imitation towards what Raymond Williams calls the 'extraordinary flowering of the creative idea',[50] it remains vital for Irish literary history to take into account the persistence of a lively popular culture of classical learning well into the nineteenth century. Recent research on what Tarlach Ó Raifeartaigh terms 'the legend of the Latin-speaking peasants' lends some credence to earlier accounts of popular classical learning in eighteenth-century culture.[51] In her study of *The Irish Classical Self*, Laurie O'Higgins finds sufficient evidence of popular classical knowledge in the eighteenth and nineteenth centuries 'to constitute a pattern, to make a mark, and create a memory in the wider culture'.[52] Irish romantic writing often locates scenes of classical learning as part of the unfolding drama of education. Owenson's *Patriotic Sketches* supplies a lively and detailed account of the figure of the scholar, scribe and hedge schoolmaster Thaddeus Connellan, whose Sligo 'lyceum' is filled with young people reading Virgil. He explains to Owenson, 'with the utmost gravity', his plan to translate 'the Eneid, and some of Terence's plays, into Irish. "The latter (he continued) I will teach to my scholars, who may play it yet upon one of the great London stages to admiration".[53] And if Owenson sounds a mocking note, her own first foray into print, her *Poems* of 1801, contains a number of pieces that are clearly written in imitation and interrogation of classical models. 'The Hawthorne Tree', for example, praises native Irish flora over both classical and British plants, while the poem makes a familiar address to Apollo as 'Dan Pol'.[54] When she died, Lady Morgan left the 'Greek and Latin classics from her library' to her grandnephew, to 'assist in his education'.[55]

Within Irish folklore, the poor scholar who travels the country in search of education, often in the classics, is a representative of longing, loss and hope. A complex figure located between oral and literate traditions, his migrant mobility becomes a source of unease in much early nineteenth-century commentary. Richard Lovell Edgeworth associated the Greek and Roman histories themselves with 'restlessness and adventure'. In a letter to the Committee of the Board of Education, he cautions against 'abridgments of these histories', arguing that 'they inculcate democracy, and a foolish hankering after undefined liberty: this is peculiarly dangerous in Ireland'.[56] Such histories surely fell into the hands of a number of the writers discussed in the book, including Jeremiah Joseph Callanan, Thomas Dermody, John Banim and Gerald Griffin. But women's names were not entirely forgotten among this male world of popular education: in 1825, an anonymous and impoverished tutor from County Limerick dedicated a manuscript volume listing teachers through the ages to 'the talents and virtues of Lady Morgan, as grateful tribute for the pleasure enjoyed in the perusal of several of her volumes wherein the subject of Education has been introduced'. Listed among the 'degraded tribe' are educators ranging from Abelard and Immanuel Kant to Theophilus O'Flanagan – listed here as O'Flaherty – whose son, Matthew, advertised 'A key to the classics' in *The Nation* on 14 June 1843.[57]

Irish Romantic Phases

Modestly phrased as it is, there remains much value in Norman Vance's suggestion that '"Romantic" probably describes the full range of writing in early nineteenth-century Ireland better than "national" or "nationalist"'.[58] But any effort to conceptualise Irish romanticism in drily discursive terms sits uneasily with the lively literary culture described in these pages. Where Marilyn Butler once warned against the Anglo-American invention of 'romanticism' as the offspring of aridly formal scholarship, in Ireland we have to guard against overweening political or philosophical explanations that seek to contain the culture in the mode of summary. A critical tendency (especially among historians) to reduce the writings of Edgeworth and Owenson to the politics of the marriage plot presents one version of the problem.[59] Moore too can be trapped within the outlines of his reputation as 'fashionable song bird, fluttering from one socially rarefied early nineteenth-century Whig salon to the next, warbling nostalgic songs and sentimental hymns to Ireland's lost glory'.[60] In my account, the category of romanticism recognises literary texture and acknowledges cultural change, whether encountered as philosophical histories, domestic novels, sharp satires, rough-hewn fictions, uneasy journalistic responses or smoothly achieved lyrics.

More generally, the term 'romanticism' now tends towards geographical diversity, cultural particularity and historical specificity, calling up a period of writing in which 'canonical order[s]', in James Chandler's description, 'feel splintered, multiple, and localized'.[61] Following Marilyn Butler's formative work, literary scholarship on romanticism has uncovered the political realities that not only underlie but also overdetermine imaginary ideals of aesthetic unity. There is also a growing awareness of what happens when Anglophone literary modes encounter other contexts: much of the work previously gathered under the rubric of 'late Romanticism' might be better thought of in terms of the new models demanded by imperial and colonial cases. That broadening of geographical frame has showcased the significance of Thomas Moore for the 'Brown Romantics', including Henry De Rozio's work in Kolkata, as shown by Manu Chander.[62] Anna Johnston and Porscha Fermanis, meanwhile, consider the case of Eliza Hamilton Dunlop, a published poet who left Ireland for Wollombi, New

South Wales with her police magistrate husband in 1838, and whose work engaged with Indigenous knowledge, languages and welfare.[63]

My study embraces the current political, generic and geographical capaciousness of the term 'romanticism' but stays true to the unifying power of a concept that enables debate and discussion across periods and places. In what follows, I proceed in the spirit of Chandler's observation that '*Romantic* and *Romanticism* share a grammar with a family of terms – say, classicist, renaissance, enlightenment, gothic, modern, even early modern – that together have been useful in the past and, going forward, will continue to work better as an ensemble than they do apart, especially in comparatist contexts'.[64] To this 'useful' collection of literary concepts we can add some terms that mesh aesthetic with political forms of judgement. *Irish Romanticism* tracks and keeps pace with the emergence of concepts – and sometimes even the coinage of terms – that have been retroactively applied to late eighteenth- and nineteenth-century literature, and which continue to do active cultural work – among them 'romantic', 'ascendancy', 'national', 'wild' and 'racy of the soil'. It is impossible fully to disentangle the books themselves from these terms, and it may be more important to note the provenance of such language: Irish romanticism realises forms of knowledge that are already embedded within and belong to the literary and oral cultures that they represent. Sydney Owenson is the most striking case of a writer who seems to invent the terms by which she will be read. In her prose we find original or very early usages of a remarkable range of terms, including 'national tale', 'wild Irish', 'wild Atlantic' and even 'romanticism' itself, as I discuss in Chapter 2. Edgeworth too concerns herself with philology as method while Moore's *Melodies* contain a repository of phrases and sounds with lasting influence.

Romanticism describes a cultural formation made up of multiple phases that played out over several decades, in part made from the materials of Ireland's relationship with Britain and its empire, in part made by writers themselves as they appraised one another, their achievements and failures. Most of all, it took shape within particular works of verse and prose. In its effort to produce a detailed account of the contoured surface across which political meanings were made, *Irish Romanticism* addresses itself primarily to literature rather than performance or the visual arts. David O'Shaugnessy has noted that, after the optimism of the 1780s, Irish dramatists found it more difficult to make their way on the London stage.[65] There were London successes – notably plays by James Sheridan Knowles (1784–1862) and Richard Lalor Sheil (1791–1851) as well as the singular case of Charles Robert Maturin's *Bertram* (1816) – and significant performances in locations including Belfast, Cork, Kilkenny and Dublin, while further research will undoubtedly reveal a fuller story.[66] The play that John Banim wrote about the Viking invasion of Ireland, for instance, may well be the same Irish historical drama that Byron mocked mercilessly in a letter to Moore, during the latter's Drury Lane days. James Sheridan Knowles was drawn to the same theme, and all are likely to have based their plays on the depiction of Brian Boru (Brian Boroimhe) found in Geoffrey Keating's *Foras Feasa ar Éirea*.[67]

A Strange Country?

Irish Romanticism depicts an Irish culture and history that is inescapably bound with other places, people and ideas, shaped by relationships that operate along a variety of different scales. To calibrate such relationships and measure Irish romanticism on its own terms is a key aim of this book. In Seamus Deane's 1984 formulation, romanticism remains fundamentally exterior to Irish cultural life, a combined problem in aesthetics and politics: 'to cast a romantic hue upon the matter represented is, in effect, to misrepresent it by lending it an aura or attraction not essentially its own'.[68] Just a few years later, Tom Dunne mapped out the contours of an 'Irish Romantic literature' but suggested that there was no Irish romanticism 'as such'; rather, he argued, Ireland saw a 'confused and introverted' period of cultural production where creative energies failed to break through the hard carapace of colonialism.

In Dunne's account, the colonial dimension is inescapable: romanticism is one phase in an Irish culture that was 'haunted by history'. It is certainly true that Irish literature is marked by violence and attuned to power, as witnessed in the prominence of plots of dispossession or in repeated references to early modern commentators including Edmund Spenser. Even the flowering of original English language fiction and poetry might be seen simply as testament to the success of the programme of anglicisation that began in the early seventeenth century. But Irish literature from the end of the eighteenth through to the middle of the nineteenth century is also intensely occupied with its own moment, whether that be a world of ballad singers, fishermen, naval service, cholera, the credit crisis or hunger and disease. Those ordinary experiences never shed their colonial markings, one aspect of which is involvement in an imperial worldview. Works by Irish writers also travelled with the empire, as evident from an exploration of the Irish titles found in Porscha Fermanis' digital archive of book catalogues from the colonial southern hemisphere.[69]

Some of Dunne's diagnosis hangs on the material facts of book production. Irish books were, at least at first, 'published mainly in London' and 'written primarily for an English audience' while a revival of Dublin publishing and a rise in English language literacy began to see changes in these patterns from around 1830. Throughout, though, 'the English focus, like the English language and English literary genres remained predominant'.[70] But Dunne's account ignores the extent to which Irish romanticism gets out ahead of literary history in inaugurating new forms, notably the national tale. Much of the Irish fiction of the early 1800s is, as R. F. Foster puts it, *'sui generis'*, characterised by a politics with an undeniably 'experimental' cast.[71] And the Englishness of Irish romanticism involved possibilities as well predicaments: questions of copying, derivativeness and 'secondariness' work their way into the texture of Irish literature as theme and metaphor, as I discuss later.[72] Finally, the rhetoric of Dunne's argument is itself worthy of close reading: to say that there was no Irish romanticism 'as such' is to fashion a verbal net that catches both a substantial body of writing and a slender set of claims to conceptual coherence. In *Irish Romanticism*, I immerse readers within a large literary archive and while also pulling those slim threads of connection in order to fashion a cohesive argument, a tension that is further explored in my Afterword via the relationship between rags and a whole coat.

In the period since Dunne's intervention, many books and essays have revived individual Irish romantic writers and revalued genres, notably the national tale, opening up a pathway to a new understanding of romanticism in the present. Yet Julia Wright's pointed description of the 'barely sketched Irish romanticism of a handful of partly known authors' remains accurate while Dunne's vital call to scholars to attempt to grasp 'the processes and traumas' of Ireland's 'cultural revolution' of the late eighteenth and early nineteenth centuries goes unanswered.[73] *Irish Romanticism* addresses the tumultuous experience of linguistic and cultural change in eighteenth- and nineteenth-century Ireland, in order to chart the contours of a literary culture on the move. It does so by mapping out three main chronological phases that give shape to a literary history whose layers unfold in the telling. All three phases in my stratigraphy overlap and interconnect. Sometimes this happens because individual authorial lives and reputations stretch across the generations. Major literary reputations – especially those of Maria Edgeworth, Sydney Owenson and Thomas Moore – appear across the three phases discussed though they sometimes fall back in my account to allow for a fuller picture of a wider range of writers to emerge. But mostly it happens because, as Edmund Burke wrote of all generations in his *Reflections on the Revolution in France* (1790), they cannot be absolutely demarcated from one another.

In Chapter 1, the first of the phases stretches from 1780 to 1815, tracking the period between the establishment of Grattan's parliament to the end of the French Revolutionary, Napoleonic and Peninsular Wars. Considering the cases of four Irish writers who at first glance seem to come from different worlds, I show how connecting them to one another requires taking a step in the direction of a more fully conceptualised Irish romanticism. Thomas Dermody, Charlotte Brooke, Mary Tighe and James Orr have all benefited from recent research that helps to restore their textual as well as biographical reputations but their reputations remain isolated from one another. I do not neglect the constitutive careers of Maria Edgeworth, Sydney Owenson and Thomas Moore in this first phase, but choose to approach them in their mediatised aspect, showing how bookish acts including copying connect their work to each other and the wider world.

Writerly networks, though sometimes quite faintly traced, emerge across my chapters. The very faintness of those connections extends, in Chapter 2, into a discussion of water in Irish romanticism, bearing in mind what Joshua Calhoun calls the 'hydrophilic' qualities of paper as a medium.[74] The second phase, explored in Chapter 2, traces a period of growing self-confidence in Irish letters that might seem surprising in the context of the post-Waterloo recession but takes some of its charge from the strength and eventual success of the campaign for Catholic Emancipation. Between 1815 and 1830, Irish writers felt able to look more closely at the island on their own terms, a scrutiny that meant for many a new interest in coastal locations and the shaping force of the sea. This is the period for which the diagnosis of Ireland as a 'strange country' seems both most apt and most contentious: writers including Gerald Griffin, Charles Robert Maturin and Jeremiah Joseph Callanan acknowledged, sought to undo and sometimes to reimagine external images of Ireland as a place that only existed in the wash of empire. The formal consequences of these varied encounters with seas and coasts include a new psychological depth in all three writers, sometimes expressed in a Gothic language, but still requiring realist modes even where introspection is the dominant note. From the end of the Napoleonic Wars to the cultural renaissance of the 1830s, Irish romanticism begins to imagine local places via their position on a world map.

Chapter 3 charts the final phase of Irish romanticism, from 1830 to 1850, when those explorations return to something of the medial self-consciousness of the earlier, bookish histories. If paper is the medium of

Chapter 1 and water of Chapter 2, the third phase offers an abundance of detail that promises to thin out the medium and create a more complete picture of Ireland in the aggregate. The very copiousness of the data is the result of state efforts to explain and understand Ireland, an enlightened political imperative that leaves a mark on literary representation, as a reach for a fuller reality becomes increasingly darkened by the detail. A new relationship takes shape, between a densely rendered colonial information infrastructure and an Irish realism that draws energy from O'Connellite mobilisation of the mass of the Irish people. This development in turn leads to an uncertain new sociology of literature that steps away from elite perspectives and is characterised by hesitations, questions and exclamations. A brief correspondence between Gerald Griffin and John Banim – begun in literary rivalry and continuing in friendly discussions of literary and political prospects – captures a note of hesitant hope, not least in the two men's confiding tones and offers of mutual help. Griffin, who travelled through County Clare during the by-election of 1828 that saw O'Connell elected, told Banim in London of the 'resolute' nature of the people: 'no drunkenness – no riot – patience and coolness beyond anything that could have been looked for. They fill the streets more like a set of Pythagorean philosophers than a mob of Munstermen'. Banim wished that he himself had seen 'the Clare heroes' and confided that he was absorbed in a collection to be called 'Songs for Irish Catholics'. Griffin meanwhile, 'on the spot', offered to renew Banim's 'acquaintance with forgotten scenes in your native country'.[75]

But the arrival of the Great Famine made it hard to sustain such shared cultural enterprises. Just when we arrive at romanticism as a recognisable episode in Irish culture, the methods by which Ireland is known make themselves visible. Their profusion is nowhere more evident than in the final famine-struck years. Within the final phase of Irish romanticism, literary abstractions of lived experience – tracking catastrophe and taking their bearings from absence and loss – appear in newspapers, journals and travel writings. The powerful writings of James Clarence Mangan, for instance, were only once gathered in book form in his own lifetime when a collection of his German translations, financed by Charles Gavan Duffy, was published in 1845. It remained for the exiled Young Irelander John Mitchel to publish *Poems by James Clarence Mangan* in New York in 1859, along with a brief but influential account of the 'life, poetry and death' of 'this new old poet'.[76] *Irish Romanticism* reflects on such gaps even as it extends into a serious and integrated consideration of the writing of the 1830s and 1840s, a period too often cast into critical darkness under the shadow of the Famine. As well as Mangan, work by Edgeworth and William Carleton is considered while Thomas Carlyle's views are also discussed. Darkness is often the dominant note, sounded even in the relatively benign period of the 1830s, when a literary revival of sorts was underway under the very shadow of what the Gaelic scholar and Ordnance Survey employee John O'Donovan called, in 1837, 'the era of infidelity'.[77]

O'Donovan's professional investments in the retrieval and storage of both memory and history can be thought of as a stage in the creation of a 'folkoristic-ethnological' understanding of Ireland: a locally grounded effort 'to renew national cultural identity' that began with elite antiquarianism and continued into the revivalist efforts of the late nineteenth century.[78] One major source of difficulty is the question of Ireland's status as strange, a culture scarred by colonial perspectives and afflicted by assumed difference.[79] In so far as Anglophone culture began with conquest and the need to subdue as well as explain a population, Ireland's standing as a 'strange country' remains a dominant force in conceptualisations of Irish romanticism. Neither emerging Enlightenment values of accurate observation nor the aesthetic recalibration of wildness in romanticism ever quite undid a persistent tendency to associate Ireland with forms of cultural inferiority. From the outset, though, strangeness has a stylistic as well as a political dimension, often realised in the form of the footnote, with its distinct visual appearance and equivocal claims to truth. Meanwhile the idea of a culture constituted by ideas of estrangement is central to no less a text than *Lyrical Ballads*, at least in Samuel Taylor Coleridge's account of his and Wordsworth's shared enterprise. Reviewing that collection in the pages of his *Biographia Literaria* (1817) – a book that borrows an Irish bull from Edgeworth and devotes a chapter to Maturin's play *Bertram* – Coleridge explained that while he wrote of supernatural things as if they were ordinary, Wordsworth looked at everyday life and estranged it with a certain 'colouring of the imagination'.[80] In a different register altogether, the Russian Formalist critic Viktor Shklovsky claimed the quality of estrangement or defamiliarization (*ostranie*) for literature itself, asking readers to break with habit and to cease seeing meaning only in silhouette or 'as though it were enveloped in a sack'.[81]

For the Afterword to the book, I turn to clothing – the heavy sack-like object that is the Irish frieze coat – in order to make a case for a culture that reckons with strangeness but on its own terms. I identify a singular and resonant set of images surrounding the coarse woollen cloth worn by the native Irish and taken up and reimagined across a remarkable series of romantic descriptions. Shklovsky can support this effort too by way of his analysis of Gogol's *The Overcoat* (1842), the tale of an impoverished clerk named Akaky Akakievich who is driven by the bitter St Petersburg weather to ask a tailor to mend his old coat. Assured that the item is quite beyond repair, Akakievich reluctantly assents to having a 'marvellous' new coat made and takes nervous steps into the complex world of '*overcoat* finance'. Once made, the new overcoat proves 'marvellous' indeed: almost like a lover or a spouse, it promises a lifetime of comfort but also begins to distract Akakievich from his work and take him into new and unfamiliar places. Finally, the '*fantastic* difference' between old and new coats leads to a violent assault, the theft of the overcoat, an encounter with bullying officialdom in the shape of an 'Important Person', followed by illness and death. The novella's self-declared 'totally unexpected, fantastic ending' involves tales of a ghostly clerk who seeks out a stolen overcoat before manifesting as Akaky Akakievich himself and taking the coat of the very same Important Person who had once traumatised him.

Gogol's *The Overcoat*, with its 'fairy-tale-like, folklore-prophetic resolution' is read by Shklovsky as a tale whose 'Gothic' architecture materialises its meanings: a thinly rendered narrative framework that is all arches and no walls. Those Gothic arches can also be thought of as strained 'power lines' along which events in the story play out. If Gogol's *Overcoat* 'transmits Petersburg and its suburbs through the thin power lines carrying the mumblings of an impoverished clerk who has been crushed by the weight of the empire' then so too do Irish romantic coats communicate a ragged relationship between ordinary Irish lives and the imperial British state.[82] Their special power to do so comes from their being at once commonplace and remarkable, possessed of an ordinariness made strange by colonialism.

The narrative arches of *Irish Romanticism* are found in a series of conceptual pairings in the realms of historiography, language use, literary media, representation, gender and environment. First of these is a relationship between past and present. The book captures the process by which a moving cultural present sifts through the centuries that preceded it. Despite Irish romanticism's reputation for history-drenched details, we find relatively few fictions of the remote past. Those that were undertaken were often unsuccessful or unremembered. Relatively recent decades, though, come into startlingly sharp focus, as when the 1798 rebellion makes its presence felt in *The Wild Irish Girl* in 1806, or Grattan's Parliament of 1782 gives shape to Edgeworth's imagination of Irish history in *Castle Rackrent* (1800). In the final phase, there is a growing effort to realise a distant past (perhaps previously thought to have been too tainted by colonial history), seen in Griffin's historical novel of the Viking invasion. As the case of William Carleton would suggest, however, cultural energy remains absorbed in a living present that is scarred by the recent past.

Second, comes Irish to English, as the book reflects upon the process by which one language community collapsed under the pressure of colonial rule. During the decades described in this book, the poorest of the poor became English speaking and literate, as the Irish language itself gradually lost ground. Numbers of Irish speakers remained very high into the 1820s and 30s, though those reflect overall booming population numbers rather than real growth.[83] But the 'large-scale language shift' from Irish to English also resulted in many moments of 'transitional bilingualism', as discussed in Margaret Kelleher's account of 'language crossings' in nineteenth-century Ireland. Her discussion of a line taken from Lady Morgan's *The O'Briens and the O'Flahertys* (1827) – the question 'Have you Irish?' – offers an insight into that changing linguistic environment.[84] The work of translation remains vital from the 1780s right through to the period of James Clarence Mangan, Samuel Ferguson and beyond.

Animated by concerns about the fading away of the practice of Irish manuscript production, the early years of the nineteenth century witnessed the beginning of 'the great push towards gathering in the manuscript refugees of Gaelic culture and civilisation', led by the Royal Irish Academy and Trinity College Dublin.[85] A third pairing concerns the relationship between manuscript and print. If, by 'the early 1820s, the last traditional poet/scribes such as the Ó Longáins and Tadhg Gaelach had just laid down the quill', it remains the case that print culture bears the marks of a manuscript culture with which it is intimately familiar and from which it freely borrows.[86] And if history itself might be thought of as 'fundamentally a literature of mediation',[87] then Irish romanticism across its phases proves to be especially alert to the potential of page space in the remaking of the deep past. A fourth paired relationship, that between originals and copies, proves a source of creative inspiration for many writers. A particular concern with copies and copying can be discerned in Irish romanticism, from the difficulties experienced by Maria Edgeworth in obtaining copies of London-published books to the artful use of metaphors drawn from print culture (including facsimile, copy, type, cliché) in the writings of the Banim brothers.[88] Working from his desk in the Admiralty, his home in Fulham and holidays in Cork, the folklorist Thomas Crofton Croker pioneered the use of lithography, a method of relief printing from stone that was particularly useful for circular letters, topography, lines of musical notation and book illustration. In 1807, the Quarter Master

General's Office in Whitehall bought the secret of the process and some materials: its first production was a map of Bantry Bay, published on 7 May 1808. Croker used lithographic illustrations of Irish life in his books while his papers in the British Library contain some fragmentary material that resemble experiments in chromolithography, including new graphic versions of St Patrick and Celtic crosses.

While such practical work in the art and techniques of copying continued, Irish literature has to wait for James Joyce's 'Counterparts' for Farrington, a clerk character akin to Gogol's Akaky Akakievich or Melville's Bartleby. But Susan Howe is sure – powered 'by shock of poetry telepathy' – that a figure from Irish literary history lies behind the American scrivener.[89] In 'Melville's Marginalia', part of *The Nonconformists' Memorial* (1989), Howe finds in James Clarence Mangan a kind of impossible original of the more American fictional copyist, traced via imaginative linkages sparked by Mitchel's US edition of Mangan's poetry. Howe, whose mother was the Irish modernist writer Mary Manning (1905-1999), recalls hearing Mangan's translation of 'Roisin Dubh' sung, during a childhood visit to Dublin. With its interest in Mangan's job as copier and transcriber for Ordnance Survey, its curiosity about Dublin journals of the nineteenth century, and its recollection of Percy Bysshe Shelley's *Address to the Irish People* (1812), we can think of Howe's book as an alternative, transatlantic, archive of Irish romanticism, made with the materials of memory, history and marginalia.

Susan Howe captures something else too: the survival of men's names over those of women. From about 1820, the senior Protestant women who ushered in a new phase of Irish literature around 1800 were eclipsed by a coming generation of Catholic men. The figure of Thomas Moore plays a key part in this transition, and his case helps me sketch in a fifth paired set of terms, the shift of cultural authority from women to men. In 1828, a letter in the *Freeman's Journal* from 'Patricius' disputed the claim made in a recent *Athenaeum* article on the appearance of 'the Wizard of the North', denying not his talent but his originality: 'For that species of *fictitious narrative* called "*the national novel*" we stand indebted conjointly to the talents and patriotism of two Irish women!'[90] A debate that we know from the 1990s about Owenson and Edgeworth's influence on Scott gathered momentum early, and, despite the brave case made by 'Patricius', women were on the losing side. Maria Edgeworth and Lady Morgan, with Moore, survived right through all three phases, and their lives and writings continue to give shape and definition to our understandings of Irish romanticism. All lived long enough to see the introduction of new and more favourable copyright arrangements and to shepherd new and revised editions of their works onto the market. Yet Edgeworth refused to authorise a collected edition in the 1840s, citing the difficulty of adding 'national explanations' to her work, and surely feeling the effects of changing times.[91] In Chapter 3, I unfold this story in a reading of her last novel, *Helen*, showing how writers including Walter Scott and Germaine de Staël play a central role in her efforts to remake her role as woman writer.

Because change does not only belong only to political history, my sixth and final set of paired terms concerns ties between people and their environment. *Irish Romanticism* suggests just how much an environmentally minded approach to nineteenth-century Irish narratives might achieve, whether Maria Edgeworth's close interest in the realities of a subsistence economy built around turf, the interest in layered anthropogenic change found in Mangan, or the weather and climate archive offered by the fictions of Carleton. Even before the Great Famine, hunger and extreme weather characterized the experience of many in the 1830s, a decade which culminated in an exceptional weather event, the 'Night of the Big Wind' of 5 January 1839, when, along with many other disasters at sea and on land, sixteen houses in Edgeworthstown lost their rooves.[92] Improvement itself, in spite of its beginnings in dispossession, can be read for the environmental information recorded as bogs were surveyed, harbours built and lines of road laid down. When the Dublin Zoological Gardens opened in 1831, Maria Edgeworth praised their role in offering 'innocent and rational recreation for the inhabitants of a populous city' but asked for further education and efforts towards 'the great scientific use' of the collection for the advancement of 'comparative anatomy'. She was writing to the Surgeon General Philip Crampton, first president of the Dublin Zoological Society and the man who obtained the land in Phoenix Park on which Dublin Zoo was founded, and the two shared interests in the new science of life.[93] Edgeworth was already strongly interested in the work of French geologist, George Cuvier, whose theories of extinction were eclipsed by Darwinist thought in the twentieth century but have become newly relevant in our Anthropocene moment.

Continuities matter too. In contrast to a critical tendency to imagine Irish romanticism as ending in the 1820s, with its creative energies hampered by improvement and broken by violence, I have sought where possible to hint at the longer history of Irish romantic books and voices, while also understanding the resilience of the discourse of improvement right through to its deadly effects during the Famine. The influence of Banim and Griffin, for instance, was felt by a young William Ewart Gladstone, who began work on his 'Irish Tale' in January 1827 and later that same month attended a debate at Eton regarding the 'conduct of England to Ireland from Revolution to 1776 justifiable? Voted, no'.[94] Gladstone's youthful views testify to the extent to which the 1820s constituted a tipping point for the discourse of improvement. In Ireland, this dissatisfaction with improvement merged with the theorisation of the romantic across Europe and led to a determination, only partly successful, to forge new forms of Irish cultural identity from native materials. It remained for the writers of the late nineteenth-century Irish Literary Revival to take up this project, and they did so in part by returning to romantic resources, even as an older Gladstone pressed ahead with a plan for Home Rule.

Most readers probably know 'Romantic Ireland' best via Yeats' lament for its passing: 'Romantic Ireland's dead and gone / It's with O'Leary in the grave'.[95] Rather than read Ireland as the very emblem of a prototypical romantic predicament, this book argues for the coherence of Irish romantic culture as a set of overlapping responses to a shifting set of circumstances, experienced by an array of writers who sought to give expression to Irish people, landscapes and histories. I have sought to read that culture from the inside and to capture the vibrant nature of the debates about literature and politics, while showing how recursive patterns of representation, adaptation and remediation made a distinctive and continuing mark. Setting the more familiar images of the romantic ruin to one side in favour of frieze fabric and its latent meanings, I end the book by arguing for an Irish romanticism that scripts its own terms and knows its own strength.

CHAPTER I

Bookish Histories, 1780–1815

From about the 1780s, Irish literature began to take on its recognisably modern shape. What the antiquarian Joseph Cooper Walker called the 'Spirit of literary enquiry' was alive and active, often exercised upon the history and antiquities of Ireland but also taking on new shapes and finding future forms.[1] The new Irish writing in English built upon a substantial body of past writing, including histories, chronicles and the emerging philosophical tradition begun earlier in the century.[2] Irish romantic writers turned to earlier authors – Spenser, Swift and Goldsmith among the poets, Keating, O'Conor and O'Halloran among the historians – as touchstones. They also looked to the classical tradition in modes ranging from elite to popular, calling upon ancient authors as their contemporaries. Across the country, a growing book, newspaper and pamphlet trade supported forms of popular politicisation that, among other forces, gave the spur to the United Irish Rebellion in 1798. That burgeoning world of popular print met and acted upon an elite Irish 'bookish culture' in existence at least since the 1720s.[3] Irish writers also shared formal, cultural and political motivations with their peers in England, Scotland and Wales while empire forged transoceanic connections.

Rather than present an ineffable Romantic Ireland that refuses to be 'safely interred in the pages of the literary canon', this chapter imagines the printed page as itself a busy site of crossings between media, forms and modes.[4] Irish romanticism was born from a late eighteenth-century impulse to tell national stories, found in such forms as antiquarian histories, travels, novels, collections of ballads and vernacular poetry. The energies and affordances of these varied forms gave texture to an emerging Irish romanticism, resulting in such features as notes, glosses and inset narratives that made space for epistolary, annalistic and chronicle modes. In all cases, what mattered was the laying down of aspects of Irish life on the printed page, an enterprise that often meant an insistent focus on the book as medium. If literature exists both as 'a thing *and* an idea', then this first phase of Irish romantic literature tends towards the former meaning, even as it sets forth concepts and begins to imagine a national culture.[5] The 'thing' that was Irish literature consisted of books, manuscripts and performances, bound at various points by political and economic circumstances to which they respond and which they work to reshape.

The body of writing that emerged in this phase of Irish culture came from the pens of writers mostly born in the 1770s and 1780s. Not all of them enjoyed success and some did not even live to see their names circulate in print, but all partook in bookish activities such as copying, transcription and transmission. Irish romantic writers invented, borrowed from and extended bookish models, meaning that literary authority is arrayed across the surface of the text, often in the form of footnotes or endnotes. But explanatory notes or glosses do not simply pin Ireland to the page as though it were a strange specimen to be observed, as critics often suggest. Rather, they operate as so many waypoints for an Irish romanticism that responds to a still palpable history of colonial conquest, rebellion and famine. Footnotes mediate memory for a divided society, bringing print culture into proximity with a palpable and varied community of knowledge.

In this chapter then, I trace that encounter through the work of four writers in particular: Thomas Dermody (1775–1802), Charlotte Brooke (c. 1740–1793), Mary Tighe (1772–1810) and James Orr (1770–1816). Each of them undertook substantial literary projects marked by the conflicts and divisions of their time and place, and all are writers whose work calls for close attention to questions of readership, circulation and transmission across bodies of knowledge. Dermody was afflicted by economic need and his writing was scarcely sustained through ruptured experiences of patronage and military service. In the case of Brooke, the separation between the English and Irish languages shapes her work as translator and editor. Mary Tighe's most significant achievement is a revisionary translation of a classical text, one that she made new for a generation of readers whose access to her work involved a variety of overlapping print and manuscript modes. James Orr wrote in both Ulster Scots and standard English and also, thanks to a brief emigration to Baltimore, helps us to see the contours of a transatlantic print culture shaped by rebellion.

Together, Dermody, Brooke, Tighe and Orr represent a series of significant meeting points between oral and print cultures, between the Irish and English languages and between manuscript and print, including patronage and subscription models. Dermody, Brooke, Tighe and Orr each express a historical sensibility that responds to the affective charge of their own time and place. They also all knew or knew of each other, even if the points of connection are not yet fully mapped. Each of the four writers has benefited from significant recent editorial and textual scholarship – Michael Griffin on Dermody, Lesa Ní Mhunghaile on Brooke, Harriet Kramer Linkin on Tighe, Carol Baraniuk on Orr – and I draw on that work as I bring these writers together to develop a detailed account of Irish romantic culture in its first phase. In order to help plot those co-ordinates more fully, the chapter also threads through discussions of the better-known cases of Edgeworth's *Castle Rackrent* (1800), Owenson's *The Wild Irish Girl* (1806) and Moore's *Irish Melodies* (1808–1834), showing how each of these texts moved between media as they sought out audiences across languages and forms and made an Irish romantic culture.

A Copious Culture

If history itself might be thought of as 'fundamentally a literature of mediation',[6] then this phase of Irish romanticism proves to be especially alert to the remaking of the deep past on the printed page. Questions of translation and transmission press upon and make demands of imaginative literature. Alex Watson speculates on a 'relationship between political and textual marginality' that may account for the special interest in its own medium found in Irish romantic writing.[7] But as footnotes break with 'illusive immediacy' and express 'the power of *visible* print', they also express a creative energy that exceeds political interpretation.[8] A further contradiction means that such creativity is often expressed in relation to copies, copying and *copia*. Behind the bookish dimension of Irish romanticism lies the older meaning of *copia* as 'abundance, plenty, multitude', an etymology that directs us to ideas of harvest and storage.[9] Books that aimed to gather up the facts of Irish life did not always hit the mark, as when the poet Mary Tighe complained to her antiquarian friend Joseph Cooper Walker of 'the *very disagreeable sensation* (at least it is so to me)' of reading Henry Boyd's 'Milesian Tales' – poems in Spenserian stanzas, many of which relate to the 1798 rebellion – and not being able to understand the references: 'alas! the notes have not been half copious enough to illuminate my dullness'.[10]

Not to be thought of as just so many vessels for an overflowing culture, Irish romantic books, newspapers and manuscripts often inscribe insufficiency as both sad plight and urgent motive. Tropes of scarcity and plenty were pervasive in this period while contrasting claims about insufficiency and overflow formed part of the texture of Irish romanticism. In April 1793, the first issue of a new Dublin literary journal, the *Anthologia Hibernica*, complained that, 'Were the abilities of the Irish to be estimated by their literary productions, they would scarcely rank higher than those nations who had just emerged from barbarism and incivility.' There may have been books – 'letters are almost universally cultivated in this isle, and the presses groan beneath the weight of voluminous and expensive publications' – but such items were not the work of 'native writers'. The language of native and natural resurfaced in the 1840s in relation to later literary insufficiencies but in this period the focus falls on factors that prevent the 'growth of authorism' in Ireland, including lack of protection for 'literary property' and insufficient patronage.[11] Yet this same journal featured new and original work by Thomas Moore and Sydney Owenson among others. And within a few years the Act of Union saw Queen Anne's copyright law extended to Ireland by the Act of Union, although, by the late 1830s, Irish writers including Maria Edgeworth and Gerald Griffin were among those campaigning with William Wordsworth for an extension of its protections. Around the same time, an established eighteenth-century culture of patronage gave way to a vigorous and commercially driven publishing industry that benefited some writers and left others floundering in the receding tide. Maria Edgeworth agreed with her father that 'the London booksellers' made the 'best patrons', yet Sydney Owenson, even after the huge success of *The Wild Irish Girl*, had to take up a dependent role in the household of the Whig grandees, the Abercorns. Thomas Moore's career was sustained by an intricate relationship between publishing and patronage: he became one of the bestselling writers of the period and yet relied upon a variety of backers and supporters throughout his life. Lord Moira even promised to create the post of Irish poet laureate for Moore and, when that did not work out, found him a position in Bermuda. And for a writer such as Thomas Dermody, discussed later in terms of the emergence of polite literature from popular contexts, patronage meant precious access to time and resources in a life otherwise marked by insecurity and scarcity.

Behind the new and emerging print culture lay a print and manuscript archive that many writers strove to access. In 1793, the antiquarian Charles Vallancey declared that the materials for Irish history were 'plenty and rich' but imperfectly translated, incorrectly interpreted and difficult to access: the original Brehon laws, he said, were '[i]mprisoned forever' in the 'manuscript closet' of Trinity College Dublin.[12] Vallancey's own views on the Irish past were highly contestable, but his description of a voluminous culture to which only scanty forms of access were available resonates across Irish romanticism in all its phases. In *The Wild Irish Girl*, Father John insists that 'Manuscripts, annals, and records, are not the treasures of a colonized or a conquered country' and instructs Mortimer in the 'plunder' of the 'literary treasures' of Ireland, meaning that 'our finest and most valuable MSS' are only to be found in France and Rome – worse than being caged within Trinity College Dublin, perhaps.[13]

Via their absence, such bookish objects call up a cultural authority made visible on Owenson's page. But in filling out that absence, Owenson often creates unstable and unpredictable aesthetic effects, characterised by Anahid Nersessian in terms of a kind of 'puppet vivacity' where culture is made to perform its own moody take on empire.[14] In *O'Donnel* (1814), that performance is one that promises to reanimate a culture via its objects. The novel depicts a rural library located in a small, whitewashed room, furnished only with deal chairs and 'hanging shelves', which is filled with 'books in almost every language' along with 'the results of scientific research, mingled with papers, manuscripts, and some mathematical instruments'.[15] The library is described as little better than a kitchen, but at its centre are antiquarian objects – an illuminated manuscript, a genealogical roll and a sword – that, thanks to their bookish collocation, already are at the work of revivification.

Such attempts to rearrange the cultural furniture often took shape within prefatory materials to novels and poems, notably so in the cases of Edgeworth, Owenson and Moore. In her preface to *Twelve Original Hibernian Melodies* (1805), discussed later, Owenson thinks about the aesthetics of location and audience in terms of sound and sentiment. The specimens of song arrayed across the volume 'afford so wild a field for reflection' that Owenson is led to open up an analysis of their affective power.[16] The claim is in part a justification of the role of the preface as a 'field' of knowledge, building perhaps on Edgeworth's self-conscious use of paratextual material in *Castle Rackrent*. Owenson further claims for her songs much the same combination of license and authority that Edgeworth grants to the gossipy revelations of Thady Quirke. Where *Castle Rackrent* suggests that an educated or polished narrator may deceive, but an Irish peasant narrator, prone to gossip, slips of the tongue and blunders, can be yield a truer picture, Owenson makes the case that native songs are made the more truthful by their artlessness: 'when, however, it is considered, that the following airs were composed by *men*, ignorant of the rules of that art they practised, it is hoped that what a celebrated personage once said of the errors of illustrious characters, will be applied to *them*, and "that their faults will be thought to bring their excuses along with them"'.[17]

Owenson makes the faults and flaws of her songs inherent to their value, but such modesty soon lost ground as her efforts to unite bardic poetry with national airs were relegated by the success of her friend and competitor

Thomas Moore, the first number of whose *Irish Melodies* appeared in 1808. In the case of the *Melodies*, we can see yet more clearly how the impulse to collect the specimens of a culture is structured according to contest and accommodation, conflict and loss. The advertisement to the first number of the *Irish Melodies* in April 1808 locates its own place in a print project with the announcement that 'Our National Music has never been properly collected.'[18] The result is cultural 'Treasures' that are left 'unclaimed and fugitive', prey to 'Composers of the Continent'.[19] Moore even suggests that these orphan airs resemble the dispossessed Catholics who fled for service in French or Spanish armies: 'Thus our airs, like too many of our Countrymen, for want of Protection at Home, have passed into the Service of Foreigners.'[20] A footnote follows: 'The Writer forgot, when he made this Assertion, that the Public are indebted to Mr. BUNTING for a very valuable Collection of Irish Music, and that the patriotic Genius of Miss OWENSON has been employed upon some of our finest Airs.'[21]

Long-term cultural loss is personalised by Moore as a matter of his own short-term memory, to be made good in the future through the reach of print. Advertisements and prefaces to subsequent numbers continue to issue calls for more materials or 'any Original Melodies' which may have 'escaped' the researches of the publisher, Power.[22] After this early hint that Moore's creative imagination is plentiful but that airs are in short supply, the prefatory material moves between predictions of lastness and the promise of continuation. Moore, meanwhile, in 1813 warned readers not to expect anything much further of the *Melodies*: the sixth number, he said, was likely to be 'the Last of the Series'.[23] Imagining his 'Volumes' as so many aged individuals while casually invoking an imperial context, Moore remarked that he would behave towards his books like 'those Indians, who put their relatives to death, when they become feeble'.[24] Moore annexes Hindu practices of assisted dying in order to promise a revival of his lyrical project: the only way to prevent this 'Euthanasia of the Irish Melodies' was for Irish readers to contribute 'sweet and expressive Songs of our Country, which either chance or research may have brought into their hands'.[25] Five more numbers were still to follow with collected editions in 1820 and 1821, while numerous reprints and translations continued throughout the nineteenth century once the Longmans' copyright expired.

Moore's advertisement to the first and second numbers of the *Melodies* not only confined works by Bunting and Owenson to a footnote but also turned its back on the print culture associated with Joseph Cooper Walker and Brooke with their careful collections of 'early songs'. But neither is his a modern popular mode in the manner that Coleridge and Wordsworth adopted for their *Lyrical Ballads* in 1798, not least because Moore stepped away from the 'ignorant and angry multitude' and addressed a polite audience.[26] Motivated by a need for professional advancement and financial success, Moore managed in the *Melodies* to find a space between elite modes of collection and the noise of popular protest. In doing so, he found a point of literary and political balance that yielded its own aesthetic effects.

Hints towards a history that could not be spoken sounded the characteristic note. The first number of the *Melodies* asserted the arrival of 'a better Period both of Politics and Music', but Moore's hints about improved Catholic hopes in 1808 hardly took notice of heated debates within the Catholic Society or agrarian insurgency in Munster in that same year, not to mind the sectarian brawls which 'became regular occurrences in the post-Union period'.[27] Number by number, the *Melodies* depict a brimming Irish culture routinely afflicted by insufficiency. The regular invocation of negative modes in Moore's lyrics helps to give aesthetic texture to this contradictory cultural formation, as found in the repeated negative injunctions ('Forget not', 'Oh breathe not', 'Fly not') and the insistent refusal of potential other views found across the poems ('There is not in the wide world a valley so sweet / As that vale in whose bosom the bright waters meet'). In prose, Moore's metaphors are often strikingly realised via references to empire. In the seventh number, a casual reference to the Dutch East India Company's conquest of the Banda Islands and their dominance of the trade in nutmeg enables him to visualise Irish musical commodities: 'we have received so many contributions of old and beautiful airs, the suppression of which, for the enhancement of those we have published, would resemble too much the policy of the Dutch in burning their spices, that I have been persuaded, though not without considerable diffidence in my success, to commence a new series of the Irish Melodies.'[28] Moore's image of imperial scarcity hardly captures the brutal behaviour of Dutch colonists who burned villages and killed and enslaved indigenous peoples so as to create in the first place the commercial conditions in which nutmeg could be traded as a commodity. The imperial context may, however, point us to an emerging romantic understanding of national culture as a resource to be exploited rather than an experience to be lived, always an uneasy relationship in Moore's writing.

Books, Paper, Patronage

It has become commonplace in studies of romanticism to invoke William St Clair's account of the rise of Britain's 'reading nation' while scholars including Ina Ferris have traced 'the equation of books with reading' in the period.[29] There are many local declarations of progress, as when the 'literary respectability of this town' began to grow with the foundation of the Belfast Literary Society in 1801.[30] But the 'unprecedented visibility and palpability of printed matter' in late eighteenth- and early nineteenth-century culture was never to be taken for granted in poor, bilingual and unevenly literate Ireland.[31] Visiting Ireland around 1807, James Hall wrote that landowners generally favoured 'dogs, dice, and jockeys' above 'books, thinking, and conversation'. 'At Dublin, Cork, and a few other places', though, he found the 'cause of elegant literature' being taken up.[32] Edgeworthstown House in County Longford was one such place, and Amy Prendergast treats the society gathered there as 'a single author salon', with conversation and discussion circulating around Maria Edgeworth's writing, regularly read aloud to family and visitors.[33] Stopping in Longford to spend time with the Edgeworth family on a geological tour taken in 1806, the chemist Humphry Davy wrote that 'Except the moral and intellectual paradise of the author of "Castle Rackrent"' he found 'nothing worthy of observation'.[34] His opinions had not changed in 1811, when Davy returned to Ireland in the company of his former lover, Anna Beddoes née Edgeworth, and remarked in a letter to his future wife, Jane Apreece, that he had nothing to say 'of the people of the west of Ireland. I returned on Wednesday to Edgeworth's Town, that oasis in the intellectual desert of this fine country; pray keep this expression a secret.'[35] Davy's first geological tour, made in the company of George Bellas Greenough to collect mineral samples for the Royal Institution, found its way into *The Absentee* (1812). Taken for a Welsh geologist in search of ore and a workable copper mine in the district, Edgeworth's hero, Lord Colambre, turns away from landscape to place his faith rather in paper documents: the main engines of the plot are a written promise erased from the back of a lease ('rubbed clean out') and a certificate of marriage entrusted to a now dead ambassador and whose papers, even when found, are in the most 'shameful disorder', 'portfolios of letters and memorials, and manifestoes and bundles of paper, of the most heterogeneous sorts'.[36] Though the commitments represented by these documents come good, the novel's drama derives from their 'heterogeneous' and frangible status, expressive of a wider uncertainty regarding the precarious reach of print culture.

The wider discourse of improvement was deeply involved in the possibilities and affordances of print, as with the preface to Arthur Young's *A Tour in Ireland* (1780), which makes an explicit connection between the need to improve the face of the country and the responsibility to publish one's own story: 'every gentleman residing in the country, and practising agriculture, should write and publish an account of so much as falls within the sphere of his observation'.[37] But such calls expressed difficulties and gaps in the record as much as they promised a more complete account.

The institutions that collected books in Romantic-era Ireland were thin on the ground and the process of 'stabilizing books' identities by assigning them fixed places within a classificatory system' proceeded unevenly.[38] Trinity College, the Royal Irish Academy and the Royal Dublin Society all had libraries and began to amass holdings of books and Gaelic manuscripts from the late eighteenth century onwards. Private libraries were relatively scarce, and a national library was not established until 1877.[39] When Robert Peel was appointed chief secretary to Ireland in 1812, he was, as K. T. Hoppen writes, 'shocked to find that Dublin Castle possessed no working library that would assist new ministers in reading their way into both the contemporary and the historical aspects of their responsibilities'. Peel made good the absence by gathering over a thousand books and pamphlets to create a 'Select Irish Library', bound in green with shamrock-stamped spines.[40] But books in general, not just books about Ireland, seemed to be in short supply. Even in 1831, when a small-scale literary revival was underway in Dublin, the newly arrived Felicia Hemans complained that 'access to new books here is not nearly as easy as in England'.[41]

In the late eighteenth- and early nineteenth century, notable private collectors and promoters of culture – including Thomas Percy (Bishop of Dromore) and Lady Moira – gathered writers, books and manuscripts about them and offered conditional forms of financial support. Their generative role meant that some important voices were preserved in print. In the case of Lady Moira in particular, her Dublin salon became 'a central location for intellectual activities in Ireland for the greater portion of the late-eighteenth century' and was regularly visited by Irish romantic writers, including Sydney Owenson (taken there by her father) and Thomas Moore (introduced while a student at Trinity College Dublin).[42] Born to the prominent Methodist Selina Hastings, Countess of Huntingdon, Elizabeth Hastings married John Rawdon of Moira House, County Down in 1752. The couple shared an interest in Irish history, and she contributed an essay on the excavation of a bog body on their estate to the journal *Archaeologia*. Their Dublin home was described as a 'temple of science and the *belles lettres*' by Samuel Walker, the brother of the antiquarian Joseph Cooper Walker.[43] As Amy Prendergast points out in her study of Irish salon culture, Moira's salon also outlived several 'other attempts at associational antiquarianism', including the men-only Physico-Historical

Society and Hibernian Antiquarian Society.[44] In the 1790s, Lady Moira supported and advised Lady Margaret Mount Cashell, the former pupil of Mary Wollstonecraft in Mitchelstown who wrote three anti-Union pamphlets before fleeing Ireland to live in Italy as part of the Shelley circle. Lady Moira still exerted an influence in the 1810s, when Edgeworth turned to her for Italian epigraphs for her *Tales of Fashionable Life*. She may have also served as a model for some of Edgeworth's many wise older women characters, including Lady Annaly in *Ormond* (1817).[45]

But patrons also exercised their cultural authority by way of particular individual relationships in the context of a highly divided society. What was in Britain a shared and 'broadly conservative gentry project of remodelling the literary past into a common "national heritage"' did not spread evenly throughout Ireland.[46] The case of Thomas Percy is instructive. In a 1953 essay charting a distinct line of Ulster literary history, the poet John Hewitt described Percy as both 'a power-house of patronage' and a man who put 'a brake on literary experiment'.[47] Percy's antiquarian approach to English literature, seen in his *Reliques of Ancient English Poetry* (1765), was rejected by Wordsworth and Coleridge in their *Lyrical Ballads* (1798) but lived on in Ireland in particular ways. Resident in County Down from 1782, following his appointment as bishop of Dromore, Percy played a role in an emerging Irish literature in the 1790s and early 1800s. He was a founding member of the Royal Irish Academy (along with Richard Lovell Edgeworth) and helped Richard Musgrave gather material for his controversial history of the 1798 rebellion. Percy's home contained antiquarian curiosities ('the complete skeleton of a deer, of a small species, in a toothpick case, made of the tree that Shakspeare [sic] planted') but also specimens of recent history, including bloody pikes, a musket modified to be carried beneath a coat and 'bludgeons, headed with lead, on the one end, for knocking out people's brains' used at the nearby Battle of Ballynahinch, all part of his collection of curiosities.[48] One cherished trophy was 'the green and white plume that had adorned the hat of Henry Munro at the Battle of Ballynahinch' which became the property of Percy's agent Crane Bush after the bishop's death in 1811.[49]

A tireless reporter of local disturbances to Dublin Castle, Percy himself contemplated a history of the rebellion.[50] Meanwhile he set about extensive agricultural improvements and patronised working-class poets via his network: Thomas Dermody's Killeigh patron, Henry Boyd, was among his circle as well as associating with Lady Moira.[51] Other writers associated with Percy include William Hamilton Drummond, a Presbyterian clergyman whose epic primitivist poem about the Giant's Causeway was published in

1811, and poet and novelist James McHenry, whose work participated in the 'social forgetting' of Presbyterian involvement in 1798.[52] Percy also helped a young man named Patrick Prunty from County Down, an apprentice blacksmith and weaver who secured a place at Cambridge via the Rev. Thomas Tighe (an uncle of the poet, Mary Tighe), where he changed his name to Brontë. All of these writers help us to think about Percy in terms of what Barnard calls print's capacity to 'sedate' as well as excite.[53]

The pattern described by Clare O'Halloran, whereby gentry antiquarianism and cultural interest in the Gaelic past both responded to and turned away from violence, militarism and conflict, can also be traced in the history of Irish music.[54] Edward Bunting (1773–1843) helped to organise the Harp Festival in Belfast in 1792 along with Henry Joy McCracken, founding member of the United Irishmen. The fact that scribes as well as musicians gathered in Belfast meant a lasting reputation for that festival. Bunting himself transcribed the tunes heard for his *General Collection of the Ancient Music* (1796), making older harp music newly available for the fashionable piano. But the majority of the Irish songs in the collection were collected by Gaelic scholar Patrick Lynch (c. 1756–1838), who noted the songs in Roman script and then copied them in the Gaelic script.[55] Lynch also travelled in Connemara 'by order of Mr E Bunting' in 1802 to collect tunes and kept a journal of his travels.[56] He had already in 1795 produced *Bolg an tSolair* (meaning 'provision bag' or miscellany), published by the same press that issued the United Irishmen's *Northern Star* newspaper and containing grammar and vocabulary as well as a selection of Charlotte Brooke's translations. The press used by United Irishmen was broken up in 1798, but the material gathered by Lynch for *Bog an tSolair* continued to have resonance. Mary Balfour, daughter of a Church of Ireland clergyman who lived in Derry and Belfast, became a member of Bunting's Harp Society, and her *Kathleen O'Neil* can be considered the first 'wholly original Irish play or melodrama based on Irish mythological and legendary materials'. The play was successfully adapted and revived in Philadelphia and New York in the 1820s.[57] Balfour also contributed lyrics – eight translations and one original work – to the second edition of Bunting's *General Collection of the Ancient Music*.[58] Guy Beiner shows how one of Balfour's poems, 'Nancy of the Branching Tresses', adopted a traditional air (*Cúil Chraobhaigh Anna*) in order to tell a quiet, evasive version of the story of Betsy Gray, a popular heroine of the United Irish turnout in County Down.[59]

This culture of patronage met and acted upon patterns of publication that were themselves in flux. For much of the eighteenth century,

British books flooded into Ireland, most often serving as copy texts for Irish reprints.[60] The copyright legislation that accompanied the Union ended a vigorous reprint industry with strong ties to the Americas and left most Irish publishers dependent on individual contracts negotiated with British firms. The Wicklow landowner and writer William Parnell did not hesitate to describe 'the 'destruction of the business of Printing' as one of the 'injuries' inflicted by a legislative measure that had a 'pernicious' effect on 'local literature'.[61] After the 1798 rebellion, many printers, publishers and bookmen with links to republican politics emigrated to the eastern United States. James McHenry's historical novel *O'Halloran; or, The Insurgent Chief: An Irish Historical Tale of 1798* (1824), which recounts events in Antrim in 1798, was published in Philadelphia some years after its author had emigrated to the United States. But original Irish publications of fiction and poetry were already unusual in the years leading up to the Union, reflecting what Benson describes as 'a weakness at the heart of the Irish book trade'.[62] Self-awareness about the reliance of the Irish book trade on markets outside the island, along with a culture of copies and reprints, meant a print culture characterised by a sense of inadequacy or insufficiency, in turn partaking of a sense of the necessary insufficiency of colonial societies. Charles O'Hara (1705–76), landlord, MP and friend of Edmund Burke, borrowed from bookmaking to express the plight of the Anglo-Irish when he told his son that 'We are a people made rather for copies than originals.'[63]

Revolution, Union and Empire

William Parnell's comments on printing make defensive reference to the value of publishing works in Ireland 'with correctness, and with that degree of decoration which Type and Paper can bestow'.[64] His *Historical Apology for the Irish Catholics* (1807) transfers that same defensive project from bookmaking onto the past at large, spelling out the growing significance of a bookish culture in Irish romanticism. Written in order to show the urgent need for better treatment of the Catholics of Ireland, Parnell's book opens on a painterly vision of a ruined contemporary Ireland, ripe for reimagination. Writing about himself in the third person, the Anglo-Irish landlord and novelist Parnell imagines the figure of a historian who 'has drawn a picture in which the distant view is gloomy and dark; but the vast ruins, the desolated landscape, and the storm, passing sullenly away, will give more brilliancy to the scenes of peace and happiness, with which the pencil of the future historian may enrich the foreground'.[65]

But what of the people who inhabited that 'desolated landscape'? From 1750 until the 1790s, the population of Ireland grew in 'a new and sustained upwards trajectory' that reached 'the unprecedented level of between 1.5 and 2 per cent per year' in spite of a high number of emigrants.[66] Living standards rose, albeit unevenly, as the dreadful famine caused by what poet William Dunkin called Ireland's 'Frosty Winters' of 1739–41 faded into memory.[67] There were no further episodes of mass mortality until the typhus epidemics and famines of 1817 and 1822, and the years leading up to the turbulent 1790s are often characterised in terms of peace and stability. The rise of the potato as a staple crop meant an increase in smaller holdings, especially in the west, while industrialisation in the northeast and the growth of a provisioning and market economy tied to empire also contributed to population growth.

Those same years saw the beginning of an earnest discussion of the issue of population, the subject of a burgeoning literature, with the dissenting minister Richard Price and the agricultural economist Arthur Young among those who investigated the vexing case of Ireland.[68] Goldsmith's stinging attack on 'stern depopulation' as the tool of a commercial society that sought to enclose the commons and extend pasturage is one of the things that make it difficult to thread his poetry into the fabric of an Irish romanticism marked by overpopulation. Edgeworth, who was deeply attuned to political economy, traces patterns in the Irish history of large-scale grazing in *Ormond* (1817), where White Connal's greedy plans exist side by side with the Gaelic island of King Corny, an oblique midlands invocation of the lives of evicted peasants who crowded along the Atlantic littoral and eked out a subsistence lifestyle. Edgeworth read Adam Smith's *The Wealth of Nations* (1776) as a young girl, and her debts to Smith are clearly expressed in the conclusion to *Castle Rackrent*, discussed later, which looks to commercial prosperity in the context of political union as the surest guarantee of national progress. When the *Edinburgh Review* was established, Edgeworth's writings became an important touchstone in British liberal understandings of the question of Ireland. Such debates extended a line of enquiry begun by Arthur Young, who arrived in Ireland in 1775 and, seeing the need for 'accurate general ideas' of the country, soon published his *Tour in Ireland* (1780).[69]

Already, the American War of Independence, a huge defeat for Britain, had seen a surge of economically oriented patriotism in Ireland with literary as well as political consequences. But what Edmund Burke described as the 'geographical morality' of American independence – the argument of distance – meant that Ireland was always going to be treated differently.[70]

James Kelly argues that the legislative independence gained in 1782 and extinguished by the Union is best understood as 'a new phase in the administration of the dependent kingdom of Ireland'.[71] The United Irish Rebellion of 1798 not only challenged Anglo-Irish authority but also tested the growing power of the British Empire. Put down by Cornwallis, the former commander in chief of British troops in India and the man who had surrendered to American and French troops at Yorktown, the rebellion resonated in European and imperial contexts. And within ten years, as Maya Jasanoff shows, 'British power regrouped, expanded, and reshaped itself across the world – in Ireland and India, Canada and the Caribbean, Africa and Australia'.[72]

The story of restive, unequal, unhappy Ireland took shape within these global contexts. In the decades to come, the 1798 rebellion came to be understood across Europe as a refutation of the proposition that integration within Britain's empire brought peace and prosperity. Locally, 1798 stayed fresh in the minds of Irish landowners as a threat to their persons and property. Coming as it did after the Union, Robert Emmet's rebellion of 1803 sharpened that sense of danger and extended a general sense of what Mary Tighe called 'the terrors of these times'.[73] Tighe's letters indicate how the 1798 rebellion engrossed elite attention, as conversation turned on the topic of 'plots & pikes' and neighbours preferred to meet for breakfast rather than risk an evening out.[74] Visiting Edgeworthstown around 1813, the travel writer James Hall observed the precautions were still taken by the family, including 'rough window-shutters' found 'all round the lower part of the house' as well as 'outer doors of plank three inches thick, and ball-proof; so that there was no fear of being attacked, either by the windows or the doors, after these were secured in the evening'.[75]

It was not only in Edgeworthstown that bookish occupations endured during violent times. The journals of apprentice notary Robert Rainey (1780–1807), which run with gaps from 1798 to 1805 contain detailed remarks on the day-to-day news of rebellion from June 1798 onwards. Beyond critical remarks on the motivations of the rebels, Rainey records his daily trips in search of scarce and sought-after news bulletins.[76] His days routinely begin and end with 'a book', and Rainey records references to fiction, history and the theatre. On 13 July 1798, for instance, Rainey 'dined alone at 5', read a book, took 'a walk in search of news' and remarked on the fate of the Sheares brothers, United Irish rebels 'to be executed tomorrow'. He heard that the nearby town of Kilcock had been taken by the rebels, noting that 'the Ballad Singers have just come into possession of a new song' that has 'the tune of "Croppies lie Down"'. Rainey transcribes some lines from the new ballad:

> Give me a needle, & give me a thread
> To sew on a tail to poor Croppy's head
>   Down down croppy's lie down.

The reference is to United Irishmen who, supposedly no longer daring to wear their hair cropped close in the French republican style, 'adopted *false tails*' or new hairpieces.[77] Rainey gives further colour to his picture of a rising tide of loyalism in an account of a theatre performance that 'concluded with the exhibition of a grand transparency which descended in a cloud – a large medallion containing a half length figure of Lord Cornwallis, supported by Justice and Mercy', 'the effect very pretty – God save the King in grand Chorus – A very loyal gallery continued exclamations of "damn the rebels" – home about 12 – Tea and toast – in bed at 11 –'.[78]

Even amidst this lively day-to-day interest in literature and culture, it is striking to arrive at *Castle Rackrent* in Robert Rainey's journal (Figure 1.1). Edgeworth's first novel, published anonymously, takes its place on his pages alongside references to travel literature, 'some new political pamphlets' and 'revolutionary poetry'. Rainey sometimes transcribes some literary material of this nature, including the ballad lines quoted earlier, but in the case of *Castle Rackrent* he copies out several pages in their entirety, a curious but not unusual example of print being remediated in manuscript form and an undertaking surely marked by uncertainty about ongoing access to a significant new novel.

On Christmas Eve, 1800, Rainey 'sat down to read "Castle Rackrent" a new production of 1 volume, its object is I believe to show the advantage we must derive from an incorporation with our more polished Sister England'. There follows a plot summary which suggests that the reading was quickly accomplished, including some remarks on the 'designing agent' who triumphs over the Rackrent family.

Rainey is clearly taken with the book's narrative achievement (though he does not know who the author is) and gives 'the following extract' as 'a specimen of old Thady's style, to support which with success is a proof of considerable ability in the author'. The transcription, which continues over three manuscript pages, all dated 24 December 1800, begins with the departure of Sir Condy's wife – 'My poor master was in great trouble after my lady left us' – and ends at the place where the last of the Rackrents signs over his estate to Jason Quirke. Having affixed Edgeworth's words to

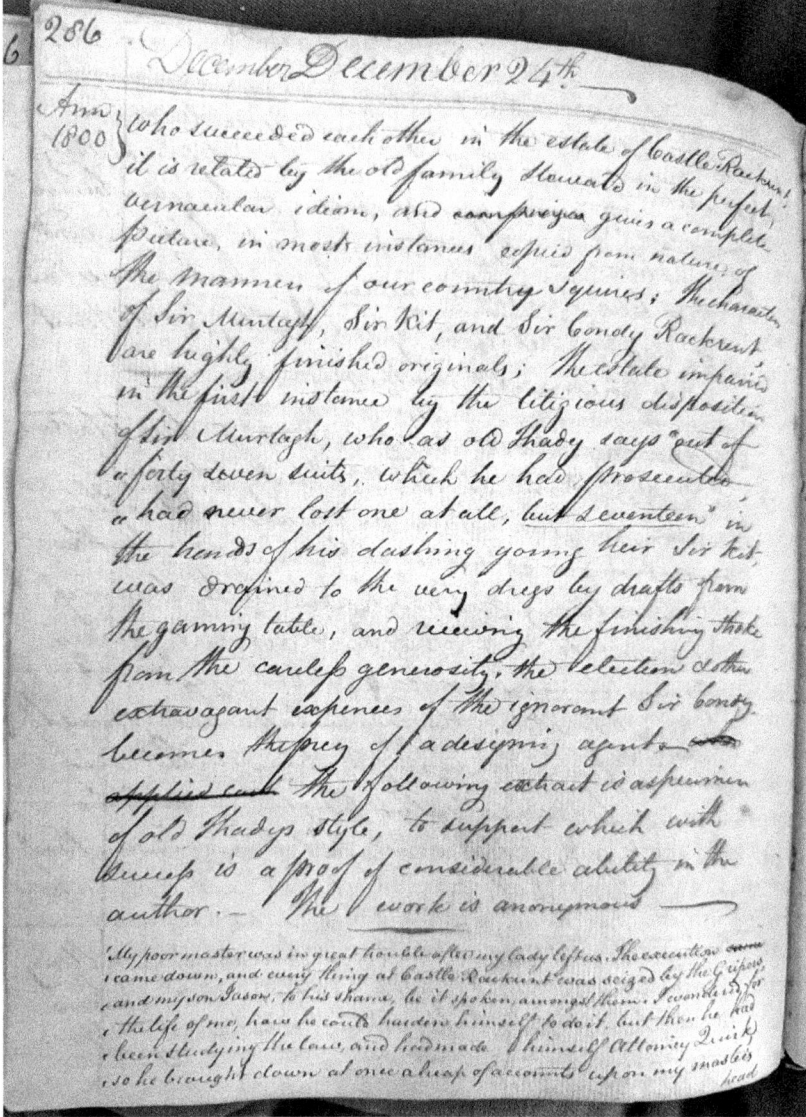

Figure 1.1   Robert Rainey, diary giving accounts of political affairs in Dublin, business and social activities while working at Crampton Court and Dame Street. National Library of Ireland MSS 34.395/1.

his own pages, Rainey turns a leaf for Christmas itself, an 'uncommonly beautiful' day which he spent at the office.[79]

In Rainey's journal, we find the text of *Castle Rackrent* not only remediated from print to manuscript but also made a tangible part of the everyday life of a young man whose day job involved him in the care, custody and certification of documents. *Castle Rackrent*, in its turn, began its life in an act of copying: Edgeworth took notes on the speech of the family steward, John Langan, and transferred these into print, achieving as she did so remarkable oral and auditory effects that made an Irish world vivid on the page. Her sister Charlotte too captured Langan's day-to-day presence in the family life in a drawing (Figure 1.2).

Edgeworth, though, was not pleased to find herself a victim of copying, as she reported in an 1816 letter to John Murray concerning Scott and pretenders to the authorship of *Waverley*. In it, she reminds Murray of

> a singular circumstance that happened about Castle Rackrent – No name was to the first edition – An officer in the Buckinghamshire militia actually took the trouble to copy from the printed book and make an Ms of it and caused himself to be surprised one morning with the Ms. on the table and then acknowledged himself to be the author! How could anyone think it worth while to do such a thing?[80]

Castle Rackrent was first published by Joseph Johnson, supporter of the French revolution. Mary Wollstonecraft met her husband William Godwin at Johnson's table in Paternoster Row, not long after her return from Mitchelstown, County Cork, where she worked as governess for the Kingsborough family and learned, as she wrote, a 'rational' love of England fostered by her general dislike of Ireland and no small measure of anti-Catholicism.[81] Richard Lovell Edgeworth too dined at Johnson's home and met Godwin and Thomas Malthus there in 1803, when he was in London to see about the publication of his daughter's *Popular Tales*. Johnson might seem an unlikely publisher for Edgeworth. But he had an interest in publishing books for younger audiences, shared connections with her father and published a number of significant women of the period, including Charlotte Smith and Anna Letitia Barbauld. In contrast to Sydney Owenson, who moved repeatedly between publishers in search of the best deal, Edgeworth remained with the firm, managed by Johnson's great nephews after he died, until her own death. But although Edgeworth, of all the writers discussed in this chapter, had the most reliable and long-lived relations with her publishers, her novel *Castle Rackrent* lived a more uncertain life.

Castle Rackrent certainly bears out Toby Barnard's warning against assuming 'any rigid barrier between orality and literacy' in our understanding of reading in eighteenth- and nineteenth-century Ireland.[82]

Figure 1.2 Charlotte Edgeworth, *John Langan with Little Harriet and Sophy*. Bodleian Libraries, University of Oxford. MS. Eng. misc. c. 903.

Edgeworth shares 'practices of extracting, quoting, and sourcing'[83] with many Romantic-era writers, but she also draws unwritten and popular forms of knowledge into these intermedial processes. And she tends to deliver such knowledge in forms that thrive at the margins of print, including the footnote and the glossary. *Castle Rackrent*'s note on the banshee, described as 'a species of aristocratic fairy', sits alongside another lengthy note on the digging up of a fairy mount by

Sir Murtagh Rackrent.[84] There is also a glossary entry on fairy belief, understood by Dáithí Ó hÓgáin as a reference to the *sí gaoithe*, 'thrust wind' or 'fairy wind' in which the fairies travelled.[85] Across this material, Edgeworth collects forms of popular knowledge and conveys them in print, a set of practices that can be thought of as 'a method for making oral genres extinct'.[86] But just as Mary Mullen describes Thady Quirke's oral performance as one that imbues a fading feudal world with a new strange kind of energy, so Edgeworth's narrative reimagines popular knowledge in a new mode.[87]

Even as it exploited the possibilities of print culture, *Castle Rackrent* never quite settled into a secure life on the shelf. In 1805, Edgeworth received an anonymous letter with a Bristol post mark, 'enclosing a page of Castle-rack on which was scrawled *lies, lies lies* in pencil'. According to Charlotte Edgeworth, Maria Edgeworth was 'all convinced' that the letter was written by their step-sister Emmeline, resident in Bristol and married to a man disliked by the family. Charlotte explained the whole affair in a letter to Emmeline, saying that 'we all thought' that the letter was 'in your own hand' and explaining that they decided not to show the offending item to their father, Richard Lovell Edgeworth. Not only does the account given by Charlotte Edgeworth help us track the movement of *Castle Rackrent* and the fame of its author along intimate family networks, it also connects the novel to wider questions of privacy, circulation and communication. Charlotte explains to Emmeline, who had just had a baby, that though she may have been curious to know 'what was said & thought here of you', that there were difficulties in conveying private information: 'every body has been so anxious about you that every body flocked to the postbox for news, so when you letter came I read them the greatest part & told them to give their opinion about the name of the little girl'.[88] Richard Lovell Edgeworth had also just had a baby girl, Sophia, with Frances Anne Beaufort, and among the tensions expressed in the letter is family disapproval of 'Zoe', the name chosen by Emmeline. The delicacies and difficulties attendant upon practices of reading aloud move between public and private modes and remained a key part of elite as well as popular literary culture.

Union and Empire

Castle Rackrent not only begins to develop a sociology of Irish difference but, as Robert Rainey noticed already in 1800, sets a distinctive aesthetic agenda that is closely tied to the passing of the Act of Union. Its distinctive style maps onto the political particularities of its moment as Union, at once a policy born of war and a reforming measure that passed into law with the help of massive corruption at state level, came to define the terms of Irish–British relations into the future. The Union, which served to buttress Britain against France and align Irish commercial interests with those of the empire, can be seen both as a natural outcome of Scottish Enlightenment and anti-feudal thinking, and as a disruptive, defensive, counter-revolutionary response to unrest. Its threat to the Anglo-Irish ascendancy was widely understood: already, in December 1798, Caroline Hamilton (née Tighe) told her cousin Mary Tighe that along with the rebellion, a Union was endlessly talked over, supplying 'an inexhaustible fund of conversation' among her circle.[89]

The Act of Union not only dominated conversations but also called up a variety of writerly models. Thomas De Quincey, passing through Dublin en route to visit his schoolfriend Lord Sligo, was in the House of Commons in Dublin for the 'final ratification of the Bill' and later invoked Robert Burns as he wrote about the 'moral' resonances of an event that he understood to have 'robbed' Ireland of its 'splendour': 'an end of an auld sang'. William Wordsworth's 'fine sonnet on the extinction of the Venetian republic had not then been published', De Quincey further commented; otherwise its final lines would have served to express his feelings: 'Men are we, and must grieve when even the shade / Of that which once was great has pass'd away.' De Quincey's elegy for Ireland's 'splendour' recognised that political centralisation was made necessary by the war with France but queried its necessity in a print- and technology-unified kingdom where 'the very furthest nook of these "nook-shotten" islands' could easily communicate with London.[90]

Owenson's *The Wild Irish Girl* might just as well have been written to make De Quincey's case. Her English hero Mortimer journeys from London, through Holyhead and Dublin and on to the west of Ireland, an area that Humphry Davy in 1811 could still characterise as 'the haunt of deserters and smugglers':

> The few persons of the middling class who reside there are delighted to see strangers, who are hailed with the same feeling of novelty and wonder as a comet in our planetary system. The lower classes are uncertain and dangerous, not unlike the natives of Owyhee; a stranger is scarcely safe amongst them.[91]

Davy in 1811 repeated myths that Owenson's novel had already set about scotching: she has Mortimer imagine 'an Esquimaux group' when he thinks of the Irish. But rather than a Pacific island or a polar desert, Mortimer finds a Connemara 'nook' that possesses a sophisticated print culture whose effects are only heightened by an air of ruin. The old oak walls of Glorvina's boudoir frame a 'rich, new, and beautiful' carpet and stylish drapery and, should we miss these marks of modernity, sheet music and recent London newspapers lay scattered on a 'pondrous Gothic table'.[92]

Owenson presses further into Ireland's 'nook-shotten' coast when a party consisting of Mortimer and Father John cross 'the imaginary line which divides the province of Connaught from that of Ulster' and stay the night at 'a sorry inn, near a tract of the sea coast, called the Magilligans'.[93] The location is a peninsula that lies to the northwest of Derry at the entrance to Lough Foyle, a place of low, flat strands and shore that was soon to serve as the baseline for the mapping of Ireland undertaken by the Ordnance Survey. Already though, in *The Wild Irish Girl*, a spatial imagination is at work as the particularities of place are mapped onto page space.

The account that *The Wild Irish Girl* gives of Ulster is often cited for its sharp distinction between a northern Ireland characterised by a Scottish devotion to industry and trade and a western seaboard whose 'genuine Irish character' is expressed in a 'warm and cordial' welcome to the stranger. Owenson even gives short shrift to the famous spectacle of the Giant's Causeway, as Mortimer makes only routine mention of its standing as 'a shrine of Nature in her grandest aspect'. Writing to his English friend, Mortimer says he will tell 'nothing' of the Causeway and instead promises to 'put into your hands a work written on the subject, from which you will derive equal pleasure and instruction'.[94] But even as Owenson downplays the Irishness of the northern counties (with their 'Scotch dialect, Scotch manners, Scotch modes') and treats minimally their known beauties, she opens up a significant space of engagement with a living representative of Ulster culture: the harper Dennis Hampson. In the late eighteenth century the Magillian peninsula was the home to the historical figure of Donnchadh Ó hAmhsaigh or Dennis Hampson, a harper whose story Owenson narrates at length, across several lavishly footnoted pages. Mortimer and Father John visit Hampson, whom they find in bed with his harp, 'cheerful and communicative' all the same.[95]

Most of the communication across this section of the novel is, however, achieved at the foot of the page rather than in the cabin described: the notes cover more than three quarters of each page, eleven pages in the original printing. She assures us in a footnote that the harper, already an elderly man by the time of Owenson's writing, had his story taken down 'from his own lips' on 3 July 1805 by a Reverend Sampson.

The transcription was then 'forwarded to the author' by a further intermediary, Dr Patterson. Sampson was a Church of Ireland rector and member of the Royal Irish Academy who produced a *Statistical Survey of the County of Londonderry* around the same time that Mary Tighe's cousin William produced his *Statistical Survey of the County of Kilkenny*. Dr Patterson was a Derry physician and fellow RIA member. Behind this network of learned informants lay Joseph Cooper Walker, who had suggested to Owenson that she incorporate an account of the harper, Hempson (sometimes Hampson), in her novel. By the early nineteenth-century, Hempson was considered one of the last keepers of many older styles of harp playing: in 1792, at the Belfast Harp Festival, he had been the only player to use the fingernail technique.

The coves, harbours and inlets along which the lines of Union also opened up to empire along watery routes that are further discussed in the next chapter. As a piece of statecraft, the Act of Union was repeated within British foreign policy after the war by Lord Castlereagh, many of whose cabinet, like George Canning and Lord Macartney, shared his Anglo-Irish Ascendancy background.[96] By taking readers deep into the Irish past and the details of its musical traditions, *The Wild Irish Girl* might seem to direct attention away from such imperial politics. But in 1809, Owenson published her *Ida of Athens* and introduced her readers to a national tale in which a learned heroine, whose lover had to flee Greece after a revolt against the Turks, is exiled to poverty in London. Her happy reunion with her lover did not impress Byron, who used one of his notes to the second canto of *Childe Harold* to criticise Owenson's lack of understanding of the Greek class system. The book sold well for Longmans though copies were scarce at home – in January, Mary Tighe boasted to Joseph Cooper Walker of having 'the only *Ida* yet in Ireland' – and soon Owenson was using the company of the Abercorns' friend Lord Castlereagh to help her negotiate a better deal with Stockdale to publish *The Missionary: An Indian Tale* (1811).[97] That novel was written in the County Tyrone house of the Abercorns and dedicated to Lady Jane Abercorn, on whose support Owenson relied until she married their physician, Sir Charles Morgan, in 1812. The plot, set in seventeenth-century Goa, sees a Hindu priestess fall in love with a Portuguese Franciscan friar who is condemned to death by immolation by the Jesuit-led Inquisition. Considered 'a divine thing' by Percy Bysshe Shelley,[98] *The Missionary* was edited and reissued in 1859, so that Owenson (now Lady Morgan) could profit from the market for tales of India in the aftermath of the Indian Rebellion of 1857.

Along with elite figures such as Castlereagh and Macartney, and socially engaged writers including Mary Leadbeater, many ordinary Irish people participated in that expanding empire. Mary Leadbeater addressed a poem to the anti-slavery activist Rushton 'on the recovery of his sight', while the first original poem found in her *Poems* of 1808 is 'The Negro', addressed to Edmund Burke. Dated 1789 and referring to a speech made by 'Great Burke' in favour of Wilberforce in that year, the poem addresses the Irish philosopher and politician as 'Freedom's firm friend, and Pity's gen'rous guide'.[99] Leadbeater situates Burke alongside abolitionist Thomas Clarkson, though her admiration for the former Ballitore pupil may have led her to overestimate the links. Burke had already in 1780 drafted the 'Sketch of a Negro Code', a plan to regulate the trade in African people and make it 'as small an evil as possible'.[100] The Code was never brought before Parliament, and Burke continued as a 'steadfast supporter and defender of the Company of Merchants Trading to Africa, a body created to maintain British forts on the African Coast and defend the interests of slave traders, for which it received annual grants from Parliament'.[101]

Leadbeater, though, not only wrote about but personally advocated for abolition. She read and admired the *Address to the People of Great Britain (Respectfully Offered to the People of Ireland) on the Utility of Refraining from the Use of West Indian Sugar and Rum* (published in London in 1791 and Dublin in 1792) and asked her friend Molly Bewley to help get it reprinted in Dublin, while other Quaker women helped to circulate it across the country via chapmen. Her poem 'To the Memory of S. E. Who Died at Calcutta, 1781. Aged 22' is critical not only of 'the wasting wrath of war' but of a guilty empire whose very geographical expansiveness spells out injustice:

> O eastern regions! Fatal climes,
>   Where stern oppression rules severe! –
> But Heav'n's broad eye beholds the crimes,
>   The cries of mis'ry Heav'n will hear.[102]

Elsewhere, in a poem dedicated to 'Dr. C. in India', she goes further in seeming to blame place rather than politics for the ills of empire: she begs the Scottish doctor to abjure 'India's wealth' and 'leave that luckless shore'.[103]

The poems written to lament the death of Irish men and women overseas call up empire as a horizon of loss but rarely invite a fuller consideration of its contours. Perhaps the literary model provided by elegy allows only narrow engagement with individual losses, as is the case with Jeremiah Joseph Callanan's 'Lines, on the Death of an Amiable and Highly Talented Young Man, Who Fell a Victim to Fever in the West Indies'.

Callanan, who is discussed in the next chapter, borrows the language of the United Irishmen to lament 'an exile of Erin', far from friends on 'his own green Isle of the Ocean'.[104] A similar and even more unpalatable interplay between the 1798 rebellion and service to the empire is found in Henry Boyd's poem 'The Recognition', which compares the plight of a group of refugee loyalists, stalled in Wexford Harbour and fearing that they will be trapped by rebels, to the fate of enslaved people awaiting transportation across the Atlantic. The unlikely and ugly proposition is that those snatched from the east coast of Africa are to be envied in their power to anticipate circumstances that will at least change, whereas Boyd's brave but threatened band of loyalists must undergo a state of terrified stasis as they await a change of tide:

> How envied they the dusky band,
>   To slavery borne from Gambia's shore,
> Where hope and fear, with even hand,
>   A changeful prospect spreads before.[105]

More familiar in the mode of British abolitionist verse of the same period is Thomas Dermody's 'On a Dead Negro', which voices the perspective of a sentimental observer of the 'iron rod' of the tyrant. Even there though, Dermody's repeated use of the word 'perchance' only reluctantly grants agency to the 'soul' and 'sable hue' of the enslaved person.[106]

The contradictions of Ireland's place in the empire are registered in Lady Morgan's novel *O'Donnel* (1814) when a group of fashionable English travellers, making a party of pleasure to the Giant's Causeway, quiz an Irish peasant character, McRory, about his travels overseas. McRory – foster brother and servant of the O'Donnel of the title, with whom he has fought for the Austrian service – is asked if he 'has seen a deal of the world'. His first reply – that he was '*twice't* in Dublin' – merits an 'Indeed! and no further?', only for him to give an ironic response worthy of Admiral Croft's wife in Austen's *Persuasion*: 'No, Sir, no further: – only once't in *Garmany*, on a little business; and a little while back in the West Indies; that's when I was sarving in th'army, your Honor.' Asked about his regiment, McRory explains that he was

> mighty near listing with the *Flaugh-na-balagh* boys, under the great Giniral Doyle, long life to him, wherever he is, only in regard of the master, who came home on account of the *troubles*. So I listed with him in the Irish Brigades; and so we went to fight the black Frinch negurs in St. Domingo. Of as fine a regimen of lads as ever you clapt your eyes on, not one of us but was kilt dead in the field, barring a handfull, as I may say, and myself and the master.[107]

The phrase '*Flaugh-na-balagh*', or *fág an bealach*, translates as 'clear the way' and served as the unofficial motto of the 87th and sometimes the 88th regiment, the Royal Irish Fusiliers and the Connaught Rangers respectively. French regiments, including Irish regiments in French service, were dispatched to put down a slave revolt in St Domingo in the early 1790s, with disastrous results. Then some years later, the Irish regiments in French service, having been disbanded by the French revolutionaries, joined the British army as an Irish Brigade and served in St Domingo, again with disastrous results. So it is quite possible that McRory could have served in both French and British services in St Domingo/Haiti in this period, as hinted at by Owenson.

The following section turns to the case of Thomas Dermody, considered against the backdrop of a culture in which books are scarce and bookish professions scarcer still. Irish romantic print culture was not only marked by the recent history of revolution or the rhetoric that accompanied the Act of Union but also bore the imprint of imperial circuits of commerce, power and knowledge. Together, these forces created a living field of culture in which a number of writers sought to make their way. Ideas of national character, though, impress or imprint themselves upon such efforts, as discussed later.

Thomas Dermody: Patronage and Possibility

Among the short lives and broken reputations that litter these years we find the name of Thomas Dermody, author of a body of work that helps to give shape to Irish literature between the French Revolution and the Act of Union.[108] His story is often told in terms of early promise betrayed by a feckless and alcoholic lifestyle, and it remains difficult to separate out his distinctive reputation from prevailing ideas of national character, discussed later.

In 1785, the same year in which the Royal Irish Academy was founded in Dublin, a ten-year-old Dermody left Ennis and struck out for the capital 'with a couple of shillings only, the second volume of Tom Jones (which, he has often said, determined him on his adventure), and a single change of linen, in his pocket'.[109] The son of a school teacher and tutor whose alcoholism meant a peripatetic family life, Dermody longed to be an author. In Dublin, he was taken on by Richard Daly, manager of the Theatre Royal at Crow Street for whom he worked as a stage-hand. There he met the actor-manager Robert Owenson, fresh from his failed 'City Theatre' enterprise on Fishamble Street, a cultural enterprise entwined with the hopes of the Volunteers and later elevated in memory by his daughter Sydney Owenson to the 'National Theatre Music Hall'.[110] The Volunteers were an elite militia established during the American War of Independence, and both father and daughter were drawn to the 'convergence of popular and elite politics' that helped to bring about legislative independence and a measure of free trade in 1782.[111] The legacy of Volunteer songs and ballads by writers including Edward Lysaght makes its way into Sydney Owenson's novels, while both she and Maria Edgeworth were drawn to the involvement of elite women in the political theatre of Patriot politics.

When Robert Owenson brought Thomas Dermody home to his family, Sydney Owenson remembered that her Methodist mother was shocked at the 'Papist' nature of the young man's name but impressed by 'the greatest prodigy that has ever appeared since Chatterton, or your own Pope, who wrote beautiful poetry at fourteen'.[112] The Owensons gave Dermody lodgings, food and clothing, while the canny Robert Owenson arranged for the young poet to wear rags when meeting prospective patrons. Dermody's new friend also took up residence in 'an eminent bookseller's shop', and offered work by Dermody 'for sale to persons who entered, sometimes relating the doleful history of the luckless bard; and even assailed the passengers that passed the door. ... by this mode he procured him considerable relief'.[113] Dermody's patrons included Patriot politicians Henry Flood (who disliked *Castle Rackrent*) and Lord Charlemont. He was also supported by Joseph Cooper Walker and addressed poems to both Walker and Owenson.

Already in 1789 a volume of Dermody's *Poems* appeared in Dublin, published by subscription. The advertisement, by a clergyman named Gilbert Austin, describes a fourteen-year-old author who had suffered 'every kind of distress' but benefited from the support of Robert Owenson. The book itself is described in terms of restrictions appropriate to a youthful and delicate talent: '*It has been thought proper not to offer this specimen to the Public at large, but to print a few copies to be circulated among* those only, who, it is hoped, will take an interest in the protection of our young Poet, and *whose protections it is of most consequence that he should obtain.*'[114] Subsequent volumes were published in 1792 and 1800. His last collection, *Poems on Various Subjects*, appeared in 1802, around the same time that he fled London for Sydenham in Kent, while a posthumous collection, *The Harp of Erin*, was published in 1807.

At his death, Dermody still enjoyed something of his early reputation as a child prodigy, but critics also agreed that he had wasted this early promise. More recently, Michael Griffin has made a case for thinking about

Dermody as a 'compelling cultural phenomenon rather than an influential literary figure', somebody who 'prefigures more substantial experiments in literary living'.[115] But any serious interest in experiment was blocked by a lifelong reliance on forms of patronage, interspersed with periods spent teaching and in the service of the army. Dermody wrote about these issues in 'The Cave of Patronage', one among those poems published in *The Harp of Erin*. With an ominous opening – 'Partitions twain this motley cave divide' – the poem shows how quickly the 'glitt'ring toy' of fame is lost, along with other forms of 'lively joy'.[116]

Invoking the 'stings of penury and woe',[117] the poem not only illustrates the dilemmas of patronage but shows Dermody's efforts to imagine a double literary lineage, British and Irish, to which he might belong, even if it is one characterised by darkness and difficulty. Dermody imagines a literary career as a cave, path and labyrinth, a 'horrid length of bog and mire', beset by dangers with only fellow poet victims for company: Spenser, Otway and Dryden.[118] Elsewhere Dermody refers to 'Mulla's Minstrel',[119] alluding to *The Faerie Queene*, where the River Awbeg, near Spenser's North Cork home, takes the name 'Mulla'. Spenser likely drew this name from the nearby town of *Cill Mullaigh* (Buttevant, County Cork), along which the river Awbeg runs.[120] In 'The Cave of Patronage', Spenser 'warbles heav'nly his dejected lay' while oppressed by political responsibilities and the demands of the Elizabethan court: 'haughty Burleigh crush'd blithe fancy's son'.[121] Spenser's name and reputation lived on in Irish romanticism where it served a code for cultural conflict: his *View of the Present State of Ireland*, with its vicious account of the starving Irish subjugated by the Crown, was published in London in 1805 and again in a Dublin edition in 1809.[122] In Lady Morgan's *Florence Macarthy* (1818), two characters arriving into Dublin by ship debate the relative merits of *The Faerie Queene* and the *View of the Present State of Ireland*. The characters traverse a mountainous route across the Ballyhoura mountains in County Cork that brings them close to Spenser's Irish home and within sight of the Elizabethan poet's 'classical scenery'. John Trotter's *Walks Through Ireland* (1817) describes that same route through places in which Spenser's name lives on in local memory (including a pilgrimage to Kilcolman castle) but also notes how little the English poet really understood of the place in which he lived.

Lady Moira offered her support to Dermody in the 1790s – though when Owenson published her own volume of poems in 1801, similar help was not forthcoming. Dermody himself thought to review her *Poems* in London, as he promised in a blustery letter to Robert Owenson in which he also asked 'Who is the *Mr. Moore* Sydney mentions? He is nobody here, I assure you, of eminence.'[123] In one of the poems published in that volume, Sydney Owenson recalled the genius of her 'some-time brother' and his influence on her own taste:

> from thy lips,
> My mind imbib'd th' enthusiastic glow;
> The love of literature, which thro' my life
> Heighten'd each bliss, and soften'd every woe.[124]

The poem in question is titled 'Retrospection', bearing the subtitle 'Written on the Author's visiting the home of her childhood, after an absence of ighte [*sic*] years.' In it, she remembers a family group that included Dermody:

> Oft does my mem'ry sketch the social group,
> At closing eve, that circled round the fire;
> Sweet hour that fondly knits each human tie,
> Unites the children, mother, friend, and sire![125]

Owenson can only have been about twenty years of age when she wrote this poem of 'dear scenes' and a former 'cot',[126] but she too is trying on a role, connecting her own literary endeavours to those of Dermody.

Michael Griffin has shown how patrons and publishers steered Dermody away from writing in the mode of Robert Burns. This is particularly true of Dermody's Killeigh poems, written over the two years he spent as a student of clergyman, poet and translator of Dante, Rev. Henry Boyd, in County Offaly, under the patronage of Lady Moira. Dermody suspected Boyd of merely wanting to 'retain him for the purpose of working at the translation' of Dante 'and copying it for him', and left Offaly to return to Dublin.[127] Only two of Dermody's raucous poems of everyday rural life were published in the 1792 volume of his *Poems*, and both of those ('Tam to Rab: An Odaic Epistle' and 'An Ode to the Collegians') followed Burns' Standard Habbie stanzaic style and irreverent, boozy tone.

By participating in the late eighteenth-century revival of Scotch verse, Dermody also turned away, as Griffin shows, from such available popular modes as Irish *amhrán* song metre (in which Carolan's 'Gracey Nugent', discussed later, was written) and macaronic poetry with its lively play between English and Irish.[128] Among the aspects of the Scots influence identified by Michael Griffin is Dermody's use of 'Wow!' in 'Tam to Rab', the exclamation signalling affective ties not only to Burns but to Allan Ramsay and Robert Fergusson.[129] But Griffin speculates that the poems written in Killeigh did not mesh well with Dermody's reputation as a classical child prodigy whose chance at fame rested on 'technical virtuosity and practised sensibility',[130] and perhaps this is why they largely remained unpublished in his lifetime. Tighe too complained of a felt need to adopt sentimental modes: 'Vain dreams, and fictions of distress and love / I idly feigned'.[131] As with Tighe, it can be difficult to link Dermody into a line of Irish poetry, though Jonas Cope makes a case for the resonances of the *aisling* form within Dermody's writing.[132] Cope discusses a late poem by Dermody, 'The Extravaganza', in which Dermody imagines a mystical female figure with clear links to his patron, Lady Moira. The woman warns him to resist the pleasures of the flesh and advises him to write poetry on more classical lines.

Issues of publication affected not only individual reputations but also blocked the emergence of a national tradition bounded by books and known names. In the 1790s, Dermody penned a 'Farewell to Ireland', a poem whose indignant opening echoes the lines composed by Jonathan Swift at Holyhead: 'Rank nurse of nonsense; on whose thankless coast / The base weed thrives, the nobler bloom is lost'. The 'sinking isle' of Ireland, propped up by a miserable populace, still inspires a pride that is vested in a line of Irish 'artists' in which the poet seeks to enrol himself: 'And haply when some native gem you see / Unknown, unfriended, lost, – oh, think on me!'[133] In another poem, though, 'Lines Written on a Blank Leaf of Swift's Works', Dermody notes that his encounter with Swift's writing was one mediated by 'bad type', 'brown paper' and poor-quality calf binding, its rough presentation contrasting favourably not only to the Morocco or goatskin covers of 'modern authors' but also Dermody's own pages, which show 'the printer's pain'.[134]

In 1793, an eighteen-year-old Dermody published a republican pamphlet in epistolary form, *The Rights of Justice, or Rational Liberty; A Letter to an Acquaintance in the Country*. This time he has Burke, not Burns, in his sights. Hailing the letter form itself as 'the only fashionable vehicle of political information', Dermody invokes the epistolary mode of Edmund Burke's *Reflections on the Revolution in France*, also acknowledging the cultural role of plays, novels and ballads as literary modes that similarly look to France and the 'Goal of Emancipation'. Setting regicide lightly to one side, Dermody weighs the blood of a country in the 'Scales of Justice' and finds that horror at the death of a monarch must be balanced against 'the happiness of our fellow creatures, and the smile of the contented peasant'.[135] The timing of the pamphlet could not have been worse: the letter is dated 20 February, three weeks after France had declared war. And within a year or so, Dermody himself had left Ireland for London only to enlist as a private in the 108th regiment of the British wagon corps. By 1795 he was already fighting against revolutionary France in France, Flanders and Germany, during which time he lost the use of his left hand. Subsequently Dermody lived in London on half-pay, where he received support from the Royal Literary Fund. He died in Kent in 1802, aged only twenty-seven, his reputation salvaged by his friend and patron James Grant Raymond, who published the poems and a biography in 1806.

In spring of that year, in Wicklow, Mary Tighe began her reading journal with a discussion of Raymond's book. She admired Dermody's talent but wondered to her friend the antiquarian scholar Joseph Cooper Walker that 'so much talent should be choak'd & embruted by a deprav'd heart'.[136] Dermody's drinking shaped his reputation for his own and future generations and contributes to a concept of Irish literature as the place where 'the potent force of the idea of a national character is most frequently and most memorably realized'.[137] In Seamus Deane's account, national character was 'an idea without a sufficient history', meaning that Irish literature was forced to step in and supply imaginative resources.[138] A kind of cultural deformation was the result, Deane says: 'The English audience lives in the everyday world; the Irish writer and the Irish culture belong to a surreal world.'[139] Mary Tighe's reading journal gives us a first-hand insight into the ways in which ideas of character circulated and mutated: in early May, 1806 she praised 'some good lines' that Dermody had addressed to Sydney Owenson and notes how they confirm a bad 'character' she already knows from reading the biography. But she is also very critical of the anti-Irish tone taken in the *Edinburgh Review* account of Raymond's biography, with its assumptions of inevitable Irish decline.[140]

The case of Dermody shows us how the 'surreal world' described by Deane was in fact already coming to know and understand itself through processes of collection, translation, publication and reading, albeit in fragmented ways. The circulation of books and manuscripts was central to this process. Joseph Cooper Walker advised Sydney Owenson to try to gain entry to the library of the Royal Irish Academy, 'where you might pass two or three hours with pleasure and advantage' and 'look over the Irish historians'.[141] He also lent her books and translations and supported Charlotte Brooke in the same way, having earlier recommended to Dermody that he write a historical novel.[142] Walker's role is difficult to reconstruct in full but suggests potential writerly networks as well as hinting at an incipient but unrealised Irish romantic associational culture.

Charlotte Brooke: Translations, Page Space, Power

Charlotte Brooke's early role in getting Irish poems onto the printed page earns her a place in many histories of Irish writing. Brooke grew up the daughter of an Anglican father, the novelist Henry Brooke, and a Methodist mother. As well as enjoying a liberal education, she knew something of the rich Gaelic culture that flourished in her home place, Mullagh, County Cavan. As Ní Mhunghaile describes it, the ancient Gaelic area of Breiffne, including sections of Donegal, Leitrim, Sligo, Fermanagh, Cavan and Meath, maintained 'a strong Gaelic literary tradition' in Brooke's time, and she would have heard Irish spoken by servants and workers. Brooke had the eyes and ears of a collector and told Joseph Cooper Walker a story that both resonates with and contrasts with Wordsworth's poem 'The Solitary Reaper', which imagines a working woman who is also a lonely, nameless singer of unknown songs. Brooke, described by Walker as a 'young lady, on whose veracity I have the firmest reliance' told him of a labourer in her father's employ 'who was in possession of two volumes of Irish manuscript poems, which, in her infancy, she often heard him read to a rustic audience in her father's fields'.[143]

In Wordsworth's poem, the oral art of the labouring class lives on in memory: 'The music in my heart I bore, / Long after it was heard no more.'[144] So too does this scene of rural reading remain with Brooke. Where the speaker of Wordsworth's poem offers a pleasingly uncertain encounter with an oral performance, however, its notes fading on the air ('Will no one tell me what she sings?'),[145] Brooke's story offers a scene of popular learning in which books – 'two volumes of Irish manuscript poems' – are inescapably present. The passage, found in a footnote to Walker's *Historical Memoirs of the Irish Bards*, further delves into the controversy regarding the Irish or Scottish origin of the Ossian poems, immersing the reader in matters of 'literary curiosity' that seek to elevate Gaelic culture and distance it via scholarly debate.[146]

In 1789 Brooke published her *Reliques of Irish Poetry*, a highly significant volume that represents 'the first major point of interaction between oral tradition in the Irish language and print culture in Ireland' as well as 'the first purely literary work ever published in Dublin containing printing in the Irish character'.[147] A second posthumous edition was published in 1816 in octavo format. The collection is important not only because of the translations themselves but also because of the way in which its preface describes and conceptualises issues of translation. That preface helped to circulate the Patriot view of Britain and Ireland as sister, interdependent kingdoms, an image also used by more radical writers: Denis Taaffe, for instance, complained of 'our haughty mistaken sister'.[148] Within a few years, public discourse was more likely to trade in images of sexual or marital relationships which in turn worked their way into the literary texture of the national tale as it developed in the hands of Irish and Scottish women writers.

Brooke's *Reliques* includes heroic poems and Ossianic material that may have later influenced W. B. Yeats' 'Wanderings of Oisin'. A substantial body of scholarly work is on display with extensive paratextual material, including footnotes and commentaries that draw on Stanihurst, Geraldus Cambrensis, Spenser and Geoffrey Keating, as well as more recent and contemporary writers such as Charles O'Conor, Sylvester O'Halloran and Theophilus O'Flanagan. Part of Brooke's documentary method involves the printing of the Gaelic originals at the end of the book, a decision that Ní Mhunghaile speculates was both a response and a rebuke to the uncertainty surrounding the originals of Macpherson's Ossian poems. Brooke also chose to set the verse out in blocks rather than in verses, in order to respect manuscript practice. But contemporaries including the antiquarian William Beauford already thought it a mistake to place the Gaelic originals at the back of the book, rather than facing the originals across the page. Neither did Brooke include musical notation for the songs that she translated, though Joseph Cooper Walker had already done this for his *Historical Memoirs of the Irish Bards* (1786). Perhaps it was the negative example of Brooke that persuaded first Owenson and then Moore to arrange lyrics and musical notation, interlined with lyrics, on facing pages of their collections of melodies. In the case of Moore, the *Melodies* grew more luxurious with success and began to feature engravings that bore italicised lines from selected songs as mottoes.

Despite what may have been Brooke's 'considerable fluency' in Irish, Lesa Ní Mhunghaile has shown that her versions of the originals 'were deficient with regard to both orthography and metre'.[149] Indeed, Brooke's translations may have been so loose as to estrange native speakers entirely from the source material, though Gregory Schirmer points out that translators well into the 1830s continued in the same mode.[150] But Brooke's treatment of the poems themselves often takes a back seat in Anglophone criticism, where the focus is on the often cited gendered and national claims made in the preface. Those claims have their own history and can be connected, as Ní Mhunghaile shows, to prefatory material in Sarah Butler's *Irish Tales* (London, 1716) and Margaret Bingham (Lady

Lucan)'s *Verses on the Present State of Ireland* (1768). Other aspects of the book itself command attention. Ní Mhunghaile's edition of the *Reliques* shows that the 1789 edition was the first book to use a new Gaelic typeface, designed to imitate manuscript writing and 'including a number of scribal contractions'. The expensive and elaborate Parker type – 'large, complex and needlessly antiquated' – was named for Stephen Parker, in whose foundry it was produced, and 'is thought to be the first Irish font to have been cut and cast in Ireland'.[151] The handsome type was at home within a substantial quarto volume, printed on very good paper and circulated among a list of elite subscribers who could afford to pay three crowns a copy. Such an elite instance of Irish romantic print nonetheless emerges from a populous oral culture which is both formed and deformed in the process.

The title of Brooke's book gestures to the authoritative mode of collection and publication established by Percy's *Reliques of Ancient English Poetry* (1765) with its claims to a national tradition at once coherent and antique. Unlike Percy, though, whose poems come from an ancient society imagined as literate but in need of progress, Brooke chose to elevate her source material by associating it with qualities of cultivated elite patriotism. In order to do so, she chose to present only love poems and Ossianic lays – 'innocuous poems from the Ulster and Fenian cycles' – and largely ignored Jacobite songs.[152] At the level of editorial choice, her work can be compared to that of Thomas Moore, whose early work consisted largely of erotic and amatory verse, though as a young man he was able to go much further in challenging social norms. Moore's racy 'Odes to Nea', for instance, were exchanged between Mary and Percy Bysshe Shelley in the first days of their courtship.

Brooke lost most of her money in 1783, the same year that her father died. She invested in the enterprise of her cousin Robert Brooke, who worked for the East India Company and recruited many Irishmen to its ranks. Thinking to profit from Irish links with the empire, he established a cotton mill in the town of Currahilly, County Kildare, a place that he renamed Prosperous. And if giving the name 'Prosperous' to a failed industrial enterprise seems ironic, then there is Charlotte Brooke's own fate. In 1787, the same year in which her relative Robert was appointed governor of St Helena, she wrote to the Royal Irish Academy asking that she be appointed to the role of housekeeper. The suggestion incurred 'resentment', as she explained to Thomas Percy, telling him that the academy secretary, John Stack, wrote to recommend a teaching role, as if to 'humble me AND get me out of the way.'[153] Two years later, the *Reliques* were published, after which Charlotte Brooke moved to live with friends in Longford, where she died in 1793.

Brooke was influential among her own class in her own time and has a place in all contemporary histories of Irish poetry. But if we encounter difficulties in fitting Brooke's *Reliques* into a narrative of Irish literature – it is often mentioned in passing but rarely engaged with outside of some detailed textual scholarship – that is because of its dual identity as a waymark in Irish poetry and a significant event in book history. In relation to the former, the original creative intervention that Brooke hoped to make with her original poetic composition, 'Maon: An Irish Tale,' 'subjoined' to her translations, did not make a lasting cultural impression. But a focus on the *Reliques* as a milestone in Irish print culture helps connect Brooke to the other writers discussed in this chapter and develop our understanding of the bookish quality of Irish romanticism in this formative phase.

Brooke engaged in what Susan Stewart would call an 'artifactualization' of the original Gaelic poems in the *Reliques*, meaning that we encounter her translations primarily as bookish objects.[154] Leith Davis notes Brooke's 'marked ambivalence to the attempt to "remediate" Gaelic musical culture through the technology of print' and shows how self-consciously she set about that task.[155] Sydney Owenson worked through similar possibilities and challenges in her *Wild Irish Girl*, where, among the many topics discussed by her protagonists, the history of Irish song can be found. Mortimer, the English traveller who arrives in Inismore in disguise, embarks on a course of study in Irish language and history, guided by the priest, Fr John. His lessons are leavened by the presence of Glorvina, Owenson's sweet-voiced protagonist, who regularly introduces 'some short poem or song' to help with pronunciation.[156] Explaining his lessons to his English correspondent, Mortimer offers 'a specimen of Irish poetry', explaining that such material is 'almost always the effusion of some blind itinerant bard, or some rustic minstrel, into whose breast the genius of his country has breathed inspiration, as he patiently drove the plough, or laboriously worked in the bog'.[157] Mortimer then transcribes three artful short poems that, made present on the page, begin to undo this account of simple, popular fare. In the process, Owenson allows the poems on the page to point readers to Mortimer's unreliability in matters of Irish culture. The first short poem is titled 'Cathbein [Cathlein or Cathleen] Nolan', and the subsequent two songs are by the famed harper and composer Turlough Carolan (1670–1738). In relation to the first poem in particular, Mortimer seems wrong-headed. The poem is reproduced as follows:

CATHBEIN NOLAN.
I.
'My love, when she floats on the mountain's brow, is like the dewy cloud of the summer's loveliest evening. Her forehead is as a pearl; her spiral locks are of gold; and I grieve that I cannot banish her from my memory.'
II.
'When she enters the forest like the bounding doe, dispersing the dew with her airy steps, her mantle on her arm, the axe in her hand, to cut the branches of flame; I know not which is the most noble – the King of the Saxons, or Cathbein Nolan.'

A footnote appended to the description of 'the King of the Saxons' explains the derivation of 'Saxon' from the Irish world *sassenach*, or 'foreigner'. Mortimer goes on to speculate that the rank of the poet 'must have been of a very humble degree', given that his lover 'is represented as cutting wood for the fire'.[158] And yet the language of the poem clearly elevates its subject via a set of images that lead up to and justify a royal comparison. Why then does he misread its meanings? Mortimer's letter in fact illustrates an apolitical and culturally insensitive reading of Irish lyrics, against which Owenson had already argued in her *Twelve Hibernian Melodies*, published in 1805 and dedicated to her father.

As with Brooke's *Reliques*, Owenson's focus is on lyrics of love and loss, even where the airs tell of political violence and 'all the horrors of anarchy and warfare'.[159] But in the published collection of sheet music, containing Irish airs adorned by English-language lyrics, Owenson gives a different translation of 'Cathleen Nolan', one that points up its politics: Cathleen carries not only a mantle, for example, but one 'of old Erin[']s green'.[160] In the novel, Mortimer next transcribes 'Gracy Nugent', a poem by Carolan in praise of a beautiful young woman. Both Walker and Brooke had already offered their translations, and Walker authenticates the historical figure of Grace Nugent, sister to John Nugent of Castle Nugent, Colambre, County Longford. Brooke repeats that same information. In the case of both Cathleen Nolan and Gracy Nugent, Owenson's translation repeats neither the version found in Walker nor Brooke. There is no source given for the translation, which may have been done by a friend or by Owenson herself, working with help. She claims these songs as instances of a 'national taste unmodified by art, uninlarged by foreign innovation, unadorned by scientific graces'.[161] She continues to insist, though, on the older significance of the airs, especially as heard in Ireland, where they are 'connected with local incidents, or public events, whose national idiom is perfectly understood and deeply felt.'[162] When

Moore came to produce his *Melodies*, only the metre was 'lawless': otherwise, Owenson's aural public context vanished.¹⁶³ These writers – Brooke, Owenson and Moore – remain at a significant distance from the sophisticated art of popular song where 'works of thought lived and breathed in the very moment of song performance itself'. All three are involved in an effort to bring print culture closer to what Tríona Ní Shíocháin calls the 'multiformity, multivocality and complex echoic texture of oral forms.'¹⁶⁴ But Ní Shíocháin has also begun to explore the ways in which the Irish language creative practices of ordinary women and men, with their distinctive forms of compositional training and aesthetic autonomy, are shadowed over by the print culture of Irish romanticism.¹⁶⁵

Maria Edgeworth used the name Grace Nugent to powerful allegorical effect in her novel of 1812, *The Absentee*, and it may be that she also borrows a 'creative framework' from Brooke.¹⁶⁶ But Marilyn Butler's edition of *The Absentee* shows how Edgeworth drew on her own local networks and knowledge in her imagination of the character of Grace Nugent. In the novel, Grace discovers her true parentage, including the fact that her real name is Reynolds, a possible reference to George Nugent Reynolds and his poem 'The Exiled Irishman's Lamentation', known for introducing the phrase *Erin go brách* or 'Ireland forever'.¹⁶⁷

Rather than read the references to Grace Nugent as a 'subtle championing of the oral over the written' in the novel,¹⁶⁸ it is clear that they form part of what Marilyn Butler calls Edgeworth's 'sophisticated textual constructions' at the level of the Irish county.¹⁶⁹ Edgeworth takes pains to integrate an oral, Gaelic world into her novel, describing how the air 'Grace Nugent' is played as the family gather at home in Clonbrony Castle. But by calling out rather than just implying layers of meaning with the song, Edgeworth's narrative breaks with the conventions of allegory and spells out Grace's role in a modernising Ireland. And as the tune plays and the narrative refuses indirection, telling details emerge: the family exit their formal dining room and gather on the terrace, from where they are at eye level with their tenants. Expressing frustration at the still visible legacy of colonial fortification in so many Irish gardens, Joseph Cooper Walker's 'Essay on the Rise and Progress of Gardening in Ireland' wished that more Anglo-Irish gentlemen would 'soften into a curve the obdurate straight line of the Dutch, to melt the terrace into a swelling bank, and to open his walks to catch the vicinal country'.¹⁷⁰ At the end of *The Absentee*, the terrace does indeed melt and swell so as to embrace the country all around, testament to Edgeworth's role in the development of realist fiction at the beginning of the nineteenth century, further discussed in the next chapter. While that realism was in its infancy, though, it contended for space with poetic practices that remained closely tied to manuscript cultures.

Mary Tighe: Between Books and Manuscript

Mary Tighe is the poet most associated with 'the still-flourishing manuscript culture of the Romantic era' in Britain and Ireland.[171] Her poems lived on manuscript pages, circulated hand to hand in elite circles and fuelled countless conversations, even as they found their way into commonplace books and letters. But since Tighe's writing also involved her in a continuing and critical relationship with the burdens and possibilities of print, it affords an important perspective on the bookish aspects of early Irish romanticism.

Like Brooke and Edgeworth, Mary Tighe received an unusually good education. Her mother, Theodosia Blatchford, was a Methodist who dedicated herself to the upbringing of her children following the death of their father. She encouraged the young Tighe to copy out works of literature, though her religious views meant a lifelong anxiety about her daughter's absorption in imaginative literature. Aged twenty, Mary Tighe married her cousin, Henry Tighe, known to her as Harry. With him she travelled to London so that he could study for the bar. They enjoyed a fashionable and literary lifestyle, travelling extensively on legal circuits and for pleasure, always with an eye on Irish affairs. When the 1798 rebellion came close to their home county of Wicklow, the Tighes were in England but returned as the Union debates ignited. In the early years of her marriage, she wrote a number of poems that feature Irish places, names and histories. Her Killarney poems, 'written during an excursion Tighe takes with friends while Henry Tighe attends the last Irish parliament on 2 August 1800, the day after George III signs the Act of Union', may be read as a kind of elegy for the Irish Protestant nation.[172] Tighe also wrote an anti-Union poem, 'There was a young lordling whose wits were all toss'd up', in which a foolish aristocrat calls for 'union!, a union!'[173]

On returning to live in Ireland in 1801, Tighe began on her great poem, *Psyche*, which she completed in 1802 and first published in 1805. *Psyche* expresses the epic ambitions of early romanticism as it revises the myth of Cupid and Psyche in order to imagine how a woman might react to being banished by her lover. Like Mary Leadbeater, who appended her translation of the thirteenth book of the *Aeneid* to a volume of her original poems published in 1810, Tighe's reinvention of the Psyche myth was a creative act, undertaken with and alongside new original work. In Leadbeater's case, she chose to publish her version of the Latin poet Maffeo Vegio's 1428 supplementary thirteenth book of Virgil's epic. Tighe too went her own way. The original story of Cupid and Psyche imagines the goddess Venus as threatened by the beauty of Psyche, the youngest of three royal daughters. Venus sends Cupid to avenger her, only for him to fall for Psyche and demand, as the price of his luxurious love, that she never look at him nor ask for his name. Tighe follows Apuleius' story in having Psyche dare to look at Cupid, but trains our focus on the young woman's adventures as she tries to win back her lover, often assisted by a knight who turns out to be Cupid in disguise. In Harriet Kramer Linkin's telling, 'by the time Psyche completes her quest and finds Cupid standing beside her, she has effectively redefined herself', a reading that finds in Tighe's poem an original and 'strong' feminist telling of the myth, confirmed by her choice to title it only for her heroine.[174]

But Tighe's feminist intervention began as a private gesture. In 1805, she printed fifty copies of the poem and shared them with friends, including Thomas Moore, William Parnell, Anna Seward, Joseph Cooper Walker and the Ladies of Llangollen. *Psyche* then circulated among friends and relatives, who often themselves transcribed parts or all of the poem and shared their copies with others: this is how Maria Edgeworth saw the poem and managed to transcribe some of the lines in 1806.[175]

Tighe drew on Romantic Spenserianism for simplified forms of allegory steeped in pathos and was also faithful at the level of form and measure: Greg Kucich counts 372 Spenserian stanzas in *Psyche*.[176] But she also acknowledged the constrictions of the literary model, and in the preface to the 1805 privately printed edition, Tighe confesses her fondness for the Spenserian stanza despite its 'many disadvantages'. She thinks of poetic form in terms of a 'restraint which I had imposed upon myself', connected to her fears and anxieties attending on publication.[177]

In April 1805 she wrote to the antiquarian scholar Joseph Cooper Walker about preparations for the private printing:

> poor Psyche continued her literary journey under very unfavourable auspices; in the course of two months I have had just four *sheets*! – I find correcting the proofs very sickening & quite endless, for as often as I get a revise as I still see something to alter, I will not say I amend it, but it goes back cover'd with scratches.

By July, she could finally look forward to seeing her 'poor verses in the respectable form of a book' but feared 'the Edinburg butchers'.[178]

Those sentiments are expressed in a letter to Joseph Cooper Walker as the two exchange gossip about Thomas Moore, at this period preparing his *Epistles, Odes and Other Poems*, to be published in 1806.

Tighe corresponded regularly with Joseph Cooper Walker, whose advice also supported the careers of Sydney Owenson and Alicia Lefanu. Her reading journal shows an early and often critical interest in Owenson's writing. Of *The Wild Irish Girl* she wrote 'A vast deal of talent surpris'd me amidst clouds of affectation & nonsense' before noting that 'without understanding Latin she quotes it almost par hazard and scarce ever correctly – with a good education, much might have been done with this mind possessed of undoubt'd genius & a great desire after superiority'. The journal records similar reactions to Owenson's *St Clair* (1803), *The Novice of St Dominick* and *The Lay of an Irish Harp* but Tighe's patience was most tested by *Patriotic Sketches* (1807), which she found to be spoiled by 'affectation, absurdity slip slops & false quotations'. *Patriotic Sketches* wastes paper, Tighe suggests, on 'margins & booksellers list & spaces', leaving only 'about twenty decent pages' of prose. Her reaction to the book – 'But what volumes!' – suggests shock at Owenson's ability to takes up space in a print culture that Tighe imagines only in terms of constraint.

From Cooper Walker, Tighe borrowed books that she in turn loaned to Thomas Moore in London. There she renewed old Irish acquaintances, including Moore, and came to know Owenson. 'I see a good deal of Miss Owenson and Moore', she remarks in one of her London letters, perhaps written around the time that Owenson was being feted for the success of *The Wild Irish Girl*.[179] Her manuscript novel, *Selena*, features a recognisable version of Thomas Moore in a character named Edwin Stanmore.[180] Lady Mary Mount Cashell probably knew Tighe (both associated with Lady Moira) and became the lover of her cousin George William Tighe when they lived alongside their friends the Shelleys in Pisa.[181] They lived in Italy as Mr and Mrs Mason (the name borrowed from Wollstonecraft's books), during which time Mount Cashell wrote a long manuscript novel entitled *Selene*, in which she imagined a utopian society on the moon that bore some resemblances to Ireland.

The violence of 1798 may not be that which Tighe imagined at the hands of the Edinburgh reviewers, but her preference for privacy and 'the repugnance I now feel to stand to the public & say Hear me' is connected to her treatment of public Irish themes.[182] Most notable in this respect is her poem 'Bryan Byrne, of Glenmalure', which was written in the autumn of 1798 and published in 1811. The poem tells the story of 'Poor Ellen, and her orphan boy', widowed because her husband has been killed by British troops in order to retaliate for the United Irish murder of three yeomen.[183] Glenmalure had been the scene of fierce fighting, and many escaped rebels hid in nearby hills. Bryan Byrne, though, was himself a loyalist, and the drama of the poem derives from the damage wrought by 'the blood-hounds of revenge'.[184] The poem later found a place in the memoir of Joseph Holt, a gardener and British army recruit turned United Irishman who led the insurgent forces in Wicklow, as well as joining battles in Wexford and Meath. As commander, he refused Cornwallis' amnesty and fought on in the Wicklow mountains and left behind a memoir, published in two volumes in 1838. A Wicklow neighbour, Sir William Betham, in collaboration with the antiquarian writer Thomas Crofton Croker, arranged its publication. Croker's interpolations and omissions cast Holt as a reluctant, uncertain United Irishman and the citation of Tighe's poem belongs to this wider renunciation of republican convictions.[185] Sydney Owenson's *The Wild Irish Girl* also turned to a domestic model infused with Gothic sensibilities when she imagined the 1798 rebellion as the occasion for the arrival of Mortimer's father to the Castle of Inismore.

After Tighe died from tuberculosis in March 1810, her poems appeared in three different collections, representing the frangible media through which a durable literary reputation was forged.[186] First, *Pysche, with Other Poems*, is a handsome octavo volume with a frontispiece engraved from Romney's portrait of the author. Published by Longmans in 1811, the volume was prepared by her husband and advertised as 'by the late Mrs Henry Tighe'. As well as *Psyche*, some thirty-nine poems by Tighe are included along with notes that refer to the manuscript of *Selena* as 'now in the possession of the editor.'[187] *Pysche, with Other Poems* sold well for Longmans and went into three editions. Among the owners of the book was John Keats, who knew Tighe's *Psyche* 'intimately' and who, as James Chandler has shown, thought of Tighe alongside Moore as a model to be disavowed and overcome.[188]

With *Pysche, with Other Poems*, Henry Tighe dispenses with gendered concerns about privacy in the interest of spreading the fame of 'a writer intimately acquainted with classical literature, and guided by a taste for real excellence'. The editor imagines himself as led by 'a sort of duty' to share personal and 'precious relics' with a wider public.[189] The 'relics' are unpublished poems, presented as a supplement to *Psyche* and simply headed 'Sonnets' in the book. Henry Tighe describes these 'Sonnets' as in need of some 'indulgence', never having been prepared or intended for publication. They are 'selected', he says 'from a larger number of poems, which were the occasional effusion of her thoughts, or productions of her leisure, but not originally intended or pointed out by herself for publication'.[190] A conventional relationship between a large body of work in manuscript and a smaller selection chosen for print is silently guided by Tighe's husband's taste. The turning of Tighe's reputation towards a wider public is aided by his choice of opening sonnet, 'Written in a Copy of Psyche Which Had Been in the Library of C. J. Fox. April, 1809'. In the poem, the author addresses her own book – 'Dear consecrated page!' – as a repository of patriot spirit and Whig hopes.[191] The book as a whole concludes with a poem by a cousin, William Tighe.

Second, an unpaginated manuscript titled *Poems by Mrs. H. Tighe* was edited by 'a friend' named E. I. Fox who 'insistently reasserts Tighe's identity as a coterie poet'. This manuscript is written for a small circle of friends who already know the Tighe poems in private circulation. It includes footnotes that give page numbers to a manuscript transcription of *Psyche* that has not been located, suggesting 'that Fox prepared the collection as another confidential manuscript for a particular community of readers who would know where to find those citations.'[192]

A third, privately printed book with 'a very few copies', possibly made on a Rosanna printing press, also appeared in 1811. That book, *Mary, a Series of Reflections during Twenty Years*, used 'a hybrid mode that interspersed poems in manuscript with poems in print'.[193] Small in size, *Mary, a Series of Reflections during Twenty Years* presents as an intimate and affective object meant to be sensed and shared. The copy held in the Houghton Library at Harvard seems to be the only survivor.[194] It contains a handwritten inscription from Tighe's mother in which she notes that the book is 'not to be given away nor lent, nor shown to any person uninterested in the subject' (Figure 1.3). On the facing page, Tighe's mother writes:

> The M.S. lines I wish'd to have printed with those which are printed here, and some others (omitting the dream) as a kind of mental history of the author, to give away to her friends and mine, but as that design was prevented, I have only had a very few copies of this selection printed *privately* by a friend to be given only to her most partial & serious friends.[195]

The book is also prefaced by a motto that more discreetly implies a select body of readers: 'Many of these Reflections were written in very early youth, and may be inaccurate; but are not the less valuable to those for whom *alone* this Selection is intended.'[196]

Unlike the Longmans volume, Tighe's mother's little book does not mention *Psyche* in its title, nor does it include any part of the

Mary Tighe: Between Books and Manuscript

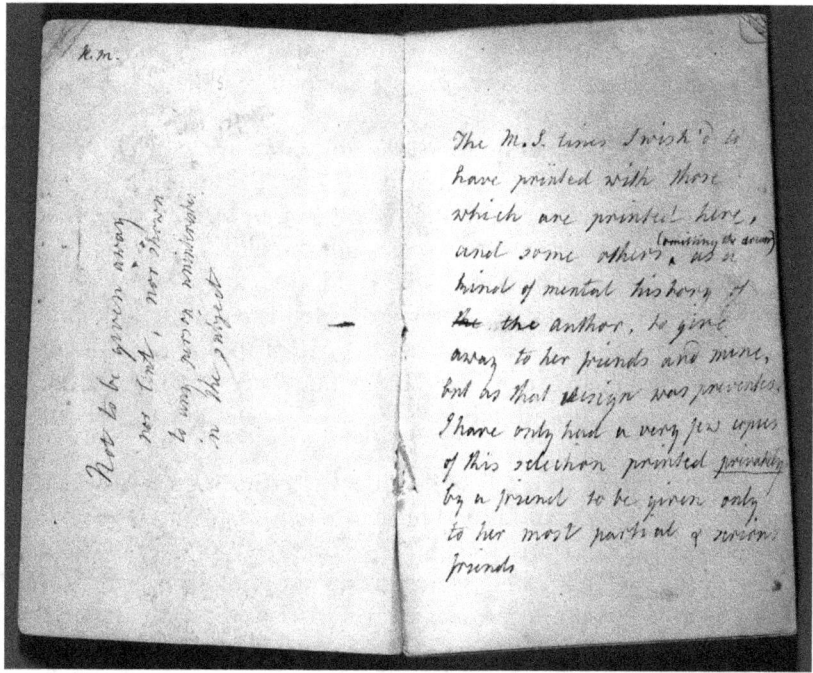

Figure 1.3 Mary Tighe, title page of *Mary, a Series of Reflections during Twenty Years*. 8.5 × 13.5 cm. *EC8 T4484 811m, Houghton Library, Harvard University.

by-then-celebrated poem, but rather offers a selection of earlier work as 'a kind of mental history of the author': thirteen previously unpublished poems, mostly likely written before her marriage and in a period where she and her mother's world entirely overlapped. Theodosia Blatchford ran into trouble, though, when she realised that Longmans now owned copyright of several of the poems. As she explains, her daughter's 'reflections in the next eight years may be found in several of the Poems annexed to her Psyche, and printed the year after her death: they would have been inserted here, but that it was supposed improper to reprint them, the copyright having been purchased.'[97] Asserting ownership at the level of family and affect, she lists a selection of eight poems judged to be 'particularly expressive' of her daughter's 'feelings'. In the Houghton copy, these are annotated by hand with page references to the Longmans edition, implying a reader who might move back and forth between the two books. The remainder of *Mary, a Series of Reflections during Twenty Years* contains some of these same poems also, along with a series of manuscript versions of some seventeen other poems, the handwriting reproduced in the printed book as both guarantor of their origin and promise of their reach into the lives and homes of the close circle of intended readers.

This curious volume intersperses manuscript with print material including some scattered reflections on Tighe's life and death. Among the final items is the narrative of a 'Remarkable Dream' experienced by Tighe aged 'seven years and three months old'.[198] The dream is a notably bookish one, opening on the child's search for 'a book on the shelf' which turns out to bear the words 'Hell is coming'. Her mother accounts for the child's fear and terror in terms of an 'attachment to fashionable studies and literature'. These, understood by her Methodist mother as the 'great hindrance' of Tighe's life, are already present in dream form.[199]

Yet Theodosia Blatchford herself worked to create a book in which to honour her daughter's writing and furthermore used an 'innovative printing mode' (possibly a private family-owned press) to transmit Tighe's writing to readers.[200] In doing so, she stakes out not only a space for private circulation but also makes a case for the persistence of manuscript as mode. *Mary, a Series of Reflections during Twenty Years* refuses a presumed progress from manuscript to print and rather preserves movement back and forth between these modes, as well as insisting on the private dimension of a public literary reputation. The book also connects handwriting and penmanship to a set of allied cultural activities, including autographs, made possible by new technologies such as lithography.

If Tighe allows us to look in on Irish history and politics via the multiple mediations of print, manuscript, class and gender, James Orr presents a different kind of case. As Tighe heard news of the Wicklow battles of 1798 from a distance, Orr was part of the great 'Turn Out' in Presbyterian Ulster. He joined the United Irishmen at the Battle of Ballynahinch and wrote about the events in the language of men whom he met.

James Orr: Poetry and Popular Politics

Born in Ballycarry, County Antrim, James Orr (1770–1816) has a literary reputation closely linked with the place in which he wrote, the politics of his time and his working identity as a weaver in Ulster's linen trade. Described by Matthew Campbell as 'the most significant poet of the region in his time', Orr wrote in both Ulster Scots and Standard English, explicitly invoking war, violence and religious conflict and remaining outwith what Campbell calls an 'incipient Gaelicism and Celticism' that characterises Irish romantic poetry more generally.[201] His work also belongs to the 'radical Belfast public sphere of the 1790s' and its continuing regional influence in the form of a 'popular intellectualism' that is deeply rooted in Presbyterian print culture and values.[202]

Orr's family came over to Ulster from Scotland in the seventeenth century. He was educated in a Presbyterian community that stressed individual responsibility founded in reading, and he came to maturity in the 'intelligent, combative and argumentative' company of the weavers who worked in Ulster's booming linen trade.[203] Though only very slightly older than Orr, his neighbour Samuel Thomson (1766–1816), teacher and weaver, was a mentor and inspiration. Jennifer Orr's account of the dissenting print culture of the period shows how a Thomson circle developed through two generations of literary, political and religious debate.[204] The United Irish newspaper, *The Northern Star*, was especially important in the 'increasing politicisation of the verse epistle', while after its demise in 1797, some labouring-class poets found an outlet in the *Belfast Newsletter*.[205] Orr addressed a poem to Thomson – 'Epistle to S. Thomson of Carngranny, a Brother Poet' – in which he imagines the two writers as disdaining 'the proud folks of patronage' in favour of 'inglorious rhymes' made noble by people and place:

> Tho' vain folk disdain folk,
> We'se sing the burns, an' bow'rs,
> O! AIRLAN', our fair lan' –
> Deel tak' *her* faes an' *ours*![206]

In the aftermath of the rebellion, though, an earlier 'fraternal project of mutual support' that centred around Thomson gave way to the conservative patronage-driven culture represented by Thomas Percy.[207] Gentry patronage succeeded writerly networks in a manner analogous to the back-and-forth movement between manuscript and print described elsewhere in this chapter.

Orr was not alone in his enlightened lower-class Presbyterian community in being drawn to the principles of the United Irishmen. On 7 June 1798, he was among the leaders of a rebel group that gathered on Donegore Hill for the Battle of Antrim. When the rebels deserted, Orr also fled. He reimagined these events in 'Donegore Hill', described by Campbell as 'one of the hitherto overlooked glories of the Irish poetry of this period'.[208] The poem, written in *braid* Ulster Scots, imagines the rebels as a body who 'Turn'd out *en masse*, as soon as ax'd', carrying 'bonnocks' of bread baked by their wives and wearing 'cockades o'green'.[209] Thomas Dermody also imagined the aftermath of the 1798 rebellion in Ulster in a poem that opens with a reference to the Giant's Causeway. 'Carrol's Complaint' invokes the perspective of a northern United Irishman who earlier, 'indignant', had responded to the rebel call but now hears only the cries of the victims.[210] Its politics are far removed from the sympathies of Dermody's earlier pamphlet on the French Revolution. Orr did not renounce his earlier commitments in quite the same way, but both 'Donegore Hill' and 'The Wanderer', like 'Bryan Byrne of Glenmalure', evince a broad scepticism about the events of 1798 and test the limits of popular involvement in the rising. The latter poem describes life on the run after the battle, as a fugitive man seeks shelter in the high ground around Slemish, a mountain east of Ballymena in County Antrim. With no explicit naming of political context and an uncertain atmosphere born of threat and danger, a man arrives himself at the house of a peasant woman and describes himself 'A frien'' who 'for common crimes / Tost thro' the country fore and aft'.[211] The poem is told in the voice of the woman, named 'Leezie' or Lizzy. She offers the wanderer shelter from 'piercin' night' and the rough winds and undertakes to keep a watch for the 'picquet bauld' or patrolling officer.[212]

Orr once more describes the hospitality he encountered among the Catholic poor in a poem written in tribute to Sydney Owenson, 'To Miss Owenson, the Authoress of the Wild Irish Girl' and published in the *Belfast Commercial Chronicle* on 8 May 1807. The poem makes a Belfast contribution to the Dublin controversy surrounding *The Wild Irish Girl*, which ran in the *Freeman's Journal* from December 1806 through the early months of 1807. Writing anonymously in the *Freeman's*, the politician and critic John Wilson Croker accused 'Miss OWENSON of having written bad novels, and worse poetry', while doing moral damage to the country.[213] The faults of her book were bound up with their bold appearance in public and in print: had *The Wild Irish Girl* been 'a novel printed at her own expence, and distributed with gratuitous kindness among her friends, embellished with all the Luxury of Letter Press, and the affluence of Book-binding', Croker would 'have read, disliked, and been silent'. But Owenson was no Mary Tighe, and Croker describes her book as one 'written professedly for the gain of sale, and ushered confidently to the public'.[214]

When the *Wild Irish Girl* controversy broke out, Croker was beginning on his political career. He stood for election in the constituency of Downpatrick, County Down, in 1806 and lost. When a general election was called in 1807 (following the collapse of the Ministry of All the Talents), he stood again and won by a small majority. That 1807 general election saw an emerging Catholic interest across a number of constituencies including Downpatrick, where Croker told Wellesley 'The popery war-whoop was sung against us', but 'we outsang them'.[215] The negatively imagined professional status that is accorded to Owenson is marked by these electoral and sectarian politics, but it also opens up a public space of literary debate, albeit one highly constrained by class and gender. Orr enters that same space with the epigraph to his 'To Miss Owenson', a quotation from playwright Joseph Atkinson (c. 1743–1818)'s opening address for the performance of Owenson's comic opera, *The First Attempt*. The play appeared on the Dublin stage in spring 1807 at the height of the *Wild Irish Girl* controversy, and the first performance was for the benefit of the actor Robert Owenson, 'to prove the comfort of a father's age', as Atkinson puts it.[216] Addressing Owenson as 'Erin's friend! and Erin's Glory!', Orr also invokes her 'fond and filial bosom'. But the real energy of the poem is reserved for Orr's account of a critical culture that fails to take account of the value of his 'compatriot' and her writing. Attacks by 'foreign men of letters' are one thing, Orr writes,

> But of sets, born in our nation,
>   On her natives slanders spread,
> May the well-earn'd execration
>   Of their land light on their head![217]

The claim to a shared nation is significant, not least given *The Wild Irish Girl*'s own reservations about Ulster as a Scotch colony. It also carries the memory of the non-sectarian promise of 1798 as the poem disdains 'bigot blindness' and recalls the 'kindness' of the Irish-speaking Catholic peasantry presumed to have offered shelter to a fugitive weaver, poet and rebel. Orr also wrote a further poem addressed to Owenson, this time in response to the publication of her *Patriotic Sketches, Written in Connaught* (1807). 'The Recluse of Connaught, Addressed to Miss Owenson on Reading her "Patriotic Sketches"' was published in the *Belfast Commercial Chronicle* on 20 April 1808.

Along with the busy traffic in letters and poems in *Freeman's*, responses to Croker's attack on Owenson appeared in Lisburn (4 February 1807) and in Liverpool (3 July 1807). Orr's poetic interventions on the topic of Owenson's writing and reputation help us to see an Irish republic of letters taking shape, even as it must be stretched across taut sectarian divisions. The Owenson poems also belong to Orr's substantial body of writing in standard English, much of it covering domestic and village affairs.

Carol Baraniuk, though, reminds us that the recovery of Orr's reputation, beginning with John Hewitt in the 1960s, was spurred on by a celebration of his Ulster Scots verse.[218] Among those Ulster Scots poems, 'The Passengers' is particularly noteworthy. It opens with an epigraph from Oliver Goldsmith's 'Deserted Village' and takes from the earlier poem a restless energy and emotional force. But where Goldsmith leaves us in the dark as to the future lives of his emigrants, Orr follows a 'melancholy band' aboard ship and imagines their experience as they cross from the port of Larne in Ulster to Newcastle on the Delaware River, just south of Philadelphia.[219] The poem recollects an intimate experience of migration, 'the time / We mov't frae Ballycarry'.[220] The place name registers both Orr's home place and the history of United Irish mobilisation, and Matthew Campbell has remarked upon the 'quality of his observations and his handling of tonal ambivalence before historical event'.[221]

In 'The Passengers', the plight of people on board and on the docks is described in ways that both naturalise the transatlantic crossing and emphasise its everyday dimension. That includes the routine violence of impressment, as when a frigate 'heaves in view', and the Irish passengers fear impressment by the British navy: 'Cried, "is she British, wat ye, / Or French, this day?"'[222] The feared vessel is plying a commercial route from Baltimore to Larne, carrying linseed. The 'poll-tax' extracted on arriving at the banks of Newfoundland represents a more casual form of violence in the poem.[223] A note explains that passengers must pay the crew a shilling, or give them 'a shilling's worth of liquor' on arriving on the banks or otherwise agree to be shaven 'without soap'.[224] Written in Ulster Scots, the poem immerses us in shipboard life, including its furniture ('creel' and 'locker') and the 'Droll leuks' of those on board. Activities on board include praying ('cantin'), making up beds, cooking, sex, knitting and reading.[225] Time on board is measured in vernacular ways and recorded as it is experienced: 'In twathree days the maist cam' to, / Few heads were sair or dizzy'.[226]

Racial contest is also invoked in Orr's poem. On board are 'blacks' who fear the sea's power and 'Lye cheepin' like a chicken' before a storm as they reflect on their bravery in other contexts: 'What gart us play? Or bouse like beasts? / Or box in fairs wi' venom?'[227] Julia Wright understands these references in terms of the circulation of African-American fighters in the Atlantic world, men who were working for plantation owners who coerced them into boxing for popular and profitable forms of entertainment.[228] Where these men are part of Orr's group of passengers, the second reference to race in the poem places African Americans outside the ship and imagines them as alien to the culture on board. On arrival, 'Creatures wha ne'er had seen a black, / Fu' scar't took to their shankies'.[229] Baraniuk speculates that 'blacks' here could mean 'blackguards' or 'blackmouths', the latter a term for Presbyterians.[230] The reference remains mysterious, but we know that Orr opposed enslavement and wrote the abolitionist poem, 'Toussaint's Farewell to Saint Domingo', discovered by Baraniuk to have been published in 1805 in the *Belfast Commercial Chronicle* before appearing in a New York newspaper in 1829.

Wright reads the 'disconnect' between the two uses of the word 'black' as mapping out a route along which we can trace the complicity of some former United Irishmen in enslavement once they reached the United States.[231] Finola O'Kane's research shows how, when Theobald Wolfe Tone and Archibald Rowan Hamilton went to Philadelphia and travelled in the United States, they opted to purchase land in Pennsylvania rather than further south. 'I will go into the woods', Tone wrote, 'but I will not kill Indians or keep slaves'.[232] But the exiled United Irishman Denis Driscol came to advocate for the rights of enslavers in Georgia, and rather 'than just rejecting the abolition of slavery, many of the United Irishmen became active participants in the institution'.[233]

Archibald Rowan Hamilton met the Anglo-Irish landowner Pierce Butler in July 1795, though he decided against taking his advice regarding property in the South. Pierce Butler, the third son of Sir Richard Butler, fifth baronet of Cloughgrenan, County Carlow, and delegate to the constitutional convention and US senator, first married into extensive landholdings around Charlestown and then developed an estate on and around the low-lying St Simon's Island in Georgia.[234] Following the death of his wife, he moved the enslaved workers (whom she left in trust to her children) to Georgia and continued to purchase enslaved labour to manage his rice fields and remake the landscape. As O'Kane shows, Butler's revolutionary landscapes wrote large the contradictions of commerce and liberty. He built an American life modelled on the 'vast transfers of property and people that were a feature of seventeenth-century Ireland'.[235]

Formally, 'The Passengers' inhabits a familiar Scots model, that provided by the medieval ballad, 'Christs Kirk on the Green'. Frank Ferguson observes that 'the genres of Scottish vernacular verse found strong purchase in Ireland and were readily appropriated', and the 'Christs Kirk on the Green' stanza was used by many late eighteenth- and early nineteenth-century poets.[236] The original poem describes a fight at a fair or festival and influenced poems including Robert Fergusson 'Leith Races' and Burns' 'The Holy Fair'. The 'Christs Kirk' literary model, relying as it does on alliterative verse and vernacular Scots, was used for 'the recounting of local events, the fair days, holidays, and carnivals and the eulogizing (and mocking) of characters in the community'.[237] In 'The Passengers', though, Orr adapts the 'Christs Kirk' stanza in order to tell the story of a scattering. He faithfully follows the pattern of twenty-two stanzas, each of which finishes on a refrain, but his use of Scots word 'skail't' vividly conveys the spreading far and wide of the passengers once they land in Delaware.[238] In 'Donegore Hill', too, the break-up of the rebel camp is described as a scattering: 'Arms, ammunition, bread-bags, brogues, / Lye skail'd in a' directions'.[239] 'Donegore Hill' also uses the 'Christs Kirk' stanza and employs the refrain to striking effect. The refrain repeats the word 'day' to sharpen the sense of historical potential betrayed: 'Were we, that day', 'Sic scenes, that day', 'Took leg, that day'.[240] The poem concludes by suggesting that the scenes of desertion witnessed at the Battle of Antrim belong not just to a beleaguered rebel group but to all who suffer oppression: 'In tryin' times, maist folk, you'll fin', / Will act like Donegore men'.[241]

Orr eventually only spent a few months in the eastern United States, returning when news of a United Irish amnesty reached Baltimore. But his poem captures the experience of life at sea, known to thousands of Irish men and women who emigrated, joined the British army or navy or served the empire. Chapter 2 moves with and beyond books and paper as it considers the shaping power of the sea and the enormous force of what Mary Leadbeater described as 'the ocean's greedy wave' in Irish letters.[242]

CHAPTER 2

Watery Prospects, 1815–1830

From the end of the Napoleonic and Peninsular Wars and through fifteen or so years characterised by economic depression, famine and rebellion, accounts of Irish culture began both to prospect hitherto unknown regional locations and explore intense inner landscapes. But in seeking new routes to understanding the island and its inhabitants, writers were drawn to imagine seas and oceans in ways that inevitably express knowledge of Britain's overseas empire. Between these two poles of insularity and expansion, a bold new literary map of the island was in the making. The co-ordinates are local, regional and global – locations prospected include Cork, Kerry, Limerick and Wicklow, as well as France, Spain and India – and this chapter charts cultural connections that flow along rivers, coastlines and oceans. In Britain, romanticism was informed by 'a maritime dynamic' that shaped ideas of nationhood and national culture. In Samuel Baker's account, a coherent idea of culture grew up with and alongside romanticism as a 'period of maximal concern with maritime affairs'. In Ireland though, that moment of 'maximal concern' is found not during the long wars at sea but rather in their aftermath.[1] Written during a period in which the age of sail gave way to steam-powered transport on the seas, Irish literature in this second phase often looks back to earlier periods of British maritime power, from early modern battles at sea to very recent victories. The romantic culture that results is fluid and uncertain, as continued bookish interests in collecting meet but fail to mesh with new and interiorised conceptions of national culture.

Across this phase of Irish romanticism, Irish writers addressed themselves to a copious culture that was coming more clearly into official view: the partial census of 1813–15 counted some four million people on the island while a more accurate exercise in 1821 enumerated a population of around seven million.[2] As surveyors began the work of mapping Ireland on a scale of six inches to one mile for the new Ordnance Survey – the office opened in Mountjoy House in Phoenix Park, Dublin in the autumn of

1824 – the face of the country became newly legible on paper. Alongside extensive measurements using trigonometry and chain links, the Survey had a topographic dimension involving studies of place names, fieldwork and historical research. The Ordnance Survey, 'a state science project of immense size, without parallel anywhere in the world', proved costly and contentious.[3] It began its operations on the shores of Lough Foyle, in the north of the country, hundreds of miles away from the Rockite rebellion that had convulsed the southern counties in the early 1820s. Maria Edgeworth received an account of the astonishing accuracy of baseline measurements from the German-born astronomer William Herschel who declared them to be the very 'Sublime of Art'.[4] But scientific and political challenges met topographic ones, with hydrographic and hydrological features posing a particular problem. Ireland's extensive and irregular shorelines served as a 'zone of vulnerability' for the Survey.[5] Then, as the Survey's topographical 'memoir' project got underway, gathering statistical, cultural, geological and meteorological information from the mid 1830s, those same coastlines were prospected for their cultural potential. In Cork in 1842, John O'Donovan describes the promise of a county that is 'particularly *Irish* especially in the mountains and along the coasts'.[6] O'Donovan expresses an everyday contradiction in his understanding of the richness of the southwest, where linguistic and cultural potential is an ironic outcome of poverty and overcrowding. Elsewhere in some Ordnance Survey notes for Cork, however, we find information concerning '[t]he first monument erected to the memory of Nelson after the Battle of Trafalgar' at Castletownshend in the west of the county: a reminder that this is a coastline closely involved in empire, war and trade.[7]

Even as Britain's relationship with its surrounding ocean shifted in the aftermath of the Napoleonic and Peninsular Wars, water comes into prominence. Already, in 1811, William Wordsworth could say in a letter that 'We have destroyed our enemies on the Sea'.[8] His correspondent, William Pasley, would soon take charge of training the sappers who worked on the Ordnance Survey in Ireland. By the time the Irish Fishery Board and Irish Coast Guard were established, in 1819 and 1822, journeys on the Irish Sea had become a matter of infrastructure and access, rather than defensive design. Irish literature continued to take its bearings also from local and intimate encounters with the coast, while travels across estuaries, rivers, lakes and seas remained an everyday aspect of Irish life. The arrival of steam from 1821 meant speedier travel times to and from Britain, as well as new avenues to the Atlantic. But the routinisation of sea travel brought little change to the legendary roughness of the Irish Sea: in 1822, a patrol vessel ran into a bank just off the coast of Wexford, unmarked on the charts.[9] Nor did new technology lessen the hold of sea crossings in the cultural imagination.[10] As the danger of coastal invasion disappeared from view, the legacy of the long wars at sea was still felt in Irish writing. Steamships berthed in newly extended and recently fortified harbours that connected with older military roads and a new stagecoach network built by the Italian entrepreneur Charles Bianconi and served by demobilised army horses. Railway lines soon followed and with them the Geological Survey of the 1830s and 40s. Along these new routes flowed the old resentments about Catholic Emancipation, not granted until 1829, and fresh concerns about law and order, exacerbated by food shortages, famine and agrarian rebellion in the south and west of the country between 1819 and 1823.

At the same time, Ireland was caught up in the wash of empire. Existing patterns of emigration were intensified after 1815, with state-sponsored schemes to the Cape Colony and Canada underway from 1820. In John Banim's novel *The Anglo-Irish of the Nineteenth Century* (1828), when a Dublin dinner group discuss their fears of Rockite violence, an English visitor asks if there is 'nothing to be done' to reconcile the people of the country with the owners of the land.[11] The answer comes by way of a reference to Britain's Cape Colony, as the Anglo-Irish diners connect their plight to that of an imperial overclass in South Africa, resented by 'the Caffers and Hottentots'.[12] The visitor in his turn hints at the ills of settler colonialism against enslaved and immiserated indigenous populations but is assured that the Irish peasantry 'are a half-savage race who hate us, our religion, our superior station, and our English descent'. The discussion is indicative of a coming watershed in British colonialism that saw a move towards an empire that understood itself in terms of free-trade politics infused by a moral agenda. What Jennifer Pitts describes as a 'sea-change in opinions on empire' meant a new liberal imperialism 'that by the 1830s provided some of the most insistent and well-developed arguments in favor of the conquest of non-European peoples and territories'.[13] That reframing of British imperialism as moral mission in the aftermath of the Peninsular and Napoleonic Wars retained strongly anti-Catholic contours, a set of relationships that helped to shape Charles Robert Maturin's global Gothic novel *Melmoth the Wanderer* (1820), discussed later in the context of a mediatised, maritime Gothic. In the same decade, Irish Catholic writers came into voice, even as debates about Emancipation seemed to stall. These writers included Gerald Griffin and Jeremiah Joseph Callanan, both of whom authored bodies of work that show the strains of intense inner explorations connected with the coast, including poems and tales that chart divided allegiances. This chapter ends with Callanan, whose original poems and translations capture the rising literary ambitions of ordinary Catholics and the complexity of language crossings in pre-Famine Ireland. In the case of Callanan, we also see how a strong urge for originality was expressed in relation to a tightly coiled relationship between collecting and creativity that is characteristic of the bilingual world in which a prolonged, varied and uneven shift from Irish to English was now underway.

If the balance of writers discussed in this chapter tends towards men rather than women, that is because the period itself saw a shift in gendered patterns. In 1814, Maria Edgeworth received her first negative reviews and from about 1820, the senior Protestant women who ushered in Irish romantic literature were eclipsed by a coming generation of men, many of them Catholic. Maturin, besides recasting the interpolated narrative structures of Ann Radcliffe and Mary Shelley, had already made a bid to masculinise the national tale with the title of his *The Wild Irish Boy* (1808) while his novel *Melmoth the Wanderer* is discussed later. The often-feminised figure of Thomas Moore played a key part in this transition.[14]

But the game was not entirely up, and writers including Henrietta Rouviere Mosse, Sarah Green and Regina Maria Roche, all published novels in the 1810s and 1820s. Lady Morgan drew the most attention, defying as well as sometimes inviting bad reviews, gossip and scandal. Forms of misrepresentation that had accreted from the early modern period continued to trouble Irish literature in this phase: writing as Sydney Owenson, Lady Morgan had already warned against stereotyped assumptions about Ireland in her *Patriotic Sketches* (1807), where she wearily recalls discussions of 'my (always termed) "unhappy country"'.[15] In 1818, she fastened the issue of representation to the figure of Edmund Spenser, subject of a long discussion in the opening pages of *Florence Macarthy*, where two characters on board a ship in Dublin Bay debate the relative values of his *Faerie Queene* and his *View of the Present State of Ireland*, a duality that already troubled Thomas Dermody in the 1790s (see Chapter 1). The shape-shifting heroine of *Florence Macarthy* has multiple roles and identities – ladies' companion, aristocrat, novelist – that bear out Angela Esterhammer's account of performance as the keynote of the culture of the 1820s.[16] The same heroine, in her guise as teller of '*tales* [and] *stories*' about 'Ireland, and Spain, and South America', goes about in fashionable company as a specimen of a 'live author', making for a knowing narrative that parades the question of representation in contemporary culture.[17] Never just a question of individual identity, representation is addressed in terms that take their bearings from Ireland's island location.

Watery Romanticism

Reading *Florence Macarthy*, Mary Russell Mitford despaired of a 'puffed-off novel' made indigestible by 'a vast deal of incredible antiquarianism'.[18] The novel has regular recourse to early modern writers and modes in its depictions of contemporary conditions, connecting as it does a famine-struck post-Waterloo landscape of Cork and Kerry to sixteenth-century documents and genealogies alongside contemporary London society. There were many 'ingredients', Mitford said, but only 'the one single sauce' – 'Ireland! Ireland! Ireland!'[19] And if Ireland were not bad enough, Mitford went on, Lady Morgan also roamed about Europe: 'if she would vigorously abstain from all French, bad or good, keep at a safe distance from that eternal Ireland (I would not trust her so near as Holyhead), and make up her mind not to allude to Napoleon – whom she is not worthy to admire – [she] might write books worth reading and worth praising'.[20]

Lady Morgan had criticised the restored Bourbon monarchy in her *France* (1817) and was still harping on Napoleon in 1827 when she set the closing scene of her final Irish historical novel, *The O'Briens and the O'Flahertys*, at the Paris Opéra. Walter Scott's sympathetic *Life of Napoleon Bonaparte* appeared that same year while William Hazlitt's biography was published in 1832. In Morgan's novel, whispers between the first consul and his wife Joséphine, overheard at the premiere of Haydn's *Creation*, help to close the curtain not only on Napoleon's regime but also on the United Irish Rebellion. The action of *Florence Macarthy* is located chiefly in Ireland, but characters carry with them memories of conflict overseas, making for a rather more extensive menu than the one mockingly described by Mitford. The movements for political independence that swept across Spanish America in the early nineteenth century serve to sketch in the background of Morgan's two main characters. These include details of General Fitzwalter's involvement with the Colombian revolutionary Antonio Nariño (1765–1823), who was imprisoned by the Spanish for publishing a translation of Thomas Paine's *The Rights of Man*. Fitzwalter is aligned with British support of resistance to Spanish power in Columbia, Venezuela and 'Terra Firma' or the so-called Spanish Main, taking in Central America, parts of the West Indies and the northwestern part of South America. His tale of exile from the Ireland of his birth earns a comparison to the Polish patriot Thaddeus Kosciusko (1746–1817), a hero of the Whigs. The novel's final union, between General Fitzwalter and Lady Clancare, sees the marriage of a man who has fought with South Americans in their wars of independence against the Spanish, to a woman whose mother was Irish and whose father fought for freedom against Spain. As the novel ends, the self-absorbed Lord Adelm Fitzadelm, dispossessed of an inheritance for which he cares little by the revelation that General Fitzwalter is the real heir, departs for the North Pole. Along with these references to Spanish America and Portugal (where Fitzadelm has undertaken a previous tour), the novel also references contemporary China, drawing on press reports of William Pitt Amherst's embassy to China in 1816–17.[21] But Morgan did not need imperial China for her description of the Crawleys, a family of agents and hangers-on that grow powerful in the absence of a resident landlord, as 'the BUREAUCRATIE, or office tyranny, by which Ireland has been so long governed.'[22] Her early use of the word that becomes 'bureaucracy' is often noted in histories of information and colonialism.

Morgan's capacious geopolitical imagination continued to take her across seas and oceans, regardless of what her critics thought. She completed the manuscript of *Florence Macarthy* on the move, as she travelled from Dublin to France via London in the winter of 1817. And in the course of her books on Italy and France, Morgan hit upon a precocious conceptualisation of the term 'romanticism' with hers as the earliest definition cited in the *OED*. Having remarked in 1821 that '[t]he vehemence with which the question of Romanticism has been debated, will have a favourable influence upon the Italians',[23] Morgan returned to the term once more in her 1830 book on France. There, she conjured up a fugitive cultural movement in search of refuge at the northern and western edges of Europe, finding sustenance where water flows: 'Romanticism', she wrote, 'still banished from France, took shelter in the meantime in the dark forests of the Rhine, hummed her Cronan on the banks of the Shannon, rhapsodized on the shores of the Clyde, and sent forth, from her abbey-cell at Newstead, such lights of song, as time will never obscure'.[24] 'Cronan' comes from the Irish word *crónán*, meaning to hum, murmur, drone or purr, a term associated with bees and cats as well as with the soughing of the wind, the babble of streams and the boom of a waterfall. Thomas Crofton Croker glossed the term to mean 'song' in his manuscript *Ballad History of Ireland*.[25] Lady Morgan's riparian vision of romanticism joins Irish to other European cultures via bodies of water across which tensions and forms of contest also flow. Burns and Byron are drawn into alliance with an Irish romanticism embodied by Morgan herself, singing sad songs at the edge of the Shannon, hearing and echoing other, Scottish and European, sounds. 'I became the martyr of romanticism', as she put it in the book on France.[26]

The idea of a 'maritime-imperial sense of a whole way of life' that 'gave rise to notions of universal culture' within British romanticism had only an uncertain hold in Ireland.[27] If not quite the union of hearts and minds promised in 1800, an idea of a shared romantic culture did flourish in the context of war and its immediate aftermath, already available to be mocked by Byron in the third canto of Don Juan (published in 1821) as a 'trimmer poet' who may be Thomas Moore easily moves from England to Spain, Portugal, Italy or Greece: 'Thus, usually, when he was asked to sing, / He gave the different nations something national; / 'Twas all the same to him'.[28]

The conflicts and convulsions described by Lady Morgan and satirised by Byron belonged to a Europe-wide theorisation of the idea of the romantic, a bookish enterprise that crossed the channel and had impact in Britain and Ireland. First Italian and then French debates about cultural identity saw classical and academic traditions under challenge from romantic writers who identified with the liberal spirit of a restored Europe. Morgan knew this context well and sought to position herself within it. The respectful comments addressed by William Wordsworth to Edmund Burke were part of this great gathering up of reputations and ideas, as the poet bowed to the politician and philosopher in recognition of 'the vital power of social ties / Endeared by Custom'.[29] Meanwhile the Irish writer William Maginn used satire to reckon with the romantic present and began his career at *Blackwood's* in November 1819 with his 'Don Juan Unread', a parody on Wordsworth's 'Yarrow Unvisited' that cashes in on Byron's popularity. With its mocking references to Byron, Coleridge, Hunt, Keats and Mary Shelley, Maginn's poem not only 'neatly collates much of what later became the "Romantic canon"' but also understands the object of its attack to be a cultural phenomenon belonging on both sides of the Irish Sea.[30] While Byron's *Don Juan* sits at the apex of fallen cultural tastes, Maturin's 'amorous themes' and Lady Morgan's 'filths' are quite 'as bad'. Meanwhile 'pleasant' Thomas Moore should know better than the pair jointly mocked as 'the parson' and 'the granny'.[31] Maginn's typically Tory attack on romantic rhetoric, made in the name of a fuller relationship with locality, took special aim against Moore, as discussed in Chapter 3. Meanwhile in 1820, Byron himself was advised by his friend and manager of his English finances, Douglas Kinnaird, to purchase mortgages on property on Dublin's Ormond Quay. Though the suggestion was not acted upon, Byron in 1822 continued to think of himself as 'a professor of love for Ireland'.[32]

Such cross-channel decisions on individual reputations, aesthetic tendencies and property deals formed part of the texture of a period that understood itself as especially marked by history: what James Chandler describes as 'the age of the spirit of the age'. As the Napoleonic Wars drew to a close, writers sought to give expression to 'the historical peculiarity of their place and time' with reactions clustering around the massacre at St Peter's Fields in Manchester in 1819.[33] In Ireland, though, rather than the singular event that was Peterloo, a post-war recession from 1817 to 1822 settled slowly and miserably into repeated patterns of famine, disease and agrarian unrest. Writing to the physician and Knutsford resident Peter Holland a week after Peterloo, Maria Edgeworth enquired as to 'whether any of your relations have suffered more than being put in bodily fear by these riots of mobs & military at Manchester'. Her perspective emerges from family experience of 1798, when a United Irish battle was fought near her home and her father was imprisoned by a suspicious militia: she is critical of the radical leader Henry Hunt but also condemns the excessive forces used by yeomanry, who 'from their local feelings & from want of discipline' are 'of all others the most improper to be employed'.[34] And in 1820, in a letter to Peter Holland's father, Henry Holland, she relayed her brother's account of the assassination of the Duc de Berry (the Bourbon heir stabbed by Louis Lavel, an anti-monarchist) and explained family plans to travel to France, saving *an explosion or a revolution in Paris*'.[35] Edgeworth's comprehensive cross-channel understanding of popular radicalism in her own moment resonates with contemporary fears that Peterloo was responsible for bringing Irish modes of violent protest and their repression over to England. The figure of Lord Castlereagh, deplored for his cruel treatment of the 1798 rebels and now despised as one who brought down state terror upon the British people epitomised the connection, as writers such as Shelley and Byron did not fail to notice. But despite the involvement of Irish radicals in 1819 on the one hand and efforts by Daniel O'Connell to contrast Irish tranquillity to an English 'revolutionary tendency' on the other,[36] an article published in the *Dublin University Magazine* some ten years later argued that Ireland had to wait until 1833 for its 1819, as if the country still had to bide its time before catching up on history.

But when Chandler analyses the year 1819 as a 'historical scene of literary activity' that is 'preoccupied with its own history-making possibilities',[37] it is to the Irish writer Thomas Moore that he turns, as a literary character intensely involved in the day-to-day process of making history. The only Irish writer mentioned in William Hazlitt's *Spirit of the Age* (1825), Moore represents the very idea of a writer of his time and place, a man of 'unpretending origin', associated with the world of newspapers and the avatar of a popular taste for writing that is 'tawdry, or superficial, or common-place'.[38] The terms of these criticisms of Moore resonated for generations: already, in the 1830s, Jeremiah Joseph Callanan repeated Hazlitt's term 'meretricious' in a discussion of Moore at a meeting of Cork writers.[39] But while the 'glossy, smooth, and beautiful' language of the poetry (Hazlitt would say 'verse') incurred criticism, Hazlitt finds in the satires a style that is 'light, agreeable, polished' and deadly.[40] Jane Moore has re-evaluated the gendered language used by Hazlitt and others and argues for Moore as a poet of sociability whose writing is intricately bound up with social scenes, identifying a 'participatory' aesthetic that is modelled in song and remediated across a range of cultural forms.[41] The latter includes writing by James Clarence Mangan, discussed in Chapter 3, and takes in both the 'heavily mediated appreciation of Moore's Anacreontic lyrics' in Mangan's drinking songs of the 1830s, as well as his 'agonised' Famine-era 'responses to the social optimism implicit in Moore's convivial Anacreontics'.[42]

What Hazlitt calls Thomas Moore's 'prettinesses'[43] is understood by Jane Moore as a form of 'self-conscious or surface artistry' that makes a distinctive 'contribution to Irish literary romanticism in its privileging of symbolic inscription and allegorical interpretation for political, transformational ends'.[44] Her account might also apply to Mary Tighe but works especially well for *Captain Rock* (1824), a kind of imaginary memoir that self-consciously goes in search of signs of the times, understood to require a deadly pursuit for evidence of Ireland in 'the Statute-book of England' where the country can be traced 'as a wounded man in a crowd is tracked by his blood'.[45] The narrator is the inheritor of a tradition of Irish insurgency regularly renewed by oppressive laws and sustained by a well-developed 'art of governing wrongly'.[46] The resulting mode of perpetual strife lands the captain himself in prison in Cork Harbour, there to await deportation to 'distant shores'.[47]

The travels undertaken in Moore's poem *The Fudge Family in Paris* (1818) are less extensive, but once more distance across the sea helps to sharpen the satiric pen. Published by Moore under a pen name, 'Thomas Brown, the Younger', *The Fudge Family in Paris* imagines an Irish family who visit post-Waterloo Paris at the service of Lord Castlereagh, already the leader of the British party at the Congress of Vienna and a notorious figure in Moore's Whig circles. The poem cleverly uses a variety of poetic metres to convey a spectrum of political opinions concerning the fate of nations. Phil Fudge, the father, is a Castlereagh stooge whose job it is to write a book in defence of the Holy Alliance of Austria, Prussia and Russia and whose iambic tetrameter lines make fun of Castlereagh's notoriously poor public speaking style, even as Moore's friend Byron would do, more savagely, in *Don Juan*. The Fudges' son Bob is in Paris to socialise and gourmandise while his sister Biddy writes home in light and breathless anapaests about fashion and romance. Bob's tutor Phelim Connor is the radical of the group, and his lines are studded with asterisks that indicate censored material as his heroic couplets call out Tory misrule in Ireland. Moore was not unusual in mocking the flight of fashionable England to Paris in these years, but it is notable that he uses an Irish family to sharpen the point of his satire. The controversial figure of Castlereagh is at the silent centre of the intrigues, and his bloody record in Ireland as well as his own Irish background is at stake. As Jane Moore shows, it is the young Irish woman Biddy who gives the deadliest account of the hypocrisies of the day.[48] Biddy's delight in writing – 'only think! – / A letter from France, with French pens and French ink' – captures the English and Irish fad for French fashions, but hers is also the first letter of the satires and her poetic style is closest to Moore's own.[49]

Moore's satire opens up a perspective on a Europe in the process of being fashioned into a network of nation states with strong local and regional identities. Its political geography, as Paul Hamilton explains, 'did not simply return nations from the uniformity of Napoleon's empire to the old order' but rather tried to shape new forms of solidarity.[50] Moore, along with Morgan, responded to that 'solidarity' in the same critical spirit as other European romantics, shaping the materials of Irish history and politics to the contours of the new geopolitics. In the case of Moore, Europe proved a safe haven when, in April 1819, dogged by his Bermuda debts, he fled to the continent, travelling from Dover to Calais and on to Paris before crossing the Alps and meeting Byron in Venice. This was how, fleeing from the consequences of his own absentee behaviour in relation to a British sinecure post granted to him in 1803, Thomas Moore became the person to whom Byron entrusted his famous memoirs.

But it is much more usual, now as then, to tell the story of an emerging romanticism as an English one. The years after Waterloo were extraordinary ones for English poetry, right up to the publication of John Keats' poems in 1820 and the death of Lord Byron in 1824. Percy Bysshe Shelley's 'A Defence of Poetry', written in 1821 and not published until 1840, expressed the political power of both reading and writing in a divided society and remains a quintessential expression of the power of poetry 'to imagine that which we know'.[51] In Ireland, those divisions were sharp and growing sharper. They could truly test the powers of imagination, as was the experience of John Keats when he crossed the North Channel from

Port Patrick in Scotland to Donaghadee in 1818. Considering 'the worse than nakedness, the rags, the dirt and misery of the poor common Irish', Keats moved through Enlightenment modes of comparison and commentary that broke down when he encountered a sick and elderly woman carried along a bog road by two girls in a chair. His nasty and ironic account of this 'Duchess of Dunghill', his Irish Lady Muck, culminates in a curious question: 'What a thing would be a history of her Life and sensations?'[52]

The rhetoric of Keats' question not only sounds a marked contrast to the 'exultant diction'[53] that characterises Romantic-era travel narratives but also is repeated and amplified through many accounts of Irish culture to the period of the Great Famine and its aftermaths. Travellers to Ireland and political economists alike expressed themselves to be baffled or astonished by the sheer numerousness of the Irish population. Such generalised exclamations, do not always take notice of the fine-grained detail of Irish social change in this period, during which population growth was concentrated in the poorest classes, who subsisted on potatoes, were already disconnected from the emerging cash-based market economy and were now hardest hit by the recession that followed victory at Waterloo.

Moore paid a visit to Ireland in the same month that Keats did, travelling to Dublin in early June 1818 to take a victory lap and celebrate the runaway success of his long poem *Lalla Rookh* (1817). Daniel O'Connell chaired the committee that organised his welcome-home dinner, and the event was widely reported. It was early January 1819, though, before Keats heard of Moore's Dublin dinner, as we know from a mocking account he gave in a letter to his brother George in Louisville, Kentucky. James Chandler argues that 'Keats tracked Moore for many reasons', including their different kinds of susceptibility to 'social ridicule' and a shared experience of nasty critical attacks.[54] Keats read of Moore's dinner in a Philadelphia democratic newspaper (reprinted from the *Dublin Evening Post*), a fact that suggests the news from Dublin was routed to London via America, only to travel back again over the same watery expanse. Keats could reasonably expect that his brother might also have heard of 'the speech Mr Tom made on his Farthers [sic] health being drank'[55] and seems to have assumed that George would think no more than he did of the gushing tribute Moore paid to his parents. The gulf separating Moore's glittering dinner from Keats' miserable trek in Ireland in the same month goes unmentioned. Come the summer of 1823, Moore himself undertook a tour of Ireland, to the disturbed south and southwestern counties, at which point his observations begin to resonate with those made by Keats in the north. Moore saw, 'for the first time in my life, some real specimens of Irish misery and filth; three or four cottages together exhibiting such a naked swarm of wretchedness as never met my eyes before'.[56] Soon after this tour, he began work on *Captain Rock*.

As the era of the celebrity poet took off, other reputations fell. When Moore's trunk briefly went missing in Dublin on his arrival – seized by an admiring crowd who 'carried it off to town' – among its contents was a manuscript copy of Mary Tighe's novel *Selena* which her friends had 'begged' him to read 'in order to decide for them the propriety of publishing it'.[57] In spite of her significantly more public profile, issues of propriety also affected Maria Edgeworth, who began to receive newly negative reviews from about 1814, not long after John Wilson Corker's savage attack on Anna Laetitia Barbauld's 'Eighteen Hundred and Eleven'. With the publication of Edgeworth's novel of English public life, *Patronage*, in that year, gendered expectations came to the fore, including censure of her plotting of public life and improper use of language.[58] The soaring reputation of *Waverley* – still anonymous but known to be a man's book – was part of the story. We can see the change already in Byron's comment to the publisher Murray, in which he describes Edgeworth, Morgan and Burney as so many failed Walter Scotts: 'Waverley is the best & most interesting novel I have redde [*sic*] since – I don't know when – I like it as much as I hate Patronage & Wanderer – & O'Donnel and all the feminine trash of the last four months.'[59] And Byron helped put into circulation Edgeworth's growing reputation for narrow morality in *Don Juan*, Canto I, where Don Juan's rigid mother resembles 'a walking calculation / Miss Edgeworth's novels stepping from their covers.'[60] Byron and Edgeworth had shared a private breakfast in May 1813 at the home of Humphry Davy, but no record of their meeting survives. By 1841, as discussed in Chapter 3, Daniel O'Connell could make sexist jokes about Edgeworth in public speeches, expressing suspicion about her father's influence on her writing and demeaning her achievements.

The rising name of Walter Scott meant that the very women writers whose influence he had acknowledged in *Waverley* were increasingly eclipsed by his achievements. When Mitford dismissed *Florence Macarthy*, for instance, she noted that the plot was 'half "Guy Mannering"'.[61] By 1828, an anonymous contributor to *The Freeman's Journal* (writing as 'Patricius') felt the need to protest against all the fuss about the originality of 'the Wizard of the North' and to call out the fading names of Edgeworth and Morgan: 'For that species of *fictitious narrative* called *"The national novel"*, we stand indebted conjointly to the talents and patriotism of two Irish-women!'[62] And when Gerald Griffin, discussed later, read

Elizabeth Hamilton's *Cottagers of Glenburnie* (1808) in the 1830s, he wondered 'whether we would ever have had the Heart of Mid Lothian' had Scott not known of Hamilton's work.[63]

Charles Robert Maturin: Wet Gothic

One writer who benefited from the newly masculinised literary sphere was Charles Robert Maturin, a Protestant vicar who lived in Dublin, from where he corresponded with Scott and enjoyed his patronage. Maturin's gothic classic *Melmoth the Wanderer* fits well in what is a period of national introspection supercharged by a wide maritime world: the novel's plot ranges across time and space and takes readers from the shores of the Irish Sea to a precipice overlooking the Indian Ocean. But the maritime romance of terror imagined by Maturin places his native island of Ireland under intense scrutiny. In doing so, it follows the contours of what Steve Mentz calls 'wet globalization', a world of oceanic expansion along trade routes that connected local shores to distant ports.[64] Not a novel of 'massive geographical sprawl' as it has been described,[65] *Melmoth* mixes highly particular topographies with invocations of abstract space that are familiar from fictions including Mary Shelley's *Frankenstein* (1818). As Siobhan Carroll has shown, romantic invocations of vast or atopic space function in relation to actual topographies: they plot rather than disperse the 'geo-imaginary' of empire.[66] In *Melmoth the Wanderer*, we find recent Irish experiences of terror submerged into a novel of global flows across bodies of water whose co-ordinates come occasionally into view. Irish and European places are imagined alongside imperial outposts and desolate regions whose connections are shaped, to borrow Carroll's formulation, via 'a shared spatial category taking many of its cues from the imaginings of the ocean'.[67]

As a man who has made an 'unutterable' diabolical bargain, the original Melmoth is one whose great 'intellectual vessel' has strayed beyond 'the narrow seas where it was coasting', leaving him stranded in time and space as he seeks out a soul to join him at the brink of damnation.[68] Within its nested narratives, the action moves from sixteenth-century Spain through the Indian Ocean, back to Spain via Switzerland and on to England during the wars of religion. *Melmoth the Wanderer* opens and closes on the Wicklow coast, where the young John Melmoth begins to unravel the secret of his infernal ancestor, *Melmoth the Wanderer*, with a portrait dated 1646 and a found manuscript (located 'among some papers of no value, such as manuscript sermons, and pamphlets on the improvement of Ireland, and such stuff') as his guides.[69] The plight of a more immediate ancestor, a dying uncle on whose goodwill his fortune depends, has brought John Melmoth to Wicklow. As he approaches the house, the very landscape seems to resist him: the 'stubborn' gate yields only slowly as it 'grated heavily through the mud and gravel stones, in which it left a deep and sloughy furrow'.[70] As John tries to navigate the 'miry' terrain along a road marked by 'an uncemented wall of loose stones', he is guided by a servant boy who goes 'plunging through the mud with all the dabbling and amphibious delight of a duck'.[71] What was once a lawn around his uncle's estate is now pasture land while grass-grown steps testify to an environment that is playing its part in the chaotic unspooling of a family history laid waste by the forces of fate. The liquid elements of the novel's co-ordinates involve mud, blood and tears as well as sea and ocean so that its wet and miry ontologies dominate even in vivid scenes of fire and destruction.

Bottles of beer, long hoarded in the cellar, are shared out in the kitchen, and whiskey appears as an honoured guest at the feast. The level of active agency assigned to these drinks is striking: 'bottles of Wicklow ale, long and surreptitiously borrowed from his "honor's" cellar, and which now made their first appearance on the kitchen hearth, and manifested their impatience of further constraint, by hissing, spitting, and bouncing in the face of the fire that provoked its animosity'.[72] As liquids fizz from their bottles indoors, we are reminded of the coastal location of the scene. 'We have already mentioned the closeness of Melmoth's abode to the seashore', remarks the narrator, noting '[t]he vicinity of Melmoth's house to what seamen call an iron-bound coast'.[73] The servants pray for those at sea and keep company with 'the bickering fire and rocking chimney' while John Melmoth hears the wind shaking the house and realises that a nearby ship is in danger.[74] Ireland's east coast was (and is) vulnerable to strong tidal currents whipped up by prevailing southwesterly winds, so that unusually steep waves break in deep water. Ships might also meet the numerous sandbanks along the east coast between Dublin and Wexford, where many vessels were wrecked by the weather. Where Gerald Griffin, for instance, describes the 'wild fishermen' of the Atlantic seaboard, whose 'livelihood was derived from the plunder of the unfortunate men who happened to be wrecked on this inhospitable shore',[75] Maturin insists on shipwreck as ordinary occurrence, an occasion for pity and not for pillage. Edgeworth too weaves a scene of shipwreck into the domestic fabric of her tales in *Patronage* (1814) and *Helen* (1834), and in all three cases such scenes belong to a longer nineteenth-century tradition of colonial adventure novels that open with disasters at sea.

Like the good Percy family in *Patronage*, John Melmoth rushes to help the unfortunate passengers. Unlike Mr Percy though, who is able to safely steer his boat away from a selfish French diplomat who threatens to overturn the rescue vessel, John Melmoth himself falls into the sea, where he experiences an oceanic loss of self. He falls backwards into 'the roaring deep' in which he is 'engulphed, then for a moment thrown to the surface': 'He struggled with nothing to grasp at. He sunk with a vague thought, that if he could reach the bottom, if he could arrive at any thing solid, he was safe.'[76] The description seems to belong to the deep ocean, rather than the narrow passage between Britain and Ireland and prepares readers for a novel that crosses and mingles bodies of water while immersing us in the elements. The character of the Wanderer defies space and time as he crosses back and forth between the eastern seaboard of Ireland, the inland expanses of Spain, the vast Indian Ocean and the north of England.

This first of the several inset narratives that make up *Melmoth the Wanderer*, 'The Tale of the Spaniard', follows a story that is first told to John Melmoth in Ireland. It tracks the story of Alonzo Monçada, a young aristocrat, born outside marriage and condemned by his parents to a monastic life to expiate their sins. 'The Tale of the Spaniard' sees Monçada finally escape the terrors of the monastery with the aid of a fellow monk. But Monçada is betrayed when the former, a man who has killed his own father and who is desperate for a promise of salvation, leads him not to the city but rather to the cells of the Inquisition. When the Inquisition itself burns to the ground and all believe him dead, Monçada makes his way onto the streets of Madrid and forces his way to precarious shelter in the home of a Jewish merchant. From that house, he becomes a horrified witness to the actions of a crowd gathered to pray for the victims of the recent fire. The crowd see the betraying monk, a known parricide, among the religious procession, and surge forward in anger with actions resembling that of the sea itself: 'the vast body that rolled and blackened beneath me, like the ocean under the first and far-felt agitations of the storm.'[77]

Monçada meanwhile lies concealed behind a curtain in the upper floor of the merchant's house, a terrified witness to the 'horrible catastrophe' as the crowd drag the parricide through 'mud and stones' and finally fling the man, now 'a mangled lump of flesh', against the door of the house where his former companion lies hidden.[78] The doubled fate of the two men, both reluctant monks, splits violently apart as one, a spectator to 'the work of blood', sees the other 'trodden in one moment into sanguine and discoloured mud by a thousand feet'.[79] The army charges across the square to aid the victim, only to find that they too are completing the terrible work of the crowd, for the man is now not only in the mud but of it: 'The officer who headed the troop dashed his horse's hoofs into a bloody formless mass, and demanded, "Where was the victim?" He was answered, "Beneath your horse's feet;" and they departed.'[80]

This scene of popular insurrection resonates with memories of the French Revolution and the United Irish Rebellion while there is a closer literary link too: the passage closely imitates the account given of the death of the Prioress in Matthew Lewis' *The Monk* (1796), where rioters, indignant on hearing of her 'inhuman' treatment of young Agnes, began to tear at her limbs and continue to attack 'her lifeless body': 'They beat it, trod upon it, and ill-used it, till it became no more than a mass of flesh, unsightly, shapeless, and disgusting.' Maturin offers an authenticating footnote, designed perhaps to distract readers from his borrowing from Lewis, or to acknowledge the difficulty of containing such a scene in time and space: 'This circumstance occurred in Ireland 1797, after the murder of the unfortunate Dr Hamilton. The officer was answered, on inquiring what was that heap of mud at his horse's feet, – "The man you came for."'[81] As the footnote does its authenticating work, mud makes the savage scene actual, and we are left with the proposition that the bodies of men really can dissolve into mire and blood. But despite its uncanny power, Maturin's note also transmits traceable information of the kind characteristic of romantic historicism. Dr William Hamilton (b. 1757), the Protestant rector of Clondavaddog, commonly Fanad, County Donegal, was assassinated by some fifty United Irishmen in March 1797. The killing took place in the house of Dr John Waller at Sharon, near Newtowncunningham, around fifteen miles from Strabane, County Tyrone. As Breandán Mac Suibhne explains, Hamilton was a target because of his 'unusually vigorous efforts to disarm United Irishmen in his own parish'.[82] Rather than flee to Derry or Dublin or England, as many well-to-do loyalists in Donegal did, Hamilton stood firm in Fanad and, with his yeomanry corps, imprisoned several republicans. At the time of his assassination, he had already seen off a United Irish effort to lay siege to his home.

Hamilton was well connected in Dublin, and his assassination resonated at national level and reverberated for decades in the northwest. The violent death of a minister – albeit one who was also a magistrate, a man of law as well as of God – precipitated the introduction of martial law in Ulster. Meanwhile his name has a place in environmental history: a fellow of Trinity College Dublin and a founding member of the Royal Irish Academy, Hamilton published essays on the temperature of the earth and Ireland's historic climate. His *Letters Concerning the Northern Coast of the*

County of Antrim (1786) established the now standard account of the volcanic origins of the Giants' Causeway in County Antrim, in argument with those who held to a 'Neptunist' or marine understanding of basalt rock as having emerged from the sea while a vast primeval ocean receded.

Maturin, in his second year at Trinity College Dublin, when the notorious assassination occurred, may have read the news in the press or heard of it in the College; meanwhile, Rev. Henry Maturin, likely a cousin, succeeded Hamilton as rector of Fanad in 1797. In 1812, John Gamble, a London-based writer who had been reared in a Presbyterian family in Strabane, met an eyewitness to the events when home on holiday. Gamble heard what had happened when Hamilton tried to hide in Waller's cellar, was 'dragged' from there and 'thrown out to his murderers, who dispatched him with as many wounds as Caesar was in the Capitol'.[83] The eyewitness was almost certainly Hamilton's servant Barney McCafferty, who was tried and acquitted for the murder at the Donegal assizes in September 1797.[84]

The Hamilton case corresponds to what Guy Beiner calls 'the dialectic of preserving and erasing memory' that marked the treatment of the 1798 United Irish Rebellion in Ulster in the first half of the nineteenth century.[85] An 'inability to openly remember insurgents in public' led to 'practices of concealment'[86] among which we might count the placing of the memory of Hamilton's violent death at the foot of the printed page. Footnotes play a special role in these patterns of memory and forgetting. In *Melmoth the Wanderer*, the Hamilton material takes its place in a group of three footnotes, a striking paratextual cluster found half way through the novel. The three notes share a focus on questions of witness and call for a multiscalar response to violence and trauma. The first note asserts the reality of a fictional description of multiple human remains buried together, '*their cinders, occupying but a single coffin*', via an account of 'the dreadful fire which consumed sixteen persons in one house, in Stephen's Green, Dublin, 1816'.[87] Maturin, who lived close by on York Street, writes in his own person as one who 'heard the screams of sufferers whom it was impossible to save'.[88] Contemporary newspapers bear out this account. Some pages on, very shortly after the account of Dr Hamilton and appended to the description of the murderous actions of a violent crowd, there follows a longer note that explores the psychological effects of terror. Invoking the authority of an eyewitness, Maturin describes how a Dublin shoemaker came to observe the notorious killing of Arthur Wolfe, Viscount Kilwarden, pulled from his carriage by rebels wielding pikes in the course of Robert Emmet's rebellion in 1803. Watching the crowd, the note asserts, the shoemaker 'stood at his window as if nailed to it; and when dragged from it, became – *an idiot for life*'.[89] And in the case of William Hamilton too, his servant McCafferty was acquitted by a judge who took into account the man's likely frozen terror.

Countless Irish writers of the Romantic period chose to gather information at the foot of the printed page, a bookish practice that is discussed in Chapter 1. The reverberations of Maturin's strange and powerful footnotes are still felt in John and Michael Banim's historical novel *Crohoore of the Bill-Hook* (1825), in a scene that rewrites the passage in which the mob attacks the Inquisition in markedly contemporary terms. Preoccupied by the anti-tithe cause of its own moment, *Crohoore of the Bill-Hook* is set in and around the 1760s. Among the scenes of agrarian violence narrated is one relating to the Whiteboys, a late eighteenth-century secret society whose members habitually wore women's clothing as they protested their access to common grazing land and challenged public order. In the novel, a company of mounted soldiers are ambushed by a group of Kilkenny Whiteboys, men dressed as women, who stage a mock funeral on the road. This time, the lone note captures not a densely rendered memory but rather stray traces of the Irish language, expressing both violence and the spatial logic of the footnote itself: launching their attack, the agrarian terrorists shout the word '*síos*', rendered in English by Banim as 'chise', and explained in the footnote as meaning 'down'.[90]

The Whiteboy victory is sudden and 'electric'. But the red-coated soldiers, seemingly 'unsaddled and disarmed', turn to fire on their assailants with hidden pistols: 'Every ball took effect, and fifteen men fell.'[91] The scene of confrontation is vividly described, as 'wretched people' who carry only sticks are trapped between and underneath the army horses. As the Whiteboys are slaughtered by the soldiers, they find themselves 'treading and trampling on the bodies of their dead companions'.[92] The whole bloody episode, we are told, 'was enacted in little over a minute' but unfolds in grim detail over several pages.[93]

Such images of ordinary people caught up in destruction suspend and prolong the experience of violence and exploit the affordances of print as living medium, joining with wider tendencies in European romanticism to engage in 'self-conscious reflection on mediality and temporality'.[94] But in the particular case of the footnote, the interconnected acts of recall and forgetting take on a spatial quality that allows the matter of history to be moved down on the page. In *Melmoth the Wanderer*, footnotes might be thought of as spaces of conceptual disorientation that drag history downward and can help move our understanding of mediation beyond 'terrestrial and anthropocentric contexts'.[95] Maturin's footnotes discussed previously realise dense and effortful moments of violence that find succour in the possibilities of page space. Drawing on the power of water and fire, footnotes achieve their effects as 'elemental media' as the printed book itself stands in relation to 'a network of infrastructural and ecological phenomena' that range from doors to streets to seascapes and hurricanes.[96]

Another of the inset narratives, 'The Tale of the Indians', unfolds in the form of a manuscript that Alonzo Monçada is set to copy while taking refuge in the home of Adonijah, a Jewish scholar. Some of the patterns discussed in Chapter 2, where copying works its way into cultural texts as material and method, re-emerge in *Melmoth the Wanderer* as Monçada feels 'a slight but painful flush tinge my cheek, at the thought of a Christian, and a peer of Spain, becoming the amanuensis of a Jew for hire'.[97] The story told retains a focus on race and privilege as Melmoth meets Immalee, the young woman with whom his fate is tied, 'not many leagues from the mouth of the Hoogly',[98] the river through which the East India Company entered western Bengal and on which they established their port of Calcutta. Immalee is orphaned on the island, having been sent for by her father, who journeyed to the East Indies from Spain in search of a fortune. When the vessel on which she travelled was wrecked, Immalee was given up for dead. Melmoth encounters her as a creature of nature who communes with animals and plants, a version of primitivism that takes its charge from a narrative that keeps 'the Eastern and Western theaters of British imperialism'[99] both in view. *Melmoth the Wanderer* connects extreme emotions across these contested bodies of water. The descriptions of the island also bring race into focus. On the island, Immalee is possessed of a desirable whiteness that is compared to 'the dark-red tint of the natives of the Bengalese islands'.[100] Her 'extraordinary colour' serves also to point up the whiteness of Melmoth himself: 'The colour of his face and hands resembled her own more than those she was accustomed to see'.[101] The same scene features several overwrought metaphors of indigeneity, as if testing out ideas of native and foreign within the frame of Immalee's island. Her smile, we are told, is properly '*a native of the face*' while she experiences the figure of the Wanderer as a '*new flower that had grown in the sand*'.[102] Such racialised language seems to fall away once she recognises the Spanish spoken by the Wanderer and falls routinely into 'the words of the Christian Catechism that had been breathed into her infant lip', at once familiar and strange in an island whose location is plotted in terms of routes laid down by European imperialism.[103]

Other watery co-ordinates are plotted in another inset narrative, 'The Lovers' Tale', set in Shrewsbury on the borders of England and Wales against the backdrop of the seventeenth-century wars of religion. A Royalist family, the Mortimers have two sons and a daughter. One son fights for the crown while a daughter who stays at home marries a Puritan preacher. The other son proves an 'apostate' like his sister and goes to Ireland with Cromwell's forces.[104] There, he leads a siege against the home of 'the ancient seat of the O'Moores, princes of Leix', only to be first 'scalded through his buff-coat by a discharge of hot water from the bartizan' and then exposed to 'drenching rain'.[105] He dies of pleurisy some days later. Maturin makes little of the sea crossing necessitated by the Cromwellian conquest of Ireland and makes no mention of the folk stories which imagined Cromwell's body churning up the Irish Sea for generations to come.[106] But his account of the death of a single drenched soldier helps to sketch a vast history of 'nations and navies on fire'[107] while the linked stories of the three Mortimer grandchildren fill in the details. Margaret Mortimer, the heiress, stays at home and represents a stable English world of birth and rank. Her cousins, though, remind us of the costs and consequences of such landed privilege. John Sandal, son of the preacher, joins the navy, fights the Dutch and comes home a hero. His naval exploits in the Anglo-Dutch war recall the emergence of British maritime power in the early seventeenth century and also partake of the glorification of the navy in the Napoleonic and Peninsular Wars. But these invocations of British power at sea are never far from the strange terrors of shipboard violence, brought into focus via the character of Elinor Mortimer, the other grandchild. Elinor's 'health, her rest, and her imagination' all fall prey to visions of distant violence.[108] It is not only her cousin's war-time exploits themselves but their contrast to a shared peaceful childhood that disturbs her as 'cherished images of the past' come to be 'fearfully and insanely contrasted in her imagination with the ideas of slaughter and blood, – of decks strewed with corses, – and of a young and terrible conqueror bestriding them amid showers of ball and clouds of fire'.[109] Maturin's vision here shares an affective power with Gerald Griffin's imagination of distant wars made vividly present on Irish shores, discussed later.

Melmoth the Wanderer ends in Ireland, where Melmoth returns to his ancestral lands, dreams of Hell as an ocean of fire and disappears into the Irish Sea, leaving only signs of a struggle with some terrible being at the edge of the coast. The dream of a fiery ocean in turn gives way to mundane details of the rainy Wicklow coast: 'damp sand or clay' captures the impress of the Wanderer's footsteps and leads John Melmoth 'through the narrow gravel walk … terminated by a broken fence, and opened on a healthy field which spread half-way up a rock whose summit overlooked the sea. The weather had been rainy, and they could trace the steps distinctly through that heathy field.'[110] The final evidence for Melmoth's fate comes from those most marginal figures who stand in here for a populous Ireland, 'poor fishermen residing on the shore'.[111] The 'gray gaping desolation' of Ireland's eastern seaboard becomes, as Vera Kreilkamp puts it, 'as terrifying as the most florid gothic nightmare of eternal doom'.[112]

The muddy miseries of the shoreline yield signs of a diabolical struggle, visible to John Melmoth and Monçada as they follow along 'a kind of tract as if a person had dragged, or been dragged, his way through it – a down-trodden track, over which no footsteps but those of one impelled by force had ever passed'.[113] With this scene, Maturin returns us to the novel's opening statements about terror as routine, repetitive reality – 'that irritating series of petty torments which constitutes the misery of life in general'[114] – now understood to have a special connection with the sea, that 'wide, waste, engulphing ocean' equally known to *Melmoth the Wanderer* and 'poor fishermen'.[115] Just such a combination of strange effects and routine dangers can be found in the writings of Gerald Griffin, where ordinary people who make their livelihoods by the coast are forced to encounter their own lives as strange and alien. Described by Tom Dunne as 'hypersensitive tortured romantics', Griffin's protagonists are caught between Ireland and empire, between speech and print and between Irish and English.[116] Plots of mistaken or misunderstood identities abound as an earlier Gothic mode of tragic repetition gives way to 'self-reflection, interiority' and broken images, described by Siobhán Kilfeather as characteristic of Irish Gothic.[117]

Gerald Griffin: Naval Service and Inner Lives

Unlike John Melmoth, who falls into the Irish Sea and feels as if he might sink to its very bottom, Immalee, in the 'Tale of the Indian', rises magically from the water 'as if' to view her island home. Immalee's identification with her island environment is connected to sea as well as land: on one occasion she experiences the sensation of being 'borne downward' into the sea with the rain, 'engulphed in the depths of the ocean – rising again to light on the swell of the enormous billows, as if she were heaved on the back of a whale'.[118] There is a strange symmetry between this scene and a similarly watery one found in Gerald Griffin's tale 'The Hand and Word', from *Holland-Tide* (1827), a story that opens with an account of a young man sitting on a rock, deep in a book, only to find himself swept up by a wave and taken 'a distins' out to sea.[119] Riding an Atlantic wave – no more or less probable than mounting a whale – he is turned back towards the coast and given a 'good sea-view' before being returned to a sloping stone on the shoreline.[120] The teller of the tale is a 'waggish host' who wishes to illustrate the power of the ocean: visitors expecting to take a 'pleasant promenade' or enjoy some sea bathing must hear of freak waves and learn to trace irregular coastal features.[121]

While Maturin's gives only loose co-ordinates for his Indian Ocean island, Griffin's story derives its drama from highly specific details of the distinctive coastal topography of the southwest of Ireland, where rocks, headlands and cliffs form 'a thousand fantastic shapes'.[122] The setting is a concave natural rock formation known as the 'amphitheatre', near Kilkee in County Clare, south of the Cliffs of Moher, where 'rocks lift themselves above the level of the sea in regular grades', as if to provide so many benches from which to view the ocean.[123] A nearby 'Puffing-hole' sends jets of water into the air at high tide while the village itself is a place of a few streets, 'scattered' over sandy, rocky land that overhangs the sea.[124] Both sites are named on the first Ordnance Survey map of the area, where the very exactness of their representation on paper presages a threat to vernacular forms of measurement, in turn connected to the kinds of intimate, oral knowledge of coasts and weather now made to inhabit the printed page.

A Catholic from Limerick who went to London to make his way as a writer, Griffin's life was marked by difficulties and depression, not least because the opportunities offered by the booming London cultural market were in journalism and fiction, where Griffin longed to make his reputation on the legitimate stage. 'The Hand and Word' is the second of the stories in *Holland-Tide*, an anonymously published series of tales that are bound together by an opening scene of shared storytelling in the home of a respectable Munster farmer on 31 October, or Halloween. The tales, originally envisaged as a series of 'Munster Anecdotes', began with Griffin's memories of life on the southwest coast. The stories that unfold in front of the burning turf fire all occur along the Shannon estuary, a place that Griffin felt would introduce some variety to the field of Irish fiction. From London, he wrote to his brother Daniel to ask him to send 'materials for a few short tales, laying the scene about the sea coast, – Kilkee – novelty at least'. He went on: 'Reality you know is all the rage now'.[125] Among the real activities described in the stories are fish jolting, seal hunting, transporting turf by boat, making manure and gathering seaweed. The anthropological impulse can result in formulaic descriptions, enlivened by the feel of notes taken in the field. Along the 'very thickly inhabited' coast described by Griffin, we meet a population who 'talk Irish – kill fish – go to sea in canoes – traffic in kind – eat potatoes and oaten bread – and exercise themselves in offices of kindness and hospitality towards strangers'.[126] In 'The Half-Sir', a disdainful woman fails to pronounce the word 'piggins' correctly, allowing Griffin to offer the following definition: 'a kind of wooden vessel used for drinking the coagulated residuum of milk, called by the peasantry thick, or skimmed milk'.[127] We also learn the meaning of 'beestings', the first milk produced by a cow after giving birth, considered a delicacy among the peasantry, along with a range of other characteristic words often rendered in a form of non-standard spelling or eye dialect that strives to capture the Irish language in print but poses challenges to modern readers.

In their detail, Griffin's fictions begin to realise the dense textures of ordinary Irish life on the coast. Such places that might seem remote today were an integral part of Britain's naval empire with littoral land often commanding high rents because of easy access to seaweed, estuarine sediment or mud scrapings from the bog. His descriptions call up a part of Ireland that is at once novel and asking to be known by its own coastal codes, similar to the ways in which Mary Russell Mitford's collection, *Our Village* (1822) walked readers around the scene of her fictions and introduced them to paths, plants and local habitation. Mitford's stories were read across the Anglophone world, in America and in British India, where her vision of village life helped to shape a world in the process of being remade by the disruptions of white settler migration from Britain. Griffin too came to find a wide readership in the United States in the years after his death, when, in 1857, the major Irish American Catholic publishing firm of D. J. Sadleir issued a ten volume series of his work. It is surely between these covers that Dion Boucicault found a copy of Griffin's novel *The Collegians* (1829) while walking down Broadway in New York, and so hit on the idea for his sensationally popular melodrama, *The Colleen Bawn* (1860).

Among the boasts of the Sadleir edition was the inclusion of Griffin's historical novel, *The Invasion* (1832) with the other works. Briefly discussed in Chapter 3, Griffin's novel opens on the shores of West Cork and its islands, describing treacherous tides and deadly waves as it imagines an ancient lordship structure threatened by the arrival of the piratical Vikings. A mention of a Martello tower near Glengarriff, County Cork, points readers to the defensive role played by that coastline in the Peninsular and Napoleonic Wars but the plot has other watery co-ordinates in mind as it moves between an ancient monastery on the Shannon, Anglo-Saxon Northumberland and East Anglia and the Swedish port of Uppsala. Despite Thomas Davis' praise of *The Invasion*'s 'invaluable and countless hints on the appearance of Ancient Ireland', quoted in the New York edition, Griffin had a hard road to travel in order to arrive at anything resembling the fashionable medievalism of Walter Scott. Where *Ivanhoe* (1820) offered readers a glittering past that surfaced in contemporary pageantry and performance, including the visits of George IV to Dublin in 1821 and Edinburgh in 1822, *The Invasion* is heavier work.

In the Irish writing of the 1820s, an ethnographic impulse persists within the wider media ecology and can take curious forms. Lady Blessington's *The Magic Lantern, or Sketches of Scenes in the Metropolis* (1822) offers a series of sketches of notable sights, including an auction, Hyde Park, the opera and Belzoni's Egyptian Tomb in Piccadilly. This was Blessington's first book, written before she and her husband left London for a seven-year tour of the Continent. Born Marguerite Agnes Power in Clonmel, County Tipperary, Blessington grew up in a garrison and was effectively sold into marriage at a young age. She later lived with Lord Blessington before their marriage in 1818. Aspects of her early life story remain difficult to figure out, but even as Lady Blessington, hers was undoubtedly an outsider's view of fashionable London.

As well as observing as everyday and unremarkable the existence of Irish points of reference in the city, what the sketches begin to bring into view is what Blessington herself calls the spectacle of 'the English ... in the aggregate'.[128] She has a marked interest in crowds and overheard conversations as she notes eddies of people moving across Hyde Park, or bumping up against one another within enclosed spaces such as the Egyptian tomb. Her only references to Ireland are to Hibernian accents or turns of phrase, experienced as part of the melee of the city. She does not seem to have known or encountered John Banim in London, and by the end of the 1820s he was in Boulogne, suffering ill health and seeking help from the Royal Literary Fund via Gerald Griffin and Thomas Moore. An 1830 letter to the publisher John Murray refers to 'two volumes of the English Tales' that Banim then had in preparation.[129]

Blessington's sketches and Banim's planned volumes help us to measure the distance between Edgeworth's scornful description of the 'frozen circles' of London in *The Absentee* (1812),[130] which her hero leaves for his tour around the much hotter society of post-Union Ireland, and her more engaged and nuanced discussion of London in *Helen* (1834), where the capital, seen from a country seat in the home counties, comes into view as a point of reference and place of movement and change. In *Helen*, discussed in more detail in Chapter 3, London fashions, London dinners and London conversation are all remarked upon just as much as Irish roads, stagecoaches and inns occupy the interest of earlier Irish tales.

If Regency London was itself a place of division and dislocation, then London-resident Irish writers encountered serial displacements that manifest themselves in the texture of their tales. In Griffin's tales, Ireland is caught in an ethnographic gaze that derives energy from the writer's uncertain location in a rapidly changing London. Griffin finds particularly rich material in the case of naval recruitment from the coastal communities of the southwest of Ireland. Across the tales, we meet people gathering 'the *dhoolamaun*' (a version of the Irish word *Dúlamán*, meaning channel wrack, a type of edible seaweed), footing turf and clubbing seals.[131] Hookers from Galway sail by carrying fish for the market in Limerick while revenue vessels ply the waters. Service in the British navy is among the ordinary activities of the place: where Thomas Moore had likened the fugitive state of Irish music publication to the Wild Geese who fled to continental Catholic brigades (see Chapter 1), Griffin wrote rather of the millions of ordinary Irish men who served the empire. Ireland consistently supplied a disproportionately high number of those men who donned British uniform: in 1830, when Ireland accounted for less than a third of the population of the United Kingdom, 'an estimated 40 per cent of the non-commissioned members of the British army was Irish-born'.[132] Griffin's eldest brother had served in the 27th regiment in Canada before returning home in 1817, while the next served as a midshipman aboard HMS *Venerable* in the English Channel. A cousin of theirs, an officer in the 9th regiment, died of cholera shortly after arriving in India in 1830, aged only 26.

Victory over the French swept away traditional British willingness to conciliate the Catholics of Ireland in the interests of recruitment to its army and navy. Already at the turn of the nineteenth century, Thomas Dermody (who himself served in the army) complained of the unequal treatment of Catholics distinguished by their bravery and sacrifice: 'Who fights our battles? who protects our coast, – / And is their gen'rous labour lost?'.[133] Griffin wrote his *Tales* just as a period of low hopes came to an end in the decade before Emancipation. The plot of 'Card Drawing' holds two kinds of knowledge in tension: that bearing British arms was widely used by Roman Catholic leaders as an argument for emancipation and that discontent with the state in which they were seeking full citizenship was a common experience among ordinary Catholics. Early nineteenth-century Ireland is more often thought of as a theatre of conflict than a population at war, but Griffin is at pains to chart the perils and illusions of competing forms of allegiance across imperial shorelines in a period that saw an unprecedented increase in recruitment give way to quick and sudden demobilisation.

The number of Irish recruits to the army and navy – over 150,000, chiefly Catholics – reflects population growth among the poorest classes, many of whom still spoke Irish, a language that grew as the numbers did. Irish romantic novels not only registered these demographic facts, as argued in Chapter 3, but were also more specifically engaged with the question of a burgeoning population that served the empire at sea. An 1827 review of Griffin's *Holland-Tide* commented that 'The Irish and Scotch divide the department of novels as they do the army, the good things in India and in other British dependencies; that is to say, pretty equal between them.'[134] In the novels themselves, 'the good things' of empire sometimes protrude in the narrative, as is the case in the tale 'Card Drawing', where the plot hinges on 'a medal ... suspended by a blue riband', earned by the peasant character Duke Dorgan for his service at the Battle of Trafalgar.[135]

'Card Drawing' was published as one of Griffin's *Tales of the Munster Festivals* in 1827, and like other pieces in that collection, it testifies to a vibrant popular culture that was coming under the scrutiny of scholars, antiquarians and novelists, moving and changing under their gaze. The plot turns on the involvement of an Irish peasant in the Napoleonic and Peninsular Wars and so draws readers' attention to a particularly intense and disruptive instance of cultural change. Paradoxically, these stories of disruption are organised around the rhythms and traditions of the Irish year: St Bridget's Day, St Stephen's Day and St John's Eve each provides the opening premise for one of the tales. In the case of 'Card Drawing', the events occur over the first and second days of February, 'The Law na Breedha or Candlemas day' as Griffin puts it.[136] While St Bridget's Day is associated with the beginning of spring, Candlemas marks the mid-point of winter, halfway between the shortest day and the spring equinox. A day of transition in the Celtic calendar, Candlemas is also associated with forms of weather divination and prophecy. Sheridan Le Fanu, who like Griffin spent his childhood in Limerick, would later use the same deeply resonant date to bring the violent and sensational events of his novel *Uncle Silas* (1864) to a close.

'Card Drawing' opens with Duke Dorgan taking leave of his ship on the Clare coast: once back on land, he plans to propose to Pennie, the sweetheart he left behind, whose forbidding father he hopes to impress with his prize money. Dorgan is presented via 'an incidental scene, which took place on the evening when his vessel arrived in the offing of Loup Head'.[137] He has completed his naval career 'with a character unspotted by any act of insubordination or servility' and with enough prize money to ensure future comfort.[138] The conceit of his return to 'his native shores' justifies a narrative excursion around the 'wild and striking' landscape as his ship moves towards port,[139] and as with *Holland-Tide*, Griffin once more renders the coastline of the southwest of Ireland in strikingly granular detail.

Once back on land, Dorgan encounters the surly figure of Pryce Kinchela. The two men had been at school together and competed for the affections of Pennie. Where Dorgan went to sea, Pryce Kinchela accepted the ignominy of rejection. There is a strong contrast between Duke Dorgan's naval success overseas and Kinchela's misfortune and poverty; they are repeatedly paired and doubled by the narrative, as if to express what Mary Favret calls 'the wayward power' of war.[140] Both men are to be understood against a backdrop of agrarian insurrection and the conditions of Munster life at the intersection of psychology and history, as the 'disturbing affective responses' described by Favret, including 'numbness, dizziness, anxiety, or a sense of being overwhelmed' make their impression on an impoverished coastal community crisscrossed by violent histories.[141]

The naval background to the story is established with a mention of 'the chronicles of Mr. James, or any other naval Tacitus of the day',[142] a reference to William James' five-volume *Naval History of Great Britain*, first published in 1822–4 and cited by Herman Melville in the text of *Billy Budd*. Griffin does not deploy footnotes quite as Maturin does, but in referring readers to an external reality while declining 'to encumber our slender narrative with any unnecessary historical detail',[143] he too expresses a concern with finding original forms of expression adequate to a copious culture that threatens to overflow the page. The narrator claims for Duke Dorgan both a place within James' history and a location outside official records:

> Whether Mr. James records the exploits of a certain Duke Dorgan, a young sailor, from the shores of Kerry, or no, I am not aware; but it is not likely that many names have been enrolled in his pages more distinguished by a modest valour (such as contents itself with doing all for duty, and nothing for vanity), than that of the person we have just mentioned.[144]

Just as the narrator serves to suspend Dorgan somewhat uneasily between fiction and reality, so the tale's plot is organised around a series of interruptions, intervals and postponements. On his first night off the ship, Duke Dorgan sleeps outdoors and suffers 'monkey-visions', Griffin's curious term for a nightmare.[145] (The monkey apparitions of Le Fanu's supernatural tale 'Green Tea' come to mind). When Duke wakes up, he overhears a young woman (who turns out to be his lover, Pennie) asking advice of the Card-Drawer, who practises 'some mystical calculation on a pack of cards'.¹⁴⁶ The narrator assures readers that 'the increasing knowledge of the peasantry' has reduced the appeal of such 'a fi'-penny or a tenpenny peep into futurity', yet lingers on the Card-Drawer's weird power over the unhappy Pennie.¹⁴⁷

Dorgan himself is tempted to draw the cards, but when the old woman asks for 'that dollar that's danglen be the ribbin to the breast o' your coat' as payment, Dorgan pulls back.¹⁴⁸ But this is not a simple distinction between stout naval reason and fickle peasant superstition. When a horrified Dorgan explains that this 'dollar' is his Trafalgar medal, the Card-Drawer herself 'drew back respectfully, and curtsied to the very ground'.¹⁴⁹ In a striking gesture of narrative doubling, the peasant prophecy woman invokes the glorious memory of Nelson, 'that great lord, that all the world is in mourning for'.¹⁵⁰ At the same time, she draws a card that promises 'voylent an' a shameful death' to Dorgan himself.¹⁵¹

Nelson's death on board the *Victory* in 1805 forms the backdrop to Griffin's tale, which sees Dorgan suspected of murdering his lover's father, the real villain proving in the end to be Pryce Kinchela, who has stolen his friend's naval uniform and medal. A priest who has overheard Dorgan and Kinchela drinking and talking helps to incriminate the former before the law so that he is sentenced to be hanged. As the Catholic Church and the British legal system prove equally inhospitable to Dorgan's injured innocence, it is to his identity within the navy that he turns for succour. In language that asks readers to consider the difference between being a 'midnight cut-throat' and spilling blood in the service of his country,¹⁵² Dorgan protests his innocence via a series of questions:

> I am a British sailor – is that the character of a ruffian or a traitor? That medal which you hold was given me as a reward for discharging my duty well and faithfully – is it likely I would stain it with the blood of a secret murder? I trod the decks of the Victory for seven years, a deck that was never pressed by the foot of a coward. – I laid my hand on the white hairs of my commander Nelson, when he lay bleeding on the bed of glory – is it likely I should hack and hew the hoary head of a defenceless fellow-creature? I stood by his side at Trafalgar, and never shrunk in the daylight from an enemy's broadside – is it likely that I would stab an old man in the dark?¹⁵³

In assigning such a pivotal role to the naval hero, Griffin recognises what Kathleen Wilson calls 'Nelson's affective power'.¹⁵⁴ Blinded in one eye in the Mediterranean and wounded again at the Nile, Nelson's fame was marked by his suffering body, while his notorious affair with Lady Emma Hamilton earned him the distrust and moral suspicion in an increasingly religious Britain. The earliest memorials to Nelson's fame were erected in Scotland and Ireland: the first Nelson memorial is usually said to be that erected by ironworkers at Bonawe in Argyllshire, although a triumphal arch was erected by Sea Fencibles in Castletownshend in County Cork only days after the battle in 1805. Work began on Dublin's Nelson's Pillar in 1808.[155]

Meanwhile, uncertainty seeps through Dorgan's questions, and even Pennie's attempted defence is permeated by ideas of fantasy: 'It is all a dream, a wild, improbable, impossible story'.[156] When Kinchela relents and confesses, it is because of a dream he has in the cabin of his aged, devout and Irish-speaking mother, who hears him disclaiming guilt for the murder while sleeping. The interior of her mud-walled cabin is described in some detail, including a turf fire in which burns 'pieces of wreck',[157] a deal table and a rush-bottomed chair. Several pages are devoted to Kinchela's strange, agitated behaviour, including his shaking, sweaty body. When a rope frays and he finds himself hanging above a cave, 'suspended between the dreadful alternative of life and death', Kinchela is overcome by a 'cold shivering'.[158] Wintry weather not only inflicts discomfort upon individual characters in the novel but also possesses its own affective force, as the tale displays a marked interest in states of cold. The day on which Dorgan is to be hanged is 'as dreary as the occasion'; the atmosphere is further characterised by 'a thick mizzle which made the air dull and gloomy, and covered the trees and herbage with a hoar and dimly glittering moistures'.[159] A 'mantle of grey and eddying mist' mingles with the prevailing air of narrative uncertainty,[160] the soft weather calling up a contrast to what Maturin in *Melmoth* describes as the 'violence' of continental rainstorms and asking readers to recall details of Irish climactic conditions.[161]

Mary Favret suggests that the weather 'can serve as a forceful wartime medium, broadcasting the voices or at least the sounds of distant violence, carrying in its currents an audible, palpable sense of suffering elsewhere'.[162] When Dorgan's cell door opens and he is taken to be hanged, he feels 'a cold thrill shooting through all his limbs'.[163] There follows a brisk summary of the death sentence followed by a curiously prolonged scene of suspension between action and inaction. The narrative lingers over his state of apprehension and anxiety and on all the mechanics of death: handcuffs, halter and noose. Telling details include the costume of the blanketed hangman, the cars ('in English, carts') in which Dorgan, the clergyman and then the hangman are carried and the 'fatal tree' from which he will be hanged.[164] As the 'awful preparations' for death continue,[165] Dorgan insists on being hanged in his naval uniform. Often interpreted as belonging to a culture of Romantic-era display, military uniforms in Georgian

Britain staged 'a continuously theatricalized encounter with authority'.[166] 'Wartime becomes modern as it becomes spectacle', as Jerome Christensen puts it.[167] In the case of Griffin's story, however, the uniform serves as a painful marker of a misapprehended and confused self as it visualises the dilemma of a sailor turned criminal.

It is the figure of 'the Card-drawer, his evil prophet' who draws narrative attention to the uniform.[168] She seeks to interest some passing sailors in Dorgan's fate by plucking their blue uniform and pointing to the prisoner, similarly clothed. When they ignore the 'old and miserably attired woman', she sings a snatch from a ballad called 'The Sailor' (a variation on the 'Constant Lovers' ballad, known around the North Atlantic rim). Griffin uses the same ballad in 'The Aylmers of Bally Aylmer' where it is described as a 'popular doggrel [*sic*]' sung to a 'naval' audience in the town. The opening lines quoted in 'The Aylmers of Bally Aylmer' are familiar ones: 'A sailor courted a farmer's dater / Who lived convanient to the Isle of Man'.[169] The Card-Drawer sings a different, later stanza:

> An' as for sailors, I don't admire them –
> I wouldn't live as a sailor's bride,
> For in their coorten, they're still discoorsen,
> Of things consarnen the ocean wide.[170]

The sung lines find another register in which to express the everyday interpenetration of land, sea and ocean along Atlantic coasts.

The details of the execution itself are intimately rendered: the 'awful preparations' complete, Dorgan stands in a cart at the foot of the 'fatal tree', with erect body, heavy eyes and tied hands. The executioner, a 'ghost-like person' covered in a heavy blanket extends a 'bony and muscular hand' and addresses the prisoner in Irish, asking for his hand: 'Therom a lauv a gra bawn' (*Tuar dom a lámh a grá bán*), meaning 'give me your hand, my love', translated in the narrative simply as 'Forgive and Forget'. The executioner's role adds another dimension to the problem of killing as profession, as the attending priest points out when he advises the owner of cart in which Dorgan stands not to take on the moral responsibility for the hanging by moving his horse along and so effecting the death of the prisoner: 'Let the man who is engaged for the purpose be the shedder of the forfeited blood'.

As the protracted period of waiting for the execution plays out, Griffin explores forms of disorientation and division that illuminate the Irish aspect of a set of connections between the form of the novel and the emergence of modernity, especially where these converge upon the psychologisation of everyday life. The mechanism by which the mystery at the heart of this tale is unravelled relies on the workings of psychology and interior reflection, rather than on legal, political or other kinds of external forces. Kinchela confesses because of his nightmares, because of his mother, a devout Irish speaker, and because of his own conscience, which is in turn deeply informed by the religious beliefs with which he has been brought up. But rather than internalising the strictures of the state or the edicts of religion, Kinchela is instead powerfully affected by this intimate encounter, in his mother's cabin, with his own language and beliefs. Just as Irish Gothic of the Romantic period works via close associations with traditional forms of supernatural belief, rather than by enacting a clear break between past and present, so 'Card Drawing' imagines a form of interiority that is intimately associated with a culture still seeking a fuller expression in the English language. The figure of the Card-Drawer herself plays a part in this process by withholding elements of the culture that the narrative seems to want to depict. She remains nameless throughout the narrative and even Duke Dorgan does not always recognise her when she makes her uncanny appearances.

By the time *Tales of the Munster Festivals* was published in London, Griffin had already returned to Ireland, exhausted and alienated by a literary culture that he understood as interested only in the 'sickly sensibility' of the Lake Poets.[171] An unfinished tale of his imagines literature as a feminised world that has turned its back on the tough talents of Moore, Campbell, Scott and Byron in order to make a fuss about Shelley, Keats, Wordsworth and Tennyson. Griffin disliked the 'weakness', 'faintishness' and 'creeping' of poems that cultivated 'originality' above all, perhaps the lingering effects of an Irish romantic culture that began in manuscripts, chronicles, glosses and footnotes.[172] The terms of Griffin's criticism suggest knowledge as well as distaste – elsewhere he describes himself as writing for literary magazines under 'five hundred different signatures'.[173] His comments take in a wider cultural world of publically oriented forms of private feeling, often associated with women, and satirised by the Irish writer Lady Blessington in her poem, 'Stock-in-Trade of Modern Poetesses', which gives a knowing account of 'the stock-in-trade / With which a modern poem's made'.[174] When William Makepeace Thackeray described this gendered field, dominated by '*Books of Beauty*', annuals, albums and souvenirs, he listed off a set of watery terms for verses 'about water-lily, chilly, stilly, shivering beside a streamlet, plighted, blighted, love-benighted, falsehood sharper than a gimlet, lost affection, recollection, cut connexion, tears in torrents, true-love token, spoken, broken, sighing, dying, girl of Florence; and so on.'[175]

Jeremiah Joseph Callanan's Coastal Poetics

It can be difficult to draw lines of connection between this burgeoning world of popular British prints, alienating as Griffin found it, and the strong and continuing presence of a Gaelic manuscript tradition in Ireland. Meidhbhín Ní Úrdail has shown that 'literature in the Irish language continued to be transmitted and disseminated in manuscripts well into the second half of the nineteenth century', and other assessments concur as to the vitality of the manuscript as a literary mode, despite limits to circulation.[176] Much Irish language material was religious in nature with prominent clerics including Bishop John Murphy of Cork providing work for scribes, sometimes commissioned to produce handwritten copies of material in print and also to translate printed sources from English into Irish. In Nicholas Wolf's account, 'the single-largest genre represented in Irish-language manuscripts and printed works of the late eighteenth and early nineteenth centuries was devotional prose'.[177] Alongside this 'voluminous and varied' body of devotional writing in Irish could be found historical, legendary, grammatical and lexicographical material.[178]

Interconnections between print and manuscript register via shared visual conventions as well as crossovers in content. As access to printed books increased, some scribes began to break with inherited traditions of Irish manuscript decoration and look to the conventions of print for their *mise-en-page*. But the relationship works in the other direction also, as the learned Gaelic manuscript tradition permeates Anglophone print culture. The characteristic reliance on paratextual material so characteristic of Irish romantic novels harks back to manuscript traditions of glossing and annotation. Even in his most watery moments, Maturin, for instance, testifies to the imaginative power of manuscript material as creative resource as well as body of knowledge. Meanwhile, a growing collection of manuscripts were housed in Trinity College Dublin, Marsh's Library and the Royal Irish Academy, close by the home of the artist, antiquarian and Ordnance Survey Superintendent George Petrie on Great Charles Street. Petrie's private collection of manuscripts further informed the place-name research of his eleven-person team, including the Irish scholar Eugene O'Curry and the poet James Clarence Mangan (discussed in Chapter 3). Cóilín Parsons reminds us that the Survey aimed at the 'preservation' not only of culture as idea but also as repository of documents, including the manuscript sources discussed in Chapter 1.[179]

The Irish writer who best allows us to think about and explore overlaps between languages, culture and media by means of their watery co-ordinates is the poet Jeremiah Joseph Callanan (1795–1829). Born in Cork, Callanan moved through many of the professional routes open to Catholics in the period just before Emancipation. He went to Maynooth to study for the priesthood but left there in 1818 before going on to study medicine at Trinity College Dublin. At the College, he won the vice-chancellor's medal for a poem on the accession of George IV but withdrew from his studies due to lack of money. On return to Cork, Callanan enlisted in the 18th regiment, the Royal Irish, bound for Malta. Friends came to his aid, and he was bought out of the army at the Isle of Wight. Back in Cork, Callanan once more tried to establish himself as a writer. He spent brief periods teaching in schools in Carlow and Cork and some time travelling around West Cork, including Clonakilty, Skibbereen, Lough Hyne, Ballydehob and Mizen Head, gathering material for a projected collection of 'Munster Melodies'. Finally he took a post as a tutor for a Cork merchant family in Lisbon, only to die in Portugal from tuberculosis.

A precocious talent, Callanan is sometimes compared to the English writer Henry Kirke White, for whom he wrote 'The Lament of Kirke White'. The son of a Nottingham butcher, Kirke White's juvenile talent earned him the praise of Wordsworth and Coleridge. Described by Byron as 'Unhappy White!' on account of his early demise,[180] Kirke White in his turn wrote a poem about the death of Thomas Dermody, in which he fashions a juvenile voice in the image of the dead Irish writer. In that poem, Dermody's 'dying scream' echoes in Kirke White's ear,[181] but his own voice too is 'out of sequence', as Laurie Langbauer puts it, as he faces a death made fateful by artistic talent.[182] In 1809, Annabella Milbanke wrote some 'Lines Supposed to be Spoken at the Grave of Dermody', later sent by her cousin Caroline Lamb to Milbanke's future husband, Lord Byron. Callanan himself did not address a poem to Dermody (whose writing is discussed in Chapter 1) but regarded him as a great talent served only by a 'semi-barbarous education which opened the world to his enterprising spirit – but launched him on its Ocean without a Chart to save him from its rocks and shoals'.[183]

This network of imperilled juvenile talent helped Callanan – himself only thirteen years old when the first number of Moore's *Melodies* was published – to shape a distinctive voice that draws on the resources of nationally inflected sensibility but also makes its own time and place. In his painterly poem about Kirke White, Callanan imagines the young man on this death bed, with 'faded cheek' and 'pale clouded brow' presaging first his own demise and second that of the 'sybil leaves of song' spread around him: 'To think when he was gone they too must die'.[184] The elegy then invokes a third hurt, that experienced by Kirke White's lover, only to conjure up from these multiple losses the figure of a 'minstrel' who blends Irish and English voices and sounds a harp for 'Albin': 'O England, O my country, despite of all my wrongs, / I love thee still my native land, thou land of sweetest songs'.[185] Callanan often relies upon such a song- or poem-within-a-poem device in order to orchestrate modes of composition founded in contradiction and contest.

An invocation of England's poetic beauties that is sounded on a minstrel's harp, 'The Lament of Kirke White' not only rescues but manufactures the 'sybil leaves of song' for a future audience on both sides of the Irish Sea. Callanan knew well the difficulties of finding an audience for his work. A Cork connection, William Maginn, helped him get some translations from the Irish published as 'Irish Popular Songs' in *Blackwood's Magazine* in 1823. Six poems were published, prefaced by a short account in which Callanan sets aside 'ancient fame' in order to focus on 'the state of popular Irish poetry' in the present via his 'literary curiosities'.[186] That refusal of the living, learned tradition of Gaelic poetry, already admired by Owenson and elegised by Moore, was important for a poet who wished to break old moulds and shape new sounds. A year later, Thomas Crofton Croker praised a lament, 'The Dirge of O'Sullivan Bear', in his *Researches in the South of Ireland* (1824), and the translations as a whole remain celebrated for their ability to carry Irish sounds over into English verse, notably the case in his 'The Convict of Clonmell'. A slightly later poem, 'The Outlaw of Loch Lene', published in *Blackwood's* in 1828, is often described as his most accomplished translation, despite uncertainty as to its original source. The poem opens by varying a short plain statement with a long, loose line: 'O many a day I made good ale in the glen, / That came not of stream, or malt, like the brewing of men'.[187] Like others of Callanan's translations, 'The Outlaw of Loch Lene' uses internal assonance – what B. G. McCarthy calls 'ingenious vowel-weaving'[188] – to create densely patterned sounds whose effect depends on the spoken patterns of the Irish language and its metrical inflections.

Gregory Schirmer shows how Callanan's artistic choices were marked by divisions and oppositions which included contests with other writers and collectors.[189] In January 1827, Callanan told his friend John Windele, a gentleman antiquarian and collector based in Cork city, that he had 'made a great harvest in the Irish way'.[190] Yet the same letter mentions unease about London-based civil servant and antiquarian, Thomas Crofton Croker, who had previously asked Callanan to undertake paid work, collecting material on his behalf in Cork for a projected 'Minstrelsy of the

South of Ireland'. Crofton Croker already had access to English-language translations of Irish songs and poems from a number of sources, including a Cork woman named Mrs Harrington whose performances he recorded and translated. He praised her 'clearness, quickness, and elegance' and, when she died, enlisted the help of the woman who keened over her grave, Mrs Leary, who in her turn introduced the indefatigable collector to the 'land surveyor and philomath', Mr Murray.[191] Crofton Croker's *The Keen of the South of Ireland* (1844) records this network of names and ends with a mock request, effectively a reprise of the fake wake at the end of *Castle Rackrent*, that Mrs Leary extemporise a lament on Crofton Croker's own death. Agreeing once she received 'a couple of shillings', Mrs Leary improvised a lament that Crofton Croker, in his own account, 'took down as recited', 'translated with the greatest fidelity' and included as the last entry in *The Keen of the South of Ireland*.[192]

It is difficult to imagine Callanan complying with Crofton Croker's 'modest request'. Instead he told Crofton Croker that the 'vast number of Songs' he had collected along with 'abundant information on all subjects he mentioned' meant that he could only accept an invitation to contribute to the projected 'Minstrelsy of the South of Ireland' in a profit-sharing and collaborative role.[193] It is curious to read Callanan informing the more experienced folklorist that he was 'determined to act in a department where I should have few or no antagonists',[194] but he clearly suspected Crofton Croker's intentions and found himself trapped between creative ambitions and the work of collecting.

Callanan's planned book never materialised and publication remained a problem, not least because the Irish writer sought an outlet in the very years that spelled an end to prestigious poetry publishing.[195] The Hennessey Press in Cork advertised *Poems by Jeremiah Joseph Callanan* as a volume to be published by subscription in 1824, but Callanan withdrew from the arrangement, citing an unease with what was, by the 1820s, a dated model of publication via subscription. Patrons were still needed though and, with help from Maginn and Windele, a volume of Callanan's poems was published in London in 1829, though the poet himself had died in Lisbon just a few weeks earlier. A Cork edition of the poems, including a new memoir, was published in 1848 and 1861. The title poem of *The Recluse of Inchidony* (1829) voices the perspective of a refugee from 'the city's din' who finds sustenance on a sweep of sandy beach near the town of Clonakilty.[196] Scarcely any topographical detail emerges as the poem moves through devout references including an invocation of 'he of Nazareth' until a song is heard 'o'er ocean's sleep'.[197] Set apart from the rest of the poem's Spenserian stanzas, the 'Song' contains references to recognisable Munster place names that seem to float on the water as a ship prepares to embark 'on th'unbounded sea'.[198] The voice of a lost Gaelic minstrel fades away just as a call is heard to sing of the plight of modern Greece: 'That moment heard ye the despairing shriek / Of Missologhi's daughters?'[199] From that point onwards, more openly political references move back and forth between Ireland and Greece, bondage and freedom, and silence and speech. Callanan does not forget to invoke Ireland's service in overseas wars, including the Battle of Waterloo and the wielding of Irish 'steel in foreign fields'.[200]

As with Griffin, Callanan presses home the position of Irish men who could serve the British Army abroad but at home must suffer in a 'cot of mud where never sound has been / But groans of famine, and disease, and woe'.[201] And just as with Griffin, these conflicted claims find voice alongside the sea. Callanan, though, shows little of Griffin's intimate knowledge of the shore. Rather, the encounter is with a body of water made strange by the contradictions of empire and liberty: 'Is this the Atlantic that before me rolls / In its eternal freedom round thy shore?', asks the speaker of 'The Recluse of Inchidony'.[202] The poem ends, as the night gives way to dawn, with another religious reference – this time to the Virgin Mary, whose traditional association with the strand at Inchydoney (in modern spelling) is referenced again by Callanan in 'The Virgin Mary's Bank', along with place names including 'the far Seven-Heads' and the 'Wild voice of Desmond'.[203] To secure the poem's place on the map, the footnote that accompanies the reference to the Seven Heads names each of the distinctive headlands along the coast, all formerly containing castles or forts, as signalled by the Irish-language prefix 'dun' – 'Dundeedy, Dunowen, Dunore, Duneene, Dunoewig, Dunworly, and Dungorly'.[204] The poem does not though, despite its war-time context, take notice of the Napoleonic-era Seven Heads signal tower built in nearby Ballymacredmond around 1808.

Callanan insisted that 'The Recluse of Inchidony' was not an imitation of *Childe Harold*, and its confined location surely proves his point. But the shared use of Spenserian stanzas to illustrate the plight of a disillusioned young man meant that the connection was often made, including by W. B. Yeats. Callanan certainly forms part of a wider Irish romantic cult of Byron, connected to the latter's invocation of the plight of the 'Irish Helots' in *Childe Harold*.[205] As has been mentioned, not long before he died and some years after his speech in favour of Catholic Emancipation in the House of Lords, Byron could still describe himself in a letter to Thomas Moore as 'a professor of love for Ireland'.[206] Among the material gathered by Thomas Crofton Croker in his manuscript ballad history of Ireland is a version of *Childe Harold* written in the form of a 'Skellig List', a popular form of verse that arose in response to the Catholic Church's rules against marriage during the Lenten period. An exception to the rules was made for couples who could travel to Skellig Michael, an island monastery off the coast of Kerry, where Lent came late. The poems, popular in Cork and Kerry, where they circulated on broadsheets, listed names of men and women who should be ashamed of their single state, with jaunty rhymes and joking, often defamatory, references to known individuals. In the case of the anonymous Skellig poem titled 'Childe Harold', an epigraph is taken from Byron's poem, while another broadsheet collected by Crofton Croker has a ballad titled after Byron's drama, *Mazeppa*. The fusion of Byron's name and works with the scandalous form of the Skellig Lists and the carnival atmosphere associated with Shrove Tuesday suggests a popular romanticism on the move, absorbing and remaking literary references from across the sea. The continuing imprint of the Irish Byron can be glimpsed in *A Portrait of the Artist as a Young Man*, when Stephen Dedalus gets into a fight with a group of school bullies who insist that Byron is 'only a poet for uneducated people'.[207]

To date, discussion of what Matthew Campbell calls the 'improvised synthetic Irish-English lyric' effects of Callanan's translations has far outstripped engagement with his original English-language poetry.[208] Bernard O'Donoghue is unusual in arguing that Callanan's translations succeed not because they are 'native' or 'natural' (as claimed by readers from W. B. Yeats to Seamus Deane) but rather because he 'brought into English poetry formal qualities that are at once entirely foreign to it and totally successful within it'.[209] For O'Donoghue, the presence of such 'vernacular freedom' on the nineteenth-century page expressed aesthetic possibilities that 'remained a permanent option within English', a romantic legacy taken up by Samuel Ferguson and Yeats himself.[210] But to review that romantic legacy in any detail is to discover a body of writing whose meanings are hard to fix, divided as it is between poems of locality, calls to the spirit of nation and a small body of loyalist verse.

Immediately following 'The Recluse of Inchidony' in Callanan's *Poems*, for instance, comes 'Accession of George IV', a triumphalist poem that adopts the voice of a boatman on the river Thames in order to praise the new king and hymn the empire. The critic B. G. McCarthy, successor to Daniel Corkery as chair of English at University College Cork and inheritor of his cultural nationalist mantle, found the poem 'slavish' while an 1861 memoir of the poet describes a 'beautiful poem' that is 'drawn down into the abyss by its subject'.[211] The political contradictions of Callanan's writing, all of which run along and beside bodies of water, can be explored further in relation to 'Gougane Barra', a poem that also adopts a riverine setting to imagine what Callanan calls in his notebooks the 'whole range of mountains at that side of the County Cork' that served as a 'retreat of the Irish when driven from the lowlands by the flint hearted Saxons'.[212]

Bodies of water not only express but explain some of the contradictions in Callanan's writing, as he seeks to salvage an Irish-language tradition on the one hand and celebrate English freedoms on the other. A writer for whom '[w]ater and its movement were powerful symbols',[213] Callanan's poem 'Gougane Barra' uses river and sea to represent different cultural possibilities that open in a traditional place of pilgrimage and end on their intermingling on the shores of Cork Harbour. The poem is often admired for a 'vowel music'[214] that is dense in place names and topographical knowledge:

> There is a green island in lone Gougane Barra,
> Where Allua of songs rushes forth as an arrow;
> In deep-vallied Desmond – a thousand wild fountains
> Come down to that lake, from their home in the mountains.[215]

As Schirmer points out, the poem works through 'patterns of internal assonance falling on stressed syllables' with every line ending 'on a two-syllable word in which the first syllable is stressed and the second unstressed, a common enough practice in Irish-language poetry'.[216] But where such regular patterns of stressed and unstressed syllables might sound comic, Callanan's rhymes insist on bardic seriousness that is in part earned by the roll call of place names. Gougane Barra itself is an ancient place of pilgrimage, a dramatic and beautiful glacial valley that sits to the west of the Iveragh Peninsula ('Ivera' in the poem). The name of *Oileáin Cléire* or Cape Clear, Ireland's most southwesterly island and a place that often features in seventeenth- and eighteenth-century maps of the Atlantic world, is also invoked as a distant location that is inferior to the 'sweet spot' of Gougane Barra.[217]

Unlike 'The Lament of Kirke White' or 'The Recluse of Inchidony', 'Gougane Barra' does not rely on inset voices or fragments of song. Rather it achieves a joining of poetic voice and subject and seems to enjoy a measure of lyric confidence as it predicts a brighter future for both country and writer. Gougane Barra, the source of the River Lee, is precious because it is removed from Callanan's 'home by the ocean', representing not only a generalised solitude but an estuarine retreat from a coastline inevitably associated with empire.²¹⁸ The final image is of a future 'Minstrel' visiting the poet's grave in a place 'Where calm Avon Buee seeks the kisses of ocean'.²¹⁹ Schirmer remarks that it seems strange that the poem does not follow the River Lee on its path to the city of Cork, instead following a different fluvial route to imagine the *Abhainn Buí* or the yellow river (anglicised as Owenboy or Owenbue), described elsewhere by Callanan as a river that 'falls into the sea at Carrigaline, the birth place of my family'.²²⁰ A small settlement on an estuary that flows into Cork Harbour, Carrigaline was a prosperous harbour town connected to Cork Harbour via a navigable river surrounded by new mills and fertile land. By taking the river on this route, the poem leaves behind Gougane Barra in the deep west and creates a literary geography that is bounded by the entrance to an imperial Atlantic. Even the wild freedom of Gougane Barra is realised via the image of a 'time-stricken willow' whose meanings are framed by the ocean: the willow must look 'chidingly down on the mirth of the billow' though those waves are many miles from its sheltered inland location.²²¹

The noun 'billow' tells its own story. A term for the swell on the sea created by the wind, 'billow' originates in and belongs to the early modern writing of empire before its later adoption as a poetic term for the sea's movement. Early *OED* examples come from Richard Hakluyt and Walter Raleigh, and we find a telling use of this archaism in Callanan's literary notebooks from the 1820s, in which a draft note for a West Cork poem reads 'the billows are humming their slogan of war'.²²² Charles Wolfe used the term too in his popular patriotic poem 'The Burial of Sir John Moore'. Famous for its depiction of stoic British heroism on the Iberian Peninsula and admired by Byron, the poem was written by an Irishman, the Kildare Anglican clergyman Charles Wolfe, for John Moore, the Scottish soldier who had served in the West Indies before being promoted to major-general in Ireland in 1798.²²³ Wolfe was with John Moore when he died in a Spanish port as the Peninsular War came to an end, and his elegy was first published in *Carrick's Morning Post* in Dublin in 1815 before appearing in London papers, including *Blackwood's Magazine* (June 1817). Despite differences in their subjects, 'The Burial of Sir John Moore' borrows from Thomas Moore's 'Oh Breathe not his Name!' a distinct romantic interest in silence and shade. What might sound like masculine imperial restraint in the first stanza ('Not a drum was heard, nor a funeral note, / As his corse to the rampart we hurried') becomes, by the poem's end, a refusal to mourn that whispers its own quiet connections to Robert Emmet and his revolutionary refusal of an epitaph: 'We carved not a line, we raised not a stone, / But we left him alone with his glory.'²²⁴ Wolfe's poem uses

Callanan's word, 'billow', in closing lines that sound a distinctly Hiberno-Irish register in their reversal of verb and subject:

> We thought, as we hallowed his narrow bed,
>   And smoothed down his lonely pillow,
> That the foe and the stranger would tread o'er his head,
>   And we far away on the billow.²²⁵

In Benedict Anderson's reading, 'The Burial of Sir John Moore' (which he describes as a poem written by one Irishman for another) enacts both the 'closed' and 'open' aspects of nationalism, addressing a confined community of mourning that defines itself by '*historical* fatality' but relies on rhythms that invite a wider audience.²²⁶ Perhaps Thomas Davis caught this contradictory note when he adopted a phrase of Wolfe's, 'racy of our soil', as the epigraph to the first issue of *The Nation*.²²⁷

For Callanan, though, it is not so much the specificities of soil as the sound of a newly charted sea that captures his imagination. In his unpublished 'Songs of the Gaskinane', Callanan tries to find in the body of water between Cape Clear and Inisherkin a portion of the wild Atlantic where freedom flourishes. Cape Clear, off the far southwesterly coast of Ireland, features on many maps of the Atlantic world and was still in this period an Irish-speaking island. Súnta an Ghaisceanáin, the Gaskinane or Gascanane Sound between Cape Clear and Sherkin Island, is said to be named for the thirteenth-century merchant Amhlaoibh Gascúnach, who 'received his nickname, "the Gascon", because of his training in the vineyards of that French province'.²²⁸ Currents run at high speed in this area, making it dangerous for navigation and treacherous in bad weather, when waves of up to ten metres high course through the channels between the offshore reefs. Cape Clear tradition has it that visitors to the island should compose a verse to quell these waters, to be recited aloud during the crossing. Callanan's short 'intended' poems include one that hails the 'Sprit of the Gaskinane / Wildest Sprit of the main', asking it to 'Guide my bark & bring her free / From thy dark stormy sea'. The draft breaks off on the word 'Billows'.²²⁹

Callanan's 'Songs of the Gaskinane' offer a glimpse into a world where Irish legends and the English language meet on the manuscript page, even as the poet's eye was fixed on print and London publishing. The balance of power clearly favoured English, understood not only to be the language of literacy but of literature itself. A note among Callanan's manuscripts, dated Easter Sunday 1829, records both a nagging sense of insufficiency and an emerging popular romanticism even as it works towards a definition of

Irish literature: 'Irish Literature – The L^{re} which flows from the rude mass of the people can never be good. May show some Genius. It is with the upper and more civilized classes it must originate to be good. It was not the case in Ireland.'[230]

Callanan's comments imagine a body of writing that tries to find a place between ordinary life and the potential 'Genius' of the place. In the same manuscript notes, Callanan speculates that the Irish language may be 'an obstacle to the improvement of the people'.[231] These manuscripts, largely written in English with some notes in Irish and in Latin, were gathered by the antiquarian John Windele following Callanan's untimely death in Lisbon in 1829. The *Literary Remains of J. J. Callanan* include scattered observations on literature, aesthetics and history, prayers and hymns, botanical notes, historical legends, letters to friends and recollections of Callanan's time in Maynooth Seminary. The notes often circle back to the question of Ireland and its culture, expressed in the self-questioning or contradictory style suggested previously. As a record of the thoughts and literary aspirations of a talented but thwarted young man, these *Literary Remains* offer a unique account of Irish romantic culture before the Famine. But Callanan's reputation remains that of a man whose life 'has only the quality of water': 'colourless, shapeless, fluid, incalculable'.[232] The writer William Carleton was also associated with the legendary instability of water. Chapter 3 explores his role alongside those of Maria Edgeworth and James Clarence Mangan in the context of a riven period of Irish romanticism that saw a brief cultural renaissance fall away in the face of the horrific changes wrought by the Great Famine.

CHAPTER 3

Darkening Skies, 1830–1850

When Catholic Emancipation passed into law in 1829, it promised an era of reform for Ireland and Britain, as the imperial state extended its influence over a growing population. The people had grown not only in number but in power and discontent, while their agitation was made worse by an irresponsible landlord class. As the military engineer, former Ordnance Survey man and later census commissioner and Under-Secretary for Ireland Thomas Larcom put it, 'thirty years ago the problem of government in Ireland was to govern a million people who governed the other six million. When they were emancipated the problem was to govern the seven million and the local machinery having been destroyed, to do so by the direct action of the executive.'[1] Many of the new 'direct action' measures seemed to promise a fuller Union, as in the assimilation of the Irish currency into sterling in 1826 or the establishment of a national primary education system from 1831. But the data collected by a centralising state efforts meant a much fuller reckoning with Irish life, suggestive of the democratisation to come. From 1838, for instance, ratepayers could vote for boards of guardians for the new Poor Law unions. Meanwhile Ordnance Survey maps facilitated the full census of 1841 and were used to mark out official boundaries for poor relief and an emerging public health infrastructure. The cultural consequences of these efforts at calculation result in a romantic realism that draws Ireland in dark and shaded hues, compelled to seek out fuller contours no matter how negative.

The Geological Survey of the island too, working northward from Hook Head in Wexford, saw new information overlaid on the six inch maps. Griffith's Valuation followed in 1855, an attempt at a full cadastral survey of Irish land. Lines of rail were constructed from the 1830s – surveyors following in the footsteps of the engineers – and travellers found themselves 'blinded and stunned by being whirled through cuttings' as they crossed a raw, newly engineered landscape.[2] But despite growing access to British markets, the majority of Irish agricultural products were still consumed at home, where about two-fifths of the population survived on a subsistence diet of potatoes. English, now the sole language of educational instruction, made slow and uneven progress across the country. When cholera came in 1831, following an earlier outbreak in 1817, it made 'fearful strides among the filthy dens of the wretched lower orders', as Lady Morgan put it.[3] Those 'lower orders' were soon telling their own story thanks to Daniel O'Connell's mass mobilisation and played a part, too, in the small-scale Young Ireland rebellion of 1848.

For Thomas Carlyle, Catholic Emancipation had already made a new world: 'Those things seemed fixed and immovable – deep as the foundations of the world; and lo! in a moment they have vanished, and their place knows them no more!'[4] Larcom also thought of the 1830s and early 1840s in terms of novelty and innovation, writing that 'the experiment in Ireland was to give reality to emancipation'.[5] Irish writing certainly gives powerful expression to ideas of change in this period, notably so in journalism and within lyric poems that shared space with radical predictions of future promise. But for ordinary Irish people, the 1830s might have felt rather more like a phase in a longer period of change underway since 1798 and its aftermath, part of the fading of revolutionary hope across Europe, confounded by the post-Waterloo economic downturn. A growing cattle economy with improved access to markets thanks to the railroads meant economic benefits for the few and vagrancy for the many, as Peter Hession explains when he describes how 'the replacement of humans by livestock through the progress of cattle capitalism in Ireland was destined not only to thin out the countryside but to bulk up a "middle class in Ireland"'.[6] When William Carleton penned his account of these shifts in 1841, it was to describe a rising generation who scarcely knew the world of their parents: 'The state of Irish society has changed so rapidly within the last thirty or forty years, that scarcely any one could believe it possible for the present generation to be looked upon in many things as the descendants of that which has immediately gone before them.' The loss of the old world was all the worse, Carleton wrote, for being irrecoverable within familiar cultural codes – 'scarcely a vestige of them will be left even to tradition itself' – though his own fictions belie that diagnosis in their search for new modes.[7] A far greater change was nonetheless in prospect. From 1845, the cultural guillotine of the Great Famine (*An Gorta Mór*) fell sharply on lives, language and landscape, meaning that this book ends on years characterised by human tragedy, political catastrophe and ecological disaster.

The transformations wrought by the Great Famine (1845–52), and its standing as a historical watershed, mean that Irish literature is normally divided into pre- and post-Famine phases. Irish literary history is further scarred by the ultimate success of a body of cultural nationalist writing that sought to invent 'a vernacular history that was romantic, heroic, and teleological'.[8] As with the revivalists that followed, the writers of the 1840s disavowed much of the literature that came before them. The editorialist and later convict and pro-slavery writer, John Mitchel, spelled out the stakes in *The Nation* in August 1847 in an article titled 'On the Individuality of a Native Literature'. Writing as deaths from disease rose, Mitchel observed that Ireland had numerous authors, some 'of the highest order', but 'no literature – in its widest sense – that we can call our own distinctly'. Oliver Goldsmith is dismissed as either 'cosmopolitan' or 'English'; Moore, along with Callanan and Banim, is 'not *nationally* Irish'; while Richard Brinsley Sheridan and Edmund Burke 'are not Irish in any exact sense'. The giant names of Griffin, Carleton and Davis 'have arisen' but the country cannot yet credit itself 'with the possession of a literature'. Neither Edgeworth nor Owenson are even mentioned, nor are any of the women poets who graced the pages of *The Nation* each fortnight named.[9] The same year in which Mitchel's call for works 'bearing marks of nationality' went up saw the publication of Charlotte Brontë's *Jane Eyre* and Emily Brontë's *Wuthering Heights*, novels written by the daughters of the County Down-born clergyman Patrick Prunty, who is discussed in Chapter 1. The character of Heathcliff has been read as 'a fragment of the Great Famine' while Jane Eyre's proposal from Rochester comes only after the threat of a hideous new position caring for the 'five daughters of Mrs. Dionysius O'Gall of Bitternutt Lodge, Connaught' fades from view. The Irish sea itself, 'that boisterous Channel', expresses the complex 'cord of communion' that connects Jane and Rochester; soon, in 1854, Charlotte Brontë was herself to cross those waters to honeymoon in Kilkee, County Clare, a place whose distinctive coastal topography is discussed in Chapter 2.[10]

But there is no clearly conceptualised body Irish Victorian literature into which we can integrate the writing of 1830s and 1840s; rather, the period can be thought of as a 'transition state'.[11] Romanticism though retains more than a provisional hold on these decades, whether as dark responses to reformist politics or nationalist calls for change in the name of a distinct culture. And as Anahid Nersessian observes, the case of Ireland calls for an 'extension of Romanticism into the nineteenth century' that allows not only for Irish experiences 'to be counted among the pressures on the Romantic imagination' but also 'makes way for a new, expansively ecological reading of Romanticism bookended on its later end by the Great Famine of the mid- to late 1840s'.[12] Adopting the environmental and epidemiological disaster of the Great Famine as a literary endpoint makes for a final phase of Irish romanticism that is riven by change, loss and catastrophe.

Yet during the key transitional decade, the 1830s, Dublin saw a short-lived cultural renaissance, as a publishing industry re-emerged in the second city of the empire. Newspapers and journals grew in number from 1830 to the mid-1840s while steam press printing became more common. Elizabeth Tilley describes 'an explosion of new titles, though the lifespan of most of them was still no more than a year'.[13] Matthew Campbell describes the 1830s and early 1840s as a period of 'extraordinary, if bitterly short-lived, renaissance of Irish nationalist culture'.[14] Most successful in terms of readership and influence was *The Nation*, which began in 1842 as a weekly newspaper tied to the cause of Repeal and was soon closely allied with the politics of the Young Irelanders. Young Ireland, like similar movements across Europe in the 1840s, voiced the opinion of middle-class and elite intellectuals with an appetite for change. Its founders broke with O'Connell in order to press the case for an Irish independent legislature, with Charles Gavan Duffy, former editor of the bi-weekly Belfast *Vindicator*, convicted for sedition in 1844. Soon, with the death of Thomas Davis, the militant journalist John Mitchel was named as the journal's leader writer, and the break with O'Connell's more conciliatory and constitutional politics was complete. Just thirty years old when he died of scarlatina, Davis was buried as potato blight began to spread in the autumn of 1845.

The other main literary organ of the period professed a different politics to those of *The Nation*, although both journals originated with meetings in Trinity College Dublin and shared talent. Founded as part of an Irish unionist reaction to Emancipation and Reform and unofficially allied to Trinity College, the *Dublin University Magazine* occupied a distinctive cultural space in mid-nineteenth-century Ireland. Its overall tone was gloomy and pessimistic, expressive of failed Tory hopes in the face of Whig reforms. Even as it decried moves towards weakening of the Union and reform of the established position of the Church of Ireland, however, the *Dublin University Magazine* also published original Irish fiction and poetry by writers including James Clarence Mangan, Charles Lever and Samuel Ferguson. When Lever took on the editorship of the journal in 1842, he called on Irish writers – 'the acknowledged staff of periodical literature in England' – to 'unite' in a literary enterprise that would bring to Ireland 'the same proud position in public estimation, that Scotsmen have won for their magazine before the eyes of Great Britain'.[15] The reference to *Blackwood's Edinburgh Magazine* and to Scotland spells out the unionist impetus of this call to Irish talent, but the diffuse and extensive cultural ambitions of the period meant that writers like William Carleton and James Clarence Mangan could move freely between the *Dublin University Magazine* and *The Nation*. In the traumatic aftermath of the Great Famine, however, what had been a broad coalition of conservative and national interests in the politically and culturally fluid years of the 1830s and early 1840s fell asunder.

Before divisions hardened and alliances narrowed, the exploration of Irish life proceeded on a broad front, aligned to what Paul Hamilton describes as the 'naturally interdisciplinary' nature of European romanticism from the 1830s onwards.[16] Forms of state-sponsored enquiry into the conditions of Irish life became more and more common after the brief post-Waterloo period that included the Year without a Summer and the Rockite rebellion in the south and west (1817–22). From the 1820s to the 1840s, Ireland was mapped, described and counted across successive state-led exercises, all of which involved a growing body of employees and a developing information infrastructure. Efforts by the colonial state to explain Ireland included select committees, surveys, government reports and the Poor Inquiry of 1833–6, amounting to a voluminous official print culture which Niall Ó Ciosáin has analysed in terms of its capacity to shape opinion and structure debate. Ó Ciosáin finds further parallels between state documentation and the emerging conventions of realism, with travel literature existing as a 'third genre' of explanation alongside reports and novels.[17]

Nor did those efforts end with the island of Ireland, as people and methods moved across the empire. The Abolition of Slavery Act passed into law in 1833 with many of the compensations to British and Irish plantation owners overseen by Lord Sligo, Governor General of Jamaica and the Cayman Islands. An old school friend of Thomas De Quincy, Lord Sligo was himself handsomely compensated for his two plantations, Kelly's Pen and Cocoa Walk, inherited from his Galway grandmother, whose father had been Chief Justice of Jamaica. Looking east, Nessa Cronin has tracked 'transnational points of contact' between the Irish Ordnance Survey and the Great Trigonometrical Survey of India, starting with George Everest's visit to Thomas Colby in Lough Foyle in the 1820s and his later modification of the instrumentation used in Ireland for India. Such imperial connections were not confined to elite circles: some 48 per cent of United Kingdom recruits to the Bengal army between 1825 and 1850 were Irish.[18]

Maria Edgeworth's youngest brother, Michael Pakenham Edgeworth (1812–1881), educated at Charterhouse and Edinburgh University, joined the East India Company in 1831, serving at Ambala, Muzaffarnagar and at Saharanpur before being appointed as a commissioner for the settlement of the Punjab in the 1850s. His botanical researches in North Africa and Egypt ensured that the family name survives across several plant species, but it is as the recipient of a letter from his sister in February 1834 that Michael Pakenham Edgeworth is best remembered in literary history. The letter is full of news about birds, trees and plants while many of its details point to the great arrival of non-native seeds and packaged hardy plants into Ireland and Britain from about 1830. Explaining the novel sight of a starling murmuration, Maria Edgeworth says that she and her sister Sophy 'would have given a crown imperial' – a beautiful flower native to Turkey, Iraq and Iran, now imported into European gardens but still scarce – for their brother to have seen the birds in formation. Edgeworth admires her brother's botanising, remarking on 'the new kingdoms of flowers' that remain for him to 'subdue' while also thanking him for his 'good observations on the state of your part of India'. Though the letter opens on plants and political economy, much of its remainder is occupied with Edgeworth's account of a journey into Connemara, a place newly accessible to tourists in the early 1830s because of roads and harbours laid out by the Scottish engineer Alexander Nimmo with some assistance from Edgeworth's other brother William.

Though Edgeworth undertook the trip west full of interest in 'the wonderful ways of going on and manners of the natives', she explains to her brother that her latest novel, *Helen* will not yield Irish material.[19] She warns her brother Pakenham that he is not likely to see the book, published that January, for at least a year but when it does arrive, he is to expect little of Irish life in its pages:

> It is impossible to draw Ireland as she now is in a book of fiction – realities are too strong, party passions are too violent to bear to see, or care to look at their faces in the looking-glass. The people would only break the glass and curse the fool who held the mirror up to nature – distorted nature, in a fever.[20]

The warning sounds a strange note amidst a letter full of lively detail about inns, fishing, fairies, muddy roads and marble quarries. But even the negative reference to *Helen* brings into focus a buoyant cultural moment during which Irish novelists began to take steps towards novels of the distant Irish past, especially in the decade following the death of Walter Scott in 1832. Edgeworth grasped the significance of this moment even if she did not herself contribute to the new Irish fiction. In her account of Connemara in 1834, she offered her brother Pakenham 'one anecdote which will show you how like the stories in Walter Scott are the scenes that have been lately passing in Connemara'.[21] The 'scenes' to which Edgeworth refers are the result of a rural revolt led by a group known as the Terry-Alts. Beginning in County Clare and spreading north and west, the Terry-Alts responded to heavy rains, ruined harvests and food scarcity with organised and communal acts of resistance that often took inspiration from parliamentary campaigns for Catholic candidates and mixed violent with non-violent acts.[22]

Edgeworth's reference to 'the glass' in which Ireland might be reflected may call up the classical tag, *veluti in speculum* (as in a mirror), used by Francis Bond Head to pitch a travel book about Ireland to the publisher John Murray.[23] Or it may catch the imprint of new media technologies, including the panoramas, dioramas and cosmoramas that fascinated London audiences from the 1820s onwards. Such spectacles were known to Edgeworth: *Helen* features a reference to 'those dioramic prints which appear all a confusion of lines till you look at them in their right point of view'.[24] Yet Edgeworth may also have been thinking of a rather less novel spectacle, that of the stage Irishman. Her letter to her brother explicitly links the difficulty of capturing Ireland in contemporary fiction to an established line of humorous representation of the Irish, judged by her to be untimely and inappropriate: 'We are in too perilous a case to laugh, humour would be out of season, worse than bad taste.'[25] She goes on to quote Walter Scott, who asked if Edgeworth could 'explain to the public why Pat, who gets forward so well in other countries, is so miserable in his own'.[26] Edgeworth likely would have thought of the question as a complex one in terms of political economy, though the offhand nature of Scott's reference to emigration sits oddly with her comment that the question is a 'very difficult' one. She offers up instead her considerable powers of observation: 'But I shall think of it continually, and listen, and look, and read'.[27]

Edgeworth's remarks vividly realise the impact of imperial networks, including the arrival of cholera from India to Britain and Ireland in 1831 and the spread of fever. She invites us to think about the ways in which fictional textures are thickened by an encounter with unfolding realities of Irish life. But even as she registers the sheer scale of population growth and the phenomenon of popular political activity on the island, she also gives us the singular image of Scott's 'Pat', who stands in for centuries of stereotypical stage Irishmen. Part of the power of O'Connellite mass mobilisation was to put pressure on representations of curious individual characters, stage Irishmen included. In 1831, an *Edinburgh Review* article on new Irish novels remarked that, while amusing characters had trod the stage since the eighteenth century, 'we never saw the Irish grouped'. Hailing a selection of new Irish novels – the Banim brothers' *The Croppy: A Tale of 1798*, John Banim's *The Denounced*, Eyre Evans Crowe's *Yesterday in Ireland* and Gerald Griffin's *The Collegians* and *The Rivals* – the reviewer welcomed a body of work that 'made *them* natural, and *us* comparatively strange and foreign'.[28]

This final chapter tracks some of the ways in which Ireland came to seem 'natural' by the numbers, tracking the aesthetic imprints of the kinds of counting, measurement and quantification made possible by a vanishing population and a growing information infrastructure. A voluminously described Ireland meant the emergence of a romantic realism that depicted Irish life as ordinary but marked: everyday, but not so commonplace as to be taken for granted or pass into unmediated existence. Many Irish writers shared a set of realistic ambitions characterised by a reach for moderation in terms of style. But they were driven also by an urgent appetite for experience that involved reliance on modes including folklore, journalism, romance and sensation. Lady Morgan describes these countervailing but related tendencies in terms of 'facts' versus 'images', or the tonal effects generated when 'statistics' contrast with 'picturesque and moral groupings'.[29] Such contrasts are threaded through the works discussed in this chapter.

Poetry as well as fiction expressed this search after truths founded in observation alongside the intimate experience of social, cultural and technological change. A County Clare poet named William Downes addressed a poem to Charles Wye Williams (1779–1866), the shipping magnate and inventor who became managing director of the first steam cargo service between Dublin and London, and whose boats plied the Shannon. Steam power provides Downes with the ultimate example of a real world contemporary spectacle, one that could be observed on the River Shannon, the Irish sea or the Atlantic. From the 1820s, the sight of steam-powered boats on Irish and British coasts, rivers and lakes meant that fossil fuels came out from the factories and penetrated 'deeply into rural ecologies', calling up new modes of representation.[30] Steam, according to Downes, surpasses even the achievements of Archimedes and his 'superhuman skill' of leverage: 'But what we *read* – not always is as true; / As what, (in modern days) we chance to view.'[31]

Downes' sense of the primacy of technological scenes observed over old books read does not pass over the extent to which the search after authentic Irish experiences met and merged with a wider culture of celebrity authorship. Downes, who published his first book of verse in Limerick via subscription, wrote for *The Nation* and published a book of *Temperance Melodies*, anti-drinking songs. The latter collection put poetry to the service of the popular abstinence movement led by Father Theobald Matthew in Cork as Downes crafted new lyrics to accompany airs from Moore's *Melodies* (including 'Away, away with the Poison'd Draught' to the tune of 'The Minstrel Boy'). Annexed to the temperance movement, Moore's lyrics might be seen to shed the Anacreontic atmosphere of the earliest poems along with the Regency licentiousness associated with the *Melodies*. And Moore himself seems to have authorised this moderated romanticism as it was remade by at least some of the new generation. His return to Dublin in 1835 was celebrated by the establishment and a statue in his honour was erected in 1857. In a letter that Downes received (and published) in 1842, Moore graciously gave the younger man his imprimatur, clear that his own bardic signature belonged quite properly alongside those bringing change to Irish society. Few things were more flattering, Moore wrote, than a story heard 'from a country-woman of ours the other day, that not long since, at a bazaar held somewhere in America for the relief of the black slaves, the autographs that bought the best prices were O'Connell's, Father Mathew's and those of my humble self'.[32]

The chapter traces a wider interest in the tactility and texture of the past via the case of Maria Edgeworth's *Helen*, a novel written by the busy head of a household who moved back and forth between estate rent books, accounts and her 'little' author's desk. In the process, Edgeworth produced literary fiction shaped by what her stepmother called 'the hard realities of life'.[33] Absorbed as it is by contemporary England and a prosperous literary culture, *Helen* nonetheless shares with other Irish writing of the period a darkness of tone that pervades even the happy atmosphere of Catholic Emancipation and prefigures disaster to come. The novel opens with Helen's 'bright' future cast into 'desolation and dismay' and sees its heroine move precariously through protracted episodes of fear, illness and disappointment before a painful arrival at her hard-won happy conclusion.[34] Darkness suffuses the work of William Carleton, whose writings immerse the reader in a known world of Irish experience, rendering rural Ireland in dense linguistic and cultural detail. At the same time, Carleton tries to thin out the medium in order to render the ordinariness of the world, as evident in his playful complaint about the need to attach introductory materials to his prose: 'It is to be wished that Prefaces were abolished', he writes in the preface to the first edition of *Traits and Stories of the Irish Peasantry*, 'there is something particularly Irish about them'.[35] His footnotes, gathered at the end of the third volume of the *Traits*, might be better 'printed in a separate pamphlet', he muses. Neither, he thinks, are dedications to lofty individuals necessary in 'the present times': 'The Public is the only Great Man at present, whose patronage is worth anything to a writer'.[36] This intense consciousness of people, place and time – the public, Ireland, the present moment – is both heightened and transcended in the work of James Clarence Mangan, who brings to Irish romantic writing a charged awareness of change as abstract force. By the time the poem discussed later, 'Lament over the Ruins of the Abbey of Teach Molaga', appeared in *The Nation* in August 1846, Ireland was facing into a winter of death from starvation and disease. Rather than social realism, though, Mangan imagines environmental change on a grand scale, as an estuary bears witness to a violent history. That sense of the scale and significance of Irish problems finds a 'scorching' spokesperson in Thomas Carlyle, whose London meeting with the editor of *The Nation* Charles Gavan Duffy was 'a key moment in the history of Irish Romanticism', as R. F. Foster has shown.[37]

Population, Politics and Reform

Mary Shelley's *The Last Man* (1826) imagines Ireland as a teeming, overflowing island whose people are an easy prey for infection – a stark vision of the people in aggregate, made possible by a plague plot and a vanishing population. When Americans flee the global plague imagined in *The Last Man*, feeling the dire effects of its second winter, they cross first to Ireland and crowd into its western seaports. There they feast on 'superabundant' food and seize stray cattle but soon rouse 'the fiery nature of the Irish'.[38] A ragged, lawless transatlantic band assembles, some travelling as far north as Belfast in order to take the short sea crossing followed by the long road to London. While the Americans are briefly described as coming from a 'populous continent', the Irish are ever present in their excess: 'disorganized multitudes', 'unnatural numbers', a 'locust visitation'.[39] The rebellious Irish and their American allies roam the land, moving south through Britain, talking of 'taking London, conquering England – calling to mind the long details of injuries which had for many years been forgotten'.[40] In turn, terrible rumours about the foreign hordes circulate in England, and Shelley reminds her readers of the ways in which communities make monsters of outsiders and migrants at times of crisis. She takes care to rescue the hordes of Irish vagrants from their likely fate at the hands of the organised English troops. As kindness prevails and hatred dissolves, both sides reckon with their shared vulnerability to the plague. The Irish are 'quartered in deserted villages' or returned to their own island as Shelley echoes Oliver Goldsmith's poem: 'the country blooms – a garden and a grave'.[41]

To gardens and graves we can add seas and coasts, as discussed in Chapter 2. Herself a practitioner of 'aquatic Romanticism',[42] Mary Shelley had already pursued her interests in the theory and politics of population in *Frankenstein* (1818), in which she sends Victor Frankenstein on his unlikely sea journey west from the Orkneys to Ireland in search of the creature.[43] Treated in fairly scant detail, Ireland surely earns its place in Shelley's famous fiction because of its prominent place in the problem of population as debated by Thomas Malthus and her father, William Godwin. After the Famine, William Carleton remarked that the Irish landlords had created a monster in their cultivation of a class of subdivided tenant farmers (the forty shilling freeholders) to do their bidding. Now disenfranchised in the aftermath of Catholic Emancipation, these forty shilling freeholders represent an evil, Carleton said, that 'Like Frankenstein in the novel … pursues them to the present moment, and must be satisfied or appeased in some way, or it will unquestionably destroy them.'[44] These images of a ragged population coming to ugly life suggest the lasting influence of Malthus, who died in 1834 but whose ideas lived on: if few of the witnesses to the Poor Law Inquiry used his name, his language proved pervasive.[45] A matter of domestic jokes as well as imperial politics, Malthus' theories were stitched into the texture of everyday Irish life, as when Sir Charles Morgan expressed concern for the health of his sister-in-law Olivia Clarke (*née* Owenson) following childbirth: he begged her to reflect upon further 'frolics' and to 'take the pains to read three thick volumes of Malthus on Population'.[46] Irish newspapers regularly made 'humorous' and 'deprecating' references to Malthus, and in 1839 the Repeal politician John O'Hagan crowed over an increase in the Catholic population of Ulster, which was 'enough to madden Miss Martineau, and make Malthus shiver in his grave'.[47]

Harriet Martineau herself, though, was soon defending rule by the majority, at least in America. When Maria Edgeworth read Martineau's *Society in America* (1837), she wrote to her friend Rachel Mordecai Lazarus in Virginia and expressed serious doubts regarding any system of representative government: 'But the point still to be proved, still to be enquired into, is whether the majority of *numbers* necessarily includes the majority of sense, judgment, moral feeling, and all that should form the legislative and governing preponderance in any nation'.[48] Edgeworth remained preoccupied with the question of numbers in relation to the 'moral feeling' of the people and their capacity for self-government. She met Malthus on a number of occasions, during visits to England. Admiring his principles and in agreement with many of his views on the poor, Edgeworth nonetheless confessed to mild shame in being disturbed by Malthus' appearance and 'snuffly' speech (he was born with a hare lip and a cleft palate). She saw him in the early months of a long visit to England from October 1830 to July 1831, writing to her stepmother of her admiration for the great man, in spite of his 'uncouth mouth and horrid voice'.[49]

At the outset of that trip, freshly arrived from the Liverpool boat and delighting in speedy rail travel, Edgeworth wrote home to Longford to share her delight in travelling through 'rich clean looking England'.[50] Yet despite her pleasure in these orderly landscapes, Edgeworth was soon reassuring relatives concerned about the Swing Riots in Kent (home to her brother Sneyd) and reporting what she heard of risings, revolutions and agitations as well as the spread of cholera. Edgeworth's farewell words are shaded by fear of popular protest: 'Wonderful England! With all your industry and all your prosperity I hope you will not be revolutionised – especially in our time. Après nous le deluge.'[51] Reacting to popular change, she adopts a Burkean language of post-revolutionary lament that, as Clíona Ó Gallchoir observes, 'sounds a very new note in Edgeworth's writing'.[52]

That note is sounded amidst a letter that recounts details of a journey from London to Birmingham, written as Edgeworth makes her way to Liverpool and the boat home, and full of brisk detail about travel. England is 'wonderful', wrote Edgeworth, because 'coaches are passing almost every hour', though in fact she had some difficulty in figuring out her booking as similarly named vehicles sped past. Finally 'hoisted' onto a coach along with her 'bag and baggage', she describes to her sister Fanny the company she kept: 'Vulgar gin-drinking man in coach with glazed eyes and hiccup', 'A very decent half lady farmers wife silent woman' and 'a very civil Birmingham man'. Stopping to eat, Edgeworth records 'lamb that was anything but tender' along with 'Stewed ducks and cabbage which all the company of 8 men, I could not say gentlemen were so eager to be helped to that I would not interfere'.[53]

Changing technologies of communication and transport afforded Edgeworth new, close-up perspectives on what Richard Menke calls the 'data of real life'.[54] At the same time, Thomas Davis and his colleagues at *The Nation* set about sorting through and lending shape to the materials of Irish history, their attention trained on the past. In 1843, for instance, Davis published a series of articles in the Whig journal *The Citizen* that recounted the history of the Irish parliament of 1689 while John Mitchel published a biography of Hugh O'Neill, Earl of Tyrone and leader of resistance to the Elizabethan conquest of Ireland. As Nicholas Canny has shown, it is wrong to dismiss these researchers as loosely romantic; rather these 'closely-argued prose histories' were published as reading rooms, railway lines and telegraph cables made progress across the country.[55] Newspapers and popular biographies, printed on steam-powered presses, were the media via which the details of the Irish past were disseminated. But that potential sense of twinned technological and cultural possibilities met real blocks and difficulties in Ireland, not least because of the sheer scale of a population busily engaged in 'the work of multiplying', as Thackeray put it.[56] When a partial effort to take a census of the Irish population in 1813–15 was supplemented in 1821, just under seven million people were counted on the island. Those exercises probably still underestimated the size of the population which continued to grow through the 1820s and 1830s, albeit at a lower rate due, as the poor delayed marriage and migration to the United States and Britain increased. Newer scholarly research builds on further censuses in 1831 and 1841 to suggest a population of about 8.5 million by the early 1840s.[57]

Contemporaries were quick to speculate on the size of the population. George Cornewall Lewis' *On Local Disturbances in Ireland* (1836) plucks a briskly efficient metaphor from the world of imperial trade when he wondered if Ireland could 'be stretched out like a piece of India rubber' in order to make more room for its people. If so, 'the peasantry would be as tranquil and contented as that of England. But as this is impossible, we must strive to do what is possible. As we cannot make more land to the inhabitants, we must make fewer inhabitants to the land.'[58] The casual, prescient cruelty of Cornewall Lewis' comment stands out, but Irish writers too produced their own imperial images: for Thomas Moore, the country figured in his mind as a 'sugar loaf', an image suggestive of a broad base that tapers off towards an upper narrow point.[59] So it was, Moore implied, that the numerous Catholic peasantry supported a small Protestant elite. Moore assumes familiarity with the conical shape described and does not invite readers to look any further into slavery as a system nor to consider the brutal and unjust conditions in which sugar was harvested before being refined and whitened in Britain and Ireland.

But it was Daniel O'Connell's use of numbers that had the most impact. The success of the popular campaign for Catholic Emancipation lingered in memory as O'Connell made powerful rhetorical use of the asymmetries of power and population. The ill and elderly Sydney Smith, now canon of St Paul's, quoted him to Edgeworth in London in 1843: 'Six millions

O Connell says seven trampled upon still by one – notwithstanding this talk of emancipation. There must be a *reformation* and redress of grievances.'[60] Lady Morgan, too, in an 1853 public letter to Cardinal Wiseman (appointed Archbishop of Westminster upon the re-establishment of the Catholic hierarchy in England and Wales in 1850) spoke of the 'now flourishing Church of seven millions of Irish Catholics' and called upon the prelate to 'dispel the dark ignorance of the lower classes'.[61]

In the 1830s and 1840s, cultural conservatives began to use claims to fuller knowledge as a way of darkening perceptions of Ireland and warning readers off earlier representations, now deemed incorrect. Writing about the 'dust and disagreeability of Ireland' in 1827, Caesar Otway described Ireland as a worthwhile destination, all the more significant for not being found 'on the lips of tourists'.[62] The negative reference to tourism stands in for Otway's own claim to expert knowledge of untrodden ways. William Maginn all but called Thomas Moore himself a tourist when he described the *Melodies* as 'unIrish', an accusation made in language that left readers in no doubt as to their author's roots: 'Were I in a savage mood, I could cut him up with as much ease as a butcher in Ormond market dissects an ox from the County of Tipperary; but I shall spare him for this time.' Where, Maginn asked, in these 'pseudo-Irish Melodies' were to be found 'our saints, fairs, wakes, rows, patrons'?[63] The general tendency was to criticise Moore for a lack of locality and the possession of what cultural nationalist Charles Gavan Duffy called 'an imperial mind'.[64] The poets of *The Nation*, too, invoked his name only to query his national spirit while the *Dublin University Magazine* found 'too much light' in the work.[65] The barrister, antiquarian and poet Samuel Ferguson though (among those involved in setting up the *Dublin University Magazine*), insisted that Moore's polite lyrics reproduce the 'rude rhymes which accompanied the same notes two centuries ago': 'the stamen and essence of each is interwoven and transfused through the whole texture and complexion of the other'. Ferguson's plant metaphor gives way to the language of blood and nationality, as Matthew Campbell observes, but it also places 'the native songs and the lyrics of Moore' in linear relationship, one originating in but also succeeding the other.[66]

But the fearful arrival of starvation, disease and death in the 1840s had already changed the face of the country. A vulnerable population, one that had trebled in number since 1750, was devastated as a 'British Famine' afflicted a country that had been part of the United Kingdom since 1800.[67] Calls upon the Imperial Parliament met an uneven, often unheeding response, and in the early 1850s Harriet Martineau remarked that the Irish expected too much of the institutions of the United Kingdom: 'the complaints of the suffering Irish that they are neglected, – that a little more law would save them, if they could but get it', she wrote, were misplaced and inappropriate.[68]

Martineau had already published a tale with the title 'Ireland' in her *Illustrations of Political Economy* (1832), in which she addressed Irish ills alongside those of Tyneside, Wales, British Guiana and Tasmania, always discovering that better political outcomes would attend rational agricultural and economic improvements. Martineau lived with her brother James in Dublin from May to September 1831, shortly after she suffered the partial loss of her hearing and before she moved to London. She returned to Ireland in 1852 in the company of a niece and, taking advantage of the new postal network, began regular reports on the state of the famine-struck country for the London *Daily News*. Martineau's descriptions are vivid, and she does not scruple to criticise government mismanagement of Irish affairs. But her clear-sightedness is borne of catastrophe as death and emigration now define the condition of Ireland. When Martineau visited Binghamstown (*An Geata Mór*) on the Mullet Peninsula in County Mayo, for instance, she took in a vista of ruined, roofless cottages from which she was able to abstract patterns of human and plant life. Noting 'more inhabitants remaining than we had expected' and looking across the empty homes, she was struck by the sight of 'crops of potatoes and cabbages grown on the floors where dead neighbours lived so lately'.[69] Travelling east from Clifden in 1851, the travel writer Francis Bond Head was startled to see profuse plant life – 'in full bloom and luxuriance, the beautiful purple loosestrife' – filling the floor of a roofless, ruined cabin.[70]

Such accounts echo across the brief boom in travel writing in the immediate post-Famine period, where deserted villages and lines of empty houses sit amidst glittering lakes and acres of brown bog. Post-Famine Ireland was newly, starkly, visible: '[a]ll was becoming clearer just as there were fewer people to see', as Breandán Mac Suibhne puts it in his study of post-Famine adjustment in West Donegal.[71] The 1851 census, the results of which became known in March 1852, emphatically spelled out the extent of loss. William Wilde, newly married to Jane Francesca Elgee, the nationalist poet and contributor ('Speranza') to *The Nation*, was assistant census commissioner in 1851, having already served as a medical commissioner for the census of 1841. He was solely responsible for two volumes of the census reports, the *Status of Disease* and the *Tables of Death*, with their remarkable level of demographic, historical and other detail.

As the quantity of new information available was analysed and reimagined, a nascent sociology of national literature emerged within the work of Irish writers themselves. Edgeworth's famous letter to her brother on the challenges of Irish realism is part of this story, as too is Oscar Wilde's picking up the threads in the Preface to *Dorian Gray* (1891) when he theorises the purpose of literature for a new century; Wilde, of course, was a son of William and Jane Wilde. Earlier in the century, writing from France, Sir Charles Morgan made his own case for the limits of fiction in the advertisement to his wife's novel, *Florence Macarthy* (1818), where he explained that she chose to write about the Anglo-Irish – the 'master caste' – rather than the 'starving, squalid, and diseased population' of Catholic Ireland. 'The people', he remarks, 'form too prominent an object in the landscape to be wholly passed over by the most indifferent observer'.[72] The Evangelical novelist Charlotte Elizabeth Tonna made an observation at once more familiar and more negative in tone when, visiting North Donegal in 1837, she described it as 'a place where every prospect pleases, and only man is vile!'[73]

During this final phase of Irish romanticism, the prominence of the people is indeed pronounced as they are at once reduced in number and summoned to the stage in representative groupings. In the place of singular figures such as Edgeworth's wily Thady Quirke, Griffin's prophecy woman or Keats' Duchess of Dunghill, we begin to encounter attempts to sketch in a whole culture. Thomas Carlyle diagnosed this tendency in terms of an unlikeable outbreak of 'Irish Reporterism', associated by him with *Fraser's Magazine* and its Cork-born editor, William Maginn along with such contributors as Francis Sylvester Mahony ('Father Prout'), and Thomas Crofton Croker.[74] But the people that remained, the 'stalking skeletons'[75] that survived the Famine, call up strangely abstract formulations such as those offered by Carlyle himself, who found in Killarney Workhouse 'the old *abominable* aspect of "human swinery"' and noticed in Gweedore, Donegal nothing but hopelessness: 'Black huts, bewildered rickety fences of crag: crag and heath, *un*subduable by *this* population, damp peat, black heather, grey stones, and ragged desolation of men and things!'[76]

Methods of calculating the relationship between Irish individuals and the people in aggregate go back at least as far as the Cromwellian conquest of Ireland and William Petty's *Political Arithmetick* and *Political Anatomy of Ireland*.[77] That relationship was further inflected by eighteenth-century conceptions of national character which returned with a vengeance in this period. As such thinking gained fresh ground in the 1830s and 40s, ugly judgements ensued. A telling case can be found in the work of Sheridan Le Fanu, a writer often associated with Irish Victorian literature but also a transitional figure in this final phase of Irish romanticism. In his early efforts to voice the rural population among whom he grew up in East County Limerick, Le Fanu registers intimately known conflicts but often in condescending mode. Le Fanu was born in 1814 and from the 1830s began a series of essays and tales that capture forms of contest between orality and literacy as he revisits the violent history of the Williamite wars in the context of the agrarian conflicts, tithe protests and faction fights of his own time. Le Fanu is particularly associated with the *Dublin University Magazine*, a journal that he owned from 1861 to 1869 and to which he began contributing in 1838 with his first ghost story, 'The Ghost and the Bone-setter'.

Across his writing of the 1830s and 1840s, Le Fanu tried to make room for the materials of Irish history and legend, always in uneasy relationship with the people and places that are represented. Ideas of contested cultural space are thematised in his 'Scraps of Hibernian Ballads', published in the *Dublin University Magazine*, part of a series that first appeared as tales that pretended to come from the files of a Catholic priest from the south of Ireland, Father Purcell, a precursor of the fictional editor that Le Fanu later used for *In a Glass Darkly* (1872). In 'Scraps of Hibernian Ballads', 'an Eighth Extract from the Legacy of the late Francis Purcell, P. P. of Drumcoolagh', we hear the story of 'one Michael Finley', a poet and 'noted song-maker' with a 'rooted aversion to pen, ink, and paper, in perfect independence of which, all his compositions were completed'. Finley is presented as one who regards 'writing materials of any kind' with 'jealousy' while 'his ever wakeful fears lest some literary pirate should transfer his *oral* poetry to paper' are considered to be justified 'inasmuch as the recitation and singing of these original pieces were to him a source of wealth and importance'. Father Purcell implicates himself in such an act of piracy as he recollects Finley's 'detecting me in the very act of following his recitation with my pencil': 'I shall not soon forget his indignant scowl, as stopping abruptly in the midst of a line, he sharply exclaimed: "Is my *pome* a pigsty, or what, that you want a surveyor's ground-plan of it?"'[78]

The idea of a map – or perhaps a political anatomy – of a poem leads to a debate about the ownership of popular culture. When Father Purcell tackles 'this man of metres', it is to dispute his 'despotic and exclusive assertion of copyright', the latter term invoked ironically for oral art.[79] The force of that mocking irony derives from the distance between the solid legal concept of copyright and a set of words that are the precarious possession of a peasant poet.

The bookish aspect of Irish romanticism, discussed in Chapter 1, persists in Le Fanu's writing but is now forced into a fuller acknowledgement of a resistant popular culture expressed via references to 1798 in 'Scraps of Hibernian Ballads'. These include a quotation from the ballad *An Sean Bhean Bhocht* (meaning 'the poor old woman', often written phonetically as 'An Shan Van Vocht' and rendered by Le Fanu as 'Shanavan Voicht'). Le Fanu cites some lines to demonstrate the assonantal power of the lyrics but does not refer to the poem's origin in radical 1790s culture. The second 1798 poem cited among his 'Scraps' names the hanged United Irish leader, Lord Edward Fitzgerald, the elite rebel beloved of Le Fanu's mother and the subject of childhood tales. Rather than address politics, though, the narrative mounts an ironic defence of peasant style, insisting on the 'strict correctness in rhyme and metre' found in the ballad tradition.[80] Le Fanu had himself turned balladeer in the late 1830s when he composed a ballad set in 1798, 'Shamus O'Brien', a celebration of the life of a fugitive United Irishman who takes refuge in the Glen of Aherlow, County Tipperary. The poem was not published until Le Fanu's brother William included the full text in his memoirs, where he described the popular piece as one 'written in a very few days' and committed to 'scraps of paper', now lost.[81]

Scattered scraps of paper prove a fitting image of the fragile forms of connection laid down in the period up to about 1840. William Le Fanu's memoirs are full of anecdotal information about Irish rural life, mixing material of anthropological and topographical value together with happy predictions of Ireland's future under the Union. An apprentice engineer who went on to lay out important lines of rail in Ireland before being appointed commissioner of public works in 1863, William Le Fanu had his own japes with Irish rural life, attending 'a fancy ball in the south of Ireland as an Irish peasant' while wearing a heavy frieze coat and wig, carrying a blackthorn stick and mimicking peasant speech.[82] As Edgeworth remarked of Sydney Smith, who lectured her about the need for fairer treatment for the Catholic Church in Ireland before going on to mock the characteristic speech of the people: 'Laughing at brogue (how easy!)'[83]

Lost Voices

While the Le Fanus pretended to peasant language and customs, and Edgeworth worried about the 'poor Protestants' who were 'to have our Church pulled down about our ears and our clergy to be buried under the rubbish and their church lands and our estates taken from us',[84] other writers foretold a different doom to come. The 1830s were 'the eleventh hour' for Irish language, according to Owen Connellan, a schoolteacher and scholar whose *A Dissertation on Irish Grammar, Comprising a Critique on the Latest Grammar of That Language* was published in Dublin in 1834, offering detailed criticism of the Evangelical Henry Joseph Monck Mason's earlier *Grammar of the Irish Language* (1830) and chiming in with John O'Donovan's earlier criticism of the same book.[85] His plea, that it was 'indispensably necessary' to provide formal learning in grammar to the Irish peasantry, rested on gains available for the English language: 'The more the Irish is studied by the peasantry of Ireland (it being their vernacular tongue) the better are their minds prepared and their taste formed to learn and understand the English.'[86]

Connellan, appointed as 'Irish Historiographer' to William IV and soon made professor of Celtic languages and literature in the newly founded Queens College Cork, describes himself as animated by 'a wish to serve the cause of Irish Literature'. His warnings were issued in the context of a culture where English-language literacy was on the rise as the price of print fell. Popular politics had grown in strength from the 1820s, helped along by English-language ballads, chapbooks and popular prints. Some of the Young Irelanders regarded the language as a lost cause: though he proposed solutions to this 'impediment', John Mitchel regarded it a sad fact 'that the tongue of our conquerors has become our vernacular'.[87] But older Irish-language material still circulated in manuscript, and Vincent Morley has shown how the much-transcribed 'Tuireamh na hÉireann' or 'Ireland's Elegy' (c. 1657) by Seán Ó Conaill both distilled and popularised Geoffrey Keating's version of the country's history, old resentments made fresh in verse.[88] Devotional works in Irish 'tended to be few in terms of titles, but potentially broad in terms of impact given their work-a-day spiritual deployment', and they testify to a short-lived boom in regional print in Irish from about the 1820s to the onset of the Famine.[89] More generally, as Nicholas Wolf reminds us, hand-written codices and non-print books remained an important presence on the literary landscape.[90]

From about 1830, serious efforts were made to lay down a pathway that would lead from the eighteenth-century Irish-language poetry that lies behind the first phase described in this book towards a future print culture that could accommodate a distinguished literary history in the Irish language: a revival in the making. In 1853, for example, Standish Hayes O'Grady and John O'Daly printed 'Eachtra Ghiolla an Amaráin', an eighteenth-century poem that recounts the accidents that befall a young man as he tries to travel to Newfoundland', and Wolf finds that same text 'being used on the secondary and university-level curriculum for Irish-language results exams by 1897, the heart of the Revival period'.[91]

Among the ordinary people, the Donegal schoolmaster Hugh Dorian left us 'the most extensive lower-class account of the Great Famine'. In it, he evokes not only a fading cultural world but also specific losses to a nascent literary tradition: with poverty and emigration, he writes, 'was lost the material for many a gem in literature – yes, many a bright and giant genius was born and did not even "blush unseen"'.[92] When Dorian quoted Thomas Gray's 'Elegy Written in a Country Churchyard', it was to use the very same line chosen by Mary Wollstonecraft to describe the literary disappointments suffered in Ireland, when she worked as a governess for the Kingston family: 'Full many a flower is born to blush unseen / And waste its sweetness on the desert air'. Wollstonecraft wrote 'Dublin' above '*Desart*'.[93] Mary Tighe, too, imagined Dublin as a place fading from view: an urban centre doomed by the coming Union, a 'poor Swan sing[ing] wonderfully before her death'.[94]

Dorian's sense of a lost literary generation finds resonances in Mac Suibhne's account of the 'faint outlines of bright futures lost in the mid-nineteenth century'.[95] Dorian himself is one such figure, his book never published in his own lifetime, while the Clare poet William Downes is another. From the evidence of Downes' published volumes, we glean a picture of a young man who went to Maynooth for a period, and travelled to the West Indies to work there before returning home and once more emigrating to the United States. Downes made a number of efforts to get his work into print, with books published in Limerick by subscription in 1833 and 1836 and a collection published in Dublin in 1839 that includes some of the earlier work. The latter volume opens with a poem hailing the accession of the young Queen Victoria to the throne and ends with a selection of songs translated from the Irish.

Yet Downes' eyes were not only fixed on Ireland. His poem 'On J. M., who Died on His Passage from the West Indies' mourns 'a man of worth' who had 'toil'd in vain for wealth' in a climate that 'Bereft him of his health'.[96] Another longer poem, 'The Soliloquy', draws together memories and scenes to create 'A Sketch of Life' and includes 'The West Indies: a Sketch'. Tracing a journey from his native Munster across the Atlantic, Downes uses the recent Abolition of Slavery Act to shape his narrative. Addressing 'vile relentless tyrants' who will 'no longer wield the rod', the poem marks a reformed present: 'By them no more are bought and sold / Our fellow-men in slavery – / A nation's voice hath made them free.'[97] A note specifies the location as Demerera (Demerara-Essequibo, merged with Berbice to form the colony of British Guiana in 1831) and dates his time there to 'six years back' when 'A modern Sodom was this coast'.[98] An attempt at a fuller reckoning with the brutality of plantation life is found in a note that reads: 'I have seen thirteen Negroes cruelly flogged for being about an hour absent from work', their manager 'one of those hard-hearted Dutch Boors who are a stigma on society in the West India Colonies'.[99] Such references, though, remain scattered and are mixed in with poems that occupy themselves with the contemporary literary world.

As with Edgeworth's *Helen*, discussed next, Downes seeks out literary waypoints to give shape to a literary scene that is passing before his eyes, with notable figures including Moore and Banim singled out for notice. Poems include 'To Thomas Moore Esq., on his Late Visit to Ireland' and 'Lines on the Intended Return of Mr Banim, from France (Written Previous to His Arrival in Ireland)'. The poem takes as an epigraph some lines addressed by Banim to his brother Michael (in which he returns 'to share the mother's tomb') and imagines the Kilkenny novelist as a 'sweet historian' who faces an early grave.[100] Downes' last volume, though, a one-canto poem called *The Exile*, remarks on William Smith O'Brien's recent rebellion, hailing the Young Ireland rebels of July 1848 as the legitimate heirs of Brian Boru, and depicts the author's planned emigration to the United States in 1850. No account of the journey survives, while the boom in Irish-American writing and publishing did not emerge until the decade after the Famine. Edgeworth did develop some ideas for a tale to be titled 'Take for Granted' that would imagine the experiences of Irish emigrants to the United States but never wrote that book. After *Ormond* (1817), her writing largely remained at a distance from ordinary Irish lives, nowhere more so than in her final novel, *Helen*.

Maria Edgeworth in Changing Times

Set in its contemporary moment, *Helen* concerns the story of a young woman made vulnerable by an inadequate inheritance from a kindly but spendthrift uncle. Her plight is echoed in later fictions by Le Fanu (including 'The Secret History of an Irish Countess', later rewritten as *Uncle Silas*, 1864) where fathers and uncles fail or even threaten the lives of the young women whom they should protect. As with Le Fanu, female friendship promises to save the day, although when Cecelia invites her friend Helen to join her in her married home, domestic security comes at the price of intrigue and tacit untruths that threaten ruin for both women. Lady Davenant, the mother of Cecelia and a friend to Helen, offers a moral compass, but her story is a complex one, involving a dangerous attraction to public life and political influence which resulted in an early lack of attention to her daughter's formation. Like Thady Quirke in *Castle Rackrent* and Lady Delacour in *Belinda*, Lady Davnenant likes to tell stories about herself and offers to Helen 'some passages of my life', a story told from a position of difficulty in the present, as she tries make sense of a changed environment.[101] Part of that effort involves charting changing attitudes to women's behaviour and the painful expectations attendant upon the settled domesticity for which the novel nonetheless aims.

Edgeworth's interest in the question of women's proper sphere of influence is more marked than ever in this last phase of Irish romanticism, perhaps the result of being herself edged out by the coming generation of male Catholic writers. As Clíona Ó Gallchoir explains, the 'long delay in granting emancipation had effectively disabled the emergence of a bourgeois public sphere in Ireland', making space for women writers – including Edgeworth and Morgan – to take on topics in history and politics.[102] By the 1830s, though, the coming of Emancipation along with a wider culture of reform meant that Irish Catholic writers (beyond the singular case of Thomas Moore) could begin to make their mark. *Helen*, in Ó Gallchoir's account, 'expresses with extraordinary poignancy the repeated banishment of the Irish woman writer to a past construed as foreign and remote'.[103]

That banishment proceeded even as Edgeworth retained her significant circle of friends and correspondents and met occasional praise in the press. In 1818, Captain Basil Hall sent her a copy of his account of a journey to the island of Okinawa, then known as Great Loo-Choo Island, with an inscription that compared his 'offering' to that of 'a common sailor scratching his name on Nelson's pillar'.[104] In May 1828, the *Freeman's Journal* carried a letter from 'Patricius' disputing the achievements of 'the Wizard of the North', denying not Walter Scott's talent but his originality: 'For that species of *fictitious narrative* called "*the national novel*" we stand indebted conjointly to the talents and patriotism of two Irish women!'[105] Such claims find a resonance in an 1834 article in the *Dublin University Magazine* on 'Irish Female Writers', a joint review of Lady Blessington's *Grace Cassidy, or the Repealers* and *Helen*. The reviewer's encomium to 'Dear Maria Edgeworth', though, does limit her range as she becomes almost a figure of childhood memory for a new generation. By 1835, Thomas Moore found her company at a London dinner to be 'any thing but agreeable'.[106]

In 1834, Edgeworth joined an array of contemporary literary figures in becoming the butt of a series of joke letters published in *Fraser's Magazine*.

A character known as the Reverend George Miller elicited letters from famous writers by addressing them in a variety of supplicatory modes only to then publish their responses in *Fraser's*. The Cork journalist William Maginn was probably behind the scheme, and *Fraser's* did not spare the blushes of the authors targeted. In the case of Edgeworth, the magazine poked particular fun at the length and detail of her response. Thomas Moore and Thomas Crofton Croker were quick to brush off the parodic request, but Edgeworth had time enough on her hands to respond twice, and at some length: 'Only to think of any body that had any thing else to do scribbling all this worrying nonsense'.[107]

Later on, Edgeworth was yet more explicitly and publicly denigrated by Daniel O'Connell, who made a blatantly sexist assault on her reputation in a speech given in 1841. O'Connell first criticised the travel writer Mrs Hall, whose books, he asserted, were actually written by her husband, 'thinking that the gallantry of the Irish people will pass over many taunts sooner than decry the works of a lady'. The only good to be found in Edgeworth's books, O'Connell claimed, came from her father, 'who understood human nature well, and published under her name several admirable works, among the best in that way of modern times; but the moment he died Maria Edgeworth ceased to publish.'[108]

Edgeworth's second letter penned in response to the 'pertinacious badgering' of the Rev. Miller was addressed from the new home of her stepsister Fanny in North Audley Street, Mayfair. *Helen* was mostly written during that long visit to England but also informed by developments in Ireland, including an 1831 election in Longford where her brother Lovell backed a Tory candidate who was a family friend. Lovell Edgeworth made his choice in the context of the perceived dangers of Reform – described by Edgeworth as *'the bill and the whole bill and nothing but the bill'* – but soon, in the 1832 election, Longford returned O'Connellite candidates.[109]

Those same London and Longford co-ordinates are faintly traced in *Helen* via the novel's comparative account of city and country life. Discussing the constant circulation of new titles and fresh literary news, Lady Davenant remarks that in London, 'one book drives out another, one impression, however deep, is effaced by the next shaking of the sand'.[110] Edgeworth's counter-intuitive proposal is that books can have much more lasting and dangerous effects in the country, as happens to Lady Davenant herself when, as a young married woman, she read Madame de Staël's *Considerations on the Principal Events of the French Revolution* and 'turned, in the first place, as every body did, eagerly to the chapter on England'.[111]

Rather than the book's advocacy of Catholic Emancipation or its praise of England with its representative institutions, commercial success and liberal approach to public opinion, Lady Davenant fastens instead on Staël's observations regarding the gendered dimensions of a society where women 'never come conspicuously forward in discourse'.[112] Staël draws an ironic contrast between the limits imposed on women who inhabit a liberal public sphere demarcated by gender and the freedom of elite women in pre-Revolutionary France where 'the conquests made by elegance were unbounded'.[113] It is hard not to hear an echo of Ó Gallchoir's account of Edgeworth's own fate, that of a woman who was granted public authority in the constrained period before Emancipation and rapidly lost ground in its reformed aftermath. And Edgeworth must have read de Staël's *Considerations* closely, for she constructed the Lady Davenant political sub-plot as if to test the observation that in England, 'the country of the greatest publicity, state secrets are kept better than any where else. … There is no example of a woman having known, or at least having told, what ought to have been kept secret.'[114] Lady Davenant herself does not tell secrets – she uses improper influence on her husband and tries to persuade him to misuse public funds – but Carlos, her page, does. It is Helen who penetrates his deceit, and the scene by which she comes upon the evidence is worthy of Le Fanu's sensation novels to come, featuring as it does candlelight, shadows, a hidden figure behind a curtain, a suspected stiletto, a stolen key and an escape through a window by means of a tree.

Part of the sensational texture of the tale derives from its rich treatment of the dramas of language, literacy and education, notably via the Carlos sub-plot. The Portuguese servant pretends to speak only his own language but in fact uses his true ability to 'speak, read, and write English' to sell political secrets.[115] Helen cannot save herself from the scandal unleashed by Carlos' treachery. He returns in the plot when he makes an attempt to use the copies of some letters written by Cecelia to Colonel D'Aubigny, documents that threaten Helen's marriage and her reputation. On being dismissed by Lady Davenant, Carlos enters into the service of D'Aubigny's brother and in that capacity gains access to old love letters which threaten both Helen and Cecelia, tied as they are in their own forms of tactful deceit. Across its episodes, the Carlos sub-plot separates out different kinds of access to English in a way that resonates with the uneven spread of literacy in nineteenth-century Ireland, while the novel as a whole treats of print culture in a manner that is distinctively marked by Edgeworth's Irish experiences.

In 1848, the year before she died, Edgeworth was herself translated into Irish when 'Maith agus Dearmad' (or 'Forgive and Forget', based on one of her *Popular Tales*) was translated into Irish for the Ulster Gaelic Society by Thomas Feenachty. The *Dublin University Magazine* review in March 1834 noted that this was one of a series of translations 'of approved English authors' undertaken by the Belfast society, while also observing that the choice of Edgeworth was 'a fit commencement to an undertaking so truly Irish'. The reviewer further noted the 'cheapness' of the translated text and expressed hopes for its 'general circulation', describing the Irish-language lessons on offer in the Belfast Academical Institution and growing cultivation of the town.[116]

Helen continues its interest in bilingual life when it sends its heroine into Wales. Fleeing London because she cannot escape the ill effects of her friend Cecelia's refusal to tell her husband the full truth of her past life, Helen takes refuge in South Wales, in the home of General Clarendon's sister and aunt. In the fictional South Wales estate of Llansillen, Helen is surrounded by Welsh speakers and begins to feel 'as if she were in a foreign land, and in a dream'.[117] The Welsh language plays its part in the unfolding history of her slow convalescence so that when she meets a former creditor of her uncle, a carpenter whose bill Helen had been sure to settle, the man's 'garrulous gratitude' can only issue forth in his 'native Welsh'.[118]

But as with Lady Davenant's praise of city life, Helen finds solace not in a rural retreat where all is 'racking suspense' but rather in a return to London and public life.[119] The hungry curiosity with which Edgeworth observed London in *Helen* is focussed in particular on books, so that even a conversation in the surgery of a gossiping fashionable dentist turns up a reference to the great Welsh naturalist, Thomas Pennant. The novel reflects upon the commodification of literature in the context of a booming popular culture. Among the challenges its heroine faces is a test of literary taste, when Helen and the man who is to become her husband, Granville Beauclerc, discuss 'albums and autographs': the collections of signatures and relics of famous writers that became popular from the 1820s in fashionable British and Irish society. Helen, who does not have an album of her own, likes to see 'the autographs of celebrated people'. Beauclerc mocks her and asks stern questions about what difference it would possibly make to our appreciation of literature to see the handwriting or the autographs of the great. What could be the value of such 'relics', wonders Beauclerc, whose 'raillery' continues as he speculates that Helen will herself turn collector and one day be the chatelaine of 'a valuable museum, in which should be preserved the old pens of great men'. Any suspicion of playfulness on Edgeworth's part – or foreknowledge of the damage her own reputation would suffer from a patriarchal Irish literary tradition – is dispelled as Helen declines this proposition and earnestly continues in defence of her 'great desire to see and know distinguished persons', a form of discerning appreciation that is distinct from 'the mere trifling vulgar taste for sight-seeing and lion-hunting'.[120]

In spite of such episodes of self-reflection, both Marilyn Butler and Ó Gallchoir admire Edgeworth's 'great naturalness of tone' in *Helen*.[121] The literary world – including its lions – forms part of that natural world, as seen in the conversation just mentioned and in a detailed discussion of Walter Scott. The discussion is promoted by Granville Beauclerc's expressed disinterest in having seen or met Scott, dead since 1832. As with his dislike of autographs, the opinion points not towards a distaste for books, but rather towards a reverence for their meanings that transcends celebrity culture. Scott, in Beauclerc's eulogy, is

> that genius, pre-eminent and unrivalled, who has so long commanded the attention of the whole reading public, arrested at will the instant order of the day by tales of other times, and in this commonplace, this every-day existence of ours, created a holiday world, where, undisturbed by vulgar cares, we may revel in a fancy region of felicity, peopled with men of other times – shades of the historic dead, more illustrious and brighter than in life![122]

The name of Scott unites all of the party, men and women, and even the name of a Scottish philosopher and Edgeworth family friend is brought in to ratify Beauclerc's perspective via Lady Davenant's remark that 'Everybody is disappointed the first time they see Hamlet, or Falstaff, as I think Dugald Stewart observes.'[123]

If *Helen* imagines a body of literature that can transcend commodification as it heralds the standing of Romantic-era prose fiction within its pages, it is notable that Edgeworth's own name is missing. She stands outside the scene observed, as befits her effort to smooth over the fictional texture and create a reality effect. Such forms of fictional self-effacement were of less interest to Lady Morgan but she also took a lively interest in the potential and capacity of novels of fashionable life. From the 1820s, Morgan became a regular reviewer for the weekly journal the *Athenaeum*, edited by her friend Charles Wentworth Dilke. She reviewed hundreds of novels anonymously, paying particular attention to fashionable or 'silver-fork' fiction. Her remarks about Catherine Gore's silver-fork novel *Preferment, or, My Uncle the Earl* (1840) position a seemingly inconsequential novel of aristocratic manners in the context of 'the history of modern times', with fiction found to be a better measure of the moment than 'the meagre records of annalists' or 'the more productive collections of state papers'.[124] Accordingly, she attributes to Gore's fiction 'a rather prominent place among the historical documents of the day' and offers to 'bind her volumes up, with those of Mr. Dickens, the forthcoming reports of the Chartist trials, and a few similar books of fact and fiction, as contributions towards an encyclopaedia of the class-morality of the nation'. Morgan once more links Gore to Dickens when she describes both authors as writing books that serve as 'sources' for understanding, just as valuable as 'the Reports of the Commissioners on Poor Laws, the Constabulary Force, or any other paid collectors' of 'facts and opinions'.[125] At the time of writing, Dickens was best known for his 'Street Sketches', published in London newspapers, and his serial *The Posthumous Papers of the Pickwick Club* (April 1836 to November 1837), works that 'offer a vivid contemporary account of the vertiginous movement of print and the increasing immersion of ordinary Londoners in a print and show culture that invites them to consider themselves as citizens and as actors in history'.[126] Irish writing of the period, although not galvanised by the same intensity of urban experience, was also absorbed in a shifting present shaped in part by official documents and reports that made ordinary Irish people actors in a historical drama.

Romantic Histories, Romanticism as History

In 1822, Edgeworth reported that she had seen the head of Cromwell at the home of the political economist David Ricardo: 'Oliver Cromwells head – not his picture – not his bust – nothing of stone or marble or plaister [*sic*] of Paris, but his real head'.[127] Cromwell belonged to a conflicted history, but also spoke to new evidentiary standards for historical research.[128] Even though Edgeworth's and Morgan's names were on the wane in this phase of Irish romanticism, their methods had gained cultural ground. The influence of their pioneering combination of history and gender can be seen in Thomas Moore's 1831 biography of Lord Edward Fitzgerald, with its focus on his subject's domestic life. By the 1840s, Young Ireland ideas of nationality were expressed in language that not only called up masculinity as a model but also expressed what Caitriona Kennedy calls 'a new emphasis on the United Irish widows as exemplary models of female national expression'. As the cultural spaces open for women narrowed, however, the widowed Matilda Tone rejected romantic attempts to novelise her loss and refused the role of 'eternal mourner', while also taking advantage of the 'degree of authority' afforded to women by 'memory work'. Matilda Tone put on the 'elegiac language of Romantic nationalism' in order to claim a bardic privilege for her own voice.[129]

In doing so, she could draw some support from the presence of women poets on the pages of *The Nation*, although their voices were often excluded from later books and anthologies. The best known of these is Jane Francesca Elgee (1821–1896), later Wilde, who from 1845 wrote as 'Speranza'. Her Famine poem, 'The Stricken Land', appeared in *The Nation* in January 1847, while, later in life, she wrote a preface for Maturin's *Melmoth the Wanderer* (1892), the work of a distant relative. Probably the most radical female voice in *The Nation* was that of Eva O'Doherty (1830–1910), who wrote as Eva Kelly or 'Eva of the Nation'. In 1848, she called upon Irish women to take up arms to secure their country's freedom, while her poem 'Hymn of the Sword', written as famine raged, calls for armed protection 'from complete and utter destruction', as Rose Novak puts it.[130] Absorbed as she was by contemporary tragedy and drawn to armed rebellion, O'Doherty did not write heroic ballads that invoked a chivalric past, the more common mode adopted by the writers of *The Nation*. Charles Gavan Duffy's edited collection, *The Ballad Poetry of Ireland* (Dublin, 1845) included 'native ballads' alongside 'Anglo Irish ballads' – 'the production of educated men, with English tongues but Irish hearts'.[131] Despite the book's 'ecumenical' approach to the Irish and its boast of 'a larger circulation than any book published in Ireland since the Union', it included only one female contributor.[132] Mary Russell Mitford, though no admirer of Lady Morgan, cherished her 'sixpenny volume of "Poetry of the Nation"' and complained that a 'friend of mine once ran off' with it 'and has not since been able to find it, either in her husband's fine library in town or at their seat in the country; and this little book I have been unable to replace'.[133]

Women novelists fared a little better than the poets, though Edgeworth complained in 1831 of having 'three authoress's books lying unread on the table before me and letters of thanks that must be penned'.[134] Among them was a novel by M. G. T. Crumpe, who also sought help from Thomas Moore and Thomas Crofton Croker in London. Edgeworth thought her historical novel of Elizabethan Ireland, *Geraldine of Desmond*, 'a book of great pretension' and was annoyed at having to return a social visit.[135] Crumpe wrote to the publisher John Murray in 1830, telling him how 'I have been furnished from a high official source with fac-similes of the autographs of the principal historical characters that are introduced into my work – Those fac-similes have been lithographed under the superintendence of my kind friend Mr Crofton Croker and will be annexed to the forthcoming edition – which I hope will invest it with a curious interest.'[136] The second edition of Crumpe's historical novel features these facsimile signatures at the opening of its first volume, while the third volume closes with the curious device of presenting most of the last paragraph (the final page of the volume) in a facsimile of the author's own manuscript hand. A facsimile reproduction of Crumpe's own signature is appended under the printed words 'The End'.[137] The edition was advertised as 'useful to the searcher after historical records': 'The value of the second edition has been considerably enhanced by the introduction of a series of autographs of the principal personages whose names are introduced into the work'.[138]

As 'writers grappled with the difficulty of giving shape to a historical sensibility no longer bounded by public transactions',[139] individual autographs accompanied by a specimen of the author's own hand might be seen to provide not just a guarantee of historical accuracy, but also a kind of personally mediated access to the inner life of the past. A mix of historical authenticity and comic effect is found in *The Davenels*, an anonymously published novel of 1829, written in the run-up to Emancipation and part of the post-1825 fad for silver-fork fiction. The novel is dedicated to the Duke of Wellington, prime minister since 1828, and contemporary reports suggest that the author is 'a lady moving in the scene of elevated society'.[140] At once 'a vulgar piece of fashionable drivel' (as the review in the *Edinburgh Literary Journal* has it)[141] and a fiction marked by a sense of the need to fathom the consequences of the concessions to Catholics, *The Davenels* mixes social visits, fashionable balls and marriage arrangements with intermittent discussions of the Catholic Association and the public personalities of Daniel O'Connell and Richard Lalor Sheil. The novel concludes with a letter in which an idle, self-absorbed and husband-hunting young lady writes to the heroine complaining that people in Dublin 'talk nothing but politics, and such *mauvais ton* politics! all about those horrid Catholics!' A collector of celebrity trivia, she is however rather delighted to own 'one of that horrid O'Connell's franks' and reports in a gushing letter that closes the novel that friends 'bore us by singing in all companies, one of Moore's melodies, which they call a prophecy'.[142]

The reference in *The Davenels* points readers to 'While History's Muse' of 1815, a poem that addresses the Duke of Wellington in the aftermath of his victory at the Battle of Waterloo. Born in Ireland to an aristocratic Irish Midlands family, Wellington was married in 1806 to a friend and neighbour of Maria Edgworth's, the second daughter of Lord Longford, 'Kitty' Pakenham. The poem exhorts Wellington to work on behalf of Catholic

Emancipation, even as it celebrates his preservation of British liberty on continental battlefields. Part of the poem's force comes from the way in which it marshals Catholic claims about the dignity earned by military and naval service, already discussed in Chapter 2. Because Wellington as prime minister did indeed see Catholic Emancipation into law, the poem's appeal to Wellington to staunch the flow of 'tears' and 'blood'[143] from his native land was later claimed by Moore himself, in an 1841 preface to the *Melodies*, as a prophecy in the bardic manner.

'History's Muse' did indeed speak to a number of Irish writers from the 1830s onwards. Lady Morgan began a novel on Grace O'Malley (c. 1530–1603) in the early 1830s, commencing work on the book just weeks after the passing of the 1832 Reform Act, though she never completed her story of this notable early modern Irish woman, whose legendary seafaring prowess formed part of the Gaelic resistance to the Tudor conquest of Ireland. Gerald Griffin turned to the yet more distant past with his novel *The Invasion* (1832), which imagined a flourishing but conflict-ridden Gaelic Ireland before the Viking incursions, and took advantage of the traditional associations of Brian Boru with well-known sites in his native County Clare. Like Morgan, Griffin consulted 'old chronicles' (as she put it) in Dublin and London: both were aware of the need to establish an evidentiary basis for the Irish past.[144]

The most stylish and successful of the new Irish historical novels was Sheridan Le Fanu's *The Cock and the Anchor* (1845), something like W. M. Thackeray's *Barry Lyndon* (1844) in the freedoms it takes with an eighteenth-century world made up of 'Old Inns and cock-fighting, and gambling rooms and duels'.[145] Although his narrator is a gentleman and not a servant, *Barry Lyndon* follows *Castle Rackrent* in using an unreliable Irish voice to sketch in a significant historical moment. But unlike Thackeray's novel, with its European canvas, Le Fanu maintains a close focus on Dublin City and its suburban surroundings. Anthony Trollope also began to write about Ireland in the 1840s, having been sent there by the Post Office. Soon, Trollope 'boasted of having visited every parish and was capable of Ordnance Survey-style descriptions of the most remote places in the country'.[146] His first novel, *The Macdermots of Ballycloran* (1847), is framed by the recollections of the mail coach guard who begins to unfold a story concerning a tragic murder in County Leitrim. Even this sensational story was understood by Trollope to have historical value: the novel, he remarked in his *Autobiography*, was 'worth reading by anyone who wishes to understand what Irish life was before the potato disease, the famine, and the Encumbered Estates Bill'.[147]

An increasing sense of the difficulty of such efforts at understanding is vividly in evidence from the period of the Great Famine onwards. As Martineau wrote, 'The world is weary of the subject of Ireland; and, above all the rest, the English reading world is weary of it. The mere name brings up images of men in long coats and women in long cloaks; of mud cabins and potatoes; the conacre, the middlemen, and the priest; the faction fight, the funeral howl.' Even well-meaning English readers were perplexed; in Martineau's account: 'Something ought to be done for Ireland; and, to readers by the fireside, it is too bewildering to say what.'[148]

Among those readers was Matthew Arnold, who characterised himself as 'an unlearned bellettristic trifler' in the 'truly vast' culture of the islands.[149] In the course of his Oxford chair of poetry lectures on the study of Celtic Literatures, Arnold recounted a story that he heard from Irish-language scholar Eugene O'Curry about Thomas Moore, who visited Ireland in 1839 in order to work on his five-volume history of Ireland and met some of the scholars working on the Ordnance Survey memoir. O'Curry and Moore had met in the Royal Irish Academy, where the former 'happened to have before me on my desk the *Book of Ballymote and Lecain*, *The Speckled Book*, *The Annals of the Four Masters*, and many other ancient books, for historical research and reference'. Moore, on 'seeing the formidable array of so many dark and time-worn volumes by which I was surrounded' was 'disconcerted' but 'listened with great attention' to the 'short explanation' offered by O'Curry and George Petrie, remarking when they had finished: 'Petrie, these huge tomes could not have been written by fools or for any foolish purpose. I never knew anything about them before, and I had no right to have undertaken the *History of Ireland*.'[150]

It was not only the history of Ireland that was 'sad work', as Moore wrote to Mary Shelley,[151] but also the current state of the country: while Griffin worked on his novel of the Viking invasion, cholera raged in his native Limerick. Writing to his doctor brother, he reported a meeting with James Kennedy, author of *The History of the Contagious Cholera; with Facts Explanatory of Its Origin and Laws, and of a Rational Method of Cure* (1831). Kennedy appears to have been brother of the Wexford-born scholar and collector of Irish folklore, Patrick Kennedy, who wrote for the *Dublin University Magazine* in the 1830s and whose *Legendary Fictions of the Irish Celts* (1866) influenced the young Yeats. In Griffin's estimation, James Kennedy 'has favoured the horror-struck English with the best book that has appeared on cholera, a subject at present far more interesting than the state of Ireland in the eighth century'.[152]

Griffin meanwhile sent an earnest letter to his brother Daniel, praying that the 1832 wave of cholera was 'the parting stroke, and that friends may once again begin to meet without the sight of the gravestone forever at their feet'.[153] Griffin's sometime friend and fellow Catholic novelist John Banim himself survived two episodes of cholera and went to convalesce in Boulogne before dying at home in Kilkenny in 1842. In 1831 Banim published a series of poems satirising British misrule of Ireland under the compelling title of *Chaunt of the Cholera*. The book, though, was 'totally unproductive' according to Banim's wife, Ellen, who sought financial assistance from the Royal Literary Fund in the early 1830s and again after the author's death.[154]

In Dublin, Felicia Hemans watched from her window as 'one of the black covered litters, which convey the cholera patients to the hospital' passed by on the street below, 'followed by policemen with sabres in their hands'. The guards were necessary, Hemans wrote, because people did not trust the medical authorities and suspected the covered carriages. Her own distance from the scene, and from the views of that 'infatuated population', is secured by a religious faith that relieves her from fear of even this 'viewless danger'. And yet Hemans too felt 'the actual presence of some dark power sweeping past' even as she was startled to see 'May-dancers in the street scarcely a moment afterwards'.[155]

Alongside the stark daily changes brought about by disease, romanticism was itself passing into history. Jane Wilde completed work on her husband's memoir of the Dutch-born artist Gabriel Beranger (d. 1817), whose romantic watercolours of ruined landscapes helped to shape the visual record of the Irish landscape. Lady Morgan and her husband travelled to France in 1829, where she complained that, rather than the 'romanticism of the Italian literati', she found a term debased by use and association with England: 'every thing English, except their politics, is now, in Paris, popular, and is deemed romantic; and we have romantic tailors, milliners, pastry-cooks, and even doctors and apothecaries'.[156] She found Anglomania in full flight in Restoration Paris, where not only cultural concepts but cakes, alcohol and clothing belonged to England. Parisian pastry shops served mince pies, plum cake and apple dumplings, aimed at the visiting English. Ireland, too, formed a part of the fad for Englishness and in a perfumer's shop where she went in search of '*eaux, essences,* and *extraits*', Morgan met 'a box of English fans and silk handkerchiefs, with O'Connell's handsome Irish face glowing in the centre'.[157] Her husband was even offered some illicit Irish spirit, *poitín*: 'Was it for this', she asked, that 'we left the snugness and oeconomical comfort of our

Irish home, and encountered the expensive inconveniences of a foreign journey?'[158] This moment of Anglomania had lasting effects on the reputation of Maturin: Delacroix painted a scene from Maturin's *Melmoth the Wanderer* in 1831, Balzac's *Melmoth Réconcilié* parodied the novel in 1835 and Pushkin included a reference in *Eugene Onegin* (1833). Soon, the adjective '*mel'moticheskii*' ('Melmoth-like') was used in Russian.[159] Meanwhile in England, Mary Russell Mitford enthused about Daniel O'Connell, writing in 1834 that he and Victor Hugo were the only two people she would 'cross the threshold to meet': 'My passion for Daniel is extraordinary'.

In Ireland itself, the reframing of romanticism happened in the hands of a new generation, chiefly writers who were born in and around 1800, and who came to a difficult and painful maturity in the 1830s. Jeremiah Joseph Callanan (discussed in Chapter 2) was born in 1795 and died in Lisbon in 1829, while John Banim was born to a family of Kilkenny shopkeepers in 1798 and died in Boulogne in 1842. Gerald Griffin visited Thomas Moore in Sloperton Cottage in November 1832 and wrote to a friend of his delight in meeting the senior Irish writer, whose songs he had known and sung 'since I was at the height of my knee'.[160] Griffin himself though ended his life in 1848 as a teaching member of a Catholic religious order dedicated to the education of the lower classes, in the North Monastery in Cork city. Mary Russell Mitford remembers Griffin warmly in her *Recollections* but wishes for a more fitting stage for his final scenes: 'One of the old Benedictine abbeys, where the consolations of religion were blended with the pursuits of learning, where the richly adorned chapel adjoined the richly stored library, would have done better.'[161] Griffin's last days were not framed by Gothic windows or arches, however, but rather by the busy streets of an overcrowded and impoverished port city at the edge of the Atlantic world.

Born in the same year as Griffin, James Clarence Mangan also grew up with the names of Edgeworth, Owenson and Moore. Late in life, ill and addicted, he penned brief entries on Maturin, Griffin, Edgeworth and William Maginn for a series published in *The Irishman*, 'Sketches and Reminiscences of Irish Writers'. The final entry concerned one James Clarence Mangan. Looking in the other direction, Edgeworth herself admired some of the coming generation. She admired Gerald Griffin and read *The Collegians* (1829) with 'horrible breathless interest'.[162] Visiting London Zoo in November 1830, she reached for an image from a recent Irish novel in order to describe her horrified fascination not only with tigers, leopards and kangaroos, but also a more familiar domestic mammal:

The otter fished for live fish thrown into his pool and bit the head of [sic] one the instant caught and played with it horridly as cat with mouse and granched it bones and blood till I was sick looking and yet could not move my eyes – like the girl looking at the murder thro the cranny in the wainscoat [sic].[163]

The scene Edgeworth remembers comes from John Banim's *The Nowlans*, a book that she described in 1827 as 'a work of great genius'.[164] Around this time, Gerald Griffin made the acquaintance of Edgeworth's friend, the Dublin surgeon Sir Philip Crampton – first president of the Dublin Zoological Society – and began to hope to mix in literary society. 'I long to meet Lady Morgan and to know Miss Edgeworth', he told his brother.[165] But it was William Carleton, 'Born and bred among the people' as both Thomas Davis and W. B. Yeats both had it,[166] whose name made the deepest impression on Edgeworth and the writers who came after her, and it is to his work that I now turn.

William Carleton and Popular Education

The youngest of fourteen children, William Carleton's (1794–1869) home place was Prillisk, in the parish of Clogher, County Tyrone. His Catholic parents both spoke Irish. His father was a tenant farmer and flax dresser whose memory, Carleton later wrote, retained 'all that the social antiquary, the man of letters, the poet, or the musician, would consider valuable', passed on to his young family by the power of 'frequent repetition' in both Irish and English. His mother, a skilled singer, keener and reciter of poetry, connected Carleton to eighteenth-century bardic traditions with her 'fine old songs' and 'airs' in Irish.[167] Carleton in his turn used his family history to create a doubled version of a romantic past that, as Marjorie Howes puts it, was at once 'available for salvage' and 'constantly slipping away'.[168]

Carleton's later reputation as the authentic voice of peasant Ireland is precariously located between presence and loss, a dilemma that is amplified by a body of writing that exists 'on the border between orality and typographically-based literacy'.[169] Carleton's own education, at home and in hedge schools, as well as his efforts as a travelling tutor and later role as journalist and novelist, meant that his narratives of rural life move between urban and rural contexts as between languages and media. Brian Earls' sharp characterisation of Carleton's 'multiple voices' catches 'the stylised intensities of keening, curses and blessings, encomium and satire, genealogical recital, the knowing extravagance of tall English, public prayer, elaborate wordplay and the extension of metaphor, professional love talk, badinage and other forms of adversarial jousting, verbal wit and high spirits, together with a non-functional delight in the use of language for its own sake'.[170] That final 'non-functional delight' marks the place where fictions that strive to represent a known world as fully as possible also begin to pull away from realism, tending towards qualities that include improvisation, melodrama and linguistic excess.

In 1819, William Carleton left his home for Dublin and soon afterwards converted to Protestantism. A change of religion offered no smooth route to professional success, however, and he spent the next seven years taking on teaching jobs in Carlow, Mullingar and Dublin. Born in the first phase of Irish romanticism and travelling the country in search of work in the second phase, this final period sees Carleton coming into literary voice through the 1830s into the 1840s as he reworks aspects of his own life and times. He met Caesar Otway around 1827 and began publishing in the *Christian Examiner*; from there, *Traits and Stories of the Irish Peasantry* was first published in 1830. The title echoes that of Griffin's *Tales of the Munster Festivals*, and Carleton, too, sought to find a space for popular historical knowledge or *stair sheanchas* within the textures of English fiction. His *Fardorougha the Miser* (1839) first appeared in serial form in the *Dublin University Magazine* from 1837 to 1838, and later novels followed: *Valentine McClutchy* (1845), *The Black Prophet* (1847) and *The Emigrants of Ahadarra* (1848).

Across his novels and stories, Carleton realises a world of ordinary peasant speech that is often coupled with passages of learned excess. The narratives use standard English to frame the fictions but make copious use of a Hiberno-English that can be difficult on the eye. Ordinary words and phrases, often transliterated from Irish, are in their turn mixed in with phrases that employ the Latin of the hedge schools, again in transliterated form. Meanwhile, Carleton's vibrant world of peasant speech stands at a distance from antiquarian and scholarly efforts to retain the contours of a distinguished literary tradition in the Irish language. James Hardiman, a native speaker born in Galway, compiled an *Irish Minstrelsy* (1831) that featured the harper Carolan on its frontispiece along with a dedication to the politician Thomas Spring Rice, the Protestant landowner whom Daniel O'Connell had recruited to the Catholic cause. Hardiman prefaces his collections by reference to a lost tradition of Irish language poetry – 'outlawed bards' writing in a 'denounced language' – that provide no resource when a writer like Thomas Dermody comes on the scene. Even Robert Burns, had he been born in Ireland would have been doomed to little more than modest literary celebrity had he not been 'cast among a literary people'.

Meanwhile John O'Donovan and Eugene O'Curry published texts relating to Ireland under the auspices of the Irish Archaeological Society (established in 1840), the Celtic Society (founded in 1845) and the Ossianic Society (1853). Invited to give evidence to a select committee on public libraries in London in 1849, O'Curry examined and catalogued Irish manuscripts held in the British Museum, and also consulted Irish-language manuscripts held at the Bodleian Library. O'Curry was made a member of the Royal Irish Academy in 1853, and later professor of Irish history and archaeology at the newly established Catholic University in Dublin. His *Lectures on the Manuscript Materials of Ancient Irish History* (1861) became a vital source for knowledge of the manuscript tradition.

Like Carleton, the writer and bookseller John O'Daly converted to Protestantism though the latter reconverted in the 1840s. The honorary secretary and publisher of the Ossianic Society, O'Daly's *Reliques of Irish Jacobite Poetry* appeared in 1844, published alongside contemporary translations by Edward Walsh. O'Daly also has the distinction of publishing the first version of the poem 'Cúirt an Mheán-Oíche', by Brian Merriman, under the title *Mediae Noctis Concilium* (1850). In Carleton's case, his change of religion remained of lasting concern to his readers and critics. Even in his own day, some suspected Carleton of writing about Irish Catholicism solely for the benefit of English Protestants, a practice likened by William Downes to 'venal prostitution' as Carleton's 'witty pen' 'falsely, shamelessly derides – / (To please J—n B—ll,) his countrymen'.[171] Seamus Heaney's later address to Carleton as 'the old fork-tongued turncoat' who 'mucked the byre of their politics' continues this dialogue.[172]

But Carleton's fictions of Irish Catholic life often understand forms of belief – such as the attraction of young men to the priesthood – as ordinary matters of observed fact, whether the account is strongly anti-Catholic or more moderate, as it became in the post-Emancipation moment. His story 'Denis O'Shaughnessy Going to Maynooth', published in Otway's *Christian Examiner* and later as one of the *Traits and Stories*, squarely takes aim at the idea of the Catholic priesthood as the apex of social and professional ambition of an Irish peasant. Denis O'Shaughnessy's father wants to show him off as a kind of a 'priestling' and, to that end, puts him 'in training for controversy'.[173] Denis, though, loves Susan, and while the first magazine version of the story ends with Denis going to Maynooth, the later version sees him come back and marry on the very day of his return from the Catholic seminary. Carleton later claimed that this change was a result of a fire at the printers with the first version of the lovers' reunion having been burned. A different version of the priest or 'young *sogarth*'[174] narrative is found in 'The Poor Scholar', a story that is drawn from Carleton's own early efforts at the priesthood. Via the character of Jemmy, who longs to raise his parents out of poverty, Carleton overlays the story of the development of a young man's education with a plot about tenant rights that focusses on poor tenant treatment by landlords. The tale opens as Jemmy and his father discuss the future, and the decision to become a priest is made amidst howling wind and the misery of eviction, the agent Yallow Sam having turned them out of their farm and left father and son to toil on a miserable hillside. Jemmy sets off for Munster to become a poor scholar, in a manner similar to the story Sydney Owenson tells in her *Patriotic Sketches* of 1807. In order to make it through to Maynooth, Jemmy must face down avaricious teachers and raging disease. Jemmy is surrounded by gifts and kindness, not only the 'thrifle' he receives from a kindly strong farmer, but also the practical community support from which he benefits while lying ill at the side of the road, suffering from typhus. His friends erect a tent beside his own rough shelter, while 'a kind of guard was set to watch and nurse-tend him; a pitchfork was got, on the prongs of which they intended to reach him bread across the ditch; and a long-shafted shovel was borrowed, on which to furnish him drink with safety to themselves'.[175] The delicacy of the details – the makeshift structure that allows scrutiny but affords distance, the long handle on the shovel meaning contagion can be kept at bay – maps onto the intricate forms of distressed sympathy invited by Jemmy's status as priest-in-waiting. Jemmy finally gets to tell his story to Colonel B., his father's landlord, who in turn indicts himself as belonging to 'a guilty race' and is depicted as ignorant rather than cruel, spending his time in London and Paris and learning nothing of his tenants.[176] Even as he details the 'curse of absenteeism', Carleton's description of the big house expresses nostalgia for a social and literary world that is already fading from view.[177] That sense of pastness is sometimes tinged by the supernatural, as when a strange power takes possession of the members of a secret society who commit a deliberate and murderous act of arson in his story *Wildgoose Lodge*, which first appeared in 1830 as *Confessions of a Reformed Ribbonman*.

Across the pages of Carleton's fictions, we find a density of social detail that jostles for space with passages of dialogue rendered in dialect, the latter in turn opening up a world of informal, oral historical knowledge, or what Brian Earls calls '*stair sheanchas*'.[178] The latter includes the prophecies of Pastorini and Colmcille, understood to predict happier times for Irish

Catholics, especially in the year 1825: 'whin Twenty-five comes, *we'll* have our own agin'.¹⁷⁹ The character of Donnel Dhu in *The Black Prophet* is fluent in such material, using it to sow dissension and create uncertainty. But Donnel Dhu also expresses uncanny forms of environmental knowledge, as when he reads epidemiological disaster in the face of the country: 'Look about you, and say what is it you see that doesn't foretell famine – famine – famine! Doesn't the dark wet day an' the rain, rain, rain, foretell it? Doesn't the rottin' crops, the unhealthy air, an' the green damp foretell it? Doesn't the sky without a sun, the heavy clouds an' the angry fire of the West foretell it? Isn't the airth a page of prophecy, an' the sky a page of prophecy, where every man may read of famine, pestilence, an' death?'¹⁸⁰ There follows an elaborate image of clouds as hearses in the sky which historian Gillen D'Arcy Wood reads in relation to Carleton's own experience of the strange skies following the explosion of Mount Tambora in 1816, the same bad weather that drove Mary Shelley, Byron and Polidori indoors at Lake Geneva to work on their dark tales. For D'Arcy Wood, *The Black Prophet*, Carleton's novel of the 1817 famine, offers not only a comment on the unfolding horrors of his own day ('the workings of death and desolation among us in the present time'), but also a rich environmental archive.¹⁸¹ In *The Black Prophet*, a sensational narrative is interspersed with detailed descriptions of the natural world and long explanatory passages characterised by striking images, including a description of the country itself as 'one vast lazar-house filled with famine, disease, and death. The very skies of heaven were hung with the black drapery of the grave'.¹⁸²

Donnel Dhu's prophecies resonate with many of the moments when Carleton's narrative turns from dialogue towards abstraction, sometimes mediated via landscape. The mixture might be understood in terms of an observation made by Hugh Dorian, who described the relationship between people and place in terms of an intimately lived experience of abstract knowledge. 'The Donegal peasant', he wrote, looks from 'the rich lands of the plantation' to 'the mountain, the bog and the seashore' and there finds 'all the historical learning he requires': 'he has his ancestors' history open before him every day he rises; it is exhibited in the large characters – the ocean, the mountain, and his own state of poverty – and if he reads anything he must read how it is that he is there and why'.¹⁸³ Dorian's emphasis on reading as a provisional act at once silences and calls out the question of literacy as part of the peasant's predicament. In Carleton, that same uncertainty means that readers inhabit a world where ordinary people both know things and are mocked for knowing things, evident in his uneven renditions of the Latin taught in hedge schools.

The fixing of Carleton as a placed peasant voice began almost as soon as his tales appeared in the 1830s. An engraving of an imaginary home place, by Henry MacManus (c. 1810–1878), Irish artist and friend of Charles Gavan Duffy, was tipped into editions of Carleton's best-known collection of stories, *Traits and Stories of the Irish Peasantry*, from 1843. And though Carleton did not approve of the image, he gave 'The Birthplace' as the title to the first chapter of his *Autobiography*. Edgeworth too began to be associated in print with the family home: the first collected edition of the works in 1825 'contains a charming vignette of the Edgeworthstown House on each title-page'.[184] An engraved image of the house accompanying an article on 'Edgeworthstown' appeared in *The Art Journal* for 1849 and was subsequently reproduced in a French magazine. The article was written by Anna Maria Hall (1800–1881), whose husband Samuel Carter Hall (1800–1889) was editor of *The Art Journal*, and the engraving originated in a drawing made by Frederick William Fairholt, on the occasion of a visit to Edgeworthstown with the Halls. Mrs Hall also noted that a photograph had recently been taken of the great writer in London, and Edgeworth herself described the 'wonderful mysterious operation' by which her image was captured in daguerreotype, 'the whole apparatus and stool on a high platform under a glass dome casting a *snap dragon blue* light making all look like spectres'.[185]

Thomas Moore too was photographed by pioneering polymath William Henry Fox Talbot, who had been experimenting with fixing images of the natural world on paper from 1834, using the power of light. He took images of leaves, lace, family members – and poems. Around this time, Fox Talbot asked Moore to write out some of his poems so that they might be copied onto a new surface using this method, a very early version of a negative to positive process. Fox Talbot's photogenic drawings involved dipping writing paper in a solution of sodium chloride then coating one side of the paper with light-sensitive silver nitrate, a compound that becomes dark with long exposure to sunlight. As Fox Talbot continued to refine his process, he made a calotype portrait of Thomas Moore as well as a family group photograph.[186]

The idea of the iconic status of the author, their family and their house gained traction in the 1830s, part of a newly confident literary culture: the County Clare poet William Downes opened his first collection, published in Limerick in 1830, with a poem entitled 'The Birthplace'.[187] Scott's Abbotsford began to receive public visitors in 1833, not long after the author's death, with a special tourist entrance built in 1847. Shakespeare's house at Stratford-upon-Avon was bought for the nation in 1847, some fifty years before Wordsworth's Dove Cottage was opened to the public.

But though Edgeworthstown, in Mrs Hall's eyes, 'may almost be regarded as public property',[188] few in famine-struck Ireland took an interest in literary tourism. Lady Morgan and her husband sold their house in Kildare Street, Dublin in January 1838 and departed for a 'dear, *very dear* house' in Knightsbridge.[189] For most Irish romantic women, though, the grave remained the site most associated with authorial reputation. Felicia Hemans visited the grave of Mary Tighe and placed 'The Grave of a Poetess' as the concluding poem in her *Records of Woman* (1828), including in a footnote a reference to the Banims' novel, *The Fetches*, which imagines the grave of the 'author of "Psyche"' in County Kilkenny as a site gaining in 'Extrinsic interest'.[190] Hemans herself died in Dublin in 1835, having moved there in 1831.

Even without opportunities to pay visits to the homes of Irish writers, however, W. B. Yeats would soon elevate a distinction between 'Miss Edgeworth's well-finished four-square house of the intelligence' and Carleton's 'rough clay "rath" of humor and passion' to the status of an abiding literary judgement.[191] But Yeats had also begun a bold reimagination of the Irish literary landscape via its absences, remarking how 'I who had never wanted to see the houses where Keats and Shelley lived would ask everybody what sort of place Inchedony was, because Callanan had named after it a bad poem in the manner of *Child Harolde*'.[192] And if Yeats never travelled to the shorelines of southwest Ireland, he had that much in common with James Clarence Mangan, who also found in Callanan's own Cork a layered image of a lost past.

James Clarence Mangan: Estuarine Histories

Mangan's father was a hedge schoolmaster, while his mother ran a grocery at 3 Fishamble Street, Dublin. He was educated in Jesuit schools and, at age fifteen, apprenticed to a scrivener as family fortunes declined. Mangan remained a legal scrivener until 1838, when he was appointed to the Ordnance Survey. In the 1830s, he came to know scholars and antiquarians, including John O'Donovan, Petrie and Owen Connellan, 'who were to inspire his interest in Irish-language material and supply him with raw translations to versify'.[193] As an employee of the Survey, Mangan was immersed in a Gaelic cultural world that was both past and present, as he consulted manuscripts at his desk in the Ordnance Survey Office.

In its practical operations, the Survey can be seen to expresses 'a sensibility that seeks out and respects indigenous forms of knowledge, Irish history, the Irish language, and the built heritage'.[194] It is within this contested context that Mangan came to know Cork and Ireland's southwest coast and, as with Yeats' longing for Inchydoney, Mangan did not follow through his reading with a visit to West Cork. While the Gaelic scholar John O'Donovan was 'tramping the roads of Ireland', engaged in 'collecting and annotating all kinds of topographical and antiquarian lore',[195] Mangan had clerical jobs, based at the home of George Petrie on Great Charles Street, Dublin. As the office of the Ordnance Survey was being wound up in 1841 and 1842, Mangan was copying down information about Cork. A letter from Larcom to Petrie asks if Mangan is 'copying the descriptive remarks from the Cork townlands of that county' and refers to the 'pressing' need for 'the copying of the inquis. for Cork'. Petrie wrote to Larcom on 25 November 1842 to say that *'Mr Mangan* is copying passages' relating to Cork from the *Pacata Hibernia*. Other letters suggest that Mangan was at work copying the Down Survey for Cork, an activity that would have brought him into close proximity to the post-Cromwellian transformation of the Irish landscape.[196]

As 'the facts and obscurities of Irish history gained immediacy and imaginative reality' for Mangan,[197] his poetry not only imparted 'imaginative reality' to the West Cork coastline but also 'engaged in a long-running critical dialogue with the modes of access to the historical past that the Survey explored'.[198] That dialogue is evident in his poem 'Lament over the Ruins of the Abbey of Teach Molaga'. First published in *The Nation* on 8 August 1846, this lyric poem in twenty quatrains gives dramatic voice to an unnamed figure who wanders at the edge of an estuary, at the head of which sits the ruined abbey of Timoleague (or Teach Molaga). The poem's topography encompasses a drowned river valley, where the Argideen River discharges into the Courtmacsherry Estuary on its way to the sea. The estuary is now designated a Special Area of Conservation because of its distinctive mudflats, sandy and shingle beaches, reedbeds and tideline vegetation, while the abbey's remains are marked on the original six-inch Ordnance Survey map for Cork: 'Timoleague Abbey. In Ruins'. On this map, the remains of the Abbey can be seen to overlook the point where the slow-moving Argideen is enclosed by sea and sand, before it discharges into the Atlantic. Gabriel Beranger's watercolours of the area, including his 'Timoleague Castle', capture the sinuous movement of water with and around a shifting shoreline. In the poem, the speaker's estuarine location ('I wandered forth at night alone / Along the dreary, shingly, billow-beaten shore') serves at once to enclose a subjective experience of loss and open the narrative up to the overlapping temporalities of anthropogenic change (Figure 3.1).[199]

James Clarence Mangan: Estuarine Histories 157

Figure 3.1 Gabriel Beranger, *Timoleague Castle, Abbey and Town*,
c. 1770–1799. Watercolour. 29.5 × 24 cm. RIA MS 3 C 30/68.
By permission of the Royal Irish Academy © RIA.

The first nineteen stanzas are translations of an earlier Irish-language poem by Sean O'Coilean of Myross in County Cork; the final, twentieth, stanza is Mangan's own addition. The title of the original poem, 'Machtnamh an Duine Dhoilgheasaig, nó Caoineadh Thighe Molaga', translates as 'Musings of a Lonely Person, or Lament for Timoleague'.[200] The poem opens with an Irish-language epigraph (*'Oidche dhámh go doilg, dúbhach'*) that is untranslated but closely echoed in the poem's opening line, 'I wandered forth at night alone'. As the speaker goes on to imagine a former clerical community as an emblem of organic wholeness and plenty, the poem voices a powerful address to a lost past. In imagining this vanished world, however, Mangan also captures the capacities of the poem's contemporary location in vivid and evocative ways. The loneliness and isolation of Mangan's lyric 'I' is intimately shaped by the 'dreary, shingly, billow-beaten shore' along which he wanders. The use of the poetic word 'billow' echoes Callanan's usage of this archaism in his literary notebooks from the 1820s, discussed in Chapter 2.

O'Coilean's original poem is sometimes thought of as a pastiche of an English romantic poem, rather than as a piece of writing that can be properly connected to Munster's rich poetic traditions, meaning that Mangan's 'Lament' arguably revives a poem that was not in the first place deeply rooted in Gaelic tradition. To be sure, O'Coilean's original is a poem that owes debts to Wordsworth's 'Tintern Abbey' and a synthetic romantic sensibility. As such, it makes up ground on which Mangan can construct a distinctive evocation of a changing place, located between languages and times.[201] Mangan himself has been understood to be unconcerned with 'natural things' and read as an urban and introspective poet who cannot reconnect the ruins of a broken sensibility with the healing qualities of the natural world.[202] His writing is, however, notably concerned with climate and with weather: states of cold and heat register layers of history in intimate ways in a number of his best poems, sometimes resulting in what Matthew Campbell describes as 'an invented prosody of frozen numbness, a sort of zombie metre'.[203]

In 'Lament over the Ruins of the Abbey of Teach Molaga', a cloudy night sky and the doleful sounds of wind and sea frame a changing historical canvas. The poem looks backwards to the Cromwellian conquest of Ireland and the destruction of monasteries and abbeys, in this case the Franciscan friary at Teach Molaga/Timoleague. In doing so, it conjures up an early modern Munster in which homeless wandering was commonplace: Dickson notes 'the disproportionately high numbers of wandering Irish poor with a south Munster background' and 'a strikingly direct association between the presence of the New English and the dislocation of the indigenous population'.[204] Nor had vagrancy passed into history. The Irish-language original of the poem was written in 1816, at the end of the Napoleonic Wars and the outset of a period of bleakly cold weather that affected the Atlantic seaboard in the aftermath of the Tambora eruption: farmers in Cork and Kerry 'witnessed the full gamut of rain-damaged crops, including waking to find their corn crop covered in red volcanic dust'.[205] Famines in 1817 and 1822 characterised these years of economic recession and food scarcity and were followed by the Rockite rebellion that convulsed the South of Ireland in the 1820s. Mangan's own translation and adaptation of the poem was undertaken during the catastrophic Famine years and appeared in print just before the cold autumn and harsh 'hunger winter' of 1846–7.

The identity of the particular place inscribed within the poem is verified via a footnote attached to the poem's title. This note not only translates what might be an unfamiliar Irish place name but also refers readers to the wider process whereby the Irish landscape was made legible in the English language via the work of the Ordnance Survey: 'Literally "The House of (St.) Molaga", and now called Timoleague. Our readers will find its position on the Map of Munster.' David Lloyd notes the many ironies involved in this note as Mangan reverts to an Irish language name now in need of translation.[206] For Lloyd, the linguistic and topographical intricacies of the footnote serve to undermine any straightforward cultural claims for authenticity that might be assumed via the poem's publication in *The Nation*. Just as the footnote suggests an opening up of provisionally placed forms of knowledge, however, so the instabilities and ironies that sound within Mangan's poetry are related to topographical as well as political forms of uncertainty. Lloyd is surely wrong when he remarks of the poem's location that '[i]t is consequently merely one more twist to this irony that, contrary to what the various versions imply, the map will show that Timoleague is not on the edge of the sea'.[207] Cóilín Parsons too queries the placing of Mangan's poem when he argues that its imagined topography confuses literary and real geographies: 'Whereas Timoleague's actual setting is closer to that of Tintern Abbey – the bend of a tranquil estuary – Mangan places it on the edge of the roaring Atlantic'.[208]

So where are the ruins of the abbey at Timoleague? The poem's topography in fact maps quite closely onto an actual marine environment comprised both of river and sea, an estuary that opens onto the Atlantic. The reference to 'the dreary, shingly, billow-beaten shore' in the first stanza of the poem signifies this estuarine location, which is also suggested in the Irish original of the poem, where the silence and lack of noise of sea or wind are mentioned. In stanzas thirteen and seventeen, the ocean is aligned with 'brutal England's Power', and the association of the Atlantic with empire and danger is familiar from Jeremiah Joseph Callanan's 1820s elegy, 'A Lay of Mizen Head', a poem that remembers the death by drowning of a young Irish midshipman on a wrecked British warship 'about a mile west of Mizen Head', on the West Cork coast.[209] These alignments of ocean and empire continued to have force in the 1840s, expressed in the 'Lament' by a distinctive coastal aesthetics that requires close attention to the very map mentioned at the poem's outset. The watery dimensions of Irish romanticism, discussed in Chapter 2, meet and reckon with detailed topographical knowledge of a marine environment that is at once estuarine and oceanic.

In the thirteenth stanza, in particular, sea, sands and history combine as active agents of change:

> Tempest and Time – the drifting sands –
> The lightnings and the rains – the seas that sweep around
> These hills in winter-nights, have awfully crowned
> The work of impious hands!

The poem's invocation of 'a continuing process of degradation'[210] can be understood in specifically environmental as well as more generally political terms. The silting up of this and other estuaries along the West Cork coast is noted by Charles Smith in his *Antient and Present State of the County and City of Cork* (first published in 1750): 'This harbour was formerly navigable, but is now quite obstructed with sand, so that only small sloops and boats can come to Timoleague, and smaller sand vessels about a mile above it'.[211] Most nineteenth-century travellers follow Smith in describing Timoleague as 'formerly a place of some note'.[212] Although by the 1830s it was a penny-post town with a constabulary station and a medical dispensary, Timoleague's most notable features remained its ruined abbey and silted up estuary. Pastness inheres not only in the abbey burned by Cromwell's soldiers but in the estuary itself, whose 'dreary' shore and 'drifting sands' supply a resonant language of change and loss.

Observing that the estuary on which the village is located is two miles from the mouth of the sea, located 'on an arm of the ocean', Smith describes how the river 'glides' in sinuous and intimate relationship to the ruined building that it 'washes' along the semicircular stretch of coastline.[213] Clear distinctions between river and sea or silence and sound do not fully hold for the mixed marine environment imagined by Mangan. The drifting, sweeping, gliding and washing of a poetic body of water that is comprised of both river and sea can cause critics of the poem to lose their bearings. In Fiona Stafford's vivid account, estuaries capture 'the essential uncertainty' of river mouths that are 'at once an end and a beginning'. The etymology is 'derived from the Latin, *aestuarium*, meaning "heating, boiling, bubbling"' and maps on to two distinct definitions. The first is an understanding of the estuary as an arm of the sea indenting the land while in its second sense, it means the tidal mouth of a great river: an inlet or an outlet both.[214]

In writing about the 'sense of an estuary as a kind of no man's land or a place of disputed power, where uncontrollable forces clash', Stafford helps us to understand the ways in which estuaries afford topographical, cultural and bodily forms of uncertainty that unfold under darkening skies. The ability of Mangan's poem to register the ambivalences of former abundance and present constraint draws on these affordances of estuaries as ending and beginning, opening and enclosure, mouth and arm. The poem's eleventh and twelfth stanzas imagine change via the lens of the natural world, as blown and unkempt flora merges with the built environment, and human and non-human worlds combine:

> Alas! alas! how dark the change!
> Now round its mouldering walls, over its pillars low,
> The grass grows rank, the yellow gowans blow,
> Looking so sad and strange!
>
> Unsightly stones choke up its wells;
> The owl hoots all night long under the altar-stairs;
> The fox and badger make their darksome lairs
> In its deserted cells!

The abbreviated lines that conclude each stanza, alongside the repeated exclamation marks, seem to enact a break with the familiar forms of consolation afforded by Romantic lyric. As the natural world darkens, the poem simultaneously registers the richness of a lost community and its susceptibility to violence. Rather than read Mangan as a poet who 'trades in evanescence' or approach 'Lament over the Ruins of the Abbey of Teach Molaga' as an 'archive of disappearances',[215] we might consider the ways in which the vision of a lost imagined community lives on, both on the map and within an imperilled natural world. Abandoned 'altar-stairs' become 'darksome lairs' for animals, while 'whitening bones half sunk / In the earth' bear witness to the lives of 'monk, / Friar, acolyte or priest'.

The critical relationship between nature and history we can discern in accounts of Irish landscape from the early modern period onwards might be seen as replicated in the unstable and invasive connection between land and sea in Mangan's poem. When the poem ends on 'the roaring of the wave', it is as a 'dirge' sounding in the ear of the poet:

> I turned away, as toward my grave,
> And, all my dark way homeward by the Atlantic's verge,
> Resounded in mine ears like to a dirge
> The roaring of the wave.

Death emerges in the specific context of the coastline with its resonant sonic effects, while the strange and uncertain rhyming of 'verge' and 'dirge', as with 'grave' and 'wave', helps us to hear some of the ways in which this poem puts in place a set of relationships between estuaries, pastness and the stylised elaboration of emotional intensity in a lyric mode. In 'Tintern

Abbey', Wordsworth writes of change in terms of a loss that is followed by 'abundant recompence'.[216] In putting a dark journey along the edge of a noisy estuary in the place of such 'recompence', Mangan's poem imagines a natural world that offers neither respite nor wreckage, but rather a fragile form of reflection beside the violent and mournful sounds of the sea.

'Lament over the Ruins of the Abbey of Teach Molaga' is rich in abstractions, perhaps evocative of the 'large characters' that Hugh Dorian had the Donegal peasant read from the landscape. Across its twenty stanzas, Mangan's poem invokes 'Life, and Death, and Fate', 'Piety and Peace: Virtue and Truth', 'Work and Will', 'Age', 'Tempest and Time', 'Wrong', 'Justice' and 'Change'. Of these, 'Change' seems the most resonant word of all, suggesting the power of language to express highly specific forms of loss even as it bends to powerful external circumstances:

> Alas, I rave! ... If Change is here,
> Is it not o'er the land? – Is it not too in me?
> Yes! I am changed even more than what I see.
> Now is my last goal near!

Such language stands at odds from the painful eyewitness accounts of mass mortality that began to appear in the British and Irish press from 1846. The West Cork town of Skibbereen, some forty kilometres east of Timoleague, featured often in the news reports. The area lost over a third of its people during the Great Famine, one of the most significant numbers seen in any Poor Law union in the country. Journalistic accounts of the impact of the Great Famine seem to already know and play upon the tones of Irish writing of the 1830s and early 1840s, where the call for a fuller picture of Ireland is also a call for darkness. William Carleton was praised by the *Dublin University Magazine* for bringing a welcome gloom to the Ireland that Edgeworth had only illuminated: where she achieved the 'first successful pourtraiture of our nation's peculiarities ... it is only its harmless wit or amiable foibles she has attempted to represent': 'though the outlines of the picture are most true to nature, yet by omitting the dark shading, she has left it imperfect, and resigned to others the task of putting in the gloomy back ground, which though sombre in itself, yet serves to throw out the brighter tints in the picture, and make it more faithful and correct.'[217] 'The genius of a people at large is not to be learned by the notes of Sunday tourists', wrote Samuel Ferguson in the *Dublin University Magazine* review of Hardiman's *Irish Melodies*.[218] Mangan's poem 'The Coming Event', published in the *Dublin University Magazine* in 1844, reworks popular prophetic modes to gesture towards an 'ungraspable' present that can only be greeted as the light dims: 'Darken the lamp, then, and bury the bowl'.[219]

Conclusion

This book has traced the emergence of a romantic relationship between past, present and future that was all but extinguished by the cataclysm of the Great Famine. In 1863 Carleton wrote to his friend Thomas Charles Steuart Corry (c. 1825–96), a doctor and poet, about his sense that his own reputation might sketch out a rough 'general history of Irish literature': 'Banim and Griffin are gone, and I will soon follow them – *ultimus Romanorum*, and after that will come a lull, an obscurity of perhaps half a century.' The 'last man' idea, already used in Mary Shelley's novel of 1826 and by Carlyle for Samuel Johnson, has deep resonance in Irish romantic writing from Thomas Moore to W. B. Yeats. But Carleton also saw a future in which other writers would come forward and take up the cause of Irish literature in the context of 'a new condition of civil society and a new phase of manners and habits among the people'. His own period, which he characterised as 'a *transition* state', was only one of a set of 'cycles of literature and taste', each of which 'appear, hold their day, displace each other, and make room for others'.[220] Carleton's predictions regarding civil society seem to call up the Literary Revival that would emerge by the century's end, while his account of literary cycles and phases might anticipate Yeats. But above and beyond Carleton's power of prophecy, and even taking account the 'tired and exhausted' state of mind in which he wrote this letter only six years before his death, we can hear his faith in a robust literary future that will yield 'new fields and new tastes'.[221] This book's Afterword takes up the idea of resilience in Irish romanticism via the much-worked image of the peasant overcoat.

Afterword
Frieze Coats and the Fabric of Irish Romanticism

The preceding chapters have described an evolving Irish romantic culture intent on originating forms of knowledge and forging its own terms of engagement with the world. In the spirit of an Irish romanticism that demands attention to its own distinctive textures, I end with a discussion of a domestic Irish product – frieze fabric – which figures a romantic culture patterned by both frangibility and force. In order to make that argument, I set the more familiar figure of romantic ruin to one side, though not before noting that ruins themselves are often busy places, containing recent London newspapers and romantic secrets as in the Castle of Inismore in *The Wild Irish Girl*, or housing aspects of everyday life, as depicted in George Petrie's delicately ironic drawing, *Hanging Washing in Lord Portlester's Chapel, Saint Audeon's* (Figure A.1). Turning to Henry McManus' painting *Reading 'The Nation'* from the 1850s (Figure A.2), it is almost as if romantic ruins – in this case, a Gothic arch, loosely rendered in the background – are in the process of giving way to the Irish peasants whose heavy clothing fills out the foreground. The painting vividly imagines growing literacy and communal reading practices as a group of men and women gather around a copy of *The Nation*. But along with the distinctive font of the newspaper itself, the range of heavy outwear depicted jostles for visual space. Our attention falls not only on the shiny black coat worn by the older man whose reading expertise gives him the central place but also on the women's red cloaks and the bulky woollen coats of the men.

Just as the 'novel persistence' of old fashions helped to create new ideas of history, so too did such heavy everyday clothing make its way into the texture of Irish romantic writing.[1] Frieze, a domestically manufactured coarse, napped woollen cloth that was commonly used to clothe the ordinary people of the country, appears in Irish literature in a range of contradictory guises: as tough and impermeable stuff, as material remnants, including tattered rags and patches, and as the makings of entire pieces

Figure A.1 George Petrie, *Hanging Washing in Lord Portlester's Chapel, Saint Audeon's, Dublin*, n.d. Graphite and wash on paper. 14.3 × 23.1 cm. NGI.6002.

of clothing (especially coats) with their own aura and near-supernatural agency. Frieze was usually spun at home before being sent to mills to be carded, thickened, teased and woven. Often coloured with natural materials including boiled mud and briars, its characteristic dark colour came, in one account, from 'colouring wool with indigo and bog-mould and branches of oak', the fabric 'then teased and the three colours were mixed – white, blue and black'.[2] Forms of coarse cloth were produced all across the country, with some regional variations, as part of an eighteenth-century Irish woollen industry that was largely rural and domestic. By 1770, some ten million yards of cloth had already been produced in Ireland. From that decade though, differences began to tell as mechanisation became the norm in Britain, and Irish woollen manufacture remained a cottage-based business. The fuller integration of British and Irish markets created difficulties for a local market in cheap coarse cloth, while Union duties in 1824 along with steam on the Irish Sea meant further setbacks for Irish industry. Still, domestically produced cloth dominated Irish markets until the 1820s, while the industry retained very close links to British manufacturing. The arrival of British woollens and then cheap cotton (which came to dominate British markets for the clothing of the poor) in Ireland from the 1830s meant the first serious setbacks.

Figure A.2   Henry McManus, *Reading 'The Nation'*, 1850s. Oil on canvas. 30.5 × 35.5 cm. National Gallery of Ireland. NGI.1917.

Over the period addressed in this book, demand for coarse woollen cloths grew in Ireland as the population did. And even after the population fell back after the Famine, it is somewhat surprising to see the establishment and survival of a number of small woollen mills in the 1850s and 60s, especially in Cork, with sites at Blarney and Dripsey. Within those mills, older practices including fulling or 'kicking' done by hand and by feet existed alongside mechanised processes. Reflecting upon woollen manufacture as 'one of the nineteenth-century success stories within the Irish industrial sector', we encounter a narrative of historic strength and strange survivals.[3] Some of these survivals can be traced in the records of the Schools' Collection of Irish folklore, material gathered from children in the 1930s, where we find the kind of details that emerge from efforts to track a vanishing history. Among the material gathered in the Schools' Collection, durability is often mentioned. Frieze, William Keaveney in Creggs, County Galway told a collector 'would last a man ten or fifteen years',[4] while Patrick Finnegan of Bushfield, County Roscommon explained to eleven-year-old Mary Finnegan that 'Frieze coats were very warm, and there was great wear in them.' Patrick Finnegan went on to say that 'Long ago most men had a frieze coat, but there are very few frieze coats to be seen nowadays.'[5]

Placenames, though, retain the history, as found in an explanation of the unusual name of the Cottoners, or Cottners River (in Irish *Abha Oileán Uachra*) in County Kerry, given to Sean O'Riordan by a Father Casey. *Abha* means river, and *oileáin* island, while *uachar* (*uachra* in the genitive) can mean the man who napped the frieze but is also the name for a plant ('the Bréide Ceann-a-bhán') that 'grows plentifully around the Cottners river', and which was used to mix in with the wool in the manufacture of frieze: 'Some people used this Ceann-a-bhán to mix with wool in making the frieze and gave it the name of Cotún or Catán and the man who napped the mixture of cotton was called the Cotner, hence the river got the name Cottner's river from the old frieze napper.'[6]

The pastness of frieze is associated with its strength and durability (affording 'great wear' as well as holding onto meanings over time) and its cultural specificity (something that needs to be explained by recursive reference to place, people and craft practices). These qualities move in and out of the figuration of frieze in the Romantic period. The value of frieze in Irish rural life can be further gauged from stories that tell of how a piece of the fabric might serve as a token in place of coin, while their power is further expressed in a Monaghan story that tells of an Orangeman who, 'contrary to custom', 'happened to be wearing a frieze coat': 'The grand master of the Order noticed this and believing him to be a catholic rode his horse over him and killed him.'[7] Violence recurs in a Longford account which sees a red-coated soldier enter a cabin after the Battle of Ballinamuck in 1798, to ask for a glass of water while carrying over his arm a new frieze coat that the woman of the house recognises as belonging to her son. She offers the soldier the water and then, as 'he raised the noggin to his head', kills him with a blow of a shovel across the throat.[8]

To further understand how frieze figures a range of meanings associated with everyday life in Ireland – including durability, concealment and threat – we need look no further than Maria Edgeworth's *Castle Rackrent* and its opening account of Thady's 'long great coat', worn 'winter and summer' over seven years, most often attached 'by a single button round my neck, cloak fashion'.[9] Thady's coat makes a distinctive textual appearance, and its layered appearance partakes of the bookish qualities of Irish romanticism described in Chapter 1. Although frieze is not specified in Thady Quirke's case, his might well be the kind of bulky garment described in James McParlan's *Statistical Survey of the County of Sligo* (1802), where he notes that the native Irish are not only clothed in 'frize [*sic*] of their own manufacture' but in layers of the stuff: a suit of frieze might only cost about thirty-five shillings but, 'as the fathers of families and settled men never can imagine a suit complete, or being decently dressed without a great coat of the same stuff, which they wear in all seasons and weathers, this increases the expence nearly one half of the whole'.[10] Edward Wakefield's *An Account of Ireland, Statistical and Political* (1812), a book that recommends *Castle Rackrent* for its contribution to 'the improvement of national manners and morals in Ireland' and claims the novel for a new literary sociology, also notes excess as an aspect of Irish clothing.[11] In Munster, Wakefield observes, 'a peasant never considers himself dressed for a fair or a pattern unless he puts on his whole wardrobe at once'. And Wakefield cites a survey of Kildare that tells of how 'Pat sweats under a heavy frieze coat' even in the dog days of summer, noting that Irish tailors like to produce items that fall loosely 'in the manner of a surtout': 'An Irishman is as awkward in a close coat, as a highlander in breeches'.[12]

The age, length and cloak-like appearance of Thady's coat further reminds attentive readers of the presence of vestigial medieval tailoring techniques and styles in ordinary Irish clothing. The connection was already made by the mid-nineteenth century, when William Wilde's list of historical objects found in the museum of the Royal Irish Academy notes not only the 'long graceful robe or cloak' worn by ancient Irish elites but also its survival in 'the heavy-caped frieze *cota-mor* of the modern Irish, so often worn hanging from the shoulders'.[13] In 1783, Richard Lovell Edgeworth wrote a letter to the Society of Antiquaries, sent to London to accompany a woollen coat found 'fifteen feet under ground, in a turf bog or peat moss' in the neighbourhood of Edgeworthstown. The letter makes a slighting reference to the reluctance of its farmer finder to give up his treasure: we are told that the unnamed man prizes it, 'like the Chinese, merely because another person wanted it'. But if the tenant farmer drove a hard bargain, then his reluctance is echoed in the 'uncouth fabric' of the coat itself, 'remarkable in nothing but its texture'.[14] A better known case is that of an early seventeenth-century coat, recovered from Killery Bog, County Sligo in 1824, found to be of knee length and made of unlined frieze, shaped in a long line style including a dip in the neckline to increase the appearance of height in the collar (Figure A.3).[15] The surviving object not only fits well

Figure A.3 A late sixteenth-century coat recovered from Killery Bog, County Sligo in 1824. © National Museum of Ireland.

with Thady's coat as described by Edgeworth, but closely resembles that worn by the teacher who occupies the foreground in Nathaniel Grogan's (c. 1740–1807) *The Country Schoolmaster*, the tails of his coat flashing about him as he beats two fleeing pupils with dried twigs (see Figure A.4).[16] The style persisted long enough for one schoolchild in Aughrim in the 1930s to refer to 'body-tail coats'.[17]

Finally, Thady's bookish coat merits its own footnote, one that proclaims the 'high antiquity' of the item and opens up rich seams of textual and historical information. The coat is first explained by reference

Figure A.4 Nathaniel Grogan, *The Country Schoolmaster*, n.d. Mezzotint and etching. 36.4 × 52.8 cm. The British Museum. 1977, U.1225.

to Edmund Spenser, whose account in turn refers us back to the fabled Scythians and ancient Greece and Rome, as well as Egypt. Authorities including Diodorus and Herodotus are cited before the note turns back to Spenser, this time in a more markedly political mode. Quoting Spenser's *View of the Present State of Ireland* and the views of one of its two speakers, Irenius, the note explains the size and bulk of ordinary Irish coats in terms of their usefulness as 'mantle, as housing, bedding, and cloathing [sic]'. Such qualities allow for disguise and escape, meaning that Irish coats such as the one worn by Thady make 'a fit house for an outlaw, a meet bed for a rebel, and an apt cloak for a thief'. Edgeworth's note cites Spenser at length:

> First, the outlaw being, for his many crimes and villanies, banished from the towns and houses of honest men, and wandering in waste places, far from danger of law, maketh his mantle his house, and under it covereth himself from the wrath of Heaven, from the offence of the earth, and from the sight of men. When it raineth, it is his penthouse; when it bloweth, it is his tent; when it freezeth, it is his tabernacle. In summer he can wear it loose; in winter he can wrap it close; at all times he can use it; never heavy,

never cumbersome. Likewise for a rebel it is as serviceable; for in this war that he maketh (if at least it deserve the name of war), when he still flieth from his foe, and lurketh in the *thick woods*, (*this should be black dogs*,) and straight passages waiting for advantages, it is his bed, yea, and almost his household stuff.[18]

The association between heavy coats and deceit is sufficiently familiar for Edgeworth to flip its meanings: in her tale 'To-morrow' (one of the *Popular Tales* from 1804), we meet Basil, the well-educated son of an English bookseller, down on his luck in Philadelphia and donning something very like Thady's greatcoat. The tale seems to reverse Spenser's terms as Basil, wrapped up in 'an old surtout' and with a hat 'slouched' over his face, walks the docks in a state of financial despair. There he meets an Irish emigrant named Barney who has gotten on in America and whose prosperous and happy family bring Basil into their comfortable home, remove his 'shabby great coat' and offer him help and hospitality.[19]

From *Castle Rackrent* onwards, coats appear in the mode of explanation: they not only clothe characters but themselves come dressed in footnotes, glosses and explanations. *The Wild Irish Girl* too threads the dense history of Irish fabrics into its paratextual material: the novel's epigraph, three lines of fourteenth-century Italian verse by the author Fazio degli Uberti, was found by Owenson in the first issue of the *Transactions of the Royal Irish Academy*, some pages into an essay written by Lord Charlemont on 'The Antiquity of the Woollen Manufacture in Ireland proved from a Passage of an Ancient Florentine Poet'.[20] The kind of claims made by Charlemont – that 'Ireland was possessed of an extensive trade in woollens at a very early period, and long before the commodity was an English export – serve to exalt ancient Ireland's standing and refute 'that idea of barbarity which is usually objected to them'.[21] Following the latter observation, Charlemont gives the translated lines of verse used by Owenson: 'This race of men, tho' savage they may seem / The country too with many a mountain rough / Yet they are sweet to him who tries and tastes them.'[22]

But the greatcoat did not shed its close connection with Spenser and nor was it easy to undo a link between glossing itself as a colonial mode of explanation with deep roots in early modern Ireland. In Lady Morgan's *Florence Macarthy*, Owney the driver wears, or rather sheds, a coat that once more comes supplied with its own footnote. 'I threw off my *cotamore*, in regard of the heat', he tells the two English travellers, describing a journey taken to Kilcolman in North Cork, the site of Edmund Spenser's

Irish home. A '*cotamore*', explains the footnote, means 'Great coat'. This literal translation from the Irish is supplemented by a further explanation that draws attention to the layered nature of coarse woollen clothing: 'The cotaigh was the upper garment anciently.'[23]

Edgeworth and Owenson both give us textual strata, layered like the clothing of the Irish poor, that lend structure to the bookish tendency of Irish romanticism in its first phase. They set in motion a process whereby footnotes mediate cultural knowledge for a divided society, making its history palpable on the page. Thady's coat shares something in common with the rag rug imagined by Carolyn Steedman in *Dust*, a domestic textile made from clippings of old clothes into a humble object that might convey the 'inwardness and harmony' of working-class lives but also speaks of a tensile strength borne of scarcity.[24]

Those dynamics of strength and scarcity come more clearly into view when we consider frieze coats alongside their regular rhetorical companion: rags. Many visitors to Ireland remarked upon the ragged clothing of the people, glimpsed on the side of the road or from the window of a coach. In Lockhart's *Memoirs of the Life of Sir Walter Scott*, before those people even come into view, it is the rags themselves that draw attention. Travelling by steam boat from Glasgow to Belfast in 1825, Scott's party shared space 'with a cargo offensive enough to the eye and the nostrils, but still more disagreeable from the anticipations and reflections it could not fail to suggest'. Indeed they saw little else: 'Hardly had our carriage been lashed on the deck before it disappeared from our view amidst mountainous packages of old clothes; the cast-off raiment of the Scotch beggars was on its way to a land where beggary is the staple of life.'[25] It is tempting to speculate that these rags were destined for the Irish paper industry, poised to play a part in the material life of literature itself. But Irish paper mills were small affairs, and it is much more likely that the malodorous bundles described by Lockhart consisted of items for reuse and resale. Ireland in the early nineteenth century was a major secondary market for old clothing, sold by the ton from the cities of England and Scotland and shipped across the sea. Such rags can scarcely cover impoverished Irish bodies (seen by Lockhart only as 'naked clamorous beggars' in Kerry), but they also possess a power of explanation at once ordinary and abundant, made evident in Scott's own remarks about Irish poverty:

> There is much less of exaggeration about the Irish than might have been suspected. Their poverty is not exaggerated; it is on the extreme verge of human misery; their cottages would scarce serve for pig-sties, even in Scotland – and their rags seem the very refuse of a rag-shop, and are disposed on their

bodies with such ingenious variety of wretchedness that you would think nothing but some sort of perverted taste could have assembled so many threads together.[26]

The version of 'human misery' to be found in Ireland seems itself to disintegrate in Scott's account, scarcely held together by the familiar images of poor cabins and tattered clothing.

Rags that are worse than rags can also express a seemingly stubborn Irish resistance to improvement. In a letter to Lord Selkirk concerning the blocks to emigration as a solution to Irish problems, Richard Lovell Edgeworth describes Irish reluctance to emigrate in terms of peasants' curious ability to satisfy themselves with rags that are less than coats. Remarking on the 'sordid content' of the peasant who would rather subsist in Ireland than settle in a British colony overseas, Edgeworth observes Ireland is 'a nursery for soldiers, but not for emigrants'.[27] Looking through the lens of the mass Irish experience of migration to come, the observation seems a strange one, but Edgeworth's concern was that that families who might otherwise emigrate (and thus free up land for grazing, as did the Scots who went to Upper Canada) were able to eke out a living on subdivided land thanks to military and naval incomes. Ireland supplied the British army and navy with around 40 per cent of its non-commissioned men, and their remittances kept relatives in their home places, poorly clad as they might be there. The relationship between abundance and scarcity so characteristic of the colonial discourse of improvement is expressed here in relation to the abundant affordances of coarse cloth and the insufficiencies of Irish ambition: 'the difference between rags and a whole coat is not much regarded amongst his neighbours'.[28]

In the case of the Edgeworths, though, improvement was not only stitched into the daily texture of family life but could also result in some unpredictable patterns. In James Hall's 1813 *Tour through Ireland*, he notes with approval that 'Mr Edgeworth's children are all instructed at home' and reports on seeing 'three of his daughters, fine little girls, busily engaged in sewing a covering of patches, of various colours, for a poor family in the vicinity, who had once been servants in the house'.[29] And yet the country around Edgeworthstown would have sustained many domestic woollen manufactures. A priest who came to Killoe, County Longford in 1917, said that the older people still remembered the time before the railways came as one of plenty, with widespread small-scale flax production, numerous looms and sheep that provided women with the materials to manufacture 'blankets, friezes and tweeds'.[30] The Edgeworth girls' coat of many colours might recognise the hard times that came after Waterloo, when ragged clothing represents the plight of those left behind by the receding tide of war-time prices. Or it might be just a misplaced act of benevolence, showing ignorance of a cottage industry that flourished just miles from the big house.

Such questions of perspective come to inhere in ragged fabrics. Looking through travellers' accounts of Ireland, the textile historian Mairead Dunlevy remarks on how often such visitors fail to notice in the 'everyday "rags"' that they describe 'the survival of traditional modes of Irish dress'.[31] Those survivals are made to seem all the more remarkable by the cultural inscription of clothing composed only of bits and pieces. In Gerald Griffin's 'Card Drawing', discussed in Chapter 2, the character of the Card-Drawer herself derives some of her strange power from the almost inconceivable and nearly non-human way in which her costume of 'shreds and rags' holds together and covers her person. The woman's potential power of prophecy is amplified in the mystery of her appearance, a matter of parts that finds comparisons only in the natural world: 'There did not appear to be two square inches about her in one piece, and her whole costume shook in the morning wind like the foliage of a tree'. In spite of resembling nothing less than 'a mountain of rags', the old woman has a 'warm and comfortable look' that leads the narrative into lengthy speculation as to the mysterious protection afforded by ragged items of clothing: 'How they were all united puzzled him more than the mystery of the tides of Negropont did the Stagyrite.' The reference to Aristotle and the Greek island of Euboea lends the narrative voice an air of distant superiority but this too dissolves in the careful catalogue of the Card-Drawer's wardrobe that follows. The tone is one of wonderment, as the inventory starts at the bottom with shoes that are 'more properly (if they must have a name) her *brogues*': they 'were in pieces, yet her feet were perfectly covered – partly with straw thrust into the fissures made in the leather, and in part with the fragments of an old woollen stocking.' Next comes her headdress, a substantial kerchief that flutters in the wind, while over her shoulder are thrown 'hare, kid, and rabbit skins'. As the description proceeds, the narrative itself appears to exfoliate into repeated expressions of amazement that recombine about the figure of the old woman in rags: 'It seemed as if her dress had been built up about her from the ground, of all manner of fragments.'[32]

Griffin's near suggestion that ordinary fragments might have a supernatural power is taken still further in Maturin's *Melmoth the Wanderer*. When John Melmoth observes the shipwreck that I discuss in Chapter 2, and the household rushes to help, they gather up 'a hundred coats, boots, and hats of their old master'. One greatcoat is found doing duty as a protective border and has to be dragged 'from the window, before which it had long hung as a blind, in total default of glass or shutters'. It is not only the window that is breached, however, as the inhabitants of the house hurry out and make for the shore, struggling against a fierce wind as they rush to help the victims of the shipwreck. A sudden burst of moonlight allows John Melmoth to achieve a 'full view' of the terrible plight of the vessel being dashed against the treacherous Wicklow coast, and he is overcome by terror, shouting into the storm 'with yells of actual insanity'. Returning to his senses, John Melmoth chooses to understand the terrible scene in terms of human capacity for sympathetic action: '"How much good there is in man," he cried, "when it is called forth by the sufferings of his fellows!"' Even as he comes to this benign conclusion, though, it is tested by the sight of a man, 'standing a few yards above him on the rock, a figure that shewed neither sympathy or terror, – uttered no sound, – offered no help'.

> Melmoth could hardly keep his footing on the slippery and rocking crag on which he stood; the figure, who stood still higher, appeared alike unmoved by the storm, as by the spectacle. Melmoth's surtout, in spite of his efforts to wrap it round him, was fluttering in rags, – not a thread of the stranger's garments seemed ruffled by the blast.

As the Wanderer remarks 'Let them perish', we see a ragged greatcoat comes under pressure of global forces, marshalled at the coast.[33] Meanwhile the Wanderer's own clothing is miraculously free from the effects of wind and weather.

John Melmoth's Gothic coat seems to lie at a great distance from the bundles of old clothing observed by Walter Scott on the boat to Ireland. And yet they share not only a maritime location but also the status of rags, once more asking readers to reflect upon and rework what Richard Lovell Edgeworth describes as 'the difference between rags and a whole coat'. A now familiar mode of bulky, miserable privation comes into view when Jane Eyre first arrives at Lowood School and has to don a 'cloak of grey frieze'.[34] Then, in the final phase of Irish romanticism and at almost the same moment as Brontë's novel appeared, frieze coats come more fully into view in their entirety. No longer the heavy item worn as a cloak by Thady Quirke or the fluttering rags imagined by Griffin and Maturin, the frieze coat of the 1830s and 40s is best represented off the page by Daniel O'Connell, who wore a heavy dark coat of domestic Irish manufacture for his debut appearance in the House of Commons. He is reported to have said: 'I leave my broadcloth at home, and I appear in frieze ... for it is through the frieze-coats I expect to get redress for Ireland's wrongs.'³⁵ O'Connell not only promoted Irish manufacture (including the so-called 'Repeal cloth') at his monster meetings but made his addresses to hundreds and thousands of followers who were themselves known as 'the frieze-coats'. Contemporary newspapers are filled with references to the '*frieze-coated* thousands' at his monster meetings, and the Oxford English Dictionary notes that the compound noun 'frieze-coat' not only means a 'coat made of frieze' but is also 'a designation applied to an Irish peasant'. (The example given comes from Benjamin Disraeli's *Sybil* of 1845).³⁶

Walking in East Lothian in the early 1840s, Thomas Carlyle shows weary familiarity with this usage as he notes the dominance of corn growing on good land, writing in a period when corn was still protected from imports so that prices were high and pastures were routinely ploughed up so as to feed the industrial cities. Complaining of a fertile Scottish landscape become a 'Corn Manchester', Carlyle described the workers, 'some 150 decent Highlanders' surrounded by 'a horde of miserable weak, wild Irish*n*, their conquerors and successors, here ... all in a ragged grey frieze, 3,000 or 4,000 of them, aimless, restless, hungry, senseless, more like apes than men; swarming ab*t*, leaping into beanfields, turnip-fields and out ag*n*, asking you "the toime, Sir"'.³⁷ The undifferentiated sea of 'ragged grey frieze' seen by Carlyle consists of seasonal migrant workers who brought money back to Ireland in order to be able to pay off debts to the gombeen men and shop owners that sold food and lent money at high interest rates in a cash scarce environment. Characterised by Carlyle in terms of restless and agitated movement, seasonal workers sometimes became permanent residents in cities like Glasgow or the industrial towns. The Scottish farmers for whom they worked needed to get the corn cut and in quickly while dry weather held, so that time to rest was scarce and the lesson of industrial clock time was taught in the fields.

Nasty as it is, Carlyle's racialised language aims at provoking British readers into an analysis of their own culture. In *Sartor Resartus* or 'the tailor re-tailored' (1831), he uses the pseudo-study of a German philosopher in order to depict a British society that consists mainly of outward representations. Originally titled 'Thoughts on Clothes', *Sartor Resartus* treats dandified aristocrats and labouring Irish as similar examples of commonplace but dangerous social groupings whose unreliability inheres in their clothing: the 'Dandiacal Body' of the aristocrat seeks safety in a swallow-tail coat with a low, rolled collar while the so-called 'Irish Poor-Slave' – also known as 'the *Drudge* Sect', 'the *White Negroes*' and 'the *Ragged-Beggar*

Sect' among a host of other offensive names – clothe themselves in 'innumerable skirts, lappets and irregular wings, of all cloths and of all colors; through the labyrinthic intricacies of which their bodies are introduced by some unknown process'.[38]

Deeply influential on a generation of British writers who came after the Romantics, *Sartor Resartus* has been understood as introducing a note of 'desperation' that ushered in Victorian literature.[39] But Irish romanticism was already wary of custom and darkened by change and, from about the 1840s, coats began to make their own case in Irish literature, taking on something of the 'vibrant' character that Colleen Taylor assigns to Irish material culture more generally.[40] When Lady Morgan reviewed Thackeray's *Irish Sketchbook* (1843), a variety of clothing stands in for a multifarious and clamorous Ireland. Guidebooks of any kind are to be treated with caution, she wrote, before offering cautious praise to Thackeray's fictional Titmarsh for the rich diversity of people and places represented. The book does not escape the 'objective' image of Ireland as a green island that lies 'shivering in unrepaled [*sic*] nakedness', Morgan writes, but it does at least open up a 'subjective' account of a well-draped Ireland: 'she may have as large a wardrobe of parti-coloured suits of clothing as would establish a masquerade warehouse, – as many as there are eyes to see, and minds to reflect'.[41]

Clothing here might stand in for realism itself, a mode responsive to a multitudinous Ireland that demands to be seen in the aggregate – thanks to the frieze coats. That romantic realism is especially associated with the work of William Carleton, who not only wrote about heavy woollen clothing but knew what it meant to wear it – 'the frieze-coated peasant of genius', as one account has it.[42] Carleton himself only gives us glimpses of this earlier world, as when in the *Autobiography* he boasts of his skill at spelling and scholarship by reference to a 'shining' coat sleeve, worn with use.[43] But the concerted cultural effort to make Carleton into the authentic peasant voice clothed him in frieze even when he wore finer fabrics: an 1847 account of meeting him on the street in Dublin looked past his 'glossy hat and broadcloth' to imagine a writer more suitably attired in 'the frieze coat and knee breeches of his forbears'.[44]

In Carleton's novel *The Black Prophet*, discussed in Chapter 3, we first meet the character of Darby Skinadre, a merchant and meal monger who takes advantage of the post-Waterloo credit crunch to exploit the needs of families whose members may be migrant workers hoping to bring back cash to pay the landlord. When Skinadre taunts a hungry man who has not recently been to mass, the poor man defends himself by way of a delicate reference to a lack of suitable clothing, explaining that his wife has 'a web of frieze half made', and that he will appear among fellow worshippers once better clad. The same meal monger is a 'blood-sucking old spider' whose 'web of mischief' is partly spun from woollen fabrics.

The commodities sold for cash in Skinadre's shop are often items that he has received in lieu of cash payment. He thinks little of appropriating the ordinary property of others to himself and Carleton gives us a list that features frieze along with butter, yarn, pigs, cows and heifers.[45] Karl Marx – writing *Das Kapital* in London as he heard news of the Irish famine and the establishment of the Encumbered Estates Court to dispose of the property of indebted Irish landlords – predicted that capitalism would penetrate agricultural production, starting in Ireland. Irish historians have debated his views, in particular his lack of understanding of the drive towards peasant proprietorship and land hunger that was to come. Less noticed within Irish Studies, however, are Marx's opening observations about coats as commodities. According to Marx, when tailoring – the making of coats from linen fabric – became a specialised activity, so began the objectification of the social value of labour and the emergence of items whose value inhered in their capacity to be exchanged on the market for money. 'Coats are not exchanged for coats' writes Marx, 'one use value is not exchanged for another of the same kind.' Coats are not quite exchanged for coats in Irish romantic culture, but neither is 'the relation between the coat and the labour that produced it' yet a matter of specialised individual work and nor has the coat taken on 'its fully developed shape, that of money'.[46] Irish coats belong to a communal world and originate in domestic manufacture. But their proximity to rags and patches endows them with a special power that hints at 'the fantastic form of a relation between things' and the emergence of commodity fetishism. Marx himself, meanwhile, took his own overcoat in and out of the pawnshop and lived a precarious relationship with its warmth and shelter.[47] Some ten years later, his friend and collaborator Friedrich Engels began to take notes on ancient Irish literature, Irish songs and the work of Jonathan Swift, all part of a projected 'History of Ireland' on which he worked in 1869 and 1870.

For W. B. Yeats, Carleton was Ireland's true historian: in lines that resonate with Hugh Dorian's account of the 'large characters' in which the country's environment writes its story, Yeats observed that *The Black Prophet* calls up 'the wild, torn, storm-clouds that lie in heaps along the western seas of Ireland'.[48] Yet the novel borrows much from Carleton's native Tyrone, a landlocked northern county that is made the scene of terrible jealousies and narrow violence. In the novel's opening scene, the character of Sarah McGowan, the daughter of the eponymous prophet, tries to stab her stepmother with a knife. A fierce girl who longs to be free of her family and thinks nothing of defying the fairies by bringing hawthorn indoors, Sarah launches at her stepmother and soon takes on the appearance of 'some beautiful vampire that was ravening for the blood of its awakened victim'. And yet it is the everyday power of ragged fabric that saves the older woman, the knife failing to penetrate 'owing to the thick layers of cloth with which the dress of the other was patched'.[49] The fight sets in motion a train of actions that include the discovery of an old dusty tobacco box in the roof of the McGowan cottage (Sarah is in search of cobwebs to stop her stepmother's blood and heal the wound) and the subsequent unearthing of a corpse near the home of their neighbours, the Sullivans.

In *The Black Prophet*, coarse fabrics belong to everyday life but also can summon states of suspended existence, made material in the plot by the pressing question of two unsolved murders that date from 1798. One of the murdered men is the uncle of the young woman Mave Sullivan, known to the community as 'the *Gra Gal*' or lovely girl. When Donnel Dhu, the Black Prophet of the title, visits the Sullivan home in the company of Mave's father, Jerry Sullivan, he is called upon to witness her parents as they upbraid her for keeping company with a young man whom they suspect to be her uncle's murderer. To drive the point home, Jerry Sullivan holds a candle to 'a great coat of frieze which hung against the wall – "there's his coat – there's my lovin' brother's coat; look upon it now, and ax yourself what do you desarve for meetin' against our will and consint the son of him that has the murdher of the man that owned it on his hands an' on his heart? What do you desarve, I say?"' It is the Black Prophet, though, not Mave who is terrified, 'struck' as he is 'by the words and the unexpected appearance of the murdered man's coat'. The two are strangely joined in this moment as she faints, supported by Donnel Dhu and at the same time marked by blood that suddenly flows from his nose. Among the many strange aspects of their uncomfortable intimacy amidst a cabin marked by poverty and hunger is their shared focus on the old frieze coat. Both observe the coat to move of its own volition, and should there be any doubt as to what happens, the narrator joins in to confirm that, 'whether from its dim flickering light, or the force of imagination, cannot be determined, one thing was certain, the coat appeared actually to move again, as if disturbed by some invisible hand'. Later, the Black Prophet dreams of the coat which returns him to a vision of his own former crime, eventually unravelled by the plot.[50]

In Carleton, as with the earlier examples discussed, the frieze coat calls for explanation but also serves to rebuff external accounts of a culture that hides itself from view. The coat is a marker of indigenous culture that is both copious and friable, excessively large and layered and yet keeping close company with the image of the poor Irish man or woman clothed only in rags. Those tensions not only remained alive in Irish romanticism but worked their way into the textures of later Irish literature too. Frieze clothing provides an easy shorthand for class and nation in Emily Lawless' novel *Hurrish: A Study* (1886). Fainter threads of connection can be traced in a mysterious late scene in E. OE. Somerville and Martin Ross' novel, *The Real Charlotte* (1894), where Charlotte Mullen, the daughter of a land agent and a true fictional descendant of Thady Quirke, dons a coat made for her by a peasant tailor named Dinny Lydon. Speaking in Irish, Charlotte commands Dinny to hand her the coat on which she observes marks made by candle wax: a sure sign that Dinny's wife has already worn the coat to a recent wake. Rather than express anger, a menacing Charlotte waits as Dinny irons the grease out of the coat using brown paper, stroking a 'half-starved cat' and extracting lethal information about recent land dealings from the unsuspecting tailor.[51]

The lineage becomes clearer with W. B. Yeats, whose 'The Circus Animals Desertion' turns to the detritus of Irish life – 'Old kettles, old bottles, and a broken can, / Old iron, old bones, old rags' – in order to fashion a dramatic vision of poetry made whole in 'the foul rag and bone shop of the heart'. Later, we find Samuel Beckett's Molloy 'in winter, under my greatcoat', 'wrapped … in swathes of newspaper', the *Times Literary Supplement* particularly admired for its 'never failing' qualities of 'toughness and impermeability'. Seamus Heaney's doomed 1798 rebels, 'the pockets of our greatcoats full of barley', carry the meanings of the *cota mór* forward into an era of commemoration.[52] As those twentieth-century examples might further suggest, rags and coats also have a tendency to keep our focus trained on Irish men rather than women, a lasting problem in a literary tradition that started off so promisingly but so partially with the writings of Protestant women.

Irish bodies continued to take shelter under strong heavy fabrics, though in 1857 William Wilde noted that 'the large-caped frieze or *cota mór*' was 'daily falling into disuse'.[53] So much was observed by William Wordsworth during his Irish tour of 1829, when he describes how, passing from Clare into Tipperary en route to Edgeworthstown, the 'Postboys' alighted the carriage just before arrival in the town of Nenagh. On the side of the road, the young Irish men 'redressed themselves' and made themselves 'dacent', 'appearing before us in smart drab jackets with gold Buttons, mounted their jaded and restive horses to their own infinite satisfaction – and not a little to our amusement'.[54]

As frieze coats were shed in favour of smart jackets, it might seem that what coats conceal is change itself. But such modest versions of progress were soon to be swept away in the coming experience of famine and mass migration. In the immediate post-Famine period, Harriet Martineau depicted Ireland as 'this land of hunger and rags'. Describing the lunatic asylum of Killarney, a 'prodigious edifice' built in a town 'where human families are huddled like swine', she turns to a metaphor drawn from clothing: 'we could not but feel that to build such an establishment in such a place was like giving a splendid waistcoat to a man without a shirt'.[55] Striving to account for that alteration on the face of the land, Thomas Carlyle concluded his *Reminiscences* of his tour in Ireland in 1849 with a metaphorical coat. A population in the process of falling away yielded for Carlyle only 'an ugly indistinct *smear*' of memories, images and sensations. The images linger, refusing to vanish into the past even as the country poses a persistent political problem in the present. But Ireland is also in the process made into a figure of tattered, frayed knowledge, coming into view via a singular metaphor: 'The whole country figures in my mind like a ragged coat; one huge beggar's gabardine, not patched, or patchable any longer.'[56]

That terrible image of the country itself as a coat serves to condense what were once the facts of Irish populousness – the sheer numbers of people, Carlyle said, constituted 'a fact that was perhaps the most eloquent that was ever written down in any language, at any date of the world's history' – alongside the shocking dissolution of those numbers in death and emigration.[57] No less eloquent for Carlyle was the wretched emptiness of famine-struck Ireland. 'Abomination of desolation! what *can* you make of it!'[58] Yet there were forms of expression and efforts at interpretation, if not as many of them as there were frieze coats, and it is to these that my book has been dedicated.

Notes

Introduction

1. Niall Ó Ciosáin, *Print and Popular Culture in Ireland, 1750–1850* (Basingstoke: Macmillan, 1997), p. 2.
2. Quoted in Clayton Koelb, *The Revivifying Word: Literature, Philosophy, and the Theory of Life in Europe's Romantic Age* (Rochester: Camden House, 2008), p. ix.
3. Peter Burke, *Popular Culture in Early Modern Europe* (New York: Harper and Row, 1978), p. 65. The phrase 'literate outsiders' is his.
4. Vincent Morley, *The Popular Mind in Eighteenth-Century Ireland* (Cork: Cork University Press, 2017), p. 2.
5. Morley, *The Popular Mind in Eighteenth-Century Ireland*, p. 270.
6. William Drennan, *Glendalloch and other Poems* (Dublin, 1859), p. 12.
7. Barry Crosbie, *Irish Imperial Networks: Migration, Social Communication and Exchange in Nineteenth-Century India* (Cambridge: Cambridge University Press, 2012), p. 62.
8. Luke Gibbons, 'Romantic Ireland: 1750–1845', in James Chandler (ed.), *The Cambridge History of English Romantic Literature* (Cambridge: Cambridge University Press, 2009), pp. 182–203 (p. 185).
9. Marilyn Butler, *Romantics, Rebels and Reactionaries: English Literature and Its Background 1760–1830* (Oxford: Oxford University Press, 1981), p. 186.
10. Jane Austen, *Jane Austen's Letters*, ed. Deirdre Le Faye, fourth ed. (Oxford: Oxford University Press, 2011), pp. 280–1.
11. [Jane Austen], *Emma*, 3 vols. (London, 1816), II, pp. 11–13, 15, 198.
12. Felicia Hemans, *The Works of Mrs. Hemans, with a Memoir by Her Sister, and an Essay on Her Genius*, 7 vols. (Philadelphia, 1840), I, p. 127.
13. [Austen], *Emma*, II, p. 152.
14. Sydney Owenson, *Patriotic Sketches of Ireland*, 2 vols. (London, 1807), II, p. 110.
15. Owenson, *Patriotic Sketches of Ireland*, I, p. vi.
16. Lord Byron, 'Debate on the Earl of Donoughmore's Motion for a Committee on the Roman Catholic Claims, April 21, 1812', in *The Parliamentary Speeches of Lord Byron* (London, 1824), p. 29.
17. [Thomas De Quincey], 'Confessions of an English Opium-Eater', *The London Magazine*, 4 (1821), pp. 293–312 (p. 300).

18. William Godwin to James Marshall, 11 July 1800. William Godwin, *The Letters of William Godwin, Volume II: 1798–1805*, ed. Pamela Clemit (Oxford: Oxford University Press, 2014), p. 147.
19. Thomas De Quincey, *Confessions of an English Opium-Eater* (London, 1856), p. 155.
20. Tim Fulford and Peter J. Kitson, 'Romanticism and Colonialism: Texts, Contexts, Issues', in Tim Fulford and Peter J. Kitson (eds.), *Romanticism and Colonialism: Writing and Empire, 1780–1830* (Cambridge: Cambridge University Press, 1998), pp. 1–12 (p. 3).
21. Catherine Hall, Nicholas Draper and Keith McClelland, 'Introduction', in Catherine Hall, Nicholas Draper, Keith McClelland, Katie Donington and Rachel Lang, *Legacies of British Slave-Ownership: Colonial Slavery and the Formation of Victorian Britain* (Cambridge: Cambridge University Press, 2014), pp. 1–33 (p. 8).
22. Ó Ciosáin, *Print and Popular Culture in Ireland*, p. 6. See also Lesa Ní Mhunghaile, 'Bilingualism, Print Culture in Irish and the Public Sphere, 1700–c. 1830', in James Kelly and Ciarán Mac Murchaidh (eds.), *Irish and English: Essays on the Irish Linguistic and Cultural Frontier, 1600–1900* (Dublin: Four Courts Press, 2012), pp. 218–42; Margaret Kelleher, *The Maamtrasna Murders: Language, Life and Death in Nineteenth-Century Ireland* (Dublin: UCD Press, 2018).
23. Tom Dunne, '"On the Boundaries of Two Languages": Representing Irish in Novels in English, 1800–1850', in John Cunningham and Niall Ó Ciosáin (eds.), *Culture and Society in Ireland since 1750: Essays in Honour of Gearóid Ó Tuathaigh* (Dublin: The Lilliput Press, 2015), pp. 44–63 (p. 45).
24. Niall Ó Ciosáin, 'Oral Culture, Literacy, and Reading, 1800–50', in James Murphy (ed.), *The Oxford History of the Irish Book, Volume IV: The Irish Book in English, 1800–1891* (Oxford: Oxford University Press, 2011), pp. 173–91 (p. 191).
25. Alan Fernihough and Cormac Ó Gráda, 'Population and Poverty in Ireland on the Eve of the Great Famine', *Demography*, 59 (2022), 1607–30.
26. William Hamilton, *Letters Concerning the Northern Coast of the Country of Antrim* (1786), quoted in Breandán Mac Suibhne, 'Whiskey, Potatoes and Paddies: Volunteering and the Construction of the Irish Nation in Northwest Ulster, 1778–1782', in Peter Jupp and Eoin Magennis (eds.), *Crowds in Ireland, c. 1720–1920* (Basingstoke: Macmillan, 2000), pp. 45–82 (p. 51).
27. Edmund Burke, *The Works of the Right Honourable Edmund Burke*, 7 vols. (Boston, 1826–7), III, p. 495.
28. William Parnell, *An Historical Apology for the Irish Catholics* (Dublin, 1807), p. 135.
29. [John Banim], *The Anglo-Irish of the Nineteenth Century*, 3 vols. (London, 1828), II, pp. 258–9.
30. Lady Morgan, *Letter to Cardinal Wiseman*, second ed. (London, 1851), p. 33.
31. Quoted in Kevin Whelan, *The Tree of Liberty: Radicalism, Catholicism and the Construction of Irish Identity 1760–1830* (Cork: Cork University Press, 1996), p. 139.

32. 'Ireland', *Edinburgh Review*, 41 (1825), pp. 356–410 (pp. 386–7). The article in the *Edinburgh Review* is anonymous. But parts of the article (including these statistics) subsequently appeared in J. R. M'Culloch's edition of Adam Smith's *The Wealth of Nations* as a discursive note. *The Wellesley Index to Victorian Periodicals* (entry 1092, p. 466) gives the author of the article as either M'Culloch or Henry Parnell; or it could have been a 'collaboration'.
33. Thomas Malthus, 'A Sketch of the State of Ireland, Past and Present', *Edinburgh Review*, 12 (1808), pp. 336–55 (p. 343).
34. Percy Bysshe Shelley, *The Masque of Anarchy* (London, 1832), p. 47.
35. Paul O'Brien, 'Shelley's Printer in Ireland', *Notes and Queries*, 50.3 (2003), pp. 313–14.
36. Percy Bysshe Shelley, 'An Address to the Irish People' [1812], in *The Prose Works of Percy Bysshe Shelley*, ed. Richard Herne Shepherd, 2 vols. (London, 1888), I, pp. 223–62 (p. 241).
37. Samuel Taylor Coleridge, *Essays on His Times*, ed. David V. Erdman, 3 vols. (Princeton: Princeton University Press, 1978), I, p. 120.
38. Shelley, 'An Address to the Irish People', p. 260.
39. Scoil na mBráthar (Enniscorthy, County Wexford), The Schools' Collection, vol. 0893, p. 259, The Dúchas Project. www.duchas.ie/en/cbes/5009309/5006264. Accessed 30 November 2024.
40. Percy Bysshe Shelley, *A Philosophical View of Reform* (Oxford: Oxford University Press, 1920), p. 53.
41. See Claire Connolly, 'Counting on the Past: Yeats and Irish Romanticism', *European Romantic Review*, 28.4 (2017), 473–87.
42. Breandán Mac Suibhne, *The End of Outrage: Post-Famine Adjustment in Rural Ireland* (Oxford: Oxford University Press, 2017), p. 5.
43. John Gamble, *Society and Manners in Early Nineteenth-Century Ireland*, ed. Breandán Mac Suibhne (Dublin: Field Day, 2011), p. 231.
44. James Orr, *Poems, on Various Subjects* (Belfast, 1804), pp. 99–100.
45. Hugh Dorian, *The Outer Edge of Ulster: A Memoir of Social Life in Nineteenth-Century Donegal*, ed. Brendán Mac Suibhne and David Dickson (Dublin: The Lilliput Press, 2000), p. 93.
46. Malthus, 'A Sketch of the State of Ireland, Past and Present', p. 339; William Makepeace Thackeray, *The Irish Sketch-Book*, second ed., 2 vols. (London, 1845), I, pp. 69, 95.
47. Sydney Owenson, *Patriotic Sketches of Ireland*, 2 vols. (London, 1807), I, p. 60.
48. Lady Morgan, *Lady Morgan's Memoirs: Autobiography, Diaries and Correspondence*, 2 vols. (London, 1862), I, p. 314.
49. Owenson, *Patriotic Sketches of Ireland*, I, pp. 96–8.
50. Raymond Williams, *The Long Revolution* (New York: Columbia University Press; London: Chatto and Windus, 1961), p. 9.
51. T. Ó Raifeartaigh, Review of W. B. Stanford's *Ireland and the Classical Tradition* (1976), *Irish Historical Studies*, 20 (1977), pp. 351–3 (p. 352).
52. Laurie O'Higgins, *The Irish Classical Self: Poets and Poor Scholars in the Eighteenth and Nineteenth Centuries* (Oxford: Oxford University Press, 2017), p. 6.

53. Owenson, *Patriotic Sketches of Ireland*, II, pp. 133, 137.
54. Sydney Owenson, *Poems* (Dublin, 1801), p. 86.
55. 'Wills and Bequests', *The Illustrated London News*, 10 September 1859, p. 252.
56. *Memoirs of Richard Lovell Edgeworth, Esq. Begun by Himself and Concluded by His Daughter, Maria Edgeworth*, 2 vols. (London, 1820), II, p. 457.
57. A Volume of Short Biographies of Tutors and Schoolmasters, Dedicated to Lady Sydney Morgan and Presented to Her, Dated in Co. Limerick, 26 August 1825. NLI MSS 19314.
58. Norman Vance, *Irish Literature since 1800* (London: Longman, 2002), p. 37.
59. See John Bew, 'Ireland Under the Union, 1801–1922', in Richard Bourke and Ian McBride (eds.), *Princeton History of Ireland* (Princeton: Princeton University Press, 2016), pp. 74–108 (pp. 78–9).
60. Jane Moore, 'Thomas Moore and the Social Life of Forms', in Claire Connolly (ed.), *Irish Literature in Transition, 1780–1830* (Cambridge: Cambridge University Press, 2020), pp. 257–72 (p. 257).
61. James Chandler, 'Figures in a Field: Revising Romantic Canonicity', *Studies in Romanticism*, 59.4 (2020), pp. 559–78 (p. 578).
62. Manu Samriti Chander, *Brown Romantics: Poetry and Nationalism in the Global Nineteenth Century* (Lewisburg: Bucknell University Press, 2017).
63. Anna Johnston and Elizabeth Webby (eds.), *Eliza Hamilton Dunlop: Writing from the Colonial Frontier* (Sydney: Sydney University Press, 2021); Porscha Fermanis, 'Suffering, Sentiment, and the Rise of Humanitarian Literature in the 1830s', in John Gardner and David Stewart (eds.), *Nineteenth-Century Literature in Transition: The 1830s* (Cambridge: Cambridge University Press, 2024), pp. 147–69. See also Sarah Comyn and Porscha Fermanis (eds.), *Worlding the South: Nineteenth-Century Literary Culture and the Southern Settler Colonies* (Manchester: Manchester University Press, 2021).
64. Chandler, 'Figures in a Field: Revising Romantic Canonicity', p. 578.
65. David O'Shaughnessy, 'Metropolitan Theatre', in Claire Connolly (ed.), *Irish Literature in Transition, 1780–1830* (Cambridge: Cambridge University Press, 2020), pp. 107–21 (p. 115).
66. See Claire Connolly, 'Theatre and Nation in Irish Romanticism: The Tragic Dramas of Charles Robert Maturin and Richard Lalor Sheil', *Eire-Ireland*, 41.3 (2006), pp. 185–214.
67. Of the rejection of *Turgesius* by Covent Garden, Banim writes: 'I tied a cord about the hopeless tragedy – all condemned criminals are manacled, you know – and I flung it into perpetual exile, into the bottom of a lumber box.' P. J. Murray, *Life of John Banim* (Dublin, 1857), p. 77. Byron wrote to Moore of a play in which Turgesius figures:

> There is a play before me from a personage who signs himself 'Hibernicus.' The hero is Malachi, the Irishman and king; and the villain and usurper, Turgesius, the Dane. The conclusion is fine. Turgesius is chained by the leg (*vide* stage direction) to a pillar on the stage; and King Malachi makes him a speech, not unlike Lord Castlereagh's about the balance of power and the lawfulness of legitimacy, which puts Turgesius into a frenzy – as Castlereagh's would, if his audience was chained by the leg. He draws a dagger and rushes at the orator; but, finding himself at

> the end of his tether, he sticks it into his own carcass, and dies, saying, he has fulfilled a prophecy.
>
> Now, this is *serious, downright matter of fact*, and the gravest part of a tragedy which is not intended for burlesque. I tell it you for the honour of Ireland. The writer hopes it will be represented: – but what is Hope? nothing but the paint on the face of Existence; the least touch of truth rubs it off, and then we see what a hollow-cheeked harlot we have got hold of. I am not sure that I have not said this last superfine reflection before. But never mind; – it will do for the tragedy of Turgesius, to which I can append it.

Lord Byron to Thomas Moore, October 28, 1815, *Letters and Journals of Lord Byron*. www.lordbyron.org. Accessed 1 December 2024.

68. Seamus Deane, *Small World: Ireland, 1798–2018* (Cambridge: Cambridge University Press, 2021), p. 106.
69. See SouthHem.org. Accessed 10 July 2024.
70. Tom Dunne, 'Haunted by History: Irish Romantic Writing, 1800–1850', in Roy Porter and Mikuláš Teich (eds.), *Romanticism in National Context* (Cambridge: Cambridge University Press, 1988), pp. 68–91 (p. 71).
71. R. F. Foster, *Words Alone: Yeats and His Inheritances* (Oxford: Oxford University Press, 2011), p. 4.
72. See Julia M. Wright, *Representing the National Landscape in Irish Romanticism* (Syracuse: Syracuse University Press, 2014), p. xxvi.
73. Wright, *Representing the National Landscape in Irish Romanticism*, p. xxvi; Dunne, 'Haunted by History', pp. 68, 70.
74. Joshua Calhoun, 'Book Microbiomes', in Alexandra Gillespie and Deidre Lynch (eds.), *The Unfinished Book* (Oxford: Oxford University Press, 2021), pp. 460–73 (p. 473).
75. Griffin, *Life of Gerald Griffin*, pp. 189–90, 191–92.
76. John Mitchel, *Poems by James Clarence Mangan with Biographical Introduction* (New York, 1859), p. 7.
77. Quoted in Breandán Mac Suibhne, *The End of Outrage*, p. 4.
78. Gearóid Ó Crualaoich, 'Folkloristic-Ethnological Studies in Ireland', in Diarmuid Ó Giolláin (ed.), *Irish Ethnologies* (South Bend: University of Notre Dame Press, 2017), pp. 75–89 (pp. 76–7).
79. Most influentially found in Seamus Deane's *Strange Country: Modernity and Nationhood in Irish Writing since 1790* (Oxford: Clarendon Press, 1997).
80. Samuel Taylor Coleridge, *Biographia Literaria*, 2 vols. (London: Routledge and Kegan Paul, 1983), II, 6–7.
81. Viktor Shklovsky, 'Art as Technique', in Lee T. Lemon and Marion J. Reis (eds. and trans.), *Russian Formalist Criticism: Four Essays* (Lincoln: University of Nebraska Press, 1965), p. 11.
82. Viktor Shklovsky, 'Prologue', *Bowstring: On the Dissimilarity of the Similar*, trans. Shushan Avagyan (Champaign: Dalkey Archive Press, 2011), pp. 17–18.
83. Nicholas M. Wolf, *An Irish-Speaking Island: State, Religion and the Linguistic Landscape in Ireland, 1770–1870* (Madison: University of Wisconsin Press, 2014), p. x.
84. Margaret Kelleher, *The Maamtrasna Murders: Language, Life and Death in Nineteenth-Century Ireland* (Dublin: UCD Press, 2018), p. 28.

85. Pádraig Ó. Macháin, 'Nineteenth-Century Irish Manuscripts', in Bernadette Cunningham and Siobhán Fitzpatrick (eds.), *Treasures of the Royal Irish Academy Library* (Dublin: Royal Irish Academy, 2009), pp. 161–71 (pp. 161, 163).
86. Joep Leerssen, *Remembrance and Imagination: Patterns in the Historical and Literary Representation of Ireland in the Nineteenth Century* (Cork: Cork University Press, 1996), p. 161.
87. Mark Salber Phillips, *On Historical Distance* (New Haven: Yale University Press, 2013), p. xi.
88. See Claire Connolly, 'A Bookish History of Irish Romanticism', in Porscha Fermanis and John Regan (eds.), *Romantic Historiography in Britain and Ireland* (Oxford: Oxford University Press, 2014), pp. 271–95.
89. Susan Howe, *The Nonconformist's Memorial* (New York: New Directions, 1989), p. 106.
90. *The Freeman's Journal*, 20 May 1828.
91. Frances Anne Edgeworth, *A Memoir of Maria Edgeworth, with a Selection from Her Letters*, 3 vols. (London, 1867), III, p. 259.
92. *Warder and Dublin Weekly Mail*, 19 January 1839.
93. Maria Edgeworth to Philip Crampton, 20 October 1837, published in Dublin newspapers.
94. William Ewart Gladstone, *The Gladstone Diaries, Volume I: 1825–1832*, ed. M. R. D. Foot (Oxford: Clarendon Press, 1968), pp. 92, 96.
95. 'September 1913', W. B. Yeats, *Responsibilities and Other Poems* (New York: Macmillan, 1916), pp. 32–3.

1 Bookish Histories, 1780–1815

1. Joseph Cooper Walker, *An Historical Essay on the Dress of the Ancient and Modern Irish* (Dublin, 1788), p. iii.
2. See Daniel Carey, 'Intellectual History: William King to Edmund Burke', in Richard Bourke and Ian McBride (eds.), *The Princeton History of Modern Ireland* (Princeton and Oxford: Princeton University Press, 2016), pp. 193–216; Ian Campbell Ross, '"We Irish": Writing and National Identity from Berkeley to Burke', in Moyra Haslett (ed.), *Irish Literature in Transition, 1700–1780* (Cambridge: Cambridge University Press, 2020), pp. 49–67.
3. Toby Barnard, 'Reading in Eighteenth-Century Ireland: Public and Private Pleasures', in Bernadette Cunningham and Máire Kennedy (eds.), *The Experience of Reading: Irish Historical Perspectives* (Dublin: Rare Book Group of the Library Association of Ireland, 1999), pp. 60–77 (p. 62).
4. Luke Gibbons, 'Romantic Ireland: 1750–1845', in James Chandler (ed.), *The Cambridge History of English Romantic Literature* (Cambridge: Cambridge University Press, 2009), pp. 182–203 (p. 203).
5. See Alexandra Gillespie and Deidre Lynch, 'The Unfinished Book: Introduction', in Alexandra Gillespie and Deidre Lynch (eds.), *The Unfinished Book* (Oxford: Oxford University Press, 2021), pp. 1–18 (p. 2).

6. Mark Salber Phillips, *On Historical Distance* (New Haven: Yale University Press, 2013), p. xi.
7. Alex Watson, *Romantic Marginality: Nation and Empire on the Borders of the Page* (London: Pickering and Chatto, 2012), p. 7.
8. Celeste Langan, 'Understanding Media in 1805: Audiovisual Hallucination in *The Lay of the Last Minstrel*', *Studies in Romanticism*, 40.1 (2001), pp. 49–70 (pp. 68–9).
9. Marcus Boon, *In Praise of Copying* (Cambridge, MA: Harvard University Press, 2010), pp. 41, 45.
10. Mary Tighe to Joseph Cooper Walker, 20 April 1806. Mary Tighe, *The Collected Letters of Mary Blachford Tighe, 1786–1810*, ed. Harriet Kramer Linkin (Bethlehem: Lehigh University Press, 2020), p. 304.
11. 'Irish Literature', *Anthologia Hibernica*, 1 (1793), pp. 295–6.
12. Charles Vallancey, *An Account of the Ancient Stone Amphitheatre Located in the County of Kerry* (Dublin, 1812), p. 59.
13. Sydney Owenson, *The Wild Irish Girl* [1806], ed. Claire Connolly and Stephen Copley (London: Pickering and Chatto, 2000), pp. 169–70.
14. Anahid Nersessian, *Utopia, Limited: Romanticism and Adjustment* (Cambridge, MA: Harvard University Press, 2015), pp. 119–20.
15. Lady Morgan, *O'Donnel*, 3 vols. (London, 1814), 1, pp. 277–8.
16. Sydney Owenson, *Twelve Original Hibernian Melodies* (London, 1805), p. 2.
17. Owenson, *Twelve Original Hibernian Melodies*, p. 2.
18. See the advertisement prefixed to *A Selection of Irish Melodies, with Symphonies and Accompaniments by Sir John Stevenson, Mus. Doc. and Characteristic Words by Thomas Moore, Esq. First Number* (London, 1808).
19. *A Selection of Irish Melodies. First Number.*
20. *A Selection of Irish Melodies. First Number.*
21. *A Selection of Irish Melodies. First Number.*
22. *A Selection of Irish Melodies. First Number.*
23. See the advertisement prefixed to *A Selection of Irish Melodies, with Symphonies and Accompaniments by Sir John Stevenson, Mus. Doc. and Characteristic Words by Thomas Moore, Esq. Fifth Number* (London, 1813).
24. *A Selection of Irish Melodies. Fifth Number.*
25. *A Selection of Irish Melodies. Fifth Number.*
26. See the prefatory letter to the Marchioness Dowager of Donegal in *A Selection of Irish Melodies, with Symphonies and Accompaniments by Sir John Stevenson, Mus. Doc. and Characteristic Words by Thomas Moore, Esq. Third Number* (London, 1810).
27. Thomas Bartlett, 'Ireland during the Revolutionary and Napoleonic Wars, 1791–1815', in James Kelly (ed.), *The Cambridge History of Ireland, Volume III: 1730–1880* (Cambridge: Cambridge University Press, 2018), pp. 74–101 (p. 97).
28. See the advertisement prefixed to *A Selection of Irish Melodies, with Symphonies and Accompaniments by Sir John Stevenson, Mus. Doc. and Characteristic Words by Thomas Moore, Esq. Seventh Number* (London, 1818).

29. William St Clair, *The Reading Nation in the Romantic Period* (Cambridge: Cambridge University Press, 2004); Ina Ferris, *Book-Men, Book Clubs, and the Romantic Literary Sphere* (Basingstoke: Palgrave, 2015), p. 2.
30. George Benn, *The History of the Town of Belfast* (Belfast, 1823), p. 128.
31. Ferris, *Book-Men*, p. 2.
32. James Hall, *Tour through Ireland, Particularly the Interior and Least Known Parts*, 2 vols. (London, 1813), II, p. 257.
33. Amy Prendergast, *Literary Salons across Britain and Ireland in the Long Eighteenth Century* (Basingstoke: Palgrave, 2015), p. 133.
34. John Davy, *Memoirs of the Life of Sir Humphry Davy*, 2 vols. (London, 1836), I, p. 278.
35. *Fragmentary Remains, Literary and Scientific, of Sir Humphry Davy*, ed. John Davy (London, 1858), p. 152.
36. Maria Edgeworth, *Tales of Fashionable Life*, 6 vols. (London, 1809–12), VI, pp. 190, 371.
37. Arthur Young, *A Tour in Ireland*, 2 vols. (Dublin, 1780), I, p. viii.
38. Gillespie and Lynch, 'The Unfinished Book: Introduction', p. 11.
39. See Barnard, 'Reading in Eighteenth-Century Ireland', p. 68.
40. K. T. Hoppen, *Governing Hibernia: British Politicians and Ireland, 1800–1921* (Oxford: Oxford University Press, 2016), pp. 51–52. Peel's collection can be found in the library of the House of Lords.
41. Felicia Hemans, *The Works of Mrs. Hemans, with a Memoir by Her Sister, and an Essay on Her Genius*, 7 vols. (Philadelphia, 1840), I, p. 260.
42. Prendergast, *Literary Salons*, p. 106.
43. Quoted in Prendergast, *Literary Salons*, p. 114.
44. Prendergast, *Literary Salons*, p. 112.
45. Prendergast, *Literary Salons*, p. 122.
46. See Ferris, *Book-Men*, p. 17.
47. John Hewitt, *Ancestral Voices: The Selected Prose of John Hewitt*, ed. Tom Clyde (Belfast: Blackstaff Press, 1987), pp. 68–9. The original essay was published in *Rann* in 1953.
48. Hall, *Tour through Ireland*, II, pp. 197, 210.
49. Guy Beiner, *Forgetful Remembrance: Social Forgetting and Vernacular Historiography of a Rebellion in Ulster* (Oxford: Oxford University Press, 2018), p. 275.
50. Frank Ferguson, 'Between the Bishop's Hall and the Hurchin: Enlightenment Legacies in Post-Union Antrim and Down', *Estudios Irlandeses*, 18.2 (2023), pp. 99–111 (p. 105).
51. Ferguson, 'Between the Bishop's Hall and the Hurchin', p. 105.
52. See Beiner, *Forgetful Remembrance*, p. 246.
53. Barnard, 'Reading in Eighteenth-Century Ireland', p. 63.
54. Clare O'Halloran, *Golden Ages and Barbarous Nations: Antiquarian Debate and Cultural Politics in Ireland, c. 1750–1800* (Cork: Cork University Press, 2004), pp. 172–7.

55. See the Edward Bunting Collection at Queen's University Belfast. https://omeka.qub.ac.uk/exhibits/show/edwardbuntingcollection/edwardbuntingmanuscripts. Accessed 1 July 2024.
56. Edward Bunting Collection MS 4/24 (Patrick Lynch's Journal), Queen's University Belfast Special Collections and Archives. https://digital-library.qub.ac.uk/digital/collection/p15979coll9/id/1131/rec/6. Accessed 1 July 2024.
57. David Clare, 'Mary Balfour's *Kathleen O'Neil* (1814): An Expression or Betrayal of Her Ulster Scots Background?', in David Clare, Fiona McDonagh and Justine Nakase (eds.), *The Golden Thread: Irish Women Playwrights, 1716–2016*, 2 vols. (Liverpool: Liverpool University Press, 2021), I, pp. 85–96 (pp. 88, 95).
58. Clare, 'Mary Balfour's *Kathleen O'Neil*', p. 89.
59. Beiner, *Forgetful Remembrance*, p. 298.
60. Charles Benson, 'The Irish Trade', in Michael F. Suarez and Michael L. Turner (eds.), *The Cambridge History of the Book in Britain, Volume V: 1695–1830* (Cambridge: Cambridge University Press, 2009), pp. 366–82 (p. 372).
61. William Parnell, preface to William Smyth, *English Lyrics* (Dublin, 1806).
62. Benson, 'The Irish Trade', p. 373.
63. Quoted in Thomas Bartlett, '"A People Made Rather for Copies than Originals": The Anglo-Irish, 1760–1800', *The International History Review*, 12.1 (1990), 11–25 (p. 25).
64. Parnell, preface.
65. William Parnell, *An Historical Apology for the Irish Catholics* (Dublin, 1807), p. vii.
66. Brian Gurrin, 'Population and Emigration, 1730–1845', in James Kelly (ed.), *The Cambridge History of Ireland, Volume III: 1730–1880* (Cambridge: Cambridge University Press, 2018), pp. 204–30 (pp. 213–14).
67. William Dunkin, *Select Poetical Works of the Late William Dunkin*, 2 vols. (Dublin, 1769–70), I, p. 431.
68. See Gurrin, 'Population and Emigration', p. 215.
69. Young, *A Tour in Ireland*, II, Part ii, p. 1.
70. Edmund Burke, *The Works of the Right Honourable Edmund Burke*, 7 vols. (Boston, 1826–7), VII, p. 104.
71. James Kelly, 'The Politics of Protestant Ascendancy, 1730–1790', in James Kelly (ed.), *The Cambridge History of Ireland, Volume III: 1730–1880* (Cambridge: Cambridge University Press, 2018), pp. 48–73 (p. 50).
72. Maya Jasanoff, *Liberty's Exiles: The Loss of America and the Remaking of the British Empire* (London: Harper Press, 2011), p. 11.
73. Mary Tighe to Joseph Cooper Walker, late July–early August 1803. Tighe, *The Collected Letters*, p. 266.
74. Mary Tighe to Joseph Cooper Walker, c. 1802. Tighe, *The Collected Letters*, p. 258.
75. Hall, *Tour through Ireland*, II, p. 17.
76. [Robert Rainey], 'Diary giving accounts of political affairs in Dublin, business and social activities while working at Crampton Court and Dame Street, 1798–1801'. National Library of Ireland MSS 34.395/1.

77. *Morning Chronicle*, 8 September 1823, p. 4. Thanks to Guy Beiner for this reference.
78. [Rainey], 'Diary'.
79. [Rainey], 'Diary'.
80. Maria Edgeworth to John Murray, 23 December 1816. National Library Scotland MSS 42181.
81. Janet Todd, 'Ascendancy: Lady Mount Cashell, Lady Moira, Mary Wollstonecraft and the Union Pamphlets', *Eighteenth-Century Ireland*, 18 (2003), 98–117 (p. 100).
82. Barnard, 'Reading in Eighteenth-Century Ireland', p. 72.
83. Dahlia Porter, *Science, Form, and the Problem of Induction in British Romanticism* (Cambridge: Cambridge University Press, 2018), p. 3.
84. [Maria Edgeworth], *Castle Rackrent* (Dublin, 1800), pp. 20–1.
85. Dáithí Ó hÓgáin, '"Said an Elderly Man …": Maria Edgeworth's Use of Folklore in *Castle Rackrent*', in Cóilín Owens (ed.), *Family Chronicles: Maria Edgeworth's 'Castle Rackrent'* (Dublin: Wolfhound Press), pp. 62–70 (pp. 65–6).
86. Susan Stewart, *Crimes of Writing: Problems in the Containment of Representation* (New York: Oxford University Press, 1991), p. 104.
87. Mary L. Mullen, *Novel Institutions: Anachronism, Irish Novels, and Nineteenth-Century Realism* (Edinburgh: Edinburgh University Press, 2019), pp. 37–67.
88. Charlotte Edgeworth to Emmeline King, 25 September 1803. National Library of Ireland MSS 10166/7/377.
89. Caroline Tighe to Mary Tighe, early December 1798. Tighe, *The Collected Letters*, p. 248.
90. Thomas De Quincey, 'Sketches of Life and Manners: From the Autobiography of an English Opium Eater', *Tait's Edinburgh Magazine*, 1 (1834), 196–204 (pp. 196–7, 200, 198).
91. *Fragmentary Remains, Literary and Scientific, of Sir Humphry Davy*, pp. 153–4.
92. Owenson, *The Wild Irish Girl*, p. 151.
93. Owenson, *The Wild Irish Girl*, p. 193.
94. Owenson, *The Wild Irish Girl*, p. 201.
95. Owenson, *The Wild Irish Girl*, p. 194.
96. Alvin Jackson, *United Kingdoms: Multinational Union States in Europe and Beyond, 1800–1925* (Oxford: Oxford University Press, 2024).
97. Mary Tighe to Joseph Cooper Walker, 21 January 1809. Tighe, *The Collected Letters*, p. 324.
98. Percy Bysshe Shelley to Thomas Jefferson Hogg, 20 June 1811. *The Letters of Percy Bysshe Shelley, Volume I: Shelley in England*, ed. Frederick L. Jones (Oxford: Oxford University Press, 1964), p. 112.
99. Mary Leadbeater, *Poems* (Dublin, 1808), p. 87.
100. Burke, *The Works*, v, p. 189.
101. Daniel I. O'Neill, 'Edmund Burke on Slavery and the Slave Trade: A Response to Gregory M. Collins', *Slavery & Abolition*, 41.4 (2020), 816–27 (pp. 818–19).

102. Leadbeater, *Poems*, pp. 134, 136.
103. Leadbeater, *Poems*, p. 306.
104. Jeremiah J. Callanan, *The Poems of J. J. Callanan* (Cork, 1861), pp. 78–9.
105. Henry Boyd, *The Woodsman's Tale* (London, 1805), p. 189.
106. Thomas Dermody, *The Harp of Erin*, 2 vols. (London, 1807), II, p. 118.
107. Morgan, *O'Donnel*, I, pp. 100–2.
108. Michael Griffin, 'Introduction', in *Thomas Dermody, Selected Writings*, ed. Michael Griffin (Dublin: Field Day, 2012), pp. 1–31 (p. 2).
109. James Grant Raymond, *The Life of Thomas Dermody*, 2 vols. (London, 1806), I, p. 11.
110. Lady Morgan, *Lady Morgan's Memoirs: Autobiography, Diaries and Correspondence*, 2 vols. (London, 1862), I, p. 23.
111. Kelly, 'The Politics of Protestant Ascendancy', p. 49.
112. Morgan, *Lady Morgan's Memoirs*, I, p. 88.
113. Raymond, *The Life of Thomas Dermody*, II, p. 8.
114. Thomas Dermody, *Poems* (Dublin, 1789), pp. iii–iv.
115. Michael Griffin, 'Infatuated to His Ruin': The Fate of Thomas Dermody, 1775–1802', *History Ireland*, 14.3 (2006). www.historyireland.com/infatuated-to-his-ruin-the-fate-of-thomas-dermody-1775-1802. Accessed 2 July 2024.
116. Dermody, *The Harp of Erin*, II, p. 145.
117. Dermody, *The Harp of Erin*, II, p. 146.
118. Dermody, *The Harp of Erin*, II, p. 145.
119. Dermody, *The Harp of Erin*, II, p. 147.
120. See P. W. Joyce, 'On Spenser's Irish Rivers', *Proceedings of the Royal Irish Academy*, 10 (1866–9), 1–13. Joyce speculates that Spenser used 'poetic license' to grant the name of the town to the river: 'the Aubeg was never called Mulla but by himself' (p. 3).
121. Dermody, *The Harp of Erin*, II, pp. 147–8.
122. Greg Kucich, *Keats, Shelley, and Romantic Spenserianism* (Pennsylvania: Pennsylvania State University Press, 1991), pp. 93–4.
123. Morgan, *Lady Morgan's Memoirs*, I, p. 204.
124. Sydney Owenson, *Poems* (Dublin, 1801), pp. 95–6.
125. Owenson, *Poems*, p. 97.
126. Owenson, *Poems*, pp. 93–4.
127. Morgan, *Lady Morgan's Memoirs*, I, p. 129.
128. Michael Griffin, 'Arcades Ambo: Robert Burns and Thomas Dermody', in David Sargeant and Fiona Stafford (eds.), *Burns and Other Poets* (Edinburgh: Edinburgh University Press, 2012), pp. 127–42 (p. 134).
129. Thomas Dermody, *Poems: Consisting of Essays, Lyric, Elegiac, &c.* (Dublin, 1792), p. 53.
130. Griffin, 'Arcades Ambo', p. 135.
131. 'From Metastasio, 1791'. Mary Tighe, *The Collected Poems and Journals of Mary Tighe*, ed. Harriet Kramer Linkin (Kentucky: The University Press of Kentucky, 2005), p. 7.

132. Jonas Cope, '"Illusive Light": Thomas Dermody, the *Aisling* and Archipelagic Romanticism', *European Romantic Review*, 26.6 (2015), pp. 757–71.
133. Dermody, *The Harp of Erin*, I, pp. 246–7.
134. Dermody, *The Harp of Erin*, II, p. 242.
135. Thomas Dermody, *The Rights of Justice, or Rational Liberty; A Letter to an Acquaintance in the Country* (Dublin, 1793), pp. xx.
136. Mary Tighe to Joseph Cooper Walker, 20 April 1806. Tighe, *The Collected Letters*, p. 304.
137. Seamus Deane, *Small World: Ireland, 1798–2018* (Cambridge: Cambridge University Press, 2021), p. 94.
138. Deane, *Small World*, p. 99.
139. Deane, *Small World*, p. 107.
140. Mary Tighe, *Reading Journal*, National Library of Ireland MS 4804.
141. Morgan, *Lady Morgan's Memoirs*, I, pp. 314–15.
142. Griffin, 'Introduction', p. 26.
143. Joseph Cooper Walker, *Historical Memoirs of the Irish Bards*, 2 vols. (Dublin, 1818), I, p. 57.
144. William Wordsworth, *Poems, in Two Volumes*, 2 vols. (London, 1807), I, p. 13.
145. Wordsworth, *Poems, in Two Volumes*, I, p. 12.
146. Walker, *Historical Memoirs*, I, p. 58.
147. Lesa Ní Mhunghaile, 'Introduction', in Charlotte Brooke, *Charlotte Brooke's Reliques of Irish Poetry*, ed. Lesa Ní Mhunghaile (Dublin: Irish Manuscripts Commission, 2009), pp. xxi–xliv (p. xxvii).
148. [Denis Taaffe], *Ireland's Mirror* (Dublin, 1796), p. vi.
149. Gregory A. Schirmer, 'English Ireland/Irish Ireland: The Poetry and Translations of J. J. Callanan', in Claire Connolly (ed.), *Irish Literature in Transition, 1780–1830* (Cambridge: Cambridge University Press, 2020), pp. 292–305 (p. 250); Ní Mhunghaile, 'Introduction', p. xxx.
150. Schirmer, 'English Ireland/Irish Ireland', p. 250.
151. Ní Mhunghaile, 'Introduction', p. xxx.
152. Ní Mhunghaile, 'Introduction', p. xxxvi.
153. Quoted in Niav Gallagher, 'Skirting the Issue: Women and the Royal Irish Academy', *Dictionary of Irish Biography*. www.dib.ie/blog/skirting-issue-women-and-royal-irish-academy. Accessed 3 July 2024.
154. Stewart, *Crimes of Writing*, p. 105.
155. Leith Davis, 'Charlotte Brooke's *Reliques of Irish Poetry*: Eighteenth-Century "Irish Song" and the Politics of Remediation', in John Kirk, Andrew Noble and Michael Brown (eds.), *United Islands? The Languages of Resistance* (London and New York: Routledge, 2012), pp. 95–108 (p. 95).
156. Owenson, *The Wild Irish Girl*, p. 86.
157. Owenson, *The Wild Irish Girl*, p. 86.
158. Owenson, *The Wild Irish Girl*, p. 86.
159. Owenson, *Twelve Original Hibernian Melodies*, p. 1.
160. Owenson, *Twelve Original Hibernian Melodies*, p. 9.
161. Owenson, *Twelve Original Hibernian Melodies*, p. 2.

162. Owenson, *Twelve Original Hibernian Melodies*, p. 2.
163. Advertisement prefixed to *A Selection of Irish Melodies. First Number*.
164. Tríona Ní Shíocháin, *Singing Ideas: Performance, Politics and Oral Poetry* (Oxford and New York: Berghahn Books, 2018), pp. 2, 11.
165. Tríona Ní Shíocháin, 'Singing from the Shadows: Undercurrents of Contestation and Resistance in Irish-Speaking Women's Song and Lament' in Julie Carlson (ed.), *The Cambridge History of Women and British Romanticism* (Cambridge: Cambridge University Press, forthcoming).
166. Murray Pittock, *Scottish and Irish Romanticism* (Oxford: Oxford University Press, 2008), p. 106.
167. Pittock, *Scottish and Irish Romanticism*, pp. 179–80.
168. Sophie Gilmartin, *Ancestry and Narrative in Nineteenth-Century British Literature: Blood Relations from Edgeworth to Hardy* (Cambridge: Cambridge University Press, 1998), p. 39.
169. See the 'Introductory Note' in Maria Edgeworth, *The Novels and Selected Works of Maria Edgeworth, Volume V: The Absentee, Madame de Fleury and Emilie de Coulanges*, ed. Heidi Van de Veire and Kim Walker with Marilyn Butler (London: Pickering and Chatto, 1999), pp. vii–xlii (p. xxviii).
170. Walker, *Historical Memoirs*, II, pp. 159–77 (p. 176).
171. Harriet Kramer Linkin, 'Mary Tighe, Thomas Moore, and the Publication of "Selena"', *Review of English Studies*, 65 (2014), pp. 711–29 (p. 712).
172. Harriet Kramer Linkin, 'Placing Mary Tighe in Irish Literary History: From Manuscript Culture to Print', in Claire Connolly (ed.), *Irish Literature in Transition, 1780–1830* (Cambridge: Cambridge University Press, 2020), pp. 173–87 (p. 183).
173. Tighe, *The Collected Poems and Journals*, p. 41.
174. Harriet Kramer Linkin, 'Introduction', in Mary Tighe, *The Collected Poems and Journals of Mary Tighe*, ed. Harriet Kramer Linkin (Kentucky: The University Press of Kentucky, 2005), pp. xv–xxxiii (p. xxiii). See Erin M. Goss, *Revealing Bodies: Anatomy, Allegory, and the Grounds of Knowledge in the Long Eighteenth Century* (Lewisburg: Bucknell University Press, 2013), pp. 127–8.
175. Prendergast, *Literary Salons*, pp. 142–3.
176. Kucich, *Keats, Shelley, and Romantic Spenserianism*, p. 92.
177. Tighe, *The Collected Poems and Journals*, p. 54.
178. Quoted in Linkin, 'Mary Tighe, Thomas Moore, and the Publication of "Selena"', pp. 722–3.
179. Quoted in Linkin, 'Mary Tighe, Thomas Moore, and the Publication of "Selena"', p. 721.
180. For the connection, see Linkin, 'Mary Tighe, Thomas Moore and the Publication of "Selena"'.
181. On George William Tighe and Percy Bysshe Shelley, see Eliza Cozzi, 'P. B. Shelley, George William Tighe and the Irish Roots of "The Sensitive Plant"', *Romanticism*, 30.1 (2024), pp. 42–55.
182. Mary Tighe to Joseph Cooper Walker, 16 August 1803. Tighe, *The Collected Letters*, p. 268.

183. Tighe, *The Collected Poems and Journals*, p. 19.
184. Tighe, *The Collected Poems and Journals*, p. 24.
185. Joseph Holt, *Memoirs of Joseph Holt, General of the Irish Rebels in 1798, Edited from His Original Manuscript, in the Possession of Sir William Betham*, ed. Thomas Crofton Croker, 2 vols. (London, 1838).
186. Gillespie and Lynch, 'The Unfinished Book: Introduction', p. 9.
187. Mary Tighe, *Psyche, with Other Poems, by the Late Mrs Henry Tighe* (London, 1811), p. 313.
188. James Chandler, *England in 1819: The Politics of Literary Culture and the Case of Romantic Historicism* (Chicago and London: University of Chicago Press, 1998), pp. 393–5.
189. Tighe, *Psyche, with Other Poems*, p. iv.
190. Tighe, *Psyche, with Other Poems*, p. v.
191. Tighe, *Psyche, with Other Poems*, p. 219.
192. Harriet Kramer Linkin, 'The Posthumous Public and Private Printing of Mary Tighe's Poetry', *Nineteenth-Century Gender Studies*, 18.2 (2022). www.ncgsjournal.com/issue182/linkin.html. Accessed 5 July 2024.
193. Kramer Linkin, 'The Posthumous Public and Private Printing of Mary Tighe's Poetry'.
194. Mary Tighe, *Mary, a Series of Reflections during Twenty Years*, Houghton Library, Harvard University EC8 T4484 811m.
195. See the front free endpaper of the copy at the Houghton Library, Harvard University (EC8 T4484 811m).
196. Tighe, *The Collected Poems and Journals*, p. 282.
197. Tighe, *Mary, a Series of Reflections during Twenty Years*, p. 13.
198. Tighe, *Mary, a Series of Reflections during Twenty Years*, p. 33.
199. Tighe, *Mary, a Series of Reflections during Twenty Years*, p. 35.
200. Linkin, 'The Posthumous Public and Private Printing of Mary Tighe's Poetry': 'Between 1912 and 1916 the *Irish Book Lover* published three articles by E. R. McClintock Dix as well as three responses (by a Reader, R. S. M., and Séamus Ó Casaide) that discussed the Tighe printing press at Rossana and whether it was used for an early copy of *Psyche* or *Mary*.'
201. Matthew Campbell, 'Whigs, Weavers, and Fire-Worshippers: Anglophone Irish Poetry in Transition', in Claire Connolly (ed.), *Irish Literature in Transition, 1780–1830* (Cambridge: Cambridge University Press, 2020), pp. 85–106 (p. 95).
202. Jennifer Orr, *Literary Networks and Dissenting Print Culture in Romantic-Period Ireland* (Basingstoke: Palgrave, 2015), p. 197; Jennifer Orr, 'Enlightened Ulster, Romantic Ulster', in Claire Connolly (ed.), *Irish Literature in Transition, 1780–1830* (Cambridge: Cambridge University Press, 2020), pp. 148–169 (p. 149).
203. Carol Baraniuk, *James Orr, Poet and Irish Radical* (London: Pickering and Chatto, 2014), p. 30.
204. Orr, *Literary Networks*, p. 3.
205. Orr, *Literary Networks*, pp. 31, 40.

206. James Orr, *Poems, on Various Subjects* (Belfast, 1804), pp. 103–4.
207. Orr, *Literary Networks*, p. 40.
208. Campbell, 'Whigs, Weavers, and Fire-Worshippers', p. 99.
209. Orr, *Poems*, p. 13.
210. Dermody, *The Harp of Erin*, I, p. 103.
211. Orr, *Poems*, p. 151.
212. Orr, *Poems*, p. 151.
213. See Claire Connolly, '"I accuse Miss Owenson": *The Wild Irish Girl* as Media Event', *Colby Quarterly*, 36.2 (2000), 98–115 (p. 98).
214. Quoted in Connolly, '"I accuse Miss Owenson"', p. 112.
215. Quoted in Connolly, '"I accuse Miss Owenson"', pp. 100–1.
216. Joseph Atkinson, 'Address, Written to be Spoken at the First Performance of Miss Owenson's Comic Opera of "The First Attempt; or, Whim of the Moment"', *New Monthly Magazine*, 24 (1807), 50–1 (p. 50).
217. James Orr, 'To Miss Owenson, the Elegant Authoress of The Wild Irish Girl', *Belfast Commercial Chronicle*, 2 May 1807.
218. Baraniuk, *James Orr*, p. 7.
219. Orr, *Poems*, p. 114.
220. Orr, *Poems*, p. 114.
221. Campbell, 'Whigs, Weavers, and Fire-Worshippers', p. 98.
222. Orr, *Poems*, pp. 119–20.
223. Orr, *Poems*, p. 119.
224. Orr, *Poems*, p. 119.
225. Orr, *Poems*, pp. 115–16.
226. Orr, *Poems*, p. 117.
227. Orr, *Poems*, p. 118.
228. Julia M. Wright, *Representing the National Landscape in Irish Romanticism* (Syracuse: Syracuse University Press, 2014), pp. 105–6.
229. Orr, *Poems*, p. 120.
230. Baraniuk, *James Orr*, pp. 128–9.
231. Wright, *Representing the National Landscape*, p. 106.
232. Quoted in O'Kane, *Landscape Design and Revolution*, p. 136.
233. See Muiris MacGiollabhuí, 'Sons of Exile: The United Irishmen in Transnational Perspective 1791–1827', unpublished PhD dissertation (University of California, Santa Cruz, 2019), pp. 164, 167. https://escholarship.org/uc/item/75x28210. Accessed 7 July 2024.
234. Finola O'Kane, *Landscape Design and Revolution in Ireland and the United States, 1688–1815* (New Haven: Yale University Press, 2023), p. 140.
235. O'Kane, *Landscape Design and Revolution*, p. 162.
236. Frank Ferguson, 'Introduction', in Frank Ferguson (ed.), *Ulster-Scots Writing: An Anthology* (Dublin: Four Courts Press, 2008), pp. 1–22 (p. 18).
237. Ferguson, 'Introduction', p. 18.
238. Orr, *Poems*, p. 120.
239. Orr, *Poems*, p. 16.
240. Orr, *Poems*, pp. 13, 15.

241. Orr, *Poems*, p. 17.
242. 'To the Memory of S. E.', Leadbeater, *Poems*, p. 135.

2 Watery Prospects, 1815–1830

1. Samuel Baker, *Written on the Water: British Romanticism and the Maritime Empire of Culture* (Charlottesville: University of Virginia Press, 2010), p. 3.
2. Brian Gurrin, 'Population and Emigration, 1730–1845', in James Kelly (ed.), *The Cambridge History of Ireland, Volume III: 1730–1880* (Cambridge: Cambridge University Press, 2018), pp. 204–30 (p. 218).
3. Patrick Joyce, *The State of Freedom: A Social History of the British State Since 1800* (Cambridge: Cambridge University Press, 2013), pp. 44–5; for praise of the 'clearness and beauty' of its engraved maps, see J. H. Andrews, *A Paper Landscape: The Ordnance Survey in Nineteenth-Century Ireland* (Oxford: Clarendon Press, 1975), p. 134.
4. Maria Edgeworth to Sophy Ruxton, 26 September 1827. Frances Anne Edgeworth, *A Memoir of Maria Edgeworth, with a Selection from Her Letters*, 3 vols. (London, 1867), II, p. 295.
5. Andrews, *A Paper Landscape*, p. 101.
6. John O'Donovan to Captain James R. E., 26 July 1842. *Cork Memoranda.* Notes relative to the Antiquities of Co. Cork, 1842–1845. [Typed copy of notes, queries, correspondence etc. written by O'Donovan, Larcom and others relative to the antiquities of County Cork, 1842–5].
7. *Cork Memoranda.* Notes relative to the Antiquities of Co. Cork, 1842–1845. [Typed copy of notes, queries, correspondence, etc. written by O'Donovan, Larcom and others relative to the antiquities of County Cork, 1842–5].
8. William Wordsworth to William Pasley, quoted in Samuel Baker, *Written on the Water: British Romanticism and the Maritime Empire of Culture* (Charlottesville: University of Virginia Press, 2010), p. 2.
9. See Andrews, *A Paper Landscape*, p. 13.
10. See Peter Hession, 'Taming the Channel: Technology, Liberalism and the Irish Sea, c. 1845–52', in Emily Mark-FitzGerald, Ciarán McCabe and Ciarán Reilly (eds.), *Dublin and the Great Famine* (Dublin: University College Dublin Press, 2022), pp. 24–35 (p. 25); Claire Connolly, 'Too Rough for Verse: Sea Crossings in Irish Culture', in Joep Leerssen (ed.), *Parnell and His Times* (Cambridge: Cambridge University Press, 2020), pp. 243–67.
11. [John Banim], *The Anglo-Irish of the Nineteenth Century*, 3 vols. (London, 1828), II, p. 262.
12. [Banim], *The Anglo-Irish of the Nineteenth Century*, II, p. 262.
13. Jennifer Pitt, *A Turn to Empire: The Rise of Imperial Liberalism in Britain and France* (Princeton: Princeton University Press, 2005), p. 2.
14. Jane Moore, 'Thomas Moore and the Social Life of Forms', in Claire Connolly (ed.), *Irish Literature in Transition, 1780–1830* (Cambridge: Cambridge University Press, 2020), pp. 257–72 (p. 257).

15. Sydney Owenson, *Patriotic Sketches of Ireland*, 2 vols. (London, 1807), I, p. v.
16. Angela Esterhammer, *Print and Performance in the 1820s: Improvisation, Speculation, Identity* (Cambridge: Cambridge University Press, 2020).
17. Lady Morgan, *Florence Macarthy*, 4 vols. (London, 1818), III, p. 109.
18. Mary Russell Mitford, *Letters of Mary Russell Mitford, Second Series*, ed. Henry Chorley, 2 vols. (London, 1872), I, p. 42.
19. Mitford, *Letters of Mary Russell Mitford*, I, p. 42.
20. Mitford, *Letters of Mary Russell Mitford*, I, p. 42.
21. I am drawing here on Jenny McAuley's edition of *Florence Macarthy* (London: Pickering and Chatto, 2012).
22. Lady Morgan, *Florence Macarthy*, 4 vols. (London, 1818), II, p. 35.
23. Lady Morgan, *Italy*, 2 vols. (London, 1821), II, p. 140.
24. Lady Morgan, *France in 1829–30*, 2 vols. (London, 1830), I, pp. 236–7.
25. Collections for a History of the Ballad Literature of Ireland, by Thomas Crofton Croker. British Library, Add MS 20091-20094.
26. Morgan, *France in 1829–30*, I, p. 250.
27. Baker, *Written on the Water*, p. 4.
28. *Lord Byron: The Major Works*, ed. Jerome J. McGann (Oxford: Worlds Classics, 2000), p. 509.
29. William Wordsworth, *The Prelude*, ed. Jonathan Wordsworth (London: Penguin, 1995), p. 281. Composed around 1831, this passage was published in *The Prelude* in 1850.
30. David Latané, *William Maginn and the British Press: A Critical Biography* (Farnham: Ashgate, 2013), p. 19.
31. William Maginn, 'Don Juan Unread', *Blackwood's Edinburgh Magazine*, 6 (1819), 194–5.

> Let Colburn's town-bred cattle snuff
> The filths of Lady Morgan
> Let Maturin to amorous themes
> Attune his barrel organ!
> We will not read them, will not hear
> The parson or the granny;
> And, I dare say, as bad as they
> Or worse, is Don Giovanni.

32. Richard Lansdown (ed.), *Byron's Letters and Journals: A New Selection* (Oxford: Oxford University Press, 2015), pp. 357, 341.
33. James Chandler, *England in 1819: The Politics of Literary Culture and the Case of Romantic Historicism* (Chicago: University of Chicago Press, 1998), p. 78.
34. Maria Edgeworth to Peter Holland, 27 August 1819. Bodleian MSS 16087/1.
35. Maria Edgeworth to Henry Holland, 20 February 1820. Bodleian MSS16087/1.
36. See James Kelly, '"The Most Portentous Event in Modern History": Ireland before and after the Peterloo Massacre', in Michael Demson and Regina Hewitt (eds.), *Commemorating Peterloo: Violence, Resilience and Claim-Making during the Romantic Era* (Edinburgh: Edinburgh University Press, 2019), pp. 140–59.
37. Chandler, *England in 1819*, p. 267.

38. William Hazlitt, *The Spirit of the Age* (London, 1825), pp. 399, 388.
39. Quoted in Gregory A. Schirmer, 'English Ireland/Irish Ireland: The Poetry and Translations of J. J. Callanan', in Claire Connolly (ed.), *Irish Literature in Transition, 1780–1830*, pp. 242–56 (p. 254).
40. Hazlitt, *The Spirit of the Age*, pp. 391, 398.
41. Moore, 'Thomas Moore and the Social Life of Forms', p. 259.
42. Moore, 'Thomas Moore and the Social Life of Forms', p. 270.
43. Hazlitt, *The Spirit of the Age*, p. 397.
44. Moore, 'Thomas Moore and the Social Life of Forms', pp. 259–60.
45. Thomas Moore, *Memoirs of Captain Rock*, fifth ed. (London, 1824), p. 368.
46. Moore, *Memoirs of Captain Rock*, p. 341.
47. Moore, *Memoirs of Captain Rock*, p. 371.
48. Jane Moore, '*The Fudge Family in Paris* (1818)', in Jane Moore (ed.), *British Satire, 1785–1840: The Satires of Thomas Moore* (London: Pickering and Chatto, 2003), pp. 121–4 (p. 122).
49. Moore (ed.), *The Satires of Thomas Moore*, p. 126.
50. Paul Hamilton, 'The "Restoration" of the Restoration', in Patrick Vincent (ed.), *The Cambridge History of European Romantic Literature* (Cambridge: Cambridge University Press, 2023), pp. 435–57 (p. 437).
51. Percy Bysshe Shelley, *Essays, Letters from Abroad, Translations and Fragments*, 2 vols. (London, 1840), I, p. 45.
52. Carol Kyros Walker, *Walking North with Keats* (New Haven: Yale University Press, 1992), p. 171. See Claire Connolly, 'Watery Romanticism: Walking and Sailing West with Keats', *Romanticism on the Net*, 79 (2022). https://ronjournal.org/articles/n79. Accessed 27 April 2024.
53. Carol Bolton, *Writing the Empire: Robert Southey and Romantic Colonialism* (London: Pickering and Chatto, 2007), p. 80.
54. Chandler, *England in 1819*, pp. 272–3.
55. John Keats, *Selected Letters*, ed. Robert Gittings and Jon Mee (Oxford: Oxford University Press, 2002), p. 176.
56. Thomas Moore, *The Journal of Thomas Moore*, ed. Wilfred S. Dowden, 6 vols. (Newark: University of Delaware Press, 1983–91), II, p. 659.
57. Quoted in Harriet Kramer Linkin, 'Mary Tighe, Thomas Moore, and the Publication of "Selena"', *Review of English Studies*, 65 (2014), 711–29 (p. 720).
58. See Claire Connolly, '"A Big Book about England"? Public and Private Meanings in *Patronage*', in Jacqueline Belanger (ed.), *The Irish Novel in the Nineteenth Century: Facts and Fictions* (Dublin: Four Courts Press, 2005), pp. 63–79.
59. Lord Byron to John Murray, 24 July 1814. *Byron's Letters and Journals*, ed. Leslie A. Marchand, 13 vols. (London: Murray, 1973–94), IV, p. 146; quoted in Peter Garside, Jacqueline Belanger and Sharon Ragaz, *British Fiction, 1800–1829*. www.british-fiction.cf.ac.uk. Accessed 20 December 2023.
60. Jerome McGann (ed.), *Lord Byron: The Major Works* (Oxford: Oxford University Press, 1986), p. 382.
61. Mitford, *Letters of Mary Russell Mitford*, I, p. 42.

62. *The Freeman's Journal*, 20 May 1828.
63. Daniel Griffin, *Life of Gerald Griffin* (London, 1843), p. 426.
64. Steve Mentz, *Ocean* (New York: Bloomsbury Academic, 2020).
65. Katarzyna Bartoszyńska, *Estranging the Novel: Poland, Ireland, and Theories of World Literature* (Baltimore: Johns Hopkins University Press, 2021), p. 71.
66. Siobhan Carroll, *An Empire of Air and Water: Uncolonizable Space in the British Imagination, 1750–1850* (Pennsylvania: University of Pennsylvania Press, 2015), p. 7.
67. Carroll, *An Empire of Air and Water*, p. 14.
68. Charles Robert Maturin, *Melmoth the Wanderer*, 4 vols. (Edinburgh, 1820), IV, pp. 337–8.
69. Maturin, *Melmoth the Wanderer*, I, pp. 40–1.
70. Maturin, *Melmoth the Wanderer*, I, p. 7.
71. Maturin, *Melmoth the Wanderer*, I, p. 7.
72. Maturin, *Melmoth the Wanderer*, I, p. 15.
73. Maturin, *Melmoth the Wanderer*, I, pp. 154, 151.
74. Maturin, *Melmoth the Wanderer*, I, pp. 151–2.
75. [Gerald Griffin], *Holland-Tide* (London, 1827), pp. 218–19.
76. Maturin, *Melmoth the Wanderer*, I, p. 166.
77. Maturin, *Melmoth the Wanderer*, III, p. 22.
78. Maturin, *Melmoth the Wanderer*, III, pp. 30–1.
79. Maturin, *Melmoth the Wanderer*, III, pp. 29, 31.
80. Maturin, *Melmoth the Wanderer*, III, pp. 31–2.
81. Maturin, *Melmoth the Wanderer*, III, p. 32.
82. Breandán Mac Suibhne, 'Editor's Introduction', in *John Gamble, Society and Manners in Early Nineteenth-Century Ireland* (Dublin: Field Day, 2011), pp. xiii–lxxx (p. lxiii).
83. Gamble, *Society and Manners in Early Nineteenth-Century Ireland*, p. 369.
84. Mac Suibhne, 'Editor's Introduction', p. lxx.
85. Guy Beiner, *Forgetful Remembrance: Social Forgetting and Vernacular Historiography of a Rebellion in Ulster* (Oxford: Oxford University Press, 2018), p. 150.
86. Beiner, *Forgetful Remembrance*, pp. 150, 248.
87. Maturin, *Melmoth the Wanderer*, III, pp. 18–19.
88. Maturin, *Melmoth the Wanderer*, III, p. 19.
89. Maturin, *Melmoth the Wanderer*, III, p. 34.
90. [John Banim and Michael Banim], *Tales, by the O'Hara Family: Containing Crohoore of the Bill-Hook, The Fetches, and John Doe*, 3 vols. (London, 1825), I, p. 234.
91. [Banim], *Tales, by the O'Hara Family*, I, pp. 235, 238.
92. [Banim], *Tales, by the O'Hara Family*, I, p. 239.
93. [Banim], *Tales, by the O'Hara Family*, I, p. 241.
94. Angela Esterhammer, 'Late Romanticism and Print Culture', in Patrick Vincent (ed.), *The Cambridge History of European Romantic Literature* (Cambridge: Cambridge University Press, 2023), pp. 458–86 (p. 463).

95. Melody Jue, *Wild Blue Media: Thinking through Seawater* (Durham, NC: Duke University Press, 2020), p. 4.
96. Nicole Starosielski, 'The Elements of Media Studies', *Media and Environment*, 1.1 (2019). https://doi.org/10.1525/001c.10780. Accessed 27 April 2024.
97. Maturin, *Melmoth the Wanderer*, III, p. 66.
98. Maturin, *Melmoth the Wanderer*, III, p. 77.
99. Ashley L. Cohen, 'The Global Indies: Historicizing Oceanic Metageographies', *Comparative Literature*, 69.1 (2017), 7–15 (p. 8).
100. Maturin, *Melmoth the Wanderer*, III, p. 96.
101. Maturin, *Melmoth the Wanderer*, III, pp. 97, 103.
102. Maturin, *Melmoth the Wanderer*, III, pp. 104–5.
103. Maturin, *Melmoth the Wanderer*, III, p. 105.
104. Maturin, *Melmoth the Wanderer*, IV, p. 199.
105. Maturin, *Melmoth the Wanderer*, IV, pp. 197–8.
106. See Claire Connolly, 'Too Rough for Verse: Sea Crossings in Irish Culture', in Joep Leerssen (ed.), *Parnell and His Times* (Cambridge: Cambridge University Press, 2020), pp. 243–67 (p. 243).
107. Maturin, *Melmoth the Wanderer*, IV, p. 237.
108. Maturin, *Melmoth the Wanderer*, IV, p. 236.
109. Maturin, *Melmoth the Wanderer*, IV, pp. 236–7.
110. Maturin, *Melmoth the Wanderer*, IV, p. 451.
111. Maturin, *Melmoth the Wanderer*, IV, p. 451.
112. Vera Kreilkamp, *The Anglo-Irish Novel and the Big House* (Syracuse: Syracuse University Press, 1998), p. 103.
113. Maturin, *Melmoth the Wanderer*, IV, p. 452.
114. Maturin, *Melmoth the Wanderer*, I, p. xi.
115. Maturin, *Melmoth the Wanderer*, IV, p. 452.
116. Tom Dunne, 'Haunted by History: Irish Romantic Writing, 1800–1850', in Roy Porter and Miklaus Teich (eds.), *Romanticism in National Context* (Cambridge: Cambridge University Press, 1989), pp. 68–91 (pp. 84–5).
117. Siobhan Kilfeather, 'Terrific Register: The Gothicization of Atrocity in Irish Romanticism', *boundary 2*, 31.1 (2004), 49–71 (p. 56).
118. Maturin, *Melmoth the Wanderer*, III, p. 102.
119. [Griffin], *Holland-Tide*, p. 218.
120. [Griffin], *Holland-Tide*, p. 218.
121. [Griffin], *Holland-Tide*, pp. 216–17.
122. [Griffin], *Holland-Tide*, p. 216.
123. [Griffin], *Holland-Tide*, p. 217.
124. [Griffin], *Holland-Tide*, pp. 219–20, 215.
125. Griffin, *Life of Gerald Griffin*, p. 199.
126. [Gerald Griffin], *Tales of the Munster Festivals*, 3 vols. (London, 1827), I, pp. 9–10.
127. [Griffin], *Tales of the Munster Festivals*, I, pp. 311–12.
128. Lady Blessington, *The Magic Lantern; or, Sketches of Scenes in the Metropolis* (London, 1822), p. 68.

129. John Banim to John Murray, 8 April 1830. National Library of Scotland MSS Acc 12604/1049 l.
130. Maria Edgeworth, *Tales of Fashionable Life*, 6 vols. (London, 1809–12), VI, p. 295.
131. [Griffin], *Tales of the Munster Festivals*, I, p. 17.
132. Christine Kinealy, *A Disunited Kingdom? England, Ireland, Scotland and Wales, 1800–1949* (Cambridge: Cambridge University Press, 1999), p. 4; see also Alvin Jackson, 'The Survival of the Union', in Joe Cleary and Claire Connolly (eds.), *The Cambridge Companion to Modern Irish Culture* (Cambridge: Cambridge University Press, 2005), pp. 25–41 (p. 35).
133. Thomas Dermody, 'Epistle, Continued', in Michael Griffin (ed.), *Thomas Dermody: Selected Writings* (Dublin: Field Day Press, 2012), p. 275.
134. *The London Magazine*, 7 (1827), 399–401 (p. 399).
135. [Griffin], *Tales of the Munster Festivals*, I, p. xi.
136. [Griffin], *Tales of the Munster Festivals*, I, p. ii.
137. [Griffin], *Tales of the Munster Festivals*, I, p. 8.
138. [Griffin], *Tales of the Munster Festivals*, I, p. 6.
139. [Griffin], *Tales of the Munster Festivals*, I, pp. 6, 8.
140. Mary A. Favret, *War at a Distance: Romanticism and the Making of Modern Wartime* (Princeton and Oxford: Princeton University Press, 2010), p. 11.
141. Favret, *War at a Distance*, p. 11.
142. [Griffin], *Tales of the Munster Festivals*, I, p. 5.
143. [Griffin], *Tales of the Munster Festivals*, I, p. 5.
144. [Griffin], *Tales of the Munster Festivals*, I, p. 6.
145. [Griffin], *Tales of the Munster Festivals*, I, p. 35.
146. [Griffin], *Tales of the Munster Festivals*, I, p. 38.
147. [Griffin], *Tales of the Munster Festivals*, I, p. 38.
148. [Griffin], *Tales of the Munster Festivals*, I, p. 47.
149. [Griffin], *Tales of the Munster Festivals*, I, p. 48.
150. [Griffin], *Tales of the Munster Festivals*, I, p. 48.
151. [Griffin], *Tales of the Munster Festivals*, I, p. 50.
152. [Griffin], *Tales of the Munster Festivals*, I, p. 73.
153. [Griffin], *Tales of the Munster Festivals*, I, p. 108.
154. Kathleen Wilson, 'Nelson and the People: Manliness, Patriotism and Body Politics', in David Cannadine (ed.), *Admiral Lord Nelson: Context and Legacy* (Basingstoke: Palgrave Macmillan, 2005), pp. 49–66 (p. 58).
155. See John M. MacKenzie, 'Nelson Goes Global: The Nelson Myth in Britain and Beyond', in David Cannadine (ed.), *Admiral Lord Nelson*, pp. 144–65.
156. [Griffin], *Tales of the Munster Festivals*, I, p. 103.
157. [Griffin], *Tales of the Munster Festivals*, I, p. 121.
158. [Griffin], *Tales of the Munster Festivals*, I, p. 150.
159. [Griffin], *Tales of the Munster Festivals*, I, pp. 162–3.
160. [Griffin], *Tales of the Munster Festivals*, I, p. 163.
161. Larcom pursued meteorological researches at Mountjoy House from 1829, including measurements of barometric pressure, rainfall and humidity records. See Andrews, *A Paper Landscape*, pp. 155–6.

162. Favret, *War at a Distance*, p. 145.
163. [Griffin], *Tales of the Munster Festivals*, I, p. 156.
164. [Griffin], *Tales of the Munster Festivals*, I, pp. 160, 168.
165. [Griffin], *Tales of the Munster Festivals*, I, p. 169.
166. Gillian Russell, *The Theatres of War Performance, Politics, and Society, 1793–1815* (Oxford: Oxford University Press, 1995), p. 20.
167. Jerome Christensen, *Romanticism at the End of History* (Baltimore: Johns Hopkins University Press, 2000), p. 4.
168. [Griffin], *Tales of the Munster Festivals*, I, p. 161.
169. [Griffin], *Holland-Tide*, p. 192.
170. [Griffin], *Tales of the Munster Festivals*, I, p. 168.
171. Griffin, *Life of Gerald Griffin*, p. 274.
172. Griffin, *Life of Gerald Griffin*, pp. 275–7.
173. Griffin, *Life of Gerald Griffin*, p. 155.
174. Lady Blessington, 'Stock-in-Trade of Modern Poetesses', *The Maids, Wives, and Widows' Penny Magazine, and Gazette of Fashion*, 1 (1832), 39.
175. [William Makepeace Thackeray], 'A Word on the Annuals', *Frazier's Magazine*, 16 (1837), 757–63 (p. 758).
176. Meidhbhín Ní Úrdail, 'From Script to Print: Some Evidence in Manuscripts Compiled in Eighteenth- and Nineteenth-Century Ireland', in Matthew Driscoll and Nioclás Mac Cathmhaoil (eds.), *Hidden Harmonies: Manuscript and Print on the North Atlantic Fringe, 1500–1900* (Copenhagen: Museum Tusculanum Press, 2021), pp. 325–61 (p. 326).
177. Nicholas M. Wolf, *An Irish-Speaking Island: State, Religion, Community, and the Linguistic Landscape in Ireland, 1770–1870* (Madison: The University of Wisconsin Press, 2014), p. 204.
178. Peadar Ó Muircheartaigh, 'Catholic Literature and Literary Culture in Welsh, Scottish Gaelic, and Irish', in Liam Chambers (ed.), *The Oxford History of British and Irish Catholicism, Volume III: Relief, Revolution, and Revival, 1746–1829* (Oxford: Oxford University Press, 2023), pp. 243–63 (p. 261). See also Ní Úrdail, 'From Script to Print'.
179. Cóilín Parsons, *The Ordnance Survey and Modern Irish Literature* (Oxford: Oxford University Press, 2016), p. 15.
180. [Lord Byron], *English Bards, and Scotch Reviewers* (London, [1809]), p. 45.
181. Henry Kirke White, *The Poetical Works of Henry Kirke White* (London, 1830), p. 179.
182. Laurie Langbauer, 'Prolepsis and the Tradition of Juvenile Writing: Henry Kirke White and Robert Southey', *PMLA*, 128 (2013), 888–906 (p. 899).
183. *Literary Remains of Jeremiah Joseph Callanan, Collected and Compiled by John Fitzpatrick Fitzthomas Windele of Blair's Castle, Cork*. Royal Irish Academy MSS 12 I 13, p. 298.
184. Jeremiah Joseph Callanan, *The Poems of J. J. Callanan* (Cork, 1861), p. 127.
185. Callanan, *The Poems of J. J. Callanan*, p. 130.
186. 'Irish Popular Songs', *Blackwood's Edinburgh Magazine*, 13 (1823), 209–15 (p. 209).

187. Callanan, *The Poems of J. J. Callanan*, p. 112.
188. B. G. MacCarthy, 'Jeremiah J. Callanan; Part II: His Poetry', *Studies: An Irish Quarterly Review*, 35 (1946), 387–99 (p. 394).
189. Schirmer, 'English Ireland/Irish Ireland', p. 243.
190. Quoted in *The Poems of J. J. Callanan* (Cork, 1848), p. xxiv.
191. Thomas Crofton Croker, *The Keen of the South of Ireland* (London, 1844), pp. xxiv, xxvi.
192. Croker, *The Keen of the South of Ireland*, p. 102. See Claire Connolly, *A Cultural History of the Irish Novel, 1790–1829* (Cambridge: Cambridge University Press, 2012), pp. 195–6.
193. *Literary Remains of Jeremiah Joseph Callanan*, p. 370.
194. J. J. Callanan (J.J.), *Recluse of Inchidony, and other Poems* (London, 1830). Four autograph letters by Callanan are inserted in the British Library copy of the book and it is from these I quote.
195. On 1824 as a threshold year, see Lee Erickson, *The Economy of Literary Form: English Literature and the Industrialization of Publishing, 1800–1850* (Baltimore: Johns Hopkins Press, 1996), p. 26: John Murray 'refused any manuscripts of poetry after Byron's death in 1824'.
196. Callanan, *The Poems of J. J. Callanan*, p. 1.
197. Callanan, *The Poems of J. J. Callanan*, pp. 2, 7.
198. Callanan, *The Poems of J. J. Callanan*, p. 9.
199. Callanan, *The Poems of J. J. Callanan*, p. 17.
200. Callanan, *The Poems of J. J. Callanan*, p. 22.
201. Callanan, *The Poems of J. J. Callanan*, p. 21.
202. Callanan, *The Poems of J. J. Callanan*, p. 20.
203. Callanan, *The Poems of J. J. Callanan*, p. 24.
204. Callanan, *The Poems of J. J. Callanan*, p. 150.
205. Lord Byron, *Childe Harold's Pilgrimage* (London, 1812), p. 161.
206. Lord Byron to Thomas Moore, 27 August 1822. *The Works of Lord Byron*, ed. Thomas Moore, 17 vols. (London, 1832–3), V, p. 353.
207. James Joyce, *A Portrait of the Artist as a Young Man*, ed. Jery Johnson (Oxford: Oxford University Press, 2000), p. 68.
208. Matthew Campbell, *Irish Poetry under the Union, 1801–1924* (Cambridge: Cambridge University Press, 2014), p. 44.
209. Bernard O'Donoghue, 'Poetry in Ireland', in Joe Cleary and Claire Connolly (eds.), *The Cambridge Companion to Modern Irish Culture*, pp. 173–89 (p. 180).
210. Bernard O'Donoghue, 'Poetry in Ireland', pp. 180–1.
211. B. G. MacCarthy, 'Jeremiah J. Callanan; Part II: His Poetry', p. 387. Callanan, *The Poems of J. J. Callanan*, p. xv.
212. Quoted in Robert Welch, *Irish Poetry from Moore to Yeats* (Gerrards Cross: Colin Smythe, 1980), p. 64.
213. Welch, *Irish Poetry from Moore to Yeats*, p. 60.
214. Schirmer, 'English Ireland/Irish Ireland', p. 248.
215. Callanan, *The Poems of J. J. Callanan*, p. 65.

216. Schirmer, 'English Ireland/Irish Ireland', p. 248.
217. Callanan, *The Poems of J. J. Callanan*, p. 66.
218. Callanan, *The Poems of J. J. Callanan*, p. 66.
219. Callanan, *The Poems of J. J. Callanan*, p. 67.
220. *Literary Remains of Jeremiah Joseph Callanan*, pp. 353–4.
221. Callanan, *The Poems of J. J. Callanan*, p. 65.
222. *Literary Remains of Jeremiah Joseph Callanan*, p. 77.
223. For both men, see the *Dictionary of Irish Biography*.
224. [Charles Wolfe], 'The Burial of Sir John Moore', *Blackwood's Edinburgh Magazine*, 1 (1817), 277–8.
225. [Charles Wolfe], 'The Burial of Sir John Moore', p. 278.
226. Benedict Anderson, *Imagined Communities: Reflections on the Origin and Spread of Nationalism* (London and New York: Verso, 2006), p. 150.
227. Described in short-lived newspaper *The Citizen* for 1841 as Wolfe's 'expressive phrase'. See also Barbara Hayley, 'A Reading and Thinking Nation: Periodicals as the Voice of Nineteenth-Century Ireland', in Barbara Hayley and Enda McKay (eds.), *Three Hundred Years of Irish Periodicals* (Mullingar: Association of Irish Learned Journals, 1987), pp. 29–48 (p. 40): 'when Peel asked what good corporations were to a country as poor as Ireland, Woulfe is reported to have replied, "they will go far to create and foster public opinion in Ireland, and make it *racy of the soil*"'.
228. John Ryan, *Ireland from A.D. 800 to A.D. 1600* (Dublin: Browne and Nolan, n.d.), p. 247.
229. *Literary Remains of Jeremiah Joseph Callanan*, p. 77.
230. *Literary Remains of Jeremiah Joseph Callanan*, p. 6.
231. *Literary Remains of Jeremiah Joseph Callanan*, p. 6.
232. B. G. MacCarthy, 'Jeremiah J. Callanan; Part 1: His Life', *Studies: An Irish Quarterly Review*, 35 (1946), 215–29 (p. 215).

3 Darkening Skies, 1830–1850

1. Quoted in Peter Hession, 'Imagining the Railway Revolution in Pre-Famine Ireland: Technology, Governance, and the Drummond Commission, 1832–39', in Richard Butler (ed.), *Dreams of the Future in Nineteenth-Century Ireland* (Liverpool: Liverpool University Press), pp. 245–70 (p. 252).
2. Harriet Martineau, 'Railway from Dublin to Galway – Bog of Allen', *Daily News*, 29 August 1852. See Harriet Martineau, *Letters from Ireland*, ed. Glenn Hooper (Dublin: Irish Academic Press, 2001), p. 69.
3. Lady Morgan, *Lady Morgan's Memoirs: Autobiography, Diaries and Correspondence*, 2 vols. (London, 1862), II, p. 339.
4. Thomas Carlyle, 'Signs of the Times', *Edinburgh Review* 49 (1829), pp. 439–59.
5. Quoted in Hession, 'Imagining the Railway Revolution in Pre-Famine Ireland', p. 263.
6. Hession, 'Imagining the Railway Revolution in Pre-Famine Ireland', p. 268.

7. William Carleton, 'The Irish Shanahus', *The Irish Penny Journal*, 1.48 (1841), pp. 378–80 (p. 378).
8. Nicholas Canny, *Imagining Ireland's Pasts: Early Modern Ireland through the Centuries* (Oxford: Oxford University Press, 2021), p. 222.
9. John Mitchel, 'The Individuality of a Native Literature', *The Nation*, 21 August 1847, p. 731.
10. Terry Eagleton, *Heathcliff and the Great Hunger: Essays in Irish Culture* (London: Verso, 1999), p. 11; Charlotte Brontë, *Jane Eyre* (Peterborough, ON: Broadview, 2022), p. 325.
11. Matthew Campbell, 'Victorian Ireland, 1830–1880: A Transition State', in Matthew Campbell (ed.), *Irish Literature in Transition, 1830–1880* (Cambridge: Cambridge University Press, 2020), pp. 3–21.
12. Anahid Nersessian, *Utopia, Limited: Romanticism and Adjustment* (Cambridge, MA: Harvard University Press, 2015), p. 237.
13. Elizabeth Tilley, 'The *Dublin Penny Journal* and Alternative Histories', in Rebecca Anne Barr, Sarah-Anne Buckley and Muireann O'Cinneide (eds.), *Literacy, Language and Reading in Nineteenth-Century Ireland* (Liverpool: Liverpool University Press, 2019), pp. 87–104 (p. 87).
14. Matthew Campbell, 'How Good Is Mangan?', *Irish Studies Review*, 13.2 (2005), pp. 227–32 (p. x).
15. 'Editor's Address', *Dublin University Magazine*, 19 (1842), pp. 423–4 (p. 424). See Elizabeth Tilley, 'Periodicals', in James H. Murphy (ed.), *The Oxford History of the Irish Book, Volume IV: The Irish Book in English, 1800–1891* (Oxford: Oxford University Press, 2011), pp. 144–70 (p. 155).
16. Paul Hamilton, 'Introduction', in Paul Hamilton (ed.), *The Oxford Handbook of European Romanticism* (Oxford: Oxford University Press, 2016), pp. 1–12 (p. 2).
17. Niall Ó Ciosáin, *Ireland in Official Print Culture, 1800–1850: A New Reading of the Poor Inquiry* (Oxford: Oxford University Press, 2014), p. 14.
18. Nessa Cronin, 'From Dublin to Dehra Dun: Language, Translation and the Mapping of Ireland and India', in Rebecca Anne Barr, Sarah-Anne Buckley and Muireann O'Cinneide (eds.), *Literacy, Language and Reading in Nineteenth-Century Ireland* (Liverpool: Liverpool University Press, 2019), pp. 159–75 (pp. 160, 162).
19. Augustus J. C. Hare (ed.), *The Life and Letters of Maria Edgeworth*, 2 vols. (London, 1894), II, p. 205.
20. Hare (ed.), *The Life and Letters of Maria Edgeworth*, II, p. 202.
21. Hare (ed.), *The Life and Letters of Maria Edgeworth*, II, p. 237.
22. James S. Donnelly, Jr., 'The Terry Alt Movement 1829–31', *History Ireland*, 2.4 (1994). www.historyireland.com/the-terry-alt-movement-1829-31-by-james-s-donnelly-jr. Accessed 19 October 2024.
23. Quoted in Glenn Hooper, 'The Charms of Ireland: Travel Writing and Tourism', in Matthew Campbell (ed.), *Irish Literature in Transition, 1830–1880* (Cambridge: Cambridge University Press, 2020), pp. 108–23 (p. 118).
24. Maria Edgeworth, *Helen* (London: Pickering and Chatto, 1999), p. 112.

25. Hare (ed.), *The Life and Letters of Maria Edgeworth*, II, p. 202.
26. Hare (ed.), *The Life and Letters of Maria Edgeworth*, II, p. 202.
27. Hare (ed.), *The Life and Letters of Maria Edgeworth*, II, p. 202.
28. 'Novels Descriptive of Irish Life', *Edinburgh Review*, 52 (1831), pp. 410–31 (p. 411).
29. Review of the first volume of A. M. Hall and S. C. Hall's *Ireland: Its Scenery, Character, &c.* (1841), *The Athenaeum*, 10 April 1841, pp. 275–7 (p. 275).
30. Ute Berns, 'Energy Ecologies in Joanna Baillie's "Address to a Steam-Vessel" (1823)', in David Kerler and Martin Middeke (eds.), *Romantic Ecologies* (Trier: Wissenschaftlicher Verlag Trier, 2023), pp. 57–74 (p. 59).
31. 'To Charles Wye Williams, Esq., Originator and Promoter of "Irish Steam Navigation"', in William M. Downes, *Poems, Epistles, Etc. Etc.* (Dublin, 1839), p. 191.
32. 'Letter of the Poet Mr Moore, to the Author', inserted as frontispiece to William M. Downes, *Temperance Melodies for the Teetotallers of Ireland* (Cork, 1843).
33. Frances Anne Edgeworth, *A Memoir of Maria Edgeworth*, 3 vols. (London, 1867), III, p. 78.
34. Edgeworth, *Helen*, pp. 5, 6.
35. William Carleton, *Traits and Stories of the Irish Peasantry: Second Series*, 3 vols. (Dublin, 1833), I, p. v.
36. Carleton, *Traits and Stories of the Irish Peasantry: Second Series*, I, pp. vi–vii.
37. R. F. Foster, *Words Alone: Yeats and His Inheritances* (Oxford: Oxford University Press, 2011), p. 50.
38. Mary Shelley, *The Last Man*, 3 vols. (Paris, 1826), II, p. 190.
39. Shelley, *The Last Man*, II, pp. 190–3.
40. Shelley, *The Last Man*, II, p. 194.
41. Shelley, *The Last Man*, II, p. 201. Oliver Goldsmith, *The Deserted Village* (London, 1770), p. 17.
42. Samuel Baker, *Written on the Water: British Romanticism and the Maritime Empire of Culture* (Charlottesville: University of Virginia Press, 2010), p. 15.
43. On Frankenstein and population, see Maureen McLane, *Romanticism and the Human Sciences: Poetry, Population and the Discourse of the Species* (Cambridge: Cambridge University Press, 2000), chapter three.
44. William Carleton, *The Emigrants of Ahadarra* (London, 1848), p. 168.
45. Ó Ciosáin, *Ireland in Official Print Culture*, p. 48.
46. Lady Morgan, *Passages from My Autobiography* (London, 1859), pp. 102–3.
47. Quoted in Ó Ciosáin, *Ireland in Official Print Culture*, p. 48.
48. Maria Edgeworth to Rachel Mordecai Lazarus, 11 July 1837. Edgar E. MacDonald (ed.), *The Education of the Heart: The Correspondence of Rachel Mordecai Lazarus and Maria Edgeworth* (Chapel Hill: The University of North Carolina Press, 1977), p. 298.
49. Maria Edgeworth, *Letters from England: 1813–1844*, ed. Christina Colvin (Oxford: Clarendon Press, 1971), pp. 331, 423–4.
50. Maria Edgeworth to Frances Anne Edgeworth, 18 October 1830. Edgeworth, *Letters from England*, p. 422.

51. Maria Edgeworth to Fanny Wilson, 11 June 1831. Edgeworth, *Letters from England*, p. 549.
52. Clíona Ó Gallchoir, *Maria Edgeworth: Women, Enlightenment and Nation* (Dublin: UCD Press, 2005), p. 163.
53. Maria Edgeworth to Fanny Wilson, 11 June 1831. Edgeworth, *Letters from England*, pp. 548–9.
54. Richard Menke, *Telegraphic Realism: Victorian Fiction and Other Information Systems* (Stanford: Stanford University Press, 2008), p. 3.
55. Canny, *Imagining Ireland's Pasts*, p. 225.
56. William Makepeace Thackeray, *Barry Lyndon*, ed. Andrew Sanders (Oxford: Oxford University Press, 1984), p. 197.
57. *Cambridge History of Ireland*. Note scholarly debate on 1831 vs 1841 censuses.
58. George Cornewall Lewis, *On Local Disturbances in Ireland* (London, 1836), p. 332.
59. Thomas Moore, *Memoirs of Captain Rock*, fifth ed. (London, 1824), p. 156.
60. Maria Edgeworth to Harriet Butler, 3 December 1843. Edgeworth, *Letters from England*, p. 598.
61. Lady Morgan, *Letter to Cardinal Wiseman*, second ed. (London, 1851), pp. 33–4.
62. Caesar Otway, *Sketches in Ireland*, second ed. (Dublin, 1839), pp. ix–x.
63. William Maginn, *The Odoherty Papers*, ed. Shelton Mackenzie, 2 vols. (New York, 1855), II, p. 104.
64. See Jim Shanahan, 'Imperial Minds: Irish Writers and Empire in the Nineteenth Century – Charles Gavan Duffy, Thomas Moore, Charles Lever and *Kim*', in Matthew Campbell (ed.), *Irish Literature in Transition, 1830–1880* (Cambridge: Cambridge University Press, 2020), pp. 143–61 (p. 143).
65. See Francesca Benatti, 'Young Ireland and the Superannuated Bard', in Sarah McCleave and Triona O'Hanlon (eds.) *The Reputations of Thomas Moore* (London: Routledge, 2019), pp. xx–xx (p. x).
66. [Samuel Ferguson], 'Hardiman's *Irish* Minstrelsy, *Dublin University Magazine* (August 1834), pp. 153–54; Matthew Campbell, *Irish Poetry under the Union, 1801–1924* (Cambridge: Cambridge University Press, 2013), p. 71.
67. See Peter Gray on the Great Famine as a 'British Famine': '"The Great British Famine of 1845–50"? Ireland, the UK and Peripherality in Famine Relief and Philanthropy', in Declan Curran, Lubomyr Luciuk and Andrew Newby (eds.), *Famines in European Economic History: The Last Great European Famines Reconsidered* (London: Routledge, 2015), pp. 83–96.
68. Harriet Martineau, 'Ireland Dying of Too Much Doctoring – The "Tenant Right" Question', *Daily News*, 20 August 1852. See Martineau, *Letters from Ireland*, p. 50.
69. Harriet Martineau, 'The Wilds of Erris', *Daily News*, 11 September 1852. See Martineau, *Letters from Ireland*, p. 102.
70. Francis B. Head, *A Fortnight in Ireland* (London, 1852), p. 186.
71. Breandán Mac Suibhne, *The End of Outrage: Post-Famine Adjustment in Rural Ireland* (Oxford: Oxford University Press, 2017), pp. 14–15.
72. Lady Morgan, *Florence Macarthy*, 4 vols. (London, 1818), I, p. iv.

73. Quoted in Mac Suibhne, *The End of Outrage*, p. 4n.
74. Thomas Carlyle to John A. Carlyle, 22 July 1834, in *The Carlyle Letters Online* www.carlyleletters.org. Accessed 1 December 2024.
75. The phrase became a common one but is quoted here from William Downes' one-canto poem *The Exile*, published in Kilrush, County Clare in 1850.
76. Thomas Carlyle, *Reminiscences of My Irish Journey in 1849* (London, 1882), pp. 133, 240.
77. See Mary Poovey, *A History of the Modern Fact: Problems of Knowledge in the Sciences of Wealth and Society* (Chicago: University of Chicago Press, 1998), p. 130.
78. Joseph Sheridan Le Fanu, *The Purcell Papers*, with a memoir by Alfred Perceval Graves, 3 vols. (London, 1880), II, pp. 262–5.
79. Le Fanu, *The Purcell Papers*, II, p. 265.
80. Le Fanu, *The Purcell Papers*, II, p. 262.
81. William Richard Le Fanu, *Seventy Years of Irish Life: Being Anecdotes and Reminiscences* (London, 1893), pp. 127–8.
82. Le Fanu, *Seventy Years of Irish Life*, p. 132.
83. Maria Edgeworth to Harriet Butler, 3 December 1843. Edgeworth, *Letters from England*, p. 599.
84. Maria Edgeworth to Harriet Butler, 3 December 1843. Edgeworth, *Letters from England*, p. 598.
85. Owen Connellan, *A Dissertation on Irish Grammar* (Dublin, 1834), p. 62.
86. Connellan, *A Dissertation on Irish Grammar*, p. 62.
87. Mitchel, 'The Individuality of a Native Literature', p. 731.
88. Vincent Morley, *The Popular Mind in Eighteenth-Century Ireland* (Cork: Cork University Press, 2018), pp. 108–10. See also Nicholas Wolf, 'Antiquarians and Authentics: Survival and Revival in Gaelic Writing', in Matthew Campbell (ed.), *Irish Literature in Transition, 1830–1880* (Cambridge: Cambridge University Press, 2020), pp. 199–217 (p. 206).
89. Wolf, 'Antiquarians and Authentics', p. 203.
90. Wolf, 'Antiquarians and Authentics', p. 202.
91. Wolf, 'Antiquarians and Authentics', p. 208.
92. Hugh Dorian, *The Outer Edge of Ulster: A Memoir of Social Life in Nineteenth-Century Donegal*, ed. Brendán Mac Suibhne and David Dickson (Dublin: The Lilliput Press, 2000), p. 84.
93. Mary Wollstonecraft, *The Collected Letters of Mary Wollstonecraft*, ed. Janet Todd (London: Allen Lane, 2003), p. 116.
94. Mary Tighe, *The Collected Letters of Mary Blachford Tighe, 1786–1810*, ed. Harriet Kramer Linkin (Bethlehem: Lehigh University Press, 2020), p. 255.
95. Mac Suibhne, *The End of Outrage*, p. 17.
96. William M. Downes, *Poetic Sketches, Rural, Pathetic, Descriptive with Tales Versified from Interesting Subjects* (Limerick, 1836), p. 133.
97. 'The Negro Slave', in William M. Downes, *Original Poems and Songs, with Notes* (Limerick, 1833), pp. 1–11.
98. Downes, *Original Poems and Songs*, p. 100n.

99. Downes, *Original Poems and Songs*, p. 105n.
100. Downes, *Poetic Sketches*, p. 32.
101. Edgeworth, *Helen*, I, p. 50.
102. Ó Gallchoir, *Maria Edgeworth*, p. 157.
103. Ó Gallchoir, *Maria Edgeworth*, p. 179.
104. Edgeworth, *A Memoir of Maria Edgeworth*, II, p. 285.
105. *The Freeman's Journal*, 20 May 1828.
106. Quoted in Ronan Kelly, *Bard of Erin: The Life of Thomas Moore* (Dublin: Penguin Ireland, 2008), p. 513.
107. 'The Miller Correspondence', *Fraser's Magazine*, 8 (1833), pp. 624–36 (p. 634).
108. *The Wexford Independent*, August 14, 1841.
109. Edgeworth, *Letters from England*, p. 543.
110. Edgeworth, *Helen*, I, p. 59.
111. Edgeworth, *Helen*, I, p. 59.
112. Madame de Staël, *Considerations on the Principal Events of the French Revolution*, 3 vols. (London, 1818), III, p. 279.
113. De Staël, *Considerations on the Principal Events*, III, p. 280.
114. De Staël, *Considerations on the Principal Events*, III, pp. 280–1.
115. Edgeworth, *Helen*, p. 218.
116. Review of Thomas Feenachty's translation of Maria Edgeworth, *Maith agus Dearmad – Rosanna* (1833), *Dublin University Magazine*, 3 (1834), 346–7.
117. Edgeworth, *Helen*, p. 335.
118. Edgeworth, *Helen*, p. 340.
119. Edgeworth, *Helen*, p. 348.
120. Edgeworth, *Helen*, p. 99.
121. Ó Gallchoir, *Maria Edgeworth*, p. 160.
122. Edgeworth, *Helen*, p. 101.
123. Edgeworth, *Helen*, p. 273.
124. Review of Catherine Gore's *Preferment, or, My Uncle the Earl* (1840) and *The Courtier of the Days of Charles II* (1839), *The Athenaeum*, 23 November 1839, pp. 888–9 (p. 888).
125. *The Athenaeum*, 23 November 1839, p. 888.
126. Clare Pettitt, *Serial Forms: The Unfinished Project of Modernity, 1815–1848* (Oxford: Oxford University Press, 2020), p. 32.
127. Maria Edgeworth to Margaret Ruxton, 9 March 1822. Edgeworth, *Letters from England*, pp. 364–5.
128. The signing of the Reform Bill in 1832 called up Cromwell in Edgeworth's imagination: in London at the time, she heard tales of 'bawling' lords: 'They say that nothing since Charles 1st and Cromwells time was ever like it.' Edgeworth, *Letters from England*, p. 537.
129. Catriona Kennedy, 'Republican Relicts: Gender, Memory, and Mourning in Irish Nationalist Culture, ca. 1798–1848', *Journal of British Studies*, 59 (2020), pp. 608–37 (pp. 636, 631, 632, 634).
130. Rose Novak, 'Reviving "Eva" of *The Nation*?: Eva O'Doherty's Young Ireland Newspaper Poetry', *Victorian Periodicals Review*, 45 (2012), pp. 436–65 (p. 442).

131. Charles Gavan Duffy (ed.), *The Ballad Poetry of Ireland*, third ed. (Dublin, 1845), pp. xi, xv.
132. See Nicholas Canny, *Imagining Ireland's Pasts: Early Modern Ireland through the Centuries* (Oxford: Oxford University Press, 2021), p. 241.
133. *The Life of Mary Russell Mitford* (London, 1852), p. 9.
134. Maria Edgeworth to Frances Anne Edgeworth, 30 April 1831. Edgeworth, *Letters from England*, pp. 528–9.
135. Maria Edgeworth to Frances Anne Edgeworth, 30 April 1831. Edgeworth, *Letters from England*, p. 529.
136. 23 January 1830. National Library of Scotland MSS Acc 12604/1298.
137. M. G. T. Crumpe, *Geraldine of Desmond: or, Ireland in the Days of Elizabeth*, second ed. (London, 1830), pp. 286–7.
138. P. D. Garside, J. E. Belanger and S. A. Ragaz, *British Fiction 1800–1829: A Database of Production, Circulation and Reception*, designer A. A. Mandal. www.british-fiction.cf.ac.uk. DBF Record No. 1829A033. Accessed 30 September 2013.
139. Mark Salber Phillips, *On Historical Distance* (New Haven: Yale University Press, 2013), p. 142.
140. Garside et al., *British Fiction*. DBF Record No. 1829A002. Accessed 20 October 2024.
141. Review of *The Davenels* (1829), *The Edinburgh Literary Journal*, 15 August 1829, pp. 148–149 (p. 148).
142. Anonymous, *The Davenels; or, A Campaign of Fashion in Dublin*, 2 vols. (London, 1829), II, pp. 268, 270.
143. *A Selection of Irish Melodies, with Symphonies and Accompaniments by Sir John Stevenson, Mus. Doc. and characteristic words by Thomas Moore, Esq. Sixth Number* (London, 1815), p. 77.
144. Lady Morgan, *Lady Morgan's Memoirs*, II, p. 336.
145. *The Cork Examiner*, 16 May 1845, p. 2.
146. John McCourt, *Writing the Frontier: Anthony Trollope between Britain and Ireland* (Oxford: Oxford University Press, 2015), p. 18.
147. Anthony Trollope, *An Autobiography*, 2 vols. (Edinburgh and London, 1883), I, p. 94.
148. [Harriet Martineau], 'Condition and Prospects of Ireland', *Westminster Review*, 59 (1853), pp. 18–32 (p. 18).
149. Matthew Arnold, *On the Study of Celtic Literature* (London, 1867), pp. 27–8.
150. Arnold, *On the Study of Celtic Literature*, pp. 46–7.
151. Quoted in Kelly, *Bard of Erin*, p. 508.
152. Daniel Griffin, *Life of Gerald Griffin* (London, 1843), p. 372.
153. Griffin, *Life of Gerald Griffin*, p. 375.
154. Royal Literary Fund, BL Loan 96 RLF 1/674/6.
155. Felicia Hemans, *Works: With a Memoir by Her Sister, and an Essay on Her Genius*, 7 vols. (Philadelphia, 1840), I, 263.
156. Lady Morgan, *France in 1829–30*, 2 vols. (London, 1830), I, p. 109.
157. Morgan, *France in 1829–30*, I, p. 107.

158. Morgan, *France in 1829–30*, I, p. 107.
159. See Delacroix, *Interior of a Dominican Convent in Madrid* (1831), oil on canvas, Philadelphia Museum of Art. https://philamuseum.org/collection/object/104366. Accessed 20 October 2024. See also Muireann Maguire, '"A Melmoth? a cosmopolitan? a patriot?": *Melmoth the Wanderer*'s Russian Epigones', *Gothic Studies*, 26.2 (2024), 148–64.
160. Griffin, *Life of Gerald Griffin*, p. 383.
161. Mary Russell Mitford, *Recollections of a Literary Life* (New York, 1852), p. 459.
162. Edgeworth, *A Memoir of Maria Edgeworth*, III, p. 35.
163. Maria Edgeworth to Frances Anne Edgeworth, 2 November 1830. Edgeworth, *Letters from England*, pp. 424–5.
164. Edgeworth, *A Memoir of Maria Edgeworth*, II, p. 280. She misremembered the book as one of Griffin's tales.
165. Daniel Griffin, *Life of Gerald Griffin* (London, 1843), p. 306.
166. Thomas Davis, *Essays and Poems with a Centenary Memoir 1845–1945* (Dublin, 1945), p. 111.
167. William Carleton, *Traits and Stories of the Irish Peasantry*, 2 vols. (Dublin, 1843), I, pp. viii–x.
168. Marjorie Howes, *Colonial Crossings: Figures in Irish Literary History* (Dublin: Field Day, 2006), p. 26.
169. Brian Earls, 'Oral Culture and Popular Autonomy', *Dublin Review of Books*, 100 (2018). https://drb.ie/articles/oral-culture-and-popular-autonomy. Accessed 20 October 2024.
170. Earls, 'Oral Culture and Popular Autonomy'.
171. 'To Samuel Lover', in Downes, *Poems, Epistles, Etc. Etc.*, p. 183.
172. Seamus Heaney, *Station Island* (London: Faber and Faber, 1984), p. 65.
173. William Carleton, *Traits and Stories of the Irish Peasantry: Second Series*, 3 vols. (Dublin, 1833), III, p. 6.
174. Carleton, *Traits and Stories of the Irish Peasantry: Second Series*, III, p. 7.
175. Carleton, *Traits and Stories of the Irish Peasantry: Second Series*, II, p. 177.
176. Carleton, *Traits and Stories of the Irish Peasantry: Second Series*, II, p. 219.
177. Carleton, *Traits and Stories of the Irish Peasantry: Second Series*, II, p. 234.
178. Brian Earls, 'Voices of the Dispossessed', *Dublin Review of Books*, December 2007. https://drb.ie/articles/voices-of-the-dispossessed/. Accessed 13 November 2024.
179. Carleton, *Traits and Stories of the Irish Peasantry: Second Series*, II, p. 61.
180. William Carleton, *The Black Prophet* (London, 1847), p. 20.
181. Carleton, *The Black Prophet*, p. vii. See Gillen D'Arcy Wood, *Tambora: The Eruption that Changed the World* (Princeton and Oxford: Princeton University Press, 2014).
182. Carleton, *The Black Prophet*, p. 211.
183. Dorian, *The Outer Edge of Ulster*, p. 130.
184. Bertha Coolidge Slade, *Maria Edgeworth, 1767–1849: A Bibliographical Tribute* (London: Constable, 1937), p. 214. See Yuri Yoshino, 'Edgeworthstown House', *European Romanticisms in Association*. www.euromanticism.org/edgeworthstown-house. Accessed 21 October 2024.

185. Maria Edgeworth to Fanny Wilson, 25 May 1841. Edgeworth, *Letters from England*, pp. 593–4. See Anna Pilz, 'The Rise of the Woman Writer', in Matthew Campbell (ed.), *Irish Literature in Transition, 1830–1880* (Cambridge: Cambridge University Press, 2020), pp. 257–79. For the daguerreotypes, see the National Portrait Gallery's website: www.npg.org.uk/collections/search/portrait/mw02020/Maria-Edgeworth. Accessed 21 October 2024.
186. Ronan Kelly, *Bard of Erin: The Life of Thomas Moore* (Dublin: Penguin Ireland, 2008), p. 536. On photogenic drawing, see https://projects.iq.harvard.edu/saltprintsatharvard/photogenic-drawing. Accessed 12 February 2025.
187. 'The Birthplace', in William Downes, *Original Poems and Songs with Notes*, pp. 1–11.
188. A. M. Hall and S. C. Hall, *Ireland: Its Scenery, Character, &c.*, 3 vols. (London, 1841–3), III, p. 276.
189. Morgan, *Lady Morgan's Memoirs*, II, p. 438.
190. Felicia Hemans, *Records of Woman: With Other Poems* (Edinburgh and London, 1828), p. 160.
191. W. B. Yeats, *Representative Irish Tales: First Series* (New York and London, [1891]), p. 8.
192. W. B. Yeats, *The Collected Works of W. B. Yeats, Volume III: Autobiographies*, ed. William H. O'Donnell, Douglas N. Archibald, with assistant editors J. Fraser Cocks III and Gretchen Schwenker (New York: Scribner, 1999), p. 104.
193. James Clarence Mangan, *Selected Writings*, ed. Seán Ryder (Dublin: UCD Press, 2004), p. 3.
194. Cóilín Parsons, *The Ordnance Survey and Modern Irish Literature* (Oxford: Oxford University Press, 2016), p. 69.
195. Robert Welch, *A History of Verse Translation from the Irish, 1789–1897* (Gerrards Cross: Colin Smythe, 1988), p. 102.
196. Ellen Shannon-Mangan, *James Clarence Mangan: A Biography* (Dublin: Irish Academic Press, 1996), pp. 247–9.
197. Welch, *A History of Verse Translation from the Irish*, p. 103.
198. Parsons, *The Ordnance Survey and Modern Irish Literature*, p. 83.
199. All quotations from the poem come from Mangan, *Selected Writings*, pp. 231–4.
200. A translation of the poem into English by Thomas Furlong appeared in James Hardiman's *Irish Minstrelsy* in 1831, while two further translations were undertaken by Samuel Ferguson and published in the *Dublin University Magazine*, October and November 1834.
201. Parsons suggests a connection to 'Elegiac Stanzas, Suggested by a Picture of Peele Castle in a Storm, Painted by Sir George Beaumont', a poem written by Wordsworth after the death by drowning of his brother, a sea-captain. The first line of 'Lament over the Ruins of the Abbey of Teach Molaga' ('I wandered forth at night alone') might also be compared to the first line of Wordsworth's poem on daffodils ('I wandered lonely as a cloud'). Both opening lines express loss and loneliness in iambic tetrameter, but are quite different in tone. Parsons, *The Ordnance Survey and Modern Irish Literature*, p. 104.

202. Robert Welch, *Irish Poetry from Moore to Yeats* (Gerrards Cross: Colin Smythe, 1980), pp. 77, 80. David Lloyd, *Nationalism and Minor Literature: James Clarence Mangan and the Emergence of Irish Cultural Nationalism* (Berkeley: University of California Press, 1987), p. 92.
203. Matthew Campbell, *Irish Poetry under the Union, 1801–1924* (Cambridge: Cambridge University Press, 2013), p. 120.
204. David Dickson, *Old World Colony: Cork and South Munster, 1630–1830* (Cork: Cork University Press, 2005), p. 27.
205. D'Arcy Wood, *Tambora*, p. 180.
206. Lloyd, *Nationalism and Minor Literature*, pp. 92–3. Check.
207. Lloyd, *Nationalism and Minor Literature*, p. 94.
208. Parsons, *The Ordnance Survey and Modern Irish Literature*, p. 105.
209. Jeremiah Joseph Callanan, *The Poems of J. J. Callanan* (Cork, 1861), p. 123.
210. Lloyd, *Nationalism and Minor Literature*, p. 91.
211. Charles Smith, *The Antient and Present State of the County and City of Cork*, 2 vols. (Cork, 1815), I, p. 242.
212. Smith, *The Antient and Present State of the County and City of Cork*, I, p. 244. G. Hansbrow, *An Improved Topographical and Historical Hibernian Gazetteer* (Dublin, 1835), p. 397.
213. Smith, *The Antient and Present State of the County and City of Cork*, I, pp. 242–3.
214. Fiona Stafford, 'The Roar of the Solway', in Nicholas Allen, Nick Groom, and Jos Smith (eds.), *Coastal Works: Cultures of the Atlantic Edge* (Oxford: Oxford University Press, 2017), pp. 41–59 (p. 45).
215. Parsons, *The Ordnance Survey and Modern Irish Literature*, p. 108.
216. William Wordsworth, *Lyrical Ballads*, 2 vols. (London, 1800), I, p. 206.
217. Review of the second series of William Carleton's *Traits and Stories of the Irish Peasantry* (1833), *Dublin University Magazine*, 1 (1833), pp. 31–41 (pp. 32–3).
218. [Samuel Ferguson], 'Irish Minstrelsy, or Bardic Remains of Ireland', *Dublin University Magazine*, 3 (1834), pp. 456–78 (p. 457).
219. Quoted in Stuart John McLean, *The Event and Its Terrors: Ireland, Famine, Modernity* (Stanford: Stanford University Press, 2004), p. 13.
220. William Carleton, *The Life of William Carleton: Being His Autobiography and Letters*, 2 vols. (London, 1896), II, p. 293.
221. Carleton, *The Life of William Carleton*, p. 293.

Afterword

1. Tim Campbell, *Historical Style: Fashion and the New Mode of History, 1740–1830* (Pennsylvania: University of Pennsylvania Press, 2016), p. 2.
2. Lacken (C.), Cill Mhichíl (Lacken, County Clare), The Schools' Collection, vol. 0602, p. 036, The Dúchas Project. www.duchas.ie/en/cbes/4922323/4870136. Accessed 2 December 2024.

3. Andy Bielenberg, 'British Competition and the Vicissitudes of the Irish Woollen Industry: 1785–1923', *Textile History*, 31 (2000), pp. 202–21 (p. 215).
4. Na Creaga (Creggs, County Galway), The Schools' Collection, vol. 0015, p. 089, The Dúchas Project. www.duchas.ie/en/cbes/4591097/4590513. Accessed 2 December 2024.
5. Enfield (Enfield, County Roscommon), The Schools' Collection, vol. 0246, p. 012, The Dúchas Project. www.duchas.ie/en/cbes/5162105/5154763. Accessed 2 December 2024.
6. Gleann na gCoileach (Glannagilliagh, County Kerry), The Schools' Collection, vol. 0472, p. 086, The Dúchas Project. www.duchas.ie/en/cbes/4742112/4737051/4936102. Accessed 2 December 2024.
7. Carrickatee (Carrickatee, County Monaghan), The Schools' Collection, vol, 0941, p. 235, The Dúchas Project. www.duchas.ie/en/cbes/4723843/4717912. Accessed 2 December 2024.
8. There are many versions of 'the woman who gave drink to the English soldier' story told in relation to the Battle of Ballinamuck. See Owen Devaney, *Killoe: History of a County Longford Parish* (Longford: Dioceses of Ardagh and Clonmacnoise, 1981), p. 128.
9. [Maria Edgeworth], *Castle Rackrent* (Dublin, 1800), pp. 2–4.
10. James McParlan, *Statistical Survey of the County of Sligo* (Dublin, 1802), p. 72.
11. Edward Wakefield, *An Account of Ireland, Statistical and Political*, 2 vols. (London, 1812), I, p. xiii.
12. Wakefield, *An Account of Ireland, Statistical and Political*, II, p. 768.
13. William Wilde, *A Descriptive Catalogue of the Antiquities of Stone, Earthen and Vegetable Materials in the Museum of the Royal Irish Academy* (Dublin, 1857), p. 308.
14. Richard Lovell Edgeworth, 'A Further Account of Discoveries in the Turf Bogs of Ireland', *Archaeologia, Or, Miscellaneous Tracts Relating to Antiquity*, 7, 1785, pp. 111–12. Richard Lovell Edgeworth's paper follows directly on from Lady Moira's 'Particulars Relative to Human Skeleton', in which she details research into a bog body found in County Down in 1780.
15. Mairead Dunlevy, *Dress in Ireland* (Cork: The Collins Press, 1999), pp. 73–5.
16. See Claudia Kinmonth, *Irish Rural Interiors in Art* (New Haven and London: Yale University Press, 2006), p. 244.
17. Caitrín Naomhtha, Eachdhruim (Aughrim, County Galway), The Schools' Collection, vol. 0029, p. 0437, The Dúchas Project. www.duchas.ie/ga/cbes/4574072/4565076. Accessed 2 December 2024.
18. [Edgeworth], *Castle Rackrent*, pp. 2–4.
19. Maria Edgeworth, *Popular Tales* (London, 1804), pp. 372, 375.
20. See notes to Claire Connolly and Stephen Copley's edition of *The Wild Irish Girl* (London: Pickering and Chatto, 2000), pp. 267–7.
21. Lord Charlemont, 'The Antiquity of the Woollen Manufacture in Ireland proved from a Passage of an Ancient Florentine Poet', *Transactions of the Royal Irish Academy*, 1, 1787, (pp. 17–24), pp. 22, 23.

22. Charlemont, 'The Antiquity of the Woollen Manufacture in Ireland proved from a Passage of an Ancient Florentine Poet', p. 24.
23. Lady Morgan, *Florence Macarthy*, 4 vols. (London, 1818), I, p. 145.
24. Carolyn Steedman, *Dust* (Manchester: Manchester University Press, 2001), p. 114.
25. J. G. Lockhart, *Memoirs of the Life of Sir Walter Scott*, 7 vols. (Edinburgh, 1837–8), VI, p. 43.
26. Lockhart, *Memoirs of the Life of Sir Walter Scott*, VI, pp. 67, 124.
27. *Memoirs of Richard Lovell Edgeworth, Esq. Begun by Himself and Concluded by His Daughter, Maria Edgeworth*, 2 vols. (London, 1820), II, pp. 308, 310.
28. *Memoirs of Richard Lovell Edgeworth*, II, p. 308.
29. James Hall, *Tour through Ireland*, 2 vols. (London, 1813), II, p. 17.
30. Owen Devaney, *Killoe: History of a County Longford Parish*, p. 218.
31. Dunlevy, *Dress in Ireland*, p. 137.
32. [Gerald Griffin], *Tales of the Munster Festivals*, 3 vols. (London, 1827), I, pp. 42–3.
33. Charles Robert Maturin, *Melmoth the Wanderer*, 4 vols. (Edinburgh, 1820), I, pp. 156, 158–9, 162–3.
34. Charlotte Brontë, *Jane Eyre* (Peterborough, ON: Broadview, 2022), p. 122.
35. C. M. O'Keeffe, *Life and Times of Daniel O'Connell*, 2 vols. (Dublin, 1864), II, p. 639.
36. 'Frieze-coat, noun', Oxford English Dictionary. https://doi.org/10.1093/OED/6038060488. Accessed 3 December 2024.
37. Thomas Carlyle's note to a letter from Jane Welsh Carlyle to Thomas Carlyle, 23 August 1843. https://carlyleletters.dukeupress.edu/volume/17/lt-18430827-JWC-TC-01. Accessed 10 December 2024.
38. Thomas Carlyle, *Sartor Resartus* (Oxford: Oxford University Press, 1999), pp. 212–213.
39. George Levine, *The Boundaries of Fiction* (Princeton: Princeton University Press, 2015), p. 71.
40. Colleen Taylor, *Irish Materialisms: The Nonhuman and the Making of Colonial Ireland, 1690–1830* (Oxford: Oxford University Press, 2024), p. 5.
41. Review of William Makepeace Thackeray's *The Irish Sketchbook* (1843), *The Athenaeum*, 13 May 1843, pp. 455–7 (p. 455).
42. John Montague, 'Tribute to William Carleton', in Gordon Brand (ed.), *William Carleton: The Authentic Voice* (Gerrards Cross: Colin Smythe, 2006), pp. 87–93 (p. 89).
43. William Carleton, *The Life of William Carleton: Being His Autobiography and Letters*, 2 vols. (London, 1896), I, p. 24.
44. Carleton, *The Life of William Carleton*, II, p. 127.
45. William Carleton, *The Black Prophet* (London, 1847), pp. 77, 81.
46. Karl Marx, *Capital: A Critique of Political Economy*, Vol. 1, trans. by Ben Fowkes (London: Penguin, 1982), p. 132.
47. Peter Stallybrass, 'Marx's Coat', in Patricia Spyer (ed.), *Border Fetishisms* (London: Routledge, 2013). See also Andy Merrifield, 'Buttoning up with

48. See R. F. Foster, *The Irish Story: Telling Tales and Making it Up in Ireland* (Oxford: Oxford University Press, 2001), p. 11.
49. Carleton, *The Black Prophet*, pp. 11–12.
50. Carleton, *The Black Prophet*, pp. 37, 39, 48.
51. E. OE. Somerville and Martin Ross' novel, *The Real Charlotte* (London: Quercus, 2024), p. 442.
52. Samuel Beckett, *Molloy*, tr. Patrick Bowles in collaboration with Samuel Beckett (New York: Grove Press, 1955), p. 39; Seamus Heaney, 'Requiem for the Croppies', in *New Selected Poems 1966–1987* (London and Boston: Faber and Faber, 1990), p. 12.
53. Wilde, *A Descriptive Catalogue*, p. 297.
54. William Wordsworth and Dorothy Wordsworth, *The Letters of William and Dorothy Wordsworth, Volume V: The Late Years, Part II, 1829–1834*, ed. Ernest de Selincourt, rev. Alan G. Hill (Oxford: Clarendon Press, 1979), p. 142.
55. Harriet Martineau, *Letters from Ireland*, ed. Glenn Hooper (Dublin: Irish Academic Press, 2001), pp. 126–7.
56. Thomas Carlyle, *Reminiscences of My Irish Journey in 1849* (London, 1882), pp. iv, 9.
57. Thomas Carlyle, *Chartism* (London, 1840), p. 25.
58. Charles Gavan Duffy, *Conversations with Carlyle* (New York, 1892), p. 119.

(Continued from previous page:)
Marx'. https://davidharvey.org/2019/03/buttoning-up-with-marx-by-andy-merrifield/#_ftn3. Accessed 5 February 2025.

Select Bibliography

Manuscript Sources

A Volume of Short Biographies of Tutors and Schoolmasters, Dedicated to Lady Sydney Morgan and Presented to Her, Dated in Co. Limerick, 26 August 1825, MSS 19314, National Library of Ireland

Collections for a History of the Ballad Literature of Ireland, by Thomas Crofton Croker. Add MS 20091–20094, British Library

Cork Memoranda. Notes relative to the Antiquities of Co. Cork, 1842–1845. [Typed copy of notes, queries, correspondence, etc. written by O'Donovan, Larcom and others relative to the antiquities of County Cork, 1842–5]

Edgeworth Papers, MS 10166/7, National Library of Ireland

John Murray Archive, Acc 12604, National Library of Scotland

Letters from Maria Edgeworth to Peter Holland, MS 16087/1, Bodleian Archives and Manuscripts

Letters from Maria Edgeworth to John Murray, MSS 42180–42181, National Library of Scotland

Literary Remains of Jeremiah Joseph Callanan, Collected and Compiled by John Fitzpatrick Fitzthomas Windele of Blair's Castle, Cork, MS 12 I 13, Royal Irish Academy

Mary Tighe, *Mary, a Series of Reflections during Twenty Years*, EC8 T4484 811m, Houghton Library, Harvard University

Mary Tighe's Reading Journal, MS 4804, National Library of Ireland

Patrick Lynch's Journal, MS 4/24, Edward Bunting Collection, Queen's University Belfast Special Collections and Archives

[Robert Rainey], 'Diary giving accounts of political affairs in Dublin, business and social activities while working at Crampton Court and Dame Street, 1798–1801'. National Library of Ireland, MSS 34.395/1

Royal Literary Fund, BL Loan 96 RLF 1/674/6

Newspapers and Journals

Anthologia Hibernica
Blackwood's Edinburgh Magazine
Fraser's Magazine

The Athenaeum
The Belfast Commercial Chronicle
The Citizen
The Cork Examiner
The Dublin University Magazine
The Edinburgh Literary Journal
The Edinburgh Review
The Freeman's Journal
The Illustrated London News
The Irish Penny Journal
The London Magazine
The Morning Chronicle
The Nation
The Westminster Review

Works Published before 1900

Anonymous, *The Davenels; or, A Campaign of Fashion in Dublin*, 2 vols. (London, 1829)
Arnold, Matthew, *On the Study of Celtic Literature* (London, 1867)
Atkinson, Joseph, 'Address, Written to Be Spoken at the First Performance of Miss Owenson's Comic Opera of "The First Attempt; or, Whim of the Moment"', *New Monthly Magazine*, 24 (1807), 50–1
Austen, Jane, *Emma*, 3 vols. (London, 1816)
Austen, Jane, *Jane Austen's Letters*, ed. Deirdre Le Faye, fourth ed. (Oxford: Oxford University Press, 2011)
Banim, John, *The Anglo-Irish of the Nineteenth Century*, 3 vols. (London, 1828)
[Banim, John and Michael Banim], *Tales, by the O'Hara Family: Containing Crohoore of the Bill-Hook, the Fetches, and John Doe*, 3 vols. (London, 1825)
Benn, George, *The History of the Town of Belfast* (Belfast, 1823)
Blessington, Marguerite Gardiner, Countess of, 'Stock-in-Trade of Modern Poetesses', *The Maids, Wives, and Widows' Penny Magazine, and Gazette of Fashion*, 1 (1832), 39
Blessington, Marguerite Gardiner, *The Magic Lantern; or, Sketches of Scenes in the Metropolis* (London, 1822)
Boyd, Henry, *The Woodsman's Tale* (London, 1805)
Burke, Edmund, *The Works of the Right Honourable Edmund Burke*, 7 vols. (Boston, 1826–7)
Byron, George Gordon Byron, Baron, 'Debate on the Earl of Donoughmore's Motion for a Committee on the Roman Catholic Claims, April 21, 1812', in *The Parliamentary Speeches of Lord Byron* (London, 1824)
Byron, George Gordon Byron, Baron, *Byron's Letters and Journals*, ed. Leslie A. Marchand, 13 vols. (London: Murray, 1973–94)
Byron, George Gordon Byron, Baron, *Don Juan* (London, 1819)

Byron, George Gordon Byron, Baron, *English Bards, and Scotch Reviewers* (London, [1809])
Byron, George Gordon Byron, Baron, *Lord Byron: The Major Works*, ed. Jerome McGann (Oxford: Oxford University Press, 1986)
Callanan, Jeremiah J., 'Irish Popular Songs', *Blackwood's Edinburgh Magazine*, 13 (1823), 209–15
Callanan, Jeremiah J., *The Poems of J. J. Callanan* (Cork, 1861)
Carleton, William, *The Black Prophet* (London, 1847)
Carleton, William, *The Emigrants of Ahadarra: A Tale of Irish Life* (London, 1848)
Carleton, William, 'The Irish Shanahus', *The Irish Penny Journal*, 1 (1841), 378–80
Carleton, William, *The Life of William Carleton: Being His Autobiography and Letters*, 2 vols. (London, 1896)
Carleton, William, *Traits and Stories of the Irish Peasantry*, 2 vols. (Dublin, 1843)
Carleton, William, *Traits and Stories of the Irish Peasantry: Second Series*, 3 vols. (Dublin, 1833)
Carlyle, Thomas, *Chartism* (London, 1840)
Carlyle, Thomas, *Reminiscences of My Irish Journey in 1849* (London, 1882)
Carlyle, Thomas, 'Signs of the Times', *Edinburgh Review*, 49 (1829), 439–59
Charlemont, James Caulfeild, Earl of, 'The Antiquity of the Woollen Manufacture in Ireland, Proved from a Passage of an Antient Florentine Poet', *Transactions of the Royal Irish Academy*, 1 (1787), 17–24
Coleridge, Samuel Taylor, *Essays on His Times*, ed. David V. Erdman, 3 vols. (Princeton: Princeton University Press, 1978)
Connellan, Owen, *A Dissertation on Irish Grammar* (Dublin, 1834)
Croker, Thomas Crofton, *The Keen of the South of Ireland* (London, 1844)
Crumpe, M. G. T., *Geraldine of Desmond: or, Ireland in the Days of Elizabeth*, second ed. (London, 1830)
Davis, Thomas, *Essays and Poems with a Centenary Memoir, 1845–1945* (Dublin: M. H. Gill and Son, 1945)
Davy, John, *Fragmentary Remains, Literary and Scientific, of Sir Humphry Davy*, ed. John Davy (London, 1858)
Davy, John, *Memoirs of the Life of Sir Humphry Davy*, 2 vols. (London, 1836)
De Quincey, Thomas, 'Confessions of an English Opium-Eater', *The London Magazine*, 4 (1821), 293–312
De Quincey, Thomas, *Confessions of an English Opium-Eater* (London, 1856)
De Quincey, Thomas, 'Sketches of Life and Manners: From the Autobiography of an English Opium Eater', *Tait's Edinburgh Magazine*, 1 (1834), 196–204
De Staël, Germaine, *Considerations on the Principal Events of the French Revolution*, 3 vols. (London, 1818)
Dermody, Thomas, *Poems* (Dublin, 1789)
Dermody, Thomas, *Poems: Consisting of Essays, Lyric, Elegiac, &c.* (Dublin, 1792)
Dermody, Thomas, *Selected Writings*, ed. Michael Griffin (Dublin: Field Day, 2012)
Dermody, Thomas, *The Harp of Erin*, 2 vols. (London, 1807)

Dermody, Thomas, *The Rights of Justice, or Rational Liberty; A Letter to an Acquaintance in the Country* (Dublin, 1793)
Dorian, Hugh, *The Outer Edge of Ulster: A Memoir of Social Life in Nineteenth-Century Donegal*, eds. Brendán Mac Suibhne and David Dickson (Dublin: The Lilliput Press, 2000)
Downes, William M., *Original Poems and Songs, with Notes* (Limerick, 1833)
Downes, William M., *Poems, Epistles, Etc. Etc.* (Dublin, 1839)
Downes, William M., *Poetic Sketches, Rural, Pathetic, and Descriptive, with Tales, Versified from Interesting Subjects* (Limerick, 1836)
Downes, William M., *Temperance Melodies for the Teetotallers of Ireland* (Cork, 1843)
Downes, William M., *The Exile: A Poem in One Canto, with Notes* (Kilrush, 1850)
Duffy, Charles Gavan, *Conversations with Carlyle* (New York, 1892)
Duffy, Charles Gavan (ed.), *The Ballad Poetry of Ireland*, third ed. (Dublin, 1845)
Dunkin, William, *Select Poetical Works of the Late William Dunkin*, 2 vols (Dublin, 1769–70)
Edgeworth, Frances Anne, *A Memoir of Maria Edgeworth, with a Selection from Her Letters*, 3 vols (London, 1867)
Edgeworth, Maria, *The Novels and Selected Works of Maria Edgeworth* (London: Pickering and Chatto, 1999)
Edgeworth, Maria, *Letters from England: 1813–1844*, ed. Christina Colvin (Oxford: Clarendon Press, 1971)
Edgeworth, Maria and Richard Lovell Edgeworth, *Memoirs of Richard Lovell Edgeworth, Esq. Begun by Himself and Concluded by His Daughter, Maria Edgeworth*, 2 vols (London, 1820)
Gamble, John, *Society and Manners in Early Nineteenth-Century Ireland*, ed. Breandán Mac Suibhne (Dublin: Field Day, 2011)
Gladstone, William Ewart, *The Gladstone Diaries, Volume I: 1825–1832*, ed. M. R. D. Foot (Oxford: Clarendon Press, 1968)
Godwin, William, *The Letters of William Godwin, Volume II: 1798–1805*, ed. Pamela Clemit (Oxford: Oxford University Press, 2014)
Goldsmith, Oliver, *The Deserted Village* (London, 1770)
Griffin, Daniel, *Life of Gerald Griffin* (London, 1843)
Griffin, Gerald, *Holland-Tide* (London, 1827)
Griffin, Gerald, *Tales of the Munster Festivals*, 3 vols (London, 1827)
Hall, A. M. and S. C. Hall, *Ireland: Its Scenery, Character, &c.*, 3 vols (London, 1841–3)
Hall, James, *Tour Through Ireland, Particularly the Interior and Least Known Parts*, 2 vols (London, 1813)
Hansbrow, G., *An Improved Topographical and Historical Hibernian Gazetteer* (Dublin, 1835)
Hardiman, James, *Irish Minstrelsy, or Bardic Remains of Ireland*, 2 vols (London, 1831)
Hare, Augustus J. C., *The Life and Letters of Maria Edgeworth*, 2 vols (London, 1894)

Hazlitt, William, *The Spirit of the Age* (London, 1825)
Head, Francis B., *A Fortnight in Ireland* (London, 1852)
Hemans, Felicia, *Records of Woman: With Other Poems* (Edinburgh and London, 1828)
Hemans, Felicia, *The Works of Mrs. Hemans, with a Memoir by Her Sister, and an Essay on Her Genius*, 7 vols (Philadelphia, 1840)
Holt, Joseph, *Memoirs of Joseph Holt, General of the Irish Rebels in 1798, Edited from His Original Manuscript, in the Possession of Sir William Betham*, ed. Thomas Crofton Croker, 2 vols (London, 1838)
Joyce, P. W., 'On Spenser's Irish Rivers', *Proceedings of the Royal Irish Academy*, 10 (1866–9), 1–13
Keats, John, *Selected Letters*, ed. Robert Gittings and Jon Mee (Oxford: Oxford University Press, 2002)
L'Estrange, A. G., *The Life of Mary Russell Mitford*, 3 vols (London, 1870)
Le Fanu, Joseph Sheridan, *The Purcell Papers*, with a memoir by Alfred Perceval Graves, 3 vols (London, 1880)
Le Fanu, William Richard, *Seventy Years of Irish Life: Being Anecdotes and Reminiscences* (London, 1893)
Leadbeater, Mary, *Poems* (Dublin, 1808)
Lewis, George Cornewall, *On Local Disturbances in Ireland* (London, 1836)
Lockhart, J. G., *Memoirs of the Life of Sir Walter Scott*, 7 vols (Edinburgh, 1837–8)
Maginn, William, 'Don Juan Unread', *Blackwood's Edinburgh Magazine*, 6 (1819), 194–5
Maginn, William, *The Odoherty Papers*, ed. Shelton Mackenzie, 2 vols (New York, 1855)
Mangan, James Clarence, *Selected Writings*, ed. Seán Ryder (Dublin: UCD Press, 2004)
Martineau, Harriet, 'Condition and Prospects of Ireland', *Westminster Review*, 59 (1853), 18–32
Martineau, Harriet, *Letters from Ireland*, ed. Glenn Hooper (Dublin: Irish Academic Press, 2001)
Maturin, Charles Robert, *Melmoth the Wanderer*, 4 vols (Edinburgh, 1820)
McParlan, James, *Statistical Survey of the County of Sligo* (Dublin, 1802)
Mitford, Mary Russell, *Letters of Mary Russell Mitford, Second Series*, ed. Henry Chorley, 2 vols (London, 1872)
Moore, Thomas, *A Selection of Irish Melodies, with Symphonies and Accompaniments by Sir John Stevenson, Mus. Doc. and Characteristic Words by Thomas Moore, Esq.* (London, 1808–34)
Moore, Thomas, *Memoirs of Captain Rock*, fifth ed. (London, 1824)
Moore, Thomas, *The Fudge Family in Paris* [1818], in *British Satire 1785–1840, Volume V: The Satires of Thomas Moore*, ed. Jane Moore (London: Pickering and Chatto, 2003)
Moore, Thomas, *The Journal of Thomas Moore*, ed. Wilfred S. Dowden, 6 vols (Newark: University of Delaware Press, 1983–91)
O'Keeffe, C. M., *Life and Times of Daniel O'Connell*, 2 vols (Dublin, 1864)

Orr, James, *Poems, on Various Subjects* (Belfast, 1804)
Orr, James, 'To Miss Owenson, the Elegant Authoress of The Wild Irish Girl', *Belfast Commercial Chronicle*, 2 May 1807
Otway, Caesar, *Sketches in Ireland*, second ed. (Dublin, 1839)
Owenson, Sydney [Lady Morgan], *Florence Macarthy*, 4 vols (London, 1818)
Owenson, Sydney *Florence Macarthy* [1818], ed. Jenny McAuley (London: Pickering and Chatto, 2012)
Owenson, Sydney *France in 1829–30*, 2 vols (London, 1830)
Owenson, Sydney *Italy*, 2 vols (London, 1821)
Owenson, Sydney *Lady Morgan's Memoirs: Autobiography, Diaries and Correspondence*, 2 vols (London, 1862)
Owenson, Sydney *Letter to Cardinal Wiseman*, second ed. (London, 1851)
Owenson, Sydney *O'Donnel*, 3 vols (London, 1814)
Owenson, Sydney *Passages from My Autobiography* (London, 1859)
Owenson, Sydney *Patriotic Sketches of Ireland*, 2 vols (London, 1807)
Owenson, Sydney *Poems* (Dublin, 1801)
Owenson, Sydney *The Wild Irish Girl* [1806], ed. Claire Connolly and Stephen Copley (London: Pickering and Chatto, 2000)
Owenson, Sydney *Twelve Original Hibernian Melodies* (London, 1805)
Parnell, William, *An Historical Apology for the Irish Catholics* (Dublin, 1807)
Raymond, James Grant, *The Life of Thomas Dermody*, 2 vols (London, 1806)
Shelley, Mary, *The Last Man*, 3 vols (Paris, 1826)
Shelley, Percy Bysshe, 'An Address to the Irish People' [1812], in *The Prose Works of Percy Bysshe Shelley*, ed. Richard Herne Shepherd, 2 vols (London, 1888), I, pp. 223–62
Shelley, Percy Bysshe, *Essays, Letters from Abroad, Translations and Fragments*, 2 vols (London, 1840)
Shelley, Percy Bysshe, *The Masque of Anarchy* (London, 1832)
Shelley, Percy Bysshe, *The Letters of Percy Bysshe Shelley, Volume I: Shelley in England*, ed. Frederick L. Jones (Oxford: Oxford University Press, 1964)
Smith, Charles, *The Antient and Present State of the County and City of Cork*, 2 vols (Cork, 1815)
Smyth, William, *English Lyrics* (Dublin, 1806)
[Taaffe, Denis], *Ireland's Mirror* (Dublin, 1796)
Thackeray, William Makepeace, 'A Word on the Annuals', *Fraser's Magazine*, 16 (1837), 757–63
Thackeray, William Makepeace, *Barry Lyndon* [1844], ed. Andrew Sanders (Oxford: Oxford University Press, 1984)
Thackeray, William Makepeace, *The Irish Sketch-Book*, second ed., 2 vols (London, 1845)
Tighe, Mary, *Psyche, with Other Poems, by the Late Mrs Henry Tighe* (London, 1811)
Tighe, Mary, *The Collected Letters of Mary Blachford Tighe, 1786–1810*, ed. Harriet Kramer Linkin (Bethlehem: Lehigh University Press, 2020)
Tighe, Mary, *The Collected Poems and Journals of Mary Tighe*, ed. Harriet Kramer Linkin (Kentucky: The University Press of Kentucky, 2005)

Tonna, Charlotte Elizabeth, *Letters from Ireland* (London, 1838)
Trollope, Anthony, *An Autobiography*, 2 vols (Edinburgh and London, 1883)
Vallancey, Charles, *An Account of the Ancient Stone Amphitheatre Located in the County of Kerry* (Dublin, 1812)
Wakefield, Edward, *An Account of Ireland, Statistical and Political*, 2 vols (London, 1812)
Walker, Joseph Cooper, *An Historical Essay on the Dress of the Ancient and Modern Irish* (Dublin, 1788)
Walker, Joseph Cooper, *Historical Memoirs of the Irish Bards*, 2 vols (Dublin, 1818)
White, Henry Kirke, *The Poetical Works of Henry Kirke White* (London, 1830)
[Wolfe, Charles], 'The Burial of Sir John Moore', *Blackwood's Edinburgh Magazine*, 1 (1817), 277–8
Wordsworth, William and Dorothy Wordsworth, *The Letters of William and Dorothy Wordsworth, Volume V: The Late Years, Part II, 1829–1834*, ed. Ernest de Selincourt, rev. Alan G. Hill (Oxford: Clarendon Press, 1979)
Wollstonecraft, Mary, *The Collected Letters of Mary Wollstonecraft*, ed. Janet Todd (London: Allen Lane, 2003)
Wordsworth, William, *Lyrical Ballads*, 2 vols (London, 1800)
Wordsworth, William, *Poems, in Two Volumes*, 2 vols (London, 1807)
Wordsworth, William, *The Prelude* [1850], ed. Jonathan Wordsworth (London: Penguin, 1995)
Yeats, W. B., *Representative Irish Tales: First Series* (New York and London, [1891])
Young, Arthur, *A Tour in Ireland*, 2 vols (Dublin, 1780)

Works Published after 1900

Anderson, Benedict, *Imagined Communities: Reflections on the Origin and Spread of Nationalism* (London and New York: Verso, 2006)
Andrews, J. H., *A Paper Landscape: The Ordnance Survey in Nineteenth-Century Ireland* (Oxford: Clarendon Press, 1975)
Baker, Samuel, *Written on the Water: British Romanticism and the Maritime Empire of Culture* (Charlottesville: University of Virginia Press, 2010)
Baraniuk, Carol, *James Orr, Poet and Irish Radical* (London: Pickering and Chatto, 2014)
Barnard, Toby, 'Reading in Eighteenth-Century Ireland: Public and Private Pleasures', in Bernadette Cunningham and Máire Kennedy (eds.), *The Experience of Reading: Irish Historical Perspectives* (Dublin: Rare Book Group of the Library Association of Ireland, 1999), pp. 60–77
Bartlett, Thomas, '"A People Made Rather for Copies than Originals": The Anglo-Irish, 1760–1800', *The International History Review*, 12.1 (1990), 11–25
Bartlett, Thomas, 'Ireland during the Revolutionary and Napoleonic Wars, 1791–1815', in James Kelly (ed.), *The Cambridge History of Ireland, Volume III: 1730–1880* (Cambridge: Cambridge University Press, 2018), pp. 74–101

Bartoszyńska, Katarzyna, *Estranging the Novel: Poland, Ireland, and Theories of World Literature* (Baltimore: Johns Hopkins University Press, 2021)

Beckett, Samuel, *Molloy*, tr. Patrick Bowles in collaboration with Samuel Beckett (New York: Grove Press, 1955)

Beiner, Guy, *Forgetful Remembrance: Social Forgetting and Vernacular Historiography of a Rebellion in Ulster* (Oxford: Oxford University Press, 2018)

Benatti, Francesca, 'Young Ireland and the Superannuated Bard: Rewriting Thomas Moore in *The Nation*', in Sarah McCleave and Triona O'Hanlon (eds.), *The Reputations of Thomas Moore* (New York and London: Routledge, 2020), pp. 214–34

Benson, Charles, 'The Irish Trade', in Michael F. Suarez S. J. and Michael L. Turner (eds.), *The Cambridge History of the Book in Britain, Volume V: 1695–1830* (Cambridge: Cambridge University Press, 2009), pp. 366–82

Berns, Ute, 'Energy Ecologies in Joanna Baillie's "Address to a Steam-Vessel" (1823)', in David Kerler and Martin Middeke (eds.), *Romantic Ecologies* (Trier: Wissenschaftlicher Verlag Trier, 2023), pp. 57–74

Bielenberg, Andy, 'British Competition and the Vicissitudes of the Irish Woollen Industry: 1785–1923', *Textile History*, 31 (2000), 202–21

Bolton, Carol, *Writing the Empire: Robert Southey and Romantic Colonialism* (London: Pickering and Chatto, 2007)

Boon, Marcus, *In Praise of Copying* (Cambridge, MA: Harvard University Press, 2010)

Burke, Peter, *Popular Culture in Early Modern Europe* (New York: Harper and Row, 1978)

Butler, Marilyn, *Romantics, Rebels and Reactionaries: English Literature and Its Background 1760–1830* (Oxford: Oxford University Press, 1981)

Calhoun, Joshua, 'Book Microbiomes', in Alexandra Gillespie and Deidre Lynch (eds.), *The Unfinished Book* (Oxford: Oxford University Press, 2021), pp. 460–73

Campbell, Matthew, 'How Good is Mangan?', *Irish Studies Review*, 13.2 (2005), 227–32

Campbell, Matthew, *Irish Poetry under the Union, 1801–1924* (Cambridge: Cambridge University Press, 2014)

Campbell, Matthew, 'Whigs, Weavers, and Fire-Worshippers: Anglophone Irish Poetry in Transition', in Claire Connolly (ed.), *Irish Literature in Transition, 1780–1830* (Cambridge: Cambridge University Press, 2020)

Canny, Nicholas, *Imagining Ireland's Pasts: Early Modern Ireland through the Centuries* (Oxford: Oxford University Press, 2021)

Carey, Daniel, 'Intellectual History: William King to Edmund Burke', in Richard Bourke and Ian McBride (eds.), *The Princeton History of Modern Ireland* (Princeton and Oxford: Princeton University Press, 2016), pp. 193–216

Carroll, Siobhan, *An Empire of Air and Water: Uncolonizable Space in the British Imagination, 1750–1850* (Pennsylvania: University of Pennsylvania Press, 2015)

Chander, Manu Samriti, *Brown Romantics: Poetry and Nationalism in the Global Nineteenth Century* (Lewisburg: Bucknell University Press, 2017)

Chandler, James, *England in 1819: The Politics of Literary Culture and the Case of Romantic Historicism* (Chicago and London: University of Chicago Press, 1998)

Chandler, James, 'Figures in a Field: Revising Romantic Canonicity', *Studies in Romanticism*, 59.4 (2020), 559–78

Christensen, Jerome, *Romanticism at the End of History* (Baltimore: Johns Hopkins University Press, 2000)

Clare, David, 'Mary Balfour's *Kathleen O'Neil* (1814): An Expression or Betrayal of Her Ulster Scots Background?', in David Clare, Fiona McDonagh and Justine Nakase (eds.), *The Golden Thread: Irish Women Playwrights, 1716–2016*, 2 vols (Liverpool: Liverpool University Press, 2021), I, pp. 85–96

Cohen, Ashley L., 'The Global Indies: Historicizing Oceanic Metageographies', *Comparative Literature*, 69.1 (2017), 7–15

Comyn, Sarah and Porscha Fermanis (eds.), *Worlding the South: Nineteenth-Century Literary Culture and the Southern Settler Colonies* (Manchester: Manchester University Press, 2021)

Connolly, Claire, '"A Big Book about England"? Public and Private Meanings in *Patronage*', in Jacqueline Belanger (ed.), *The Irish Novel in the Nineteenth Century: Facts and Fictions* (Dublin: Four Courts Press, 2005), pp. 63–79

Connolly, Claire, *A Cultural History of the Irish Novel, 1790–1829* (Cambridge: Cambridge University Press, 2012)

Connolly, Claire, 'Counting on the Past: Yeats and Irish Romanticism', *European Romantic Review*, 28.4 (2017), 473–87

Connolly, Claire, '"I accuse Miss Owenson": *The Wild Irish Girl* as Media Event', *Colby Quarterly*, 36.2 (2000), 98–115

Connolly, Claire, 'Introduction: Making Maps', in Claire Connolly (ed.), *Irish Literature in Transition, 1780–1830* (Cambridge: Cambridge University Press, 2020), pp. 1–34

Connolly, Claire, 'Too Rough for Verse: Sea Crossings in Irish Culture', in Joep Leerssen (ed.), *Parnell and His Times* (Cambridge: Cambridge University Press, 2020), pp. 243–67

Connolly, Claire, 'Watery Romanticism: Walking and Sailing West with Keats', *Romanticism on the Net*, 79 (2022), https://ronjournal.org/articles/n79 (accessed 27 April 2024)

Cope, Jonas, '"Illusive Light": Thomas Dermody, the *Aisling* and Archipelagic Romanticism', *European Romantic Review*, 26.6 (2015), 757–71

Cozzi, Eliza, 'P. B. Shelley, George William Tighe and the Irish Roots of "The Sensitive Plant"', *Romanticism*, 30.1 (2024), 42–55

Cronin, Nessa, 'From Dublin to Dehra Dun: Language, Translation and the Mapping of Ireland and India', in Rebecca Anne Barr, Sarah-Anne Buckley and Muireann O'Cinneide (eds.), *Literacy, Language and Reading in Nineteenth-Century Ireland* (Liverpool: Liverpool University Press, 2019), pp. 159–75

Crosbie, Barry, *Irish Imperial Networks: Migration, Social Communication and Exchange in Nineteenth-Century India* (Cambridge: Cambridge University Press, 2012)

Davis, Leith, 'Charlotte Brooke's *Reliques of Irish Poetry*: Eighteenth-Century "Irish Song" and the Politics of Remediation', in John Kirk, Andrew Noble and Michael Brown (eds.), *United Islands? The Languages of Resistance* (London and New York: Routledge, 2012), pp. 95–108

Deane, Seamus, *Small World: Ireland, 1798–2018* (Cambridge: Cambridge University Press, 2021)

Deane, Seamus, *Strange Country: Modernity and Nationhood in Irish Writing since 1790* (Oxford: Clarendon Press, 1997)

Devaney, Owen, *Killoe: History of a County Longford Parish* (Longford: Dioceses of Ardagh and Clonmacnoise, 1981)

Dickson, David, *Old World Colony: Cork and South Munster, 1630–1830* (Cork: Cork University Press, 2005)

Donnelly, James S., Jr., 'The Terry Alt Movement 1829–31', *History Ireland*, 2.4 (1994), www.historyireland.com/the-terry-alt-movement-1829-31-by-james-s-donnelly-jr (accessed 19 October 2024)

Dunlevy, Mairead, *Dress in Ireland* (Cork: The Collins Press, 1999)

Dunne, Tom, 'Haunted by History: Irish Romantic Writing, 1800–1850', in Roy Porter and Mikuláš Teich (eds.), *Romanticism in National Context* (Cambridge: Cambridge University Press, 1988), pp. 68–91

Dunne, Tom, '"On the boundaries of two languages": Representing Irish in Novels in English, 1800–1850', in John Cunningham and Niall Ó Ciosáin (eds.), *Culture and Society in Ireland Since 1750: Essays in Honour of Gearóid Ó Tuathaigh* (Dublin: The Lilliput Press, 2015), pp. 44–63

Earls, Brian, 'Oral Culture and Popular Autonomy', *Dublin Review of Books*, 100 (2018), https://drb.ie/articles/oral-culture-and-popular-autonomy (accessed 20 October 2024)

Erickson, Lee, *The Economy of Literary Form: English Literature and the Industrialization of Publishing, 1800–1850* (Baltimore: Johns Hopkins University Press, 1996)

Esterhammer, Angela, 'Late Romanticism and Print Culture', in Patrick Vincent (ed.), *The Cambridge History of European Romantic Literature* (Cambridge: Cambridge University Press, 2023), pp. 458–86

Esterhammer, Angela, *Print and Performance in the 1820s: Improvisation, Speculation, Identity* (Cambridge: Cambridge University Press, 2020)

Favret, Mary A., *War at a Distance: Romanticism and the Making of Modern Wartime* (Princeton and Oxford: Princeton University Press, 2010)

Ferguson, Frank, 'Between the Bishop's Hall and the Hurchin: Enlightenment legacies in Post-Union Antrim and Down', *Estudios Irlandeses*, 18.2 (2023), 99–111

Ferguson, Frank, 'Introduction', in Frank Ferguson (ed.), *Ulster-Scots Writing: An Anthology* (Dublin: Four Courts Press, 2008), pp. 1–22

Fermanis, Porscha, 'Suffering, Sentiment, and the Rise of Humanitarian Literature in the 1830s', in John Gardner and David Stewart (eds.), *Nineteenth-Century Literature in Transition: The 1830s* (Cambridge: Cambridge University Press, 2024), pp. 147–169

Fernihough, Alan and Cormac Ó Gráda, 'Population and Poverty in Ireland on the Eve of the Great Famine', *Demography*, 59 (2022), 1607–30

Ferris, Ina, *Book-men, Book Clubs, and the Romantic Literary Sphere* (Basingstoke: Palgrave, 2015)

Fulford, Tim and Peter J. Kitson, 'Romanticism and Colonialism: Texts, Contexts, Issues', in Tim Fulford and Peter J. Kitson (eds.), *Romanticism and Colonialism: Writing and Empire, 1780–1830* (Cambridge: Cambridge University Press, 1998)

Gallagher, Niav, 'Skirting the Issue: Women and the Royal Irish Academy', *Dictionary of Irish Biography*, www.dib.ie/blog/skirting-issue-women-and-royal-irish-academy. Accessed 3 July 2024

Gibbons, Luke, 'Romantic Ireland: 1750–1845', in James Chandler (ed.), *The Cambridge History of English Romantic Literature* (Cambridge: Cambridge University Press, 2009), pp. 182–203

Gillespie, Alexandra and Deidre Lynch, 'The Unfinished Book: Introduction', in Alexandra Gillespie and Deidre Lynch (eds.), *The Unfinished Book* (Oxford: Oxford University Press, 2021), pp. 1–18

Gilmartin, Sophie, *Ancestry and Narrative in Nineteenth-Century British Literature: Blood Relations from Edgeworth to Hardy* (Cambridge: Cambridge University Press, 1998)

Goss, Erin M., *Revealing Bodies: Anatomy, Allegory, and the Grounds of Knowledge in the Long Eighteenth Century* (Lewisburg: Bucknell University Press, 2013)

Gray, Peter, '"The Great British Famine of 1845–50"? Ireland, the UK and Peripherality in Famine Relief and Philanthropy', in Declan Curran, Lubomyr Luciuk and Andrew Newby (eds.), *Famines in European Economic History: The Last Great European Famines Reconsidered* (London: Routledge, 2015)

Griffin, Michael, 'Arcades Ambo: Robert Burns and Thomas Dermody', in David Sargeant and Fiona Stafford (eds.), *Burns and Other Poets* (Edinburgh: Edinburgh University Press, 2012), pp. 127–42

Griffin, Michael, '"Infatuated to His Ruin": The Fate of Thomas Dermody, 1775–1802', *History Ireland*, 14.3 (2006), www.historyireland.com/infatuated-to-his-ruin-the-fate-of-thomas-dermody-1775-1802. Accessed 2 July 2024

Griffin, Michael, 'Introduction', in Thomas Dermody, *Selected Writings*, ed. Michael Griffin (Dublin: Field Day, 2012), pp. 1–31

Gurrin, Brian, 'Population and Emigration, 1730–1845', in James Kelly (ed.), *The Cambridge History of Ireland, Volume III: 1730–1880* (Cambridge: Cambridge University Press, 2018), pp. 204–30

Hall, Catherine, Nicholas Draper and Keith McClelland, 'Introduction', in Catherine Hall, Nicholas Draper, Keith McClelland, Katie Donington and Rachel Lang (eds.), *Legacies of British Slave-Ownership: Colonial Slavery and the Formation of Victorian Britain* (Cambridge: Cambridge University Press, 2014), pp. 1–33

Hamilton, Paul, 'Introduction', in Paul Hamilton (ed.), *The Oxford Handbook of European Romanticism* (Oxford: Oxford University Press, 2016), pp. 1–12

Hamilton, Paul, 'The "Restoration" of the Restoration', in Patrick Vincent (ed.), *The Cambridge History of European Romantic Literature* (Cambridge: Cambridge University Press, 2023), pp. 435–57

Hayley, Barbara, 'A Reading and Thinking Nation: Periodicals as the Voice of Nineteenth-Century Ireland', in Barbara Hayley and Enda McKay (eds.), *Three Hundred Years of Irish Periodicals* (Mullingar: Association of Irish Learned Journals, 1987), pp. 29–48

Heaney, Seamus, *New Selected Poems 1966–1987* (London and Boston: Faber and Faber, 1990)

Heaney, Seamus, *Station Island* (London: Faber and Faber, 1984)

Hession, Peter, 'Taming the Channel: Technology, Liberalism and the Irish Sea, c. 1845–52', in Emily Mark-FitzGerald, Ciarán McCabe and Ciarán Reilly (eds.), *Dublin and the Great Famine* (Dublin: UCD Press, 2022), pp. 24–35

Hewitt, John, *Ancestral Voices: The Selected Prose of John Hewitt*, ed. Tom Clyde (Belfast: Blackstaff Press, 1987)

Hooper, Glenn, 'The Charms of Ireland: Travel Writing and Tourism', in Matthew Campbell (ed.), *Irish Literature in Transition, 1830–1880* (Cambridge: Cambridge University Press, 2020), pp. 108–23

Howes, Marjorie, *Colonial Crossings: Figures in Irish Literary History* (Dublin: Field Day, 2006)

Jackson, Alvin, 'The Survival of the Union', in Joe Cleary and Claire Connolly (eds.), *The Cambridge Companion to Modern Irish Culture* (Cambridge: Cambridge University Press, 2005), pp. 25–41

Jackson, Alvin, *United Kingdoms: Multinational Union States in Europe and Beyond, 1800–1925* (Oxford: Oxford University Press, 2024)

Jasanoff, Maya, *Liberty's Exiles: The Loss of America and the Remaking of the British Empire* (London: Harper Press, 2011)

Johnston, Anna and Elizabeth Webby (eds.), *Eliza Hamilton Dunlop: Writing from the Colonial Frontier* (Sydney: Sydney University Press, 2021)

Joyce, James, *A Portrait of the Artist as a Young Man* [1916], ed. Jery Johnson (Oxford: Oxford University Press, 2000)

Joyce, Patrick, *The State of Freedom: A Social History of the British State Since 1800* (Cambridge: Cambridge University Press, 2013)

Jue, Melody, *Wild Blue Media: Thinking through Seawater* (Durham, NC: Duke University Press, 2020)

Kelleher, Margaret, *The Maamtrasna Murders: Language, Life and Death in Nineteenth-Century Ireland* (Dublin: UCD Press, 2018)

Kelly, James, '"The Most Portentous Event in Modern History": Ireland Before and After the Peterloo Massacre', in Michael Demson and Regina Hewitt (eds.), *Commemorating Peterloo: Violence, Resilience and Claim-Making During the Romantic Era* (Edinburgh: Edinburgh University Press, 2019), pp. 140–59

Kelly, James, 'The Politics of Protestant Ascendancy, 1730–1790', in James Kelly (ed.), *The Cambridge History of Ireland, Volume III: 1730–1880* (Cambridge: Cambridge University Press, 2018), pp. 48–73

Kelly, Ronan, *Bard of Erin: The Life of Thomas Moore* (Dublin: Penguin Ireland, 2008)

Kennedy, Catriona, 'Republican Relicts: Gender, Memory, and Mourning in Irish Nationalist Culture, ca. 1798–1848', *Journal of British Studies*, 59 (2020), 608–37

Kilfeather, Siobhan, 'Terrific Register: The Gothicization of Atrocity in Irish Romanticism', *boundary 2*, 31.1 (2004), 49–71

Kinealy, Christine, *A Disunited Kingdom? England, Ireland, Scotland and Wales, 1800–1949* (Cambridge: Cambridge University Press, 1999)

Kinmonth, Claudia, *Irish Rural Interiors in Art* (New Haven and London: Yale University Press, 2006)

Koelb, Clayton, *The Revivifying Word: Literature, Philosophy, and the Theory of Life in Europe's Romantic Age* (Rochester: Camden House, 2008)

Kreilkamp, Vera, *The Anglo-Irish Novel and the Big House* (Syracuse: Syracuse University Press, 1998)

Kucich, Greg, *Keats, Shelley, and Romantic Spenserianism* (Pennsylvania: Pennsylvania State University Press, 1991)

Langan, Celeste, 'Understanding Media in 1805: Audiovisual Hallucination in *The Lay of the Last Minstrel*', *Studies in Romanticism*, 40.1 (2001), 49–70

Langbauer, Laurie, 'Prolepsis and the Tradition of Juvenile Writing: Henry Kirke White and Robert Southey', *PMLA*, 128 (2013), 888–906

Latané, David, *William Maginn and the British Press: A Critical Biography* (Farnham: Ashgate, 2013)

Leerssen, Joep, 'Ossian and the Rise of Literary Historicism', in Howard Gaskill (ed.), *The Reception of Ossian in Europe* (London: Thoemmes Continuum, 2004), pp. 109–25

Leerssen, Joep, *Remembrance and Imagination: Patterns in the Historical and Literary Representation of Ireland in the Nineteenth Century* (Cork: Cork University Press, 1996)

Linkin, Harriet Kramer, 'Mary Tighe, Thomas Moore, and the Publication of "Selena"', *Review of English Studies*, 65 (2014), 711–29

Linkin, Harriet Kramer, 'Placing Mary Tighe in Irish Literary History: From Manuscript Culture to Print', in Claire Connolly (ed.), *Irish Literature in Transition, 1780–1830* (Cambridge: Cambridge University Press, 2020), pp. 173–87

Linkin, Harriet Kramer, 'The Posthumous Public and Private Printing of Mary Tighe's Poetry', *Nineteenth-Century Gender Studies*, 18.2 (2022), www.ncgsjournal.com/issue182/linkin.html. Accessed 5 July 2024

Lloyd, David, *Nationalism and Minor Literature: James Clarence Mangan and the Emergence of Irish Cultural Nationalism* (Berkeley: University of California Press, 1987)

Mac Suibhne, Breandán, 'Editor's Introduction', in *John Gamble, Society and Manners in Early Nineteenth-Century Ireland*, ed. Breandán Mac Suibhne (Dublin: Field Day, 2011), pp. xiii–lxxv

Mac Suibhne, Breandán, *The End of Outrage: Post-Famine Adjustment in Rural Ireland* (Oxford: Oxford University Press, 2017)

Mac Suibhne, Breandán, 'Whiskey, Potatoes and Paddies: Volunteering and the Construction of the Irish Nation in Northwest Ulster, 1778–1782', in Peter Jupp and Eoin Magennis (eds.), *Crowds in Ireland, c. 1720–1920* (Basingstoke: Macmillan, 2000), pp. 45–82

MacCarthy, B. G., 'Jeremiah J. Callanan; Part i: His Life', *Studies: An Irish Quarterly Review*, 35 (1946), 215–29

MacCarthy, B. G., 'Jeremiah J. Callanan; Part ii: His Poetry', *Studies: An Irish Quarterly Review*, 35 (1946), 387–99

MacDonald, Edgar E. (ed.), *The Education of the Heart: The Correspondence of Rachel Mordecai Lazarus and Maria Edgeworth* (Chapel Hill: The University of North Carolina Press, 1977)

MacGiollabhuí, Muiris, 'Sons of Exile: The United Irishmen in Transnational Perspective 1791–1827', unpublished PhD dissertation (University of California, Santa Cruz, 2019), https://escholarship.org/uc/item/75x28210. Accessed 7 July 2024

MacKenzie, John M., 'Nelson Goes Global: The Nelson Myth in Britain and Beyond', in David Cannadine (ed.), *Admiral Lord Nelson: Context and Legacy* (Basingstoke: Palgrave Macmillan, 2005), pp. 144–65

Maguire, Muireann, '"A Melmoth? a cosmopolitan? a patriot?": *Melmoth the Wanderer*'s Russian Epigones', *Gothic Studies*, 26.2 (2024), 148–64

Manly, Susan, 'Intertextuality, Slavery and Abolition in Maria Edgeworth's "The Good Aunt" and "The Grateful Negro"', *Essays in Romanticism*, 20.1 (2013), 19–36

McCormack, W. J., 'The Tedium of History: An Approach to Maria Edgeworth's *Patronage* (1814)', in Ciarán Brady (ed.), *Ideology and the Historians* (Dublin: The Lilliput Press, 1991), pp. 77–98

McCourt, John, *Writing the Frontier: Anthony Trollope between Britain and Ireland* (Oxford: Oxford University Press, 2015)

McLean, Stuart John, *The Event and Its Terrors: Ireland, Famine, Modernity* (Stanford: Stanford University Press, 2004)

Menke, Richard, *Telegraphic Realism: Victorian Fiction and Other Information Systems* (Stanford: Stanford University Press, 2008)

Mentz, Steve, *Ocean* (New York: Bloomsbury Academic, 2020)

Montague, John, 'Tribute to William Carleton' [1952], in Gordon Brand (ed.), *William Carleton: The Authentic Voice* (Gerrards Cross: Colin Smythe, 2006), pp. 87–93

Moore, Jane, 'Thomas Moore and the Social Life of Forms', in Claire Connolly (ed.), *Irish Literature in Transition, 1780–1830* (Cambridge: Cambridge University Press, 2020), pp. 257–72

Morley, Vincent, *The Popular Mind in Eighteenth-Century Ireland* (Cork: Cork University Press, 2017)

Mullen, Mary L., *Novel Institutions: Anachronism, Irish Novels, and Nineteenth-Century Realism* (Edinburgh: Edinburgh University Press, 2019)

Murphy, James H., *Irish Novelists of the Victorian Age* (Oxford: Oxford University Press, 2011)

Nersessian, Anahid, *Utopia, Limited: Romanticism and Adjustment* (Cambridge, MA: Harvard University Press, 2015)

Ní Mhunghaile, Lesa, 'Bilingualism, Print Culture in Irish and the Public Sphere, 1700–*c*. 1830', in James Kelly and Ciarán Mac Murchaidh (eds.), *Irish and English: Essays on the Irish Linguistic and Cultural Frontier, 1600–1900* (Dublin: Four Courts Press, 2012), pp. 218–42

Ní Mhunghaile, Lesa, 'Introduction', in Charlotte Brooke, *Charlotte Brooke's Reliques of Irish Poetry*, ed. Lesa Ní Mhunghaile (Dublin: Irish Manuscripts Commission, 2009), pp. xxi–xliv

Ní Shíocháin, Tríona, *Singing Ideas: Performance, Politics and Oral Poetry* (Oxford and New York: Berghahn Books, 2018)

Ní Úrdail, Meidhbhín, 'From Script to Print: Some Evidence in Manuscripts Compiled in Eighteenth- and Nineteenth-Century Ireland', in Matthew Driscoll and Nioclás Mac Cathmhaoil (eds.), *Hidden Harmonies: Manuscript and Print on the North Atlantic Fringe, 1500–1900* (Copenhagen: Museum Tusculanum Press, 2021), pp. 325–61

Novak, Rose, 'Reviving "Eva" of *The Nation*?: Eva O'Doherty's Young Ireland Newspaper Poetry', *Victorian Periodicals Review*, 45 (2012), 436–65

Ó Ciosáin, Niall, *Ireland in Official Print Culture, 1800–1850: A New Reading of the Poor Inquiry* (Oxford: Oxford University Press, 2014)

Ó Ciosáin, Niall, 'Oral Culture, Literacy, and Reading, 1800–50', in James Murphy (ed.), *The Oxford History of the Irish Book, Volume IV: The Irish Book in English, 1800–1891* (Oxford: Oxford University Press, 2011), pp. 173–91

Ó Ciosáin, Niall, *Print and Popular Culture in Ireland, 1750–1850* (Basingstoke: Macmillan, 1997)

Ó Gallchoir, Clíona, *Maria Edgeworth: Women, Enlightenment and Nation* (Dublin: UCD Press, 2005)

Ó Giolláin, Diarmuid, (ed.), *Irish Ethnologies* (South Bend: University of Notre Dame Press, 2017)

Ó hÓgáin, Dáithí, '"Said an Elderly Man …": Maria Edgeworth's Use of Folklore in *Castle Rackrent*', in Cóilín Owens (ed.), *Family Chronicles: Maria Edgeworth's 'Castle Rackrent'* (Dublin: Wolfhound Press), pp. 62–70

Ó Macháin, Pádraig, 'Nineteenth-Century Irish Manuscripts', in Bernadette Cunningham and Siobhán Fitzpatrick (eds.), *Treasures of the Royal Irish Academy Library* (Dublin: Royal Irish Academy, 2009), pp. 161–71

Ó Muircheartaigh, Peadar, 'Catholic Literature and Literary Culture in Welsh, Scottish Gaelic, and Irish', in Liam Chambers (ed.), *The Oxford History of British and Irish Catholicism, Volume III: Relief, Revolution, and Revival, 1746–1829* (Oxford: Oxford University Press, 2023), pp. 243–63

Ó Raifeartaigh, T., Review of W. B. Stanford's *Ireland and the Classical Tradition* (1976), *Irish Historical Studies*, 20 (1977), 351–3

O'Donoghue, Bernard, 'Poetry in Ireland', in Joe Cleary and Claire Connolly (eds.), *The Cambridge Companion to Modern Irish Culture* (Cambridge: Cambridge University Press, 2005), pp. 173–89

O'Halloran, Clare, *Golden Ages and Barbarous Nations: Antiquarian Debate and Cultural Politics in Ireland, c. 1750–1800* (Cork: Cork University Press, 2004)

O'Higgins, Laurie, *The Irish Classical Self: Poets and Poor Scholars in the Eighteenth and Nineteenth Centuries* (Oxford: Oxford University Press, 2017)
O'Kane, Finola, *Landscape Design and Revolution in Ireland and the United States, 1688–1815* (London: Paul Mellon Centre for Studies in British Art, 2023)
O'Neill, Daniel I., 'Edmund Burke on Slavery and the Slave Trade: A Response to Gregory M. Collins', *Slavery & Abolition*, 41.4 (2020), 816–27
Orr, Jennifer, *Literary Networks and Dissenting Print Culture in Romantic-Period Ireland* (Basingstoke: Palgrave, 2015)
Parsons, Cóilín, *The Ordnance Survey and Modern Irish Literature* (Oxford: Oxford University Press, 2016)
Pettitt, Clare, *Serial Forms: The Unfinished Project of Modernity, 1815–1848* (Oxford: Oxford University Press, 2020)
Phillips, Mark Salber, *On Historical Distance* (New Haven and London: Yale University Press, 2013)
Pilz, Anna, 'The Rise of the Woman Writer', in Matthew Campbell (ed.), *Irish Literature in Transition, 1830–1880* (Cambridge: Cambridge University Press, 2020), pp. 257–79
Pittock, Murray, *Scottish and Irish Romanticism* (Oxford: Oxford University Press, 2008)
Porter, Dahlia, *Science, Form, and the Problem of Induction in British Romanticism* (Cambridge: Cambridge University Press, 2018)
Prendergast, Amy, *Literary Salons Across Britain and Ireland in the Long Eighteenth Century* (Basingstoke: Palgrave, 2015)
Rodgers, Nini, 'Two Quakers and a Utilitarian: The Reaction of Three Irish Women Writers to the Problem of Slavery, 1789–1807', *Proceedings of the Royal Irish Academy*, 100C.4 (2000), 137–57
Ross, Ian Campbell, '"We Irish": Writing and National Identity from Berkeley to Burke', in Moyra Haslett (ed.), *Irish Literature in Transition, 1700–1780* (Cambridge: Cambridge University Press, 2020), pp. 49–67
Ryan, John, *Ireland from A.D. 800 to A.D. 1600* (Dublin: Browne and Nolan, n.d.)
Schirmer, Gregory A., 'English Ireland/Irish Ireland: The Poetry and Translations of J. J. Callanan', in Claire Connolly (ed.), *Irish Literature in Transition, 1780–1830* (Cambridge: Cambridge University Press, 2020), pp. 242–56
Shanahan, Jim, 'Imperial Minds: Irish Writers and Empire in the Nineteenth Century – Charles Gavan Duffy, Thomas Moore, Charles Lever and *Kim*', in Matthew Campbell (ed.), *Irish Literature in Transition, 1830–1880* (Cambridge: Cambridge University Press, 2020), pp. 143–61
Shannon-Mangan, Ellen, *James Clarence Mangan: A Biography* (Dublin: Irish Academic Press, 1996)
Shklovsky, Viktor, 'Art as Technique' in Lee T. Lemon and Marion J. Reis (eds. and trans.), *Russian Formalist Criticism: Four Essays* (Lincoln: University of Nebraska Press, 1965)
Shklovsky, Viktor, *Bowstring: On the Dissimilarity of the Similar*, trans. Shushan Avagyan (Champaign: Dalkey Archive Press, 2011)
Slade, Bertha Coolidge, *Maria Edgeworth, 1767–1849: A Bibliographical Tribute* (London: Constable, 1937)

St Clair, William, *The Reading Nation in the Romantic Period* (Cambridge: Cambridge University Press, 2004)
Stafford, Fiona, 'The Roar of the Solway' in Nicholas Allen, Nick Groom, and Jos Smith (eds.), *Coastal Works: Cultures of the Atlantic Edge* (Oxford: Oxford University Press, 2017)
Starosielski, Nicole, 'The Elements of Media Studies', *Media and Environment*, 1.1 (2019), https://doi.org/10.1525/001c.10780 (accessed 27 April 2024)
Steedman, Carolyn, *Dust* (Manchester: Manchester University Press, 2001)
Stewart, Susan, *Crimes of Writing: Problems in the Containment of Representation* (New York: Oxford University Press, 1991)
Tilley, Elizabeth, 'Periodicals', in James H. Murphy (ed.), *The Oxford History of the Irish Book, Volume IV: The Irish Book in English, 1800–1891* (Oxford: Oxford University Press, 2011), pp. 144–70
Tilley, Elizabeth, 'The *Dublin Penny Journal* and Alternative Histories', in Rebecca Anne Barr, Sarah-Anne Buckley and Muireann O'Cinneide (eds.), *Literacy, Language and Reading in Nineteenth-Century Ireland* (Liverpool: Liverpool University Press, 2019), pp. 87–104
Todd, Janet, 'Ascendancy: Lady Mount Cashell, Lady Moira, Mary Wollstonecraft and the Union Pamphlets', *Eighteenth-Century Ireland*, 18 (2003), 98–117
Vance, Norman, *Irish Literature Since 1800* (London: Longman, 2002)
Walker, Carol Kyros, *Walking North with Keats* (New Haven and London: Yale University Press, 1992)
Watson, Alex, *Romantic Marginality: Nation and Empire on the Borders of the Page* (London: Pickering and Chatto, 2012)
Welch, Robert, *A History of Verse Translation from the Irish, 1789–1897* (Gerrards Cross: Colin Smythe, 1988)
Welch, Robert, *Irish Poetry from Moore to Yeats* (Gerrards Cross: Colin Smythe, 1980)
Whelan, Kevin, *The Tree of Liberty: Radicalism, Catholicism and the Construction of Irish Identity 1760–1830* (Cork: Cork University Press, 1996)
Williams, Raymond, *The Long Revolution* (New York: Columbia University Press, 1961)
Wilson, Kathleen, 'Nelson and the People: Manliness, Patriotism and Body Politics', in David Cannadine (ed.), *Admiral Lord Nelson: Context and Legacy* (Basingstoke: Palgrave Macmillan, 2005), pp. 49–66
Wolf, Nicholas M., *An Irish-Speaking Island: State, Religion, and the Linguistic Landscape in Ireland, 1770–1870* (Madison: University of Wisconsin Press, 2014)
Wolf, Nicholas M., 'Antiquarians and Authentics: Survival and Revival in Gaelic Writing', in Matthew Campbell (ed.), *Irish Literature in Transition, 1830–1880* (Cambridge: Cambridge University Press, 2020), pp. 199–217
Wood, Gillen D'Arcy, *Tambora: The Eruption That Changed the World* (Princeton and Oxford: Princeton University Press, 2014)
Wright, Julia M., *Representing the National Landscape in Irish Romanticism* (Syracuse: Syracuse University Press, 2014)
Yeats, W. B., *Responsibilities and Other Poems* (New York: Macmillan, 1916)

Yeats, W. B., *The Collected Works of W. B. Yeats, Volume III: Autobiographies*, ed. William H. O'Donnell and Douglas N. Archibald, with assistant editors J. Fraser Cocks III and Gretchen Schwenker (New York: Scribner, 1999)
Yoshino, Yuri, 'Edgeworthstown House', *European Romanticisms in Association*, www.euromanticism.org/edgeworthstown-house. Accessed 21 October 2024

Online Resources

Dictionary of Irish Biography, www.dib.ie
Oxford English Dictionary, www.oed.com
P. D. Garside, J. E. Belanger and S. A. Ragaz, British Fiction 1800–1829: A Database of Production, Circulation and Reception, designer A. A. Mandal, www.british-fiction.cf.ac.uk
The Schools' Collection, Dúchas, www.duchas.ie/en/cbes/volumes

Index

1798. *See* United Irish rebellion

Abelard, Peter, 14
Abolition of Slavery Act, 1833, 120
Act of Union, 3
 copyright law, 29
 and shared romantic culture, 81
America
 African-American boxers, 72
 American Revolution, 2
 Baltimore, 27
 Louisiana Purchase, 3
 New York, 97
 Philadelphia, 37, 72
 Pierce Butler and St Simon's Island, Georgia, 73
Amherst, William Pitt, 80
An Gorta Mór, 117
An Sean Bhean Bhocht (ballad), 133
Anderson, Benedict, 114
anonymous
 The Davenels, 144
Anthologia Hibernica, 28
Apollo, 13
Aristotle, 174
Arnold, Matthew, 146
Athenaeum, 23
 and Lady Morgan as reviewer, 141
Atkinson, Joseph
 and Sydney Owenson, 71
Austen, Jane
 Persuasion, 49
 references to Ireland, 4
Australia
 New South Wales, 15
 Tasmania, 130
Austria, 83

Baker, Samuel, 75
Balfour, Mary
 Kathleen O'Neil, 36

Balzac, Honoré de
 parody of *Melmoth the Wanderer*, 148
Banim, John
 The Anglo-Irish of the Nineteenth Century, 77
 Chaunt of the Cholera, 147
 The Nowlans, 149
 surviving cholera, 147
Banim, John & Michael
 Crohoore of the Bill-Hook, 92
Baraniuk, Carol, 72, 73
Barbauld, Anna Laetitia
 'Eighteen Hundred and Eleven', 86
Barnard, Toby, 42
Battle of Antrim, 74
Battle of Ballinamuck, 167
Battle of Waterloo
 English poetry after, 84
 and Jeremiah Joseph Callanan, 110
Beaufort, Frances Anne, 44
Beckett, Samuel
 Molloy, 180
Beiner, Guy, 36, 91
Belfast Academical Institution, 140
Belfast Commercial Chronicle, 70, 71, 73
Belfast Literary Society, 33
Belfast News-letter, 69
Bellas Greenough, George, 33
Bengal, 3
Bengal army
 and Irish recruits, 120
Beranger, Gabriel, 147
 watercolour 'Timoleague Castle', 156
Betham, Sir William, 65
Bewley, Molly, 48
Bingham, Margaret
 Verses on the Present State of Ireland, 58
Blackwood's Magazine, 108, 113, 119
Blatchford, Theodosia, 68
 as editor of *Mary, a Series of Reflections during Twenty Years*, 66
 mother of Mary Tighe, 62

236

Blessington, Lady
  The Magic Lantern, 98
  'Stock-in-Trade of Modern Poetesses', 105
Boucicault, Dion
  The Colleen Bawn, 97
Boyd, Henry
  'Milesian Tales', 28
  'The Recognition', 49
Boyd, Rev. Henry
  and Thomas Dermody, 53
Brehon laws, 29
Britain and Ireland as sisters, 56
British colonialism, 77
British Guiana, 130, 136
British military uniforms, 103
British Museum, 151
British romanticism
  shaped by Ireland, 4
Brontë, Charlotte
  Jane Eyre, 118
Brontë, Emily
  Wuthering Heights, 118
Brooke, Charlotte, 27, 56–7
  comparison with Thomas Moore, 58
  and cousin Robert Brooke, East India Company, 58
  and Gaelic culture, 56
  and influence on W. B. Yeats, 57
  and Joseph Cooper Walker, 56
  'Maon: An Irish Tale', 59
  and Percy's *Reliques of Ancient English Poetry*, 58
  Reliques of Irish Poetry, 56
  and William Beauford, 57
  and Wordsworth's poem 'The Solitary Reaper', 56
Bunting, Edward
  and Belfast Harp Festival, 36
  General Collection of the Ancient Music, 36
Burke, Edmund, 7, 118
  and American independence, 38
  'Letter to Hercules Langrishe', 8
  and Mary Leadbeater, 48
  Reflections on the Revolution in France, 54
  'Sketch of a Negro Code', 48
Burke, Peter, 2
Burns, Robert, 45, 53
  'The Holy Fair', 73
Butler, Marilyn, 4, 14
  and *The Absentee*, 61
  and *Helen*, 141
Butler, Pierce, 73
Butler, Sarah
  Irish Tales, 57
Byron, Lord George Gordon
  and criticism of Owenson's *Ida of Athens*, 47
  Don Juan, 81
  professed love for Ireland, 81

Calhoun, Joshua, 18
Callanan, Jeremiah Joseph, 48, 77, 106–30
  'The Convict of Clonmell', 108
  his definition of Irish literature, 114
  'Gougane Barra', 112
  'The Lament of Kirke White', 107
  'A Lay of Mizen Head', 159
  Lisbon, 107
  'The Outlaw of Loch Lene', 108
  and Moore as meretricious, 83
  and poem-within-a-poem device, 108
  The Recluse of Inchidony, 109
  and Royal Irish regiment, 107
  'Songs of the Gaskinane', 114
  and translations from Irish, 108
Cambrensis, Geraldus, 57
Campbell, Matthew, 68, 72, 111, 119, 158
Canada, 77
  Newfoundland, 72
  Upper Canada, 173
Canning, George, 47
Canny, Nicholas, 128
Cape Colony, 77
Carleton, William, 117, 149–55
  as authentic voice of peasant Ireland, 149
  Autobiography, 177
  The Black Prophet, 150, 153, 177
  conversion to Protestantism, 150
  'Denis O'Shaughnessy Going to Maynooth', 151
  The Emigrants of Ahadarra, 150
  Fardorougha the Miser, 150
  and Hiberno-English, 150
  and Irish tenant farmers as Frankenstein, 126
  and literary revival, 163
  priesthood narratives, 152
  and *stair sheanchas*, 150
  and state of Irish society, 117
  Traits and Stories of the Irish Peasantry, 124, 150
  Valentine McClutchy, 150
Carlyle, Thomas, 181
  and Catholic Emancipation, 117
  Sartor Resartus, 176
Carolan, Turlough, 59
Carrick's Morning Post, 113
Carroll, Siobhan, 87
Castlereagh, Lord, 47
  treatment of 1798 rebels, 82
Catholic Emancipation, 18, 77, 116
Catholic University in Dublin, 151

cattle capitalism, 117
Cayman Islands, 120
Celtic Society, 151
census of 1821, 8
Chander, Manu, 14
Chandler, James, 14, 65, 82, 85
Charlemont, Lord James, 51, 171
Charles Bianconi, 77
China, 80
cholera outbreaks in 1817 & 1831, 117, 146
Christensen, Jerome, 104
Christian Examiner, 150
Clarkson, Thomas, 48
Coleridge, Samuel Taylor & Wordsworth, William
    Lyrical Ballads, 20, 32
colonial adventure novels, 88
Colum, Padraic, 12
Columbia, 79
Congress of Vienna, 83
Connaught, 12
Connellan, Owen
    A Dissertation on Irish Grammar, 134
    as professor of Celtic languages at Queens College Cork, 134
Cooper Walker, Joseph
    and brother Samuel Walker, 34
Cope, Jonas, 54
copies and copying, 28, 37
copyright law, 29, 37
Cornewall Lewis, Sir George
    On Local Disturbances in Ireland, 128
Cornwallis, Marquess Charles, 39, 65
cota mór, 180, 181
County Antrim, 37, 68, 70, 91
County Carlow
    and Sir Richard Butler, 73
County Cavan, 56
    Breiffne, 56
County Clare, 19, 96, 122
    Charlotte Brontë, honeymoon in Kilkee, 118
County Cork, 52
    Bantry Bay, 23
    Blarney, 166
    Buttevant, 52
    Cape Clear, 112, 114
    Carrigaline, 113
    Castletownshend, Nelson monument, 76
    Clonakilty, 109
    Cork harbour, 112
    Dripsey, 166
    Glengarriff, 97
    Gougane Barra, 112
    Inchydoney, 156
    Iveragh Peninsula, 112
    Mizen Head, 159
    Seven Heads, 110
    Sherkin Island, 114
    Skibbereen, 162
    Timoleague, 156
    West Cork, 107
County Donegal, 56, 90
    loyalists, 90
County Down, 34, 35, 70
County Fermanagh, 56
County Galway, 166
County Kerry
    Cottoners River, 167
    Killarney lunatic asylum, 181
    Skellig Michael, 111
County Kildare, 168
    Prosperous, 58
County Leitrim, 56
County Limerick, 13
County Longford, 33, 60, 167, 173
County Mayo, 130
County Meath, 56, 65
County Monaghan, 167
County Offaly, 53
County Roscommon, 167
County Sligo, 12, 56, 168
    Killery Bog, 168
County Tipperary, 98, 133
    Nenagh, 180
County Tyrone, 47, 90
    birthplace of William Carleton, 149
County Wexford, 65
    Hook Head, 116
County Wicklow, 62, 65
Croker, John Wilson
    anonymous criticism of Sydney Owenson, 70
    political career, 70
Croker, Thomas Crofton, 65
    Ballad History of Ireland, 80
    The Keen of the South of Ireland, 109
    and lithography, 22
    Researches in the South of Ireland, 108
Cromwell, Oliver
    conquest of Ireland, 94
    Edgeworth sees his head, 142
crónán, 80
Cronin, Nessa, 120
Crumpe, M.G.T., 143
    Geraldine of Desmond, 143
Curran, John Philpott, 6
Cuvier, George, 24

D'Arcy Wood, Gillen, 153
Daily News, 130

Davis, Leith, 59
Davis, Thomas, 119, 127
Davy, Humphry, 45
  and breakfast for Byron and Edgeworth, 86
  1806 and 1811 visits to Edgeworthstown, 33
de Berry, Duc Charles-Ferdinand, 82
De Quincey, Thomas
  and Act of Union, 45
  Confessions of an English Opium-Eater, 6
De Rozio, Henry, 14
de Staël, Madame Germaine, 24
  Considerations on the Principal Events of the French Revolution, 138
Deane, Seamus, 16
  and national character, 55
Delacroix, Eugéne
  painting scene from *Melmoth the Wanderer*, 148
Dermody, Thomas, 27, 50–55, 99
  admired by Mary Tighe, 55
  and aisling form, 54
  arrival at Owenson home, 51
  and Burns's Standard Habbie stanzaic style, 53
  'Carrol's Complaint', 70
  'The Cave of Patronage', 52
  and Edmund Burke, 54
  and *The Faerie Queene*, 52
  'Farewell to Ireland', 54
  'Goal of Emancipation', 54
  The Harp of Erin, 51
  and Henry Flood, 51
  and Lady Moira, 52
  'Lines Written on a Blank Leaf of Swift's Works', 54
  military career, 55
  'On a Dead Negro', 49
  Poems on Various Subjects, 51
  poems published by subscription, 51
  The Rights of Justice, or Rational Liberty, 54
  and Royal Literary Fund, 55
  and Scotch verse, 53
Dickens, Charles
  The Posthumous Papers of the Pickwick Club, 142
Dickson, David, 158
Dilke, Charles Wentworth, 141
Disraeli, Benjamin
  Sybil, 176
Dorian, Hugh, 135
  account of the Famine, 153
  customs around letters from America, 11
Downes, William, 123, 135
  and Abolition of Savery Act, 135
  'On J. M., who Died on His Passage from the West Indies', 135
  Temperance Melodies, 124
  and *The Nation*, 124
Drennan, William
  'Glendalloch', 2
Driscol, Denis
  advocate of enslavers, 73
Dublin
  in literary decline, 135
  visit of George IV, 98
Dublin Evening Post, 85
Dublin University Magazine, 82, 119, 129, 140, 146, 162
  joint review of Lady Blessington and Edgeworth, 137
Dublin Zoological Society, 24, 149
Duffy, Charles Gavan, 119
  The Ballad Poetry of Ireland, 143
  and Moore as possessing an imperial mind, 129
Dunkin, William, 38
Dunlevy, Mairead, 174
Dunne, Tom, 16, 95
During, Simon, 99

Earls, Brian, 149
East India Company, 93, 121
Edgeworth, Maria
  The Absentee, 33, 61
  and Adam Smith's *The Wealth of Nations*, 38
  admiration of Gerald Griffin, 148
  Castle Rackrent, 28, 30, 167
  Castle Rackrent and the Act of Union, 44
  correspondence with Rachel Mordecai Lazarus, 126
  daguerreotype, 154
  denigration by Daniel O'Connell, 138
  and depictions of London, 98
  and fairy belief, 44
  first negative reviews, 78
  Helen, 98, 124, 136–42
  her account of Connemara, 121
  and her publisher Joseph Johnson, 42
  her understanding of popular radicalism, 82
  and letter to John Murray concerning Scott, 42
  Ormond, 35, 38
  and otter, 149
  Patronage, 86
  and Peterloo, 82
  and political economy, 38
  Popular Tales, 171
  Tales of Fashionable Life, 35
  and Thomas Malthus, 127

Edgeworth, Maria (cont.)
  translation into Irish, 140
  visiting London Zoo, 148
  and Walter Scott's view of the Irish, 122
  and William Herschel, 76
Edgeworth, Michael Pakenham
  his botanical researches, 121
Edgeworth, Richard Lovell, 13, 168
  and Frances Anne Beaufort, 44
  and Irish reluctance to emigration, 173
  and Joseph Johnson, 42
Edgeworthstown
  visit of Mr & Mrs Hall, 154
Edinburgh Literary Journal, 144
Edinburgh Review, 9, 38
  critcism by Mary Tighe, 55
  and Irish novels, 122
Edinburgh University, 120
Elgee, Jane Francesca, 130
  'The Stricken Land', 143
Emmet, Robert, 113
  and 1803 rebellion, 39
Engels, Friedrich
  and Ireland, 178
Esterhammer, Angela, 78
European romanticism, 81, 84, 92, 120

Fairholt, Frederick William
  drawing of Edgeworthstown House, 154
Father Prout. *See* Mahony, Francis Sylvester
Favret, Mary, 101, 103
Ferguson, Frank, 73
Ferguson, Samuel, 129, 162
Fergusson, Robert
  'Leith Races', 73
Fermanis, Porscha, 14, 16
Ferris, Ina, 33
Fitzgerald, Lord Edward, 133
  biography by Thomas Moore, 142
footnotes
  role in memory and forgetting, 91
Foster, R. F., 125
Fox Talbot, William Henry
  photographed Thomas Moore, 154
France, 45, 75
Fraser's Magazine, 131
  and joke letters to literary figures, 137
Freeman's Journal, 23, 70, 137
French Revolution, 2, 50, 90
Friel, Brian, 12
Frieze coats, 20, 181
  and ancient Greece and Rome, 170
  found in bog near Edgeworthstown, 168
  found in Killery Bog, Co. Sligo, 168
  and medieval tailoring techniques, 168

  in Schools' Collection of Irish folklore, 166
  and Thomas Carlyle, 176
Fulford, Tim, 6

Gaelic manuscript tradition, 106
Galperin, William, 1
Gamble, John, 10
  and eyewitness to Hamilton murder, 91
Gascúnach, Amhlaoibh, 114
general election, 1807, 71
Geological Survey, 77
Gladstone, William Ewart, 24
Godwin, William, 6
Gogol, Nikolai
  The Overcoat, 21
Goldsmith, Oliver, 118
Gore, Catherine
  compared by Lady Morgan to Dickens, 142
  Preferment, or, My Uncle the Earl, 141
Grattan, Henry, 6
Grattan's Parliament, 18
Gray, Thomas
  'Elegy Written in a Country Churchyard', 135
Great Famine, 1, 117
Greece
  as setting for Owenson's novels, 5
  island of Euboea, 174
Green, Sarah, 78
Griffin, Gerald, 77, 94, 95–20
  'The Aylmers of Bally Aylmer', 104
  'Card Drawing', 100, 174
  criticism of the Lake Poets, 105
  and Dion Boucicault, 97
  and family in British military, 99
  'The Half-Sir', 97
  Holland-Tide, 95, 101
  The Invasion, 97, 145
  'Munster Anecdotes', 96
  and naval recruitment, 99
  and North Monastery, Cork City, 148
Griffin, Michael, 51, 53
Griffith's Valuation, 116
Grogan, Nathaniel
  The Country Schoolmaster, 169

Haiti
  Haitian revolution, 3, 50
  James Orr's abolitionist poem, 73
  Toussaint Louverture in Paris jail, 3
Hall, Captain Basil
  account of journey to Okinawa, 137
Hall, James, 33
  Tour Through Ireland, 173
  and visit to Edgeworthstown, 39
Hamilton Dunlop, Eliza, 14

Hamilton, Archibald Rowan, 73
Hamilton, Dr William
  assasination, 90
  Letters Concerning the Northern Coast of the County of Antrim, 91
  and Presbyterians, 7
  Royal Irish Academy, 90
Hamilton, Elizabeth
  Cottagers of Glenburnie, 87
Hamilton, Paul, 84, 120
Hampson, Dennis
  and Belfast Harp Festival, 47
Hardiman, James
  Irish Minstrelsy, 150
Hastings, Elizabeth, 34
Haydn, Joseph
  Creation, 79
Hazlitt, William
  Spirit of the Age, 82
Head, Francis Bond, 122
  travelling in Connemara, 130
Heaney, Seamus, 12, 180
  and Carleton as turncoat, 151
Hemans, Felicia, 34
  Records of Woman, 5, 155
Hession, Peter, 117
Hewitt, John, 72
  description of Thomas Percy, 35
Hibernian Antiquarian Society, 35
Holland, Peter, 82
Holt, Joseph, 65
Home Rule, 25
Hoppen, K.T., 34
Houghton Library, Harvard, 66
House of Commons, Dublin, 45
House of Commons, London, 175
House of Lords, 6
Howe, Susan
  The Nonconformists' Memorial, 23
Hunt, Henry, 82

India, 75
  as setting for Owenson's *The Missionary*, 5
Ireland populousness, 1
Irish Archaeological Society, 151
Irish Coast Guard, 76
Irish Fishery Board, 76
Irish folklore, 123
  Patrick Kennedy, 146
  and poor scholar motif, 13
Irish gardens
  and colonial fortification, 61
Irish language
  bilingual society in 18th and 19th century, 7
  language shift, 22

literature in 19thC, 106
loss, 2
manuscripts held at the Bodleian Library, 151
metrical inflections, 108
revival, 134
Irish manuscript production, 22
Irish population, 38, 128
Irish populousness, 7, 181
Irish romanticism
  Burns and Byron, 80
  colonial dimension, 16
  copies and copying, 22
  cult of Byron, 110
  definitions, 3
  Edgeworth and women's proper sphere of influence, 137
  and Edmund Burke, 8
  and everyday clothing, 164
  final phase, 131
  frieze coats, 175
  and the Great Famine, 117
  and Great Famine as a literary endpoint, 119
  and Ireland as a strange country, 20
  and Irish Gothic, 105
  and 'last man' idea, 163
  and maritime affairs, 75
  and the national tale, 17
  phases, 14
  and performance and visual arts, 15
  and popular classicism, 12
  and population, 75
  Sheridan Le Fanu, 132
Irish Schools Collection, 9
Irish Sea, 76
  and Cromwell's body, 94
  and legendary roughness, 76
Irish Victorian literature, 118
  and Sheridan Le Fanu, 132
Irish woollens, 165
  supposed antiquity of trade, 171
Irish writing
  and ethnographic impulse, 98
Italy
  Shelleys in Pisa, 64

Jamaica, 120
James, William
  Naval History of Great Britain, 101
Jasanoff, Maya, 39
Johnson, Joseph
  and Mary Wollstonecraft, 42
  and publication of *Castle Rackrent*, 42
Johnston, Anna, 14
Joyce, James
  A Portrait of the Artist as a Young Man, 111

Kant, Immanuel, 14
Keating, Geoffrey, 57
    Foras Feasa ar Éirea, 16
Keats, John, 84
    his 'Duchess of Dunghill', 85
    visit to Northern Ireland, 84
Kelleher, Margaret, 22
Kelly, James, 39
Kennedy, Caitriona, 142
Kennedy, George
    The History of the Contagious Cholera, 146
Kennedy, Patrick
    Legendary Fictions of the Irish Celts, 146
Kinnaird, Douglas, 81
Kirke White, Henry, 107
    and poem about death of Thomas Dermody, 107
Kitson, Peter, 6
Kramer Linkin, Harriet, 63
Kreilkamp, Vera, 95
Kucich, Greg, 63

Ladies of Llangollen
    and Mary Tighe, 63
Lady Morgan. *See* Owenson, Sydney
Langbauer, Laurie, 107
Larcom, Thomas, 116, 117
Lavel, Louis, 82
Lawless, Emily
    Hurrish, a Study, 180
Le Fanu, Sheridan
    The Cock and the Anchor, 145
    'The Ghost and the Bone-setter', 132
    In a Glass Darkly, 132
    and *Dublin University Magazine*, 132
    'Scraps of Hibernian Ballads', 132
    'Shamus O'Brien', 133
    Uncle Silas, 100
    Uncle Silas plot echoing Edgeworth's *Helen*, 136
Le Fanu, William
    as Commissioner of Public Works, 133
    and Irish rural life, 133
    mimicking peasant speech, 133
Leadbeater, Mary
    and abolition, 48
    and Latin poet Maffeo Vegio, 63
    The Negro, 48
    'To the Memory of S. E. Who Died at Calcutta, 1781. Aged 22', 48
Lee, John, 11
Lefanu, Alicia, 64
Lewis, Matthew
    The Monk, 90
Lloyd, David, 159

Lockhart, John Gibson
    Memoirs of the Life of Sir Walter Scott, 172
Lough Foyle, 46, 76
Louverture, Toussaint, 3
Lucan, Lady. *See* Bingham, Margaret
Lynch, Patrick
    Bolg an tSolair, 36
Lysaght, Edward
    and Volunteer songs and ballads, 51

Mac Suibhne, Breandán, 10, 90
    and post-Famine Donegal, 130
Macartney, Lord, 47
Maginn, William, 81, 108
    career at *Blackwood's Magazine*, 81
    describes Moore's *Melodies* as unIrish, 129
    editor of *Fraser's Magazine*, 131
Mahony, Francis Sylvester, 131
Malthus, Thomas, 7, 42
    and William Godwin, 126
Mangan, James Clarence, 83, 106
    and environmental change, 125
    'Lament over the Ruins of the Abbey of Teach Molaga', 155–86
    and Ordnance Survey, 155
Marsh's Library, 106
Martineau, Harriet, 181
    and expectations of the Irish, 129
    Famine reports from Ireland, 130
    Illustrations of Political Economy, 130
    Society in America, 126
    weary of the subject of Ireland, 146
Marx, Karl
    and coats as commodities, 178
    and Irish agricultural production, 178
    Das Kapital, 178
Matthew, Father Theobald, 124
Maturin, Charles Robert, 95
    Bertram, 15
    Melmoth the Wanderer, 77, 87, 174
    reception in Paris, 148
    The Wild Irish Boy, 78
Maturin, Rev. Henry, 91
McCafferty, Barney
    and Hamilton murder, 91
McCarthy, B.G., 108, 111
McCracken, Henry Joy, 36
McHenry, James
    O'Halloran, 37
McManus, Henry
    Reading 'The Nation', 164
McParlan, James
    Statistical Survey of the County of Sligo, 168

Index

Melville, Herman
  Billy Budd, 101
Menke, Richard, 127
Merriman, Brian
  'Cúirt an Mheán-Oíche', 151
Milbanke, Annabella
  'Lines Supposed to be Spoken at the Grave of Dermody', 107
Ministry of All the Talents, 70
Mitchel, John, 118, 119
  biography of Hugh O'Neill, 127
  editor of *Poems by James Clarence Mangan*, 19
  and Irishness of Irish literature, 118
Mitford, Mary Russell
  enthusiasm for Daniel O'Connell, 148
Moira, Lady, 34, 53
  and her literary salon, 34
  and Italian epigraphs for Edgeworth, 35
Monck Mason, Henry Joseph
  Grammar of the Irish Language, 134
Moore, Jane, 84
  gendered language used by Hazlitt, 83
Moore, Thomas, 29, 34
  Bermuda, 29
  Bermuda debts, 84
  and disagreeable company of Edgeworth, 137
  Dutch colonists and nutmeg, 32
  and Dutch East India Company, 32
  entrusted with Byron's memoirs, 84
  Epistles, Odes and Other Poems, 64
  as feminised figure, 78
  'The Fudge Family in Paris', 83
  and Hinduism, 31
  Irish Melodies, 28, 31
  and Irish population, 128
  Lalla Rookh, 85
  Lord Moira and Irish poet laureate, 29
  and Mary Tighe's novel *Selena*, 86
  Melodies, 57
  and negative modes in lyrics, 32
  and photograph by Fox Talbot, 154
  tour of Ireland, 85
Morgan, Lady. *See* Sydney Owenson
Morgan, Sir Charles, 126
  and Anglo-Irish as the master caste, 131
Morley, Vincent, 2, 134
Moryson, Fynes, 5
Mount Cashell, Lady Margaret, 35
  lover of George William Tighe, 64
  Selene, 64
  and the Shelley circle in Italy, 35
Mount Tambora eruption, 153, 158
  Year without a Summer, 120
Mullen, Mary, 44
Munster
  and agrarian insurgency, 32
Murphy, Bishop John, 106
Murray, John, 42
Musgrave, Richard, 8, 35

Napoleonic Wars, 75, 82, 97, 100
Nariño, Antonio, 79
national tale, 57
  and masculinisation by Charles Robert Maturin, 78
Nelson, Horatio, 102
  affair with Lady Emma Hamilton, 102
  memorial in Argyllshire, 103
  memorial in Castletownshend, 103
  memorial in Dublin, 103
Nersessian, Anahid, 30, 118
Newenham, Edward, 9
Ní Mhunghaile, Lesa, 56, 57
  and Charlotte Brooke's translations from Irish, 57
Ní Shíocháin, Tríona, 61
Ní Úrdail, Meidhbhín, 106
Night of the Big Wind, 24
Nimmo, Alexander, 121
Novak, Rose, 143

Ó Ciosáin, Niall, 1, 120
Ó Conaill, Seán
  'Tuireamh na hÉireann' or 'Ireland's Elegy', 134
Ó Gallchoir, Clíona, 127, 137, 139, 141
Ó Raifeartaigh, Tarlach, 13
O'Brien, Paul, 9
O'Coilean, Sean
  'Machtnamh an Duine Dhoilgheasaig, nó Caoineadh Thighe Molaga', 157
  and Wordsworth's 'Tintern Abbey', 158
O'Connell, Daniel, 19, 82, 117
  and denigration of Maria Edgeworth, 86
  his frieze coat, 175
  and welcome home dinner for Thomas Moore, 85
  on asymmetries of Irish power and population, 128
O'Conor, Charles, 57
O'Curry, Eugene, 146
  Lectures on the Manuscript Materials of Ancient Irish History, 151
O'Curry, Eugene, 106
O'Daly, John
  Reliques of Irish Jacobite Poetry, 151
O'Doherty, Eva
  'Hymn of the Sword', 143
O'Donoghue, Bernard, 111

O'Donovan, John, 20, 134
　and Irish Archaeological Society, 151
　and Southwest Ireland, 76
O'Flanagan, Theophilus, 14, 57
O'Hagan, John, 126
O'Halloran, Clare, 36
O'Halloran, Sylvester, 57
O'Hara, Charles, 37
O'Higgins, Laurie, 13
O'Kane, Finola, 73
O'Shaugnessy, David, 15
Okinawa
　known as Great Loo-Choo Island, 137
Ordnance Survey, 46, 75
　and the Great Trigonometrical Survey of India, 120
　and James Clarence Mangan, 155
Orr, James, 27, 68–9
　and Battle of Antrim, 69
　Battle of Ballynahinch, 68
　'Donegore Hill', 69, 74
　'Epistle to S. Thomson of Carngranny, a Brother Poet', 69
　Owenson poems, 71
　'The Passengers', 72
　and Presbyterian print culture, 69
　and race, 72
　'The Recluse of Connaught, Addressed to Miss Owenson', 71
　and Scottish origins, 69
　and Thomas Percy, 69
　'To Miss Owenson, the Authoress of the Wild Irish Girl', 70
　'Toussaint's Farewell to Saint Domingo', 73
　and Ulster Scots, 68
　and United Irishmen, 69
　'The Wanderer', 70
　in the United States, 74
　Ulster Scots, 27
　use of 'Christs Kirk on the Green', 73
Orr, Jennifer, 69
Ossianic Society, 151
Otway, Caesar, 129
Owenson, Robert
　and Thomas Dermody, 50
Owenson, Sydney, 29, 34
　and Abercorn, Lady Jane, 47
　and American War of Independence, 51
　criticism of Bourbon monarchy in *France*, 79
　early definition of romanticism, 80
　The First Attempt, 71
　Florence Macarthy, 52, 171
　and Giant's Causeway, 46
　and Grace O'Malley, 145
　'The Hawthorne Tree', 13
　her translation of 'Cathleen Nolan', 60
　Ida of Athens, 47
　and marriage to Sir Charles Morgan (1812), 47
　The Missionary: An Indian Tale, 47
　The O'Briens and the O'Flahertys, 79
　O'Donnel, 30, 49
　Patriotic Sketches, 78
　public letter to Cardinal Wiseman, 129
　'Retrospection', 53
　review of Thackeray's *Irish Sketchbook*, 177
　The Wild Irish Girl, 28, 29, 45
　The Wild Irish Girl and 1798 rebellion, 65
　Twelve Hibernian Melodies, 60
　Twelve Original Hibernian Melodies, 30
Oxford University, 146

Pacata Hibernia, 156
Paine, Thomas
　The Rights of Man, 79
Paris, 84
　and Anglomania, 147
Parker, Stephen
　and new Gaelic typeface, 58
Parnell, William, 8, 37
　Historical Apology for the Irish Catholics, 37
Parsons, Cóilín, 106, 159
Pasley, William, 76
Peel, Robert, 34
Peninsular Wars, 75
Percy, Thomas, 34
　agricultural improvements, 35
　and Battle of Ballynahinch, 35
　and James McHenry, 36
　and Patrick Prunty (Brontë), 36
　Reliques of Ancient English Poetry, 35, 58
　and reporting to Dublin Castle, 35
　and William Hamilton Drummond, 35
Peterloo Massacre, 9, 82
Petrie, George, 146
　and place-name research, 106
　Hanging Washing in Lord Portlester's Chapel, Saint Audeon's, 164
Petty, William
　Political Arithmetick and Political Anatomy of Ireland, 131
Physico-Historical Society, 35
Pitts, Jennifer, 77
Poor Law Inquiry
　and Thomas Malthus, 126
Poor Law unions, 116
Prendergast, Amy, 33, 34
Price, Robert
　and Irish population, 38

Prussia, 83
Publishers
   D.J. Sadleir, 97
   Hennessey Press, 109
   John Murray, 86, 98, 122
   John Stockdale, 9
   Joseph Johnson, 42
   Longmans, 67
   Power, 31
Pushkin, Alexander
   reference to *Melmoth the Wanderer* in *Eugene Onegin*, 148

Queens College Cork, 134

Rainey, Robert
   and rebel ballads, 40
   and *Castle Rackrent*, 40
   and his journals, 39
Rawdon, John, 34
Reform Act, 1832, 145
Reynolds, George Nugent, 61
   Erin go brách, 61
   'The Exiled Irishman's Lamentation', 61
Ricardo, David
   and Cromwell's head, 142
River Shannon, 80, 96, 123
Roche, Regina Maria, 78
Rockite rebellion, 76, 158
Rouviere Mosse, Henrietta, 78
Royal Dublin Society, 34
Royal Irish Academy, 22, 34, 50, 106, 168
   and Richard Lovell Edgeworth as founding member, 35
   and Thomas Percy as founding member, 35
Royal Irish Fusiliers
   fág an bealach, 50
Royal Literary Fund, 98
Russell Mitford, Mary
   and Owenson's *Florence Macarthy*, 79
   Our Village, 97
Russia, 83
   '*mel'moticheskii*' ('Melmoth-like'), 148

Sampson, Reverend Vaughan G.
   Statistical Survey of the *County of Londonderry*, 47
Schirmer, Gregory, 57, 108, 112, 113
Scott, Walter, 24
   Abbotsford, 154
   and Irish poverty, 172
   Ivanhoe, 98
   Life of Napoleon Bonaparte, 79
   Waverley, 86
Scottish Enlightenment, 45

Shelley, Mary, 58
   and aquatic Romanticism, 126
   Frankenstein, 87, 126
   The Last Man, 125
Shelley, Percy Bysshe, 9
   Address to the Irish People, 9
   criticism of Lord Castlereagh, 9
   Declaration of Rights, 9
   'A Defence of Poetry', 84
   'The Masque of Anarchy', 9
   and Moore's 'Odes to Nea', 58
   and Owenson's *The Missionary*, 47
   Philosophical View of Reform, 9
Sheridan, Richard Brinsley, 118
shipwrecks, 88
Shklovsky, Viktor, 20
sí gaoithe, 44
Sligo, Lord, 45, 120
   and Abolition of Slavery Act, 1833, 120
   friendship with Thomas De Quincey, 120
   Governor General of Jamaica and the Cayman Island, 120
Smith, Charles
   Antient and Present State of the County and City of Cork, 160
Smith, Sydney, 128
Somerville, E. OE. & Ross, Martin
   The Real Charlotte, 180
Spain, 75
Spanish Main, 79
Spenser, Edmund
   in Owenson's *Florence Macarthy*, 78
   View of the Present State of Ireland, 52, 170
Speranza. *See* Elgee, Jane Francesca
St Clair, William, 32
St Domingo. *See* Haiti
St Helena, 58
St Peter's Fields massacre. *See* Peterloo Massacre
Stafford, Fiona, 160
stage Irishmen, 122
Steedman, Carolyn, 172
Stewart, Susan, 59
Sweden
   Uppsala, 97
Swift, Jonathan, 54
Switzerland
   Lake Geneva, 153

Taaffe, Denis, 57
Taylor, Colleen, 177
Teach Molaga. *See* County Cork, Timoleague
Terry-Alts, 122
Thackeray, William Makepeace, 105
   Barry Lyndon, 145
   Irish Sketchbook, 177

The Art Journal, 154
The Citizen, 127
The Freeman's Journal, 86
The Nation, 114, 119, 129, 159
   and women poets, 143
The Northern Star, 69
The Vindicator, 119
The Volunteers, 51
Theatre Royal Dublin, 50
Thomson, Samuel, 69
Tighe, Mary, 27, 39, 62–68
   and 1798 rebellion, 62
   Act of Union poems, 62
   and Anna Seward, 63
   'Bryan Byrne, of Glenmalure', 64
   copyright and Longmans, 67
   death from tuberculosis, 65
   and Dublin in literary decline, 135
   and her cousin Caroline Hamilton, 45
   her reading journal, 55
   her uncle Rev Thomas Tighe, 36
   and John Keats, 65
   and Joseph Cooper Walker, 63
   and Maria Edgeworth, 63
   marriage to cousin Henry, 62
   Mary, a Series of Reflections during Twenty Years, 66
   and mother Theodosia Blatchford, 62
   and posthumous publication by Henry Tighe, 65
   Psyche, 62
   and Romantic Spenserianism, 63
   Selena, 64
   and Sydney Owenson's novels, 64
   and the Ladies of Llangollern, 63
   and Thomas Moore, 63
   and William Parnell, 63
Tighe, William
   Statistical Survey of the County of Kilkenny, 47
Tilley, Elizabeth, 119
Tone, Matilda
   rejection of role as eternal mourner, 142
Tonna, Charlotte Elizabeth, 131
Trinity College Dublin, 22, 29, 34, 90, 106, 119
Trollope, Anthony
   The Macdermots of Ballycloran, 145
Trotter, John
   Walks Through Ireland, 52
Tyneside, 130

Uberti, Fazio degli, 171
Ulster
   and 1798 rebellion, 70
   depiction in *The Wild Irish Girl*, 46
   and Irishness of the northern counties, 46
   and James Orr, 68
   martial law, 90
   as Scotch colony in *The Wild Irish Girl*, 71
Ulster Gaelic Society
   and Thomas Feenachty, 140
United Irish rebellion, 2, 26, 37, 39, 79, 90
   in Ulster, 91
United Irishmen
   and complicity with enslavement, 73
   Northern Star newspaper, 36
University College Cork, 111

Vallancey, Charles, 29
Vance, Norman, 14
veluti in speculum, 122
Venezuela, 79
Virgil, 13

Wakefield, Edward
   An Account of Ireland, Statistical and Political, 168
Wales, 130
Walker, Joseph Cooper, 26
   'Essay on the Rise and Progress of Gardening in Ireland', 61
   Historical Memoirs of the Irish Bards, 56
   and orgins of Ossian poems, 56
   support to Alicia Lefanu, 64
   support to Sydney Owenson, 64
Watson, Alex, 28
Wellington, Duke of, 144
   and Catholic Emancipation, 145
West India, 136
Whiteboys, 92
Wilberforce, William, 48
Wilde, Oscar
   Dorian Gray, 131
Wilde, William, 130, 168
   census reports
   Status of Disease & Tables of Death, 130
Williams, Raymond, 12
Wilson, Kathleen, 102
Windele, John, 108
   Literary Remains of J. J. Callanan, 115
Wolf, Nicholas, 106, 134
Wolfe Tone, Theobald, 73
Wolfe, Charles
   'The Burial of Sir John Moore', 113
Wolfe, Viscount Arthur Kilwarden
   killing, 91
Wolfson, Susan, 1

Wollstonecraft, Mary, 35, 135
  and dislike of Ireland, 42
  and Mitchelstown, 42
Wordsworth, William, 45, 76
  and Dove Cottage, 154
Wright, Julia, 17, 72

Yeats, W. B.
  'The Circus Animals Desertion', 180
  his distinction between Edgeworth & Carleton, 155
  views on William Carleton, 178
Young Ireland
  and break with O'Connell, 119
  ideas of nationality, 142
  and Irish language, 134
  rebellion, 117
  rebels of 1848, 136
Young, Arthur
  and Irish population, 38
  A Tour in Ireland, 33

For EU product safety concerns, contact us at Calle de José Abascal, 56–1°,
28003 Madrid, Spain or eugpsr@cambridge.org.

www.ingramcontent.com/pod-product-compliance
Lightning Source LLC
LaVergne TN
LVHW011813060526
838200LV00053B/3759